D0461983

[Front cover] Will it hold? Marek Raganowicz
starts pitch 26, Bushido, Great Trango Tower
(p.297). *Marcin Tomaszewski* [This page]
Quinn Brett and Prairie Kearney in Greenland.
The big towers above: Baronet (left) and
Baron (right) (p.182). *John Dickey*

[This page] Whit Magro on the first one-day free ascent of Jaded Lady, Mt. Hooker, Wyoming (p.132). *John Dickey*

CONTENTS

RECON [UNEXPLORED & OVERLOOKED]

CLIMBS AND EXPEDITIONS

New books from Steph Davis, Marni Jackson, Tony Whittome, Doug Robinson, Harriet Pugh, Jerry Auld, Tom Walker, Nick Bullock, Yvon Chouinard, Dick Dorworth, Chris Jones, Lito Tejada-Flores, Doug Tompkins, David Roberts, Jim Perrin, Peter H. Hansen, and Jonathan Waterman

Remembering Doug Abromeit, Stanley Boucher, John Ewbank, Artur Hajzer, Pop Hollandsworth, Layton Kor, Theodore (Nick) Nicolai, Denali Schmidt, Marty Schmidt, and William Thomas

[This page] Final steps toward the summit of Khunyang Chhish East (p.32). *Simon Anthamatten*

CORPORATE PARTNERS

SUMMIT PARTNER $50,000

HIGH CAMP $25,000

BASECAMP $15,000

PATRON $10,000

The American Alpine Journal, 710 Tenth St. Suite 100, Golden, Colorado 80401
Telephone: (303) 384-0110 Fax: (303) 384-0111
E-mail: aaj@americanalpineclub.org
www.americanalpineclub.org

ISSN: 0065-6925
ISBN: 978-1-933056-83-8
ISBN: (e-book): 978-1-933056-84-5

WE THANK THE FOLLOWING FOR THEIR GENEROUS FINANCIAL SUPPORT:

GREAT RANGES FELLOWSHIP

$10,000+

Douglas Beall
Richard Blum
Yvon Chouinard
Anonymous
Kevin Duncan &
Duncan Family Foundation
Ken Ehrhart

Clark Gerhardt Jr.
Todd Hoffman
David Koch
Mark Kroese
McKibben/Merner Family-
Foundation
Peter Metcalf

Anonymous
NY Section, AAC
Mark & Teresa Richey
David Riggs
Steve Schwartz
Steven Swenson & Ann Dalton
Doug and Maggie Walker

$5,000-$9,999

Ansara Family Fund
Yonsuk Derby
Charles Fleischman
Bruce Franks
Gerald Gallwas
Sandy Hill
Louis Kasischke

George McCown
Amy Meredith
Vanessa O'Brien
Wolf Riehle
Cody J Smith
Travis Spitzer
William & Barbra Straka

Theodore Streibert
Peter Sulick
Lawrence True & Linda Brown
Ronald Ulrich
The Estate of Paul Wiseman

$2,500-$4,999

Warren Adelman
Steve Barrett
George Basch
Sherman Bull M.D.
Thomas Burch
John Catto
Mike Collins
James Donini
James & Cheryl Duckworth
Jim Edwards
Dan Emmett
Charlotte Fox
Marilyn Geninatti

Peter, Sam, Addis, &
Gus Goldman
Syed Haider
Robert Hall
Helene Hill
Michael Hodges
Thomas Hornbein M.D.
Mark Kassner
Phil Lakin Jr
George Lowe III
Jeff Martin
Anonymous
Linda McMillan

James Morrissey
Miriam Nelson & Kinloch Earle
David Olsen
Charles Peck
Marshall Peterson
Charles Sassara III
Howard Sebold
Alan Spielberg
Bob Street
Paul Underwood
Theodore Weicker
John (Jed) Williamson
Keegan Young

$1,000-$2,499

Robert Anderson
Larry Arthur
William Atkinson
Gail Bates
COL Christopher Bates
Gali Beh
Vaclav Benes
Gordon A. Benner M.D.
Laurie Berliner
Tanya Bradby & Martin Slovacek
John Bragg
Wesley Brown
Paul Brunner
William Burd
Deirdre Byers
Edmund &
Betsy Cabot Foundation
Robert J. Campbell
Peter Carter
Jeffrey Cohen
Douglas Colwell
Kevin Cooney
Matt & Charlotte Culberson
Karen Daubert
Joseph Davidson
Tom Degenhardt
Stanley Dempsey
David Dingman
Jennifer Dow M.D.
Jeff Dozier
Richard Draves
Jesse Dwyer
Charles Eilers
H. Newcomb Eldredge

Stuart Ellison
Lee Elman
Denise Elmer
Terrence English
Philip Erard
Timothy Forbes
James Frank
James Frush
James & Franziska Garrett
Bill Givens
David Goeddel
Anonymous
Wayne & Cynthia Griffin
Richard Griffith
Scot Hillman
Marley & Jennifer Hodgson
Richard E. Hoffman M.D.
Robert Hyman & Deborah
Atwood
Thomas Janson
John Kascenska
William Krause M.D.
Ellen Lapham
Leo Lebon
Paul Lego
Gerald Lofthouse
Jamie Logan
Gail Loveman
Chris Lynch
Brent Manning
Edward Matthews
James McCarthy
Peter McGann
Hacksaw

Paul Morrow
Ted Morton
Amy Paradis
Will Phillips
James Pinter-Lucke
John Pope
Matthew Pruis
Eugene Rehfeld
Louis Reichardt
Prof John Reppy
Andrea Resnick
Ryan Rich
Michael Riley
Carey Roberts
Joel Robinson
John Rudolph
Stephen Scofield
George Shaw
Jay Smith
George N. Smith
Brian Sohn
Allen Steck
Robert & Jennifer Stephenson
Seth Switzer
Pat & Jack Tackle
Thomas Taplin
David Thoenen
Martin J. Torresquintero
John Tracy
Dieter Von Hennig
James Whittaker
Todd Winzenried
Joseph Yannuzzi
Rob Ziegler

FRIENDS OF THE AMERICAN ALPINE JOURNAL

[This page] If you're climbing Cerro Mariposa, there's only one approach: Will Stanhope and Marc-Andre Leclerc paddle out from the wall (p.224). *Matt Van Biene*

THE AMERICAN ALPINE JOURNAL

EXECUTIVE EDITOR
Dougald MacDonald

SENIOR EDITOR
Lindsay Griffin

ASSISTANT EDITOR
Erik Rieger

ART DIRECTOR
Erik Rieger

PUBLICATIONS INTERN
Michiko Arai

CONTRIBUTING EDITORS
Frederick O. Johnson, *Club Activities*
David Stevenson, *Book Reviews*
David Wilkes, *In Memoriam*

ILLUSTRATIONS AND MAPS
Jeremy Collins, Jesse Crock, Joe Iurato,
Mike Clelland, Anna Riling

INDEXERS
Ralph Ferrara, Eve Tallman

TRANSLATORS
Peter Jensen-Choi, Zbysek Cesenek,
Tamotsu Nakamura, Henry Pickford, Simone
Sturm, Ekaterina Vorotnikova, Xia Zhongming

REGIONAL CONTACTS
Steve Gruhn, *Alaska*; Drew Brayshaw, Rapahel
Slawinski, *Canada*; Sevi Bohorquez, Sergio
Ramirez Carrascal, *Peru*; Damien Gildea,
Antarctica; Rolando Garibotti, Marcelo Scanu,
Daniel Seeliger, *Argentina/Chile*; Rajesh
Gadgil, Harish Kapadia, *India*; Elizabeth
Hawley, Rodolphe Popier, Richard Salisbury,
Nepal; Tamotsu Nakamura, Hiroshi Hagiwara,
Japanese climbs; Peter Jensen-Choi, *Korean
climbs*; Anna Piunova, *Russia, Tajikistan*, and
Kyrgyzstan, Xia Zhongming, *China*

ONLINE EDITORS
Doug Haller, Chris Harrington, Joel Peach,
Tom Prigg, Cris Valerio

ADVISORY BOARD
Andrew Bisharat, Kelly Cordes, Damien Gildea,
Colin Haley, Mark Richey, Freddie Wilkinson,
Emily Stifler Wolfe

WITH HEARTFELT THANKS TO
David Boersma, Claude Gardien, Maro
Lablance, Erik Lambert, Anna Piunova, Tucker,
and all *AAJ* donors and supporters

[This page] Approaching the
Doublets in East Rosebud Canyon,
Montana (p.127). *Ian Cavanaugh*

THE AMERICAN ALPINE CLUB

OFFICIALS FOR THE YEAR 2014
*DIRECTORS EX-OFFICIO

[EXECUTIVE COMMITTEE]

Honorary President
James P. McCarthy

Honorary Treasurer
Theodore (Sam) Streibert

President
Mark Kroese

Vice President
Doug Walker

Secretary
Clark Gerhardt

Treasurer
Paul Gagner

[DIRECTORS]

Term Ending 2015
Brad Brooks
Matt Culberson
Karen Daubert
Ken Ehrhart
John Heilprin
Rebecca Schild

Term Ending 2016
Deanne Buck
Philip Duff
Chuck Fleischman

Term Ending 2017
Janet Wilkinson
Phil Lakin
Kit DesLauriers

[SECTION CHAIRS]

Alaska
Harry Hunt & Cindi Squire
Arizona
Erik Filsinger & Jeff Snyder
Cascade
Joshua Brandon & Truc Allen
DC
Simon Carr & David Giacomin
Deep South
Michael Kidder
Front Range
Carol Kotchek
Great Lakes
Bill Thompson
Heartland
Jeremy Collins
Idaho
Kammie Cuneo & Jason Luthy

Mid Atlantic
Barry Rusnock &
James Kunz
Midwest
Ray Kopcinski
Montana
Kevin Brumbach
New England
Nancy Savickas & Rick Merritt
New Mexico
Pat Gioanninni
NY Metro
Philip Erard
NY Upstate
Will Roth & Mark Scott
North Central
Mark Jobman

Oregon
Jesse Bernier & Heidi Medema
Sierra Nevada
Karen Zazzi & Kristen Nute
Southern Appalachian
Danny McCracken
Southwest
James Pinter-Lucke & Tony
Yeary
Texas
Adam Mitchell
Utah
Blake Summers
Western Slope
Lee Jenkins
Wyoming
Micah Rush

[STAFF]

Executive Driector, Phil Powers
Director of Operations, Penn Burris
Executive Assistant and Grants Manager, Janet Miller
Information & Marketing Director, Erik Lambert
Director, Regional Programs & Development, Keegan Young
Library Director, Dana Gerschel
IT Director, Craig Hoffman
Accountant, Carol Kotchek
Develpment Manager, Vickie Hormuth
Development Coordinator, Ben Edwards
Membership Coordinator, Lauren Shockey
Online Store Manager, Allison Levy
Marketing Manager, Jonny Griffith

Social Media Manager, Whitney Bradberry
Graphic Designer, David Boersma
Conservation & Volunteer Coordinator, Remy Rodriguez
Digitization Librarian, Allison Bailey
Library Manager, Katie Sauter
Facilities Director, Philip Swiny
Publications, Executive Editor, Dougald MacDonald
Publications, Assistant Editor & Art Director, Erik Rieger
Northwest Regional Manager, Eddie Espinosa
Western Regional Manager, Jeff Deikis
Rocky Mountain & Central Regional Manager, Adam Peters
Southeast Regional Manager, Lisa Hummel
Museum Director, Shelby Arnold

PREFACE

TRUST BUT VERIFY

THE AAJ EXISTS TO DOCUMENT IMPORTANT ASCENTS, and so it may be surprising that we will publish reports of great climbs with no proof they actually happened. The notable example from 2013, of course, is Ueli Steck's solo new route on the south face of Annapurna. Steck lost his camera low on the climb, carried no tracking device, and passed the crucial sections of the route, including the summit, late at night. You will find his account of this climb starting on page 12.

It seems almost inconceivable that a heavily sponsored athlete could fail to document the most important ascent of his career. Yet, other than a possible sighting of Steck's headlamp high on the wall from advanced base camp, we have only his word that he climbed up and down Annapurna in 28 hours. That's good enough for the two French climbers, Stéphane Benoist and Yannick Graziani, who followed in Steck's footsteps two weeks later—metaphorically, as his footprints had been erased by snow and wind—and who staunchly defend Steck's ascent against detractors. Given the Swiss climber's extraordinary fitness and unique track record, his ascent seems plausible, and so, unless we receive real proof to the contrary, his word is good enough for us, too.

Countless climbers reach summits without producing any evidence—there are ample aesthetic, stylistic, and practical reasons why someone might not carry or use a phone, GPS unit, or even a camera. We also believe the great majority of climbers—even those paid for their successes in the mountains—are honest about their accomplishments, even though we recognize a few will exploit the general trust of the climbing community. When climbers are not honest, we will not hesitate to say so. To cite just two examples: Bradford Washburn reported extensively in these pages on his long campaign to debunk Cook's claims for the first ascent of Denali, and Rolando Garibotti definitively rebutted Maestri's claims on Cerro Torre in *AAJ 2004*. In this edition you will find several revisions of the historical record. We derive no pleasure from countering climbers' claims. We simply want to get it right.

We ask a lot of questions even when we have zero reason to suspect dishonesty. In this age of intensive self-reporting through blogs, sponsor websites, Facebook and Instagram feeds, certain key details of an ascent—even whether a summit was reached—often are omitted in the initial accounts. Names are misspelled. East becomes west. We check the facts, clarify descriptions, and provide historical context. When we receive new information on previously published reports, we update the stories at our website (*publications.americanalpineclub.org*). It is the job of magazines, news sites, and marketing departments to churn out the first drafts of history. We take the longer view.

DOUGALD MACDONALD, *Executive Editor*

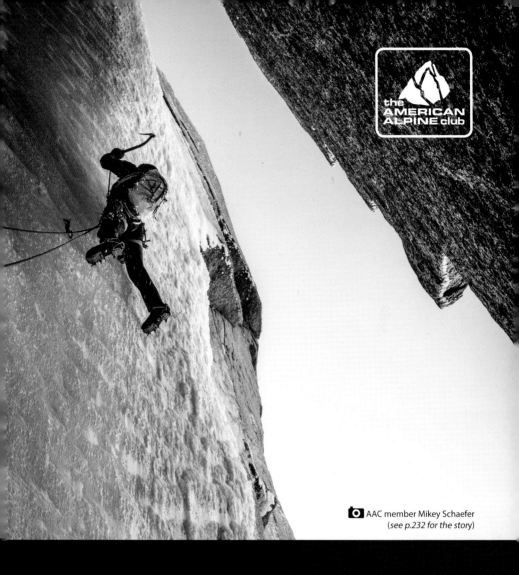

ANNAPURNA

TWO EXTRAORDINARY ASCENTS

ALONE ON ANNAPURNA

BY UELI STECK

In 1984, Swiss alpinists Norbert Joos and Erhard Loretan ventured with a small team up the seven-kilometer-long east ridge of Annapurna, which borders the south face in a rippling line of subpeaks and summits. For the final four days on the crest, the two men continued alone in alpine style through squalls of wind, committing themselves to total solitude between heaven and earth. In *Les 8000 Rugissants*, Loretan wrote, "I've never felt as far away from the living and as close to the dead."

Loretan became my idol. He helped bring a revolutionary approach to the Himalaya, achieving the best results by moving remarkably fast and light across vast stretches of terrain. In 1986 he and Jean Troillet climbed and descended the north face of Everest in a mere 43 hours. Years later, Loretan and I went to the Himalaya together, and I pestered him with questions about Everest. He was very clever: Because they'd free-soloed through the darkness, he and Troillet didn't have to bring ropes or a tent: They only stopped climbing during the day, when the temperatures were warm. With less time up high, they felt they had less risk of objective hazards and altitude sickness. It was a simple, efficient, and intelligent solution. The Polish alpinist Voytek Kurtyka proposed that such ultra-minimalism could change everything. But the 1986 Everest climb baffled most climbers, and no one has managed to replicate it.

[Previous page] "Annapurna," original 10-by-20-inch acrylic painting by Colorado artist Jesse Crock *(jessecrockart.com)*. [This page] October 8: Ueli Steck begins his solo ascent of the south face. *PatitucciPhoto.com*

Then, in 1992, two French climbers, Pierre Béghin and Jean-Christophe Lafaille, envisioned another beautiful ascent: a direct path up the south face of Annapurna that could be climbed in lightweight style. They reached 7,400 meters before they had to retreat in a gale. Béghin fell to his death when a single-cam rappel anchor failed, and Lafaille clung to an ice slab without a partner or a rope. A five-day descent began. Although he found a 20-meter cord in a lower camp, he soon ran out of food. Rockfall broke his arm. "I thought about letting go, about joining Pierre," he admitted.

Only Lafaille's technical abilities allowed him to survive. For years afterward, he felt like a "prisoner of Annapurna," and he reattempted the south face in 1995 and 1998. In 2002, Lafaille and Alberto Iñurrategi traversed the east ridge to the top, and he felt, "for the first time, I could think of Annapurna not as merely a place of morbid statistics and personal loss, but as the Goddess of Abundance."

In 2007, I arrived beneath the south face of Annapurna, determined to complete Béghin and Lafaille's brilliant, unfinished line. My first attempt, solo, ended after a couple of hundred meters. The air was too warm, and a stone hit my head, knocking me unconscious. Only luck kept me from dying. By then, like Lafaille, I was possessed. I wanted at all costs to climb this route. A year later, Simon Anthamatten and I advanced to 6,000 meters before we realized it was hopeless. Snow fell every day, and the avalanche risk was too high. One night a call for help reached us: Iñaki Ochoa de Olza was dangerously ill in Camp IV (7,500m), halfway along the east ridge. Two days later I reached Iñaki, but he didn't survive. Afterward, I just wanted to go home and forget Annapurna. It took years before I could accept what had happened.

By the autumn of 2013, I felt ready to return to Annapurna, together with Don Bowie from Canada. Our team established an advanced base camp at 5,000 meters, where Tenji Sherpa and Nima Sherpa kept us supplied with fresh food. On October 8, at 5:30 a.m., Don and I climbed toward the foot of the wall. Finally, everything seemed to be yielding for us, although a strong wind blew. When we arrived at the bergschrund, however, Don stared up at the glaze of ice that coated the rocks, and he concluded that the route was too close to his limits to climb without a rope. There aren't many words for such moments. "See you," I said.

At first it was difficult to get used to being alone, but the hard snow helped me focus. I had no

[This page] Back in Kathmandu, Steck goes over the details of his ascent with Elizabeth Hawley. *PatitucciPhoto.com*

firm plans, and thought I might just acclimatize some more, but the great conditions kept pulling me upward. I picked up the tent and stove that Don and I had stashed at 6,100 meters, but I left the rope since I was already carrying a 6mm cord. Higher up, as I photographed the face, a heavy flow of spindrift swept over me and I grabbed onto both of my ice tools, dropping my camera and one of my gloves. From then on, I had to climb in my lighter gloves.

Above 6,800 meters I climbed inside a thickening cloud. Before me, the headwall crested in a giant band of gray and brown rock, striated with runnels of ice and snow. I decided to set up my tent. There were two possible outcomes: Either the wind would ease and I'd be able to go higher, or I'd have to retreat in the morning. Since I couldn't find a sheltered spot right there, I began to climb down. One hundred meters lower, a crevasse offered a perfect bivouac site. I was now inside the mountain, surrounded and protected by its blue ice and white snow. The last rays of sun vanished, and the mountain grew quiet, just as I'd noticed the previous evening from advanced base camp. Night fell quickly. This was my chance. The only way I'd reach this summit would be to climb into the dark.

A silvery line of ice and firn crossed most of the headwall—it seemed it would be possible to find the way. And I like climbing in the dark. When you shrink your field of vision to a headlamp's lighted cone, you're forced to concentrate on the task at hand. Everything else becomes unimportant. Merely the next step, the next movement, is decisive.

I felt as if I were moving inside a luminous bubble. The rest of the world had vanished, apart from this small light moving through the sharp, black air. Flows of ice and snow surged into each other, forming an ideal surface for soloing. Although the cold was a little tiresome, a kind of happiness filled me: I was climbing on, and I felt at home. The terrain reminded me of the Eiger north face in peak winter conditions—demanding, yet not so difficult that I needed to tether myself to the mountain.

It's hard to say how many pitches I climbed, but I sensed that I arrived relatively fast at the upper end of the headwall. There, for the first time, I became aware of where I actually was and what that meant. The rest of the climb would be a race between me and the wind. Either I'd make it to the top before the gusts picked up again or I'd be forced back down. Step by step, I regained my rhythm, and the noises in my head grew quieter. *Now you just have to fight on a bit.*

When I stood on the summit ridge, I could hardly believe the landscape that spread out before me. Nothing seemed real. Yet at the same time, I still felt rational. There was no place in my mind for anything except the light of my headlamp, the search for the way ahead and the night sky blazing with stars. I checked my altimeter and followed the crest to the highest point. *Up, OK, now down.* I felt electrified with energy: I wanted to get down as soon as possible, before the wind came up or the rising sun melted the good névé. The bergschrund far below was my real summit. Scarcely five minutes passed before I began to descend. At a few steep sections I stopped to rappel. The cold stiffened my hands, and I kept having to warm them. My tracks faded endlessly into the deep. *If only I were already down!*

Around 4 a.m. I crawled inside my tent without taking off my crampons. I rested for as long as it took to boil water. My calves felt as hard as rocks. In the east, the sun slowly breached the horizon. But I didn't notice the colors of the dawn. I merely hoped the wind would hold back a little. On the other side of the bergschrund I saw only white, empty snow. I continued down alone, traversing the glacier. When Tenji, Don, and photographer Dan Patitucci arrived, my first words were, "We can go home!" Tenji gave me some soda, bread,

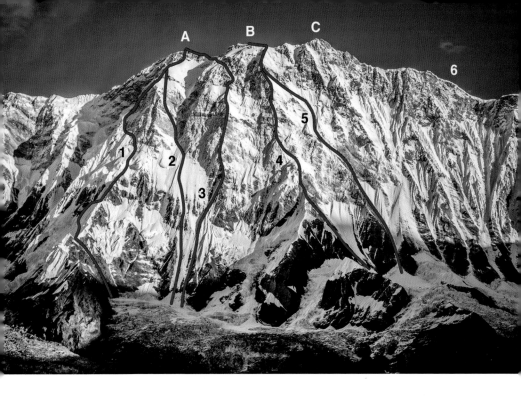

[This page] The ca 2,500-meter south face of Annapurna. (A) Main Summit (8,091m). (B) Middle Summit (8,051m). (C) East Summit (8,026m). (1) British Route (Haston-Whillans, 1970). (2) Steck Route (2013); climbed to ca 7,400m by Pierre Béghin and Jean-Christophe Lafaille in 1992; repeated alpine-style by Stéphane Benoist and Yannick Graziani two weeks after Steck. (3) Japanese Route (Aota-Yanagisawa, 1981). (4) Polish Route (Berbeka-Probulski, 1981), to central summit. (5) Catalan Route (Bohigas-Lucas, 1984, first alpine-style ascent of the south face, to central summit). This route was climbed to 7,150m, alpine-style, by Alex MacIntyre and René Ghilini, in 1982. (6) East Ridge (Joos-Loretan, 1984). *PatitucciPhoto.com*

and an apple. I could hardly summon any words—I didn't know what I should say. It was all over. It felt like deliverance. At last.

SUMMARY

New route on the south face of Annapurna (8,091m), climbed solo by Ueli Steck on October 8–9, 2013. The Swiss climber completed the route started by Pierre Béghin and Jean-Christophe Lafaille (1992, to 7,400m). He reached the summit around 1 a.m., after a brief stop at ca 6,800m. He downclimbed most of the face, making only eight rappels with a single 6mm rope, and returned to the bergschrund 28 hours after starting.

ABOUT THE AUTHOR

Ueli Steck, 37, lives outside Interlaken, Switzerland. A note on this article: The author requested that the AAJ adapt his story from Alpinist 45 (Winter 2013), and this was done with the kind permission of Alpinist's editor. The original story was translated from German by Adam Oberlin.

SOLO, ALPINE-STYLE, NEW ROUTE, 8,000 METERS

WITH HIS ANNAPURNA ASCENT, Steck joined a small, highly elite club: Only a handful of people have made an alpine-style solo ascent of an independent new route to the main summit of an 8,000-meter peak.

The most famous example is Reinhold Messner on the Diamir Face of Nanga Parbat in 1978. While the route was non-technical, it was committing and had considerable objective danger—a line that could only be contemplated by a fast-moving climber. The route is now 35 years old and has not been repeated.

In 1981, Jerzy Kukuczka soloed Makalu's northwest ridge, though his approach to 7,400 meters involved variants to the normal route. Pierre Béghin made a solo traverse of Makalu in 1989, a year no one else summited the mountain, via a new route up the south face—it was the pinnacle of his mountaineering career. However, with two other climbers he'd already fixed rope to 7,200 meters, and the upper part of his line was common to the Slovenian Route.

In 1993 Polish legend Krzysztof Wielicki soloed the southwest face of Xixabangma, following a previously unclimbed 50° snow couloir to the right of the 1982 British route. From 7,700 meters he followed the previously climbed south ridge to the summit,. This was the first time a new route on an 8,000-meter peak had been soloed in a single push and in a day.

The following year saw the remarkable two-day solo of a new route on the 2,000-meter southwest face of Cho Oyu by the Japanese Yasushi Yamanoi. On the same mountain, in 2006, Slovenian Pavle Kozjek soloed a partial new route on the south face, joining the previously climbed west ridge after crossing a technical section at 7,200 meters. Kozjek reached the summit in less than 15 hours.

Asked to name the climbers and routes that most inspired his Annapurna solo, Steck cited Erhard Loretan, first and foremost, but also the first alpine-style ascent of Annapurna's south face (Bohigas-Lucas, 1984), Reinhold Messner's solo of Mt. Everest (1980), the Béghin-Profit alpine-style partial new route on K2 in 1991, and, more recently, the ski mountaineer and speed climber Kilian Jornet. "At present I am inspired by the whole ski mountaineering scene. To see how fast those guys are able to climb is crazy." —Lindsay Griffin

ANNAPURNA AT LAST

BY YANNICK GRAZIANI

After a committing eight-day climb, my friend Stéphane Benoist and I reached the summit of Annapurna via the south face. I had been to Annapurna twice before: once in 2000 with Christian Trommsdorff and Patrick Wagnon, and then in 2010 with Stéphane. Last fall we finally completed the climb, but not without consequences. When we returned to Europe I had a mild case of frostbite, and Stéphane lost his toes and parts of the fingers on his right hand. It will be a while before he can climb again. So you could say we did not succeed 100 percent, but only around 51 percent.

Stéphane and I both work as guides in Europe, and the weather last summer was good day after day, so we very busy. Despite this we somehow got on the plane to Nepal on August 15. We looked forward to our adventure with a mix of anticipation and confidence in our fitness and preparation.

Instead of setting up a base camp, we planned to stay at the Annapurna Sanctuary Lodge between acclimatization climbs, so our logistics were fast and easy. Our plan was to acclimatize in the valley leading up to Annapurna III and Gangapurna. We did the first ascent of a nice, unnamed 6,505-meter peak and ended up spending two nights on top. After a month of

[Previous page] Nil Bohigas during the breakthrough alpine-style ascent of Annapurna's south face in 1984. *Enric Lucas* [This page] Yannick Graziani below the headwall at ca 7,000m. Steck described "once in a century" ice conditions on the face. *Stéphane Benoist*

training, we left the lodge on October 16 to approach the big south face of Annapurna. We had spent the past month going over and over our plan for the climb: which line to try, what equipment to carry, and how long we expected it would take. We also talked with Ueli Steck at the Sanctuary about his plans and ours, but by the time we returned from our last acclimatization climb he had already done the face and left. The five-hour approach up the glacier gives you time to think. Now I cannot remember much of what went through my mind, but I think everyone who has been through a similar experience understands what I mean.

At 5,000 meters we set up our tent, and the next day we got an early start, making an exhausting push through deep snow to the base of the route. The south wall is so massive and vertical that the top disappears as you get close to the bottom. It's nearly impossible to find even one square meter of flat ground for the tent. In the afternoon we set our first camp at around 6,100 meters and talked about the coming days. The forecast seemed a bit less stable than what we had expected, but we decided to continue. At about 6,650 meters, we found an uncomfortable yet magical place for a tent site, chopped out of a snow rib. In the end, we stayed three nights there and waited for better weather, because it would be pure suicide to ascend a vertical mountain when it is snowing every afternoon.

On the morning of the 20th we set off again. After hours on steep slopes, we reached the yellow rock band above 7,000 meters and climbed a few of the most difficult pitches of the entire climb. Stéphane climbed beautifully—it was as if I were at the theater! Night forced us to improvise a bivouac on a small ledge at 7,100 meters, without our tent. My mattress was

dead because of a small leak. Hell, I thought, I will freeze my ass off the rest of the climb!

The morning sun warmed us as we melted some ice for tea before setting off. That day, October 22, was the kind of day you will remember for a long time. Runnels of ice gave us a natural line to follow through the yellow rock—difficult but nice. We skirted a large black roof by climbing a frozen waterfall. The natural line led us right to what we thought would be our final

[This page] Stéphane Benoist leads steep ice at ca 7,300m. Descending from his solo ascent, Steck rappelled the steepest sections but downclimbed all but about 200 meters. *Yannick Graziani* [Next page] Graziani approaches the summit. Behind him is Annapurna South (7,219m), Behind left: Hiunchuli. *Stéphane Benoist*

bivouac, at 7,450 meters. But the following morning we discovered that we were too far left and we had to traverse back to the right. We were moving very slowly now, and we lost a few hours finding the way, and so after one more very technical pitch we dug another bivouac ledge at 7,600 meters.

At 11 a.m. we stood on the summit of Annapurna, filled with an immense feeling of happiness and satisfaction. October 24 was my 40th birthday, and the summit was a wonderful place to celebrate with my old friend from St. Jeannet (a crag near Nice), where we both started climbing at age 15.

That night we slept on the same ledge at 7,600 meters and tried to recover. The wind picked up to about 100 km/h. I didn't feel well that night, and I nearly froze outside the tent as I organized the gear to assure an early start the next morning. Our plan was to rappel to our first bivouac at 6,100 meters—a long way down. Stéphane felt weak, and we didn't yet understand that he was suffering from pneumonia and frostbite. I had to manage the rappels for both of us. Everything felt "prearranged" in my mind, as if someone else had taken hold of me—not because of the altitude but because I was in survival mode.

Finally, at 2 or 3 in the morning, we reached that first bivy ledge. Now I knew we would survive, but I also knew that a rescue would be essential for Stéphane. The next day, on the 26th, we called for a helicopter. Standing on the snow at 5,000 meters, with only half a cartridge of gas and a few cookies left, I waited for the helicopter to arrive. Normally I hate helicopters, but at that moment I thought, *What a wonderful machine!* I am grateful to JB Gurung from the Annapurna Sanctuary Lodge and all of the pilots of Simrik Air. Annapurna is behind us now, and life will go on. Stéphane is recovering in Nice, and I am in Chamonix. The cold weather has passed and spring is around the corner, with the renewal that warmth brings. Life is full of good things.

SUMMARY

Alpine-style second ascent of the Steck Route on Annapurna by Stéphane Benoist and Yannick Graziani (France), October 16–26, 2013. The French pair used a different start than Steck and made a few variations through the headwall. They reported difficulties approaching WI5 and M5+/M6 above 7,000m, and M4/M5 at ca 7,500m.

ABOUT THE AUTHOR
Yannick Graziani, 40, is a mountain guide based in Chamonix, France.

NO WEAK SHIT

A TEN-YEAR OBSESSION
WITH THE MOOSES TOOTH

SCOTT ADAMSON

It all started with a mistake, as some things do. I was with my friend James Stover, somewhere near the summit of the Mooses Tooth. We had just finished the last of our food: a little can of Vienna sausages. I was cold from nearly 24 hours on the go without many calories. Belaying that last pitch in a funnel of spindrift hadn't helped. I had been packed in snow up to my chest for what seemed like a long time.

It was late May of 2004, our first trip to the Alaska Range. We weren't too excited about it at the time, but we had just climbed a direct new route up the south face of the Mooses Tooth, to the right of the classic Ham and Eggs ice couloir (AAJ 2005). If getting lost on a corniced ridge in a whiteout had been the norm for me, I might have had a slightly bigger grin.

After topping out the headwall, we shortened the rope and traversed the Tooth's infamous wavy ridgeline. Our plan had been to rappel Ham and Eggs, which we'd done a week earlier; there were fixed anchors the whole way down. But now we couldn't see much farther than our nose, and we headed the wrong way on the ridge, traversing to the east. After hours of wallowing, the ridge dropped off drastically. That couldn't be right.

We had carried only a single, very light pack between us, with no bivy gear, not even a stove. Our plan had worked well, as far as it went. We'd blasted up that steep face, feeling so comfortable with our speed that we allowed ourselves a nap in the sun atop a rock pillar. But now we were shivering and almost out of gas, and blindly trying to navigate a convoluted cornice in a whiteout at night.

We ate those little weenies. I slurped the last bit of gelatin slime out of the can just to get the last bit of fat. I could feel some warmth inside, but it wasn't much. We decided to backtrack and rap the new route we'd just climbed.

Our tracks along the ridge had vanished. We climbed back to what we thought was our top-out, built a snow anchor, and threw the ropes into the white void. I made it about three-quarters of the way down the ropes before it started to feel very wrong. By now it had gotten light and stopped snowing, and I was looking down at a glacier that didn't seem familiar. This definitely wasn't the Ruth or the Root Canal. It must have been the Buckskin, below

the east face. The clouds wisped by, and I kept getting little glimpses of the face below me. Even in the state we were in, the face looked very attractive. Really quite sexy. By the time I'd climbed back up to James, the clouds had parted in a Hollywood ending. We got our bearings back, traversed over the summit, and rapped Ham and Eggs.

Back home, I couldn't stop thinking about our wrong turn on the Mooses Tooth. That radical-looking face, half-seen from above. We had used one point of aid for a tension traverse on Levitation and Hail Marys, our new route on the south face, and now I wanted madly to go back and do another new line, all free. Over the next couple of years I dabbled in the Ruth, but I couldn't stop thinking about the Mooses Tooth.

IN 2008, I TALKED MY BROTHER Tom into flying onto the Buckskin to sink our tools into the east face. In photos I had eyeballed a couple of options, all of which looked steep and challenging. In mid-April our bags sat on the runway as Paul Roderick from Talkeetna Air Taxi pulled our ride around and dropped off two British climbers, fresh out the range. Jon Bracey and Matt Helliker stepped out of the plane sunburned and sporting grins. They had fired up some new ground to the right of Arctic Rage (Gilmore-Mahoney, 2004) on the Mooses Tooth. They said it was steep, with not much ice. *Damn!* I thought. *That was one of our options!*

With our gear loaded on the plane, I thought for a second about flying to the Kichatna instead, but something told me we should still head to the Buckskin. Not counting the British ascent (which hadn't quite topped out), there were still only two full-length routes up the broad east face, and no route had gone free.

As soon as we landed, a few miles down the glacier from the Mooses Tooth, Tom and I threw our bags out and skied to the base of the wall. The skies were clear, and we could see the line the Brits had followed. A distinct ribbon cut down the face between their line and Arctic Rage. I couldn't tell if it was ice or snow. When we got to camp, my brother said, "Have you seen that thing to the...." "Yup," I said, cutting him off. We quickly agreed to try it.

Now it was time to sit and watch, getting to know the face's moods. The Buckskin was quiet other than the rumble of falling ice from a huge serac on the north face, named the Menace by the late Seth Shaw. A few times a day, you could faintly recognize the low hum of an aircraft flying sightseers or climbers into the Ruth, on the other side of the mountain. I lay in the tent with my brother, listening to Rage Against the Machine. "Know Your Enemy" reverberated in my brain. I thought about the looming axe these mountains hold above our necks. We train hard, develop our skills, and become as indestructible as we can. We get to know our enemy. That becomes our ticket to trespass.

We packed three days of food, a small tent, and two sleeping bags. A little heavy, but I'd learned my lesson about going too light on the Mooses Tooth back in 2004. A year later, Tom and I had gotten backhanded on Kyzyl Asker in Asia with one bag between us and no tent. We'd retreated with our tail between our legs, Tom with frostbite and me with slight hypothermia. This time we planned to dig in and wait out any funk, rather than bail at the first sight of snowfall.

It was dark as we crossed the bergschrund. We simul-climbed until the horizon turned pink, then pitched out a steep roof with good pro as the light went from pink to orange. After a few more pitches of simul-climbing, we hit the first band of steep rock. It was blue sky and Tom's lead. He made multiple attempts to get past a dripping-wet, flaring offwidth, lowered off, and then found a way around to the right. In a full pitch he didn't find any pro. It was powder snow over 70-degree granite. When I pulled into the belay I found him giving me a body belay. "If you went winging off, I would have jumped down this other couloir," he said. *Yeah, I guess that would have worked.*

I got on the sharp end, swinging and torquing my tools up mixed ground. By the time we reached a big snow slope up above, it was snowing heavily. We postholed to a safe-looking bivy site under the main rock headwall and spent an hour chipping a flat spot for the tent. A quarter

[Previous page] Nearing the summit ridge of the Mooses Tooth, in a rising storm, in 2004. *James Stover* **[This page]** Tom Adamson traverses back onto the line after a storm in 2008. Broken Tooth is in the center background. *Scott Adamson*

of the tent hung off the ledge. Inside, we clipped everything to the anchor.

When the sun came out nearly two full days later, we swam up rotten, snow-filled chimneys. You'd bounce-test and rip your tool through soft snow until finally it held body weight just long enough to do one move and repeat the process. If you chossled in too deep, looking for real ice, you'd hit dry rock. This would create a small bulge that you'd have to crawl over, feet scratching at the rock underneath.

Several pitches of this led us to a 15-foot roof. Through the binos it had seemed like there was a fang of ice dripping from the right corner of the roof, but now we saw it was just a sugary snow cone. If it had been pink or blue you could have called it cotton candy. When I tried to place a piton above the belay, the rock disintegrated and rained down on Tom like kitty litter. The crappy rock and free-hanging snow fang made for an easy decision. We bailed. A friend met us with warm food at camp. He had seen the massive slides tearing down our line and thought we'd perished. As a result, he drank all the whiskey, so we had nothing left to help us swallow our failure.

I had carried a picture of the face, torn out of an *Alpinist* article, as a topo for our route. Back home in Utah, I folded it and put it on the shelf.

IN 2010 I RECEIVED THE MUGS STUMP AWARD for another try on the Mooses Tooth. I unfolded that photo from the *Alpinist* and applied a layer of climbing tape along the back of the weakened creases.

My brother couldn't get away from life's pull this time, and so Matt Tuttle signed up for the mission. He and I climb well together. We've spent winters training in the Wasatch.

Once again the plane's echoing hum faded away, leaving us alone on the Buckskin Glacier. We had flown in earlier this time, in late March. Colder sounded better for this route, and we thought we might catch some of the ice left over from the previous fall, making for better conditions.

A day later, with stable-looking weather, we skied with light packs toward the bergschrund. This time my plan was slightly different. We had four days of food, if rationed, two 15°F bags, but no tent, only a shovel head that we could use to dig in if we had to.

Above the 'schrund we chose a more direct line to access the headwall, and Matt gave it a go as the sun popped above the horizon. It was –10°F when we left camp, and I hadn't been warm since. Matt downclimbed to the belay. No ice, no gear. We juked around to the left, found a weakness, and burned a few rope lengths simul-climbing. At the headwall where Tom had started his sketchy traverse, we found a bit of thin ice leading directly into the main ribbon. Climbing ice where there hadn't been any in 2008 gave me hope for the roof pitch. I kept

[Previous page] The author, stuck in another bivy, in 2010. *Matt Tuttle* **[This page]** The east faces of the Mooses Tooth (right) and Bears Tooth in April 2013. See Climbs and Expeditions for a photo showing all routes on the east face of the Mooses Tooth. *Pete Tapley*

peering up and imagining myself pulling those moves. The sky turned gray and started to drop.

As I followed a sticky ice pitch that brought us to the same height as our two-day bivy in 2008, it started to snow. I told Matt I didn't want to commit to the headwall with the weather change. We decided to climb a steep ice pitch that led us away from the blow-out zone, and then spent a good hour digging a snow cave. It wasn't five-star, but it was home for the next 24 hours. On Easter morning I surprised Matt with some Peeps. We dunked those cute little marshmallow birds in delicious instant coffee, which made things better but not alright, and then rapped off as soon as we felt it was safe.

Back at camp we rested a couple of days. When the sky seemed to be clearing, we climbed to our high point in half the time. With a good feeling that we could blast the upper headwall and rap back to our snug cave in a push, we left a pack with extra food, our shovel, and sleeping bags, and we kept climbing. We had been keeping an eye on a peak maybe 15 miles away, and now it was getting hit hard with wind. We could see snow blowing thousands of feet from its summit. But the sky was still cloud-free, and we felt good about our progress.

Matt led steep ice to a belay just below the crux. As he belayed me in, I noticed him fidgeting and cursing. He was holding up a large rock with his shoulder. The rock was still clipped to him with a sling, and now he was anchored only to a shabby, two-lobe cam. "This horn came loose! Put in a piece and clip me in!" I hammered in a semi-good Pecker, and with an ugly mess of slings we equalized the Pecker and the sketchy cam. Matt let the horn go whizzing off. I laughed as I told him that the cord he'd clipped was the anchor I had rapped off in 2008. *It must have been frozen in better then.*

It was getting dark. I could see some ice in the roof, but very little. I dry-tooled up about 30 feet, slung another horn for protection, and found a good stance before I had to start tapping into the verglas. Months of spindrift had formed a transparent windowpane contouring along the steep belly of the granite roof. There was no icicle hanging off the lip. This ice followed different rules than I was used to.

I yelled "Watch me!" as if that was going to help. I was facing out, down the glacier toward base camp. My left tool stuck first swing. My stomach churned. I breathed deep and committed, swinging around on my left arm so I was facing the ice, feet scratching. A stick for my right tool. Still no ice for my feet. I pressed my crampons onto the granite, locked off with my right, and swung the left just as my feet skated. My crampons bit ice, and soon I put in a stubby that looked strong and moved up to a small stance. Feeling like I'd barely pulled it off, I let out a scream that echoed off the Broken Tooth. I couldn't tell if Matt was pissed off at the committing lead or stoked for our progress. Regardless, that was out of the way.

In the time it took me to belay Matt up, the chimney system had started to spindrift. It was still dark. After a couple more pitches, the spindrift was constant. As I belayed Matt up to what would be our high point, I could hear him yelling and cursing the snow slides. I was in a sheltered stance, but he was in the gut of it. When he came into the belay, I still couldn't see him. He swung his tool right between my legs. *Matt, I'm right here!* He had a lens of hard ice covering one side of his face. I had to chip it off with a carabiner. We were about three quarters of the way up the route, but it was time to get out of there. When our ropes got stuck we had to cut one of them, leaving us with 100-foot rappels. We rapped some more.

Seconds after Matt flopped into our bivy cave, the mountain rumbled and debris slammed all around us. At some point the next day the weather let up, and 100 feet at a time we rappelled to the glacier. It snowed for eight straight days before we flew back to the land of green.

IN THE FALL OF 2012, I moved into the basement of a buddy's place and pinned that topo photo of the Mooses Tooth above my bed. It's not that I had forgotten about the route—I just hadn't been ready to start thinking about it yet. Well, now I had all winter to think about it.

I had a great ice season, but as usual I was broke come February. The chances of a trip to Alaska were looking pretty slim. I was climbing in Vail when a friend invited me to do a local mixed-climbing comp. I had stood atop a lot of things but never on a podium. But I took second, and the $1,200 prize was just enough to pay for an Alaska trip. It was on.

I had a plan but no partner, only one "maybe" from Pete Tapley. I decided to fly out to the range alone, contemplating a solo attempt. But after four days of heavy snow, they couldn't fly me to the Buckskin. Alone on the Ruth, I skied around in –30° temps. I had plenty of time to think about that route and all the attempts. I knew my skills were well-tempered from six months of ice climbing. I was strong, I knew my enemy. It was time for another round. A week later, after a failed solo attempt on the Snow Patrol route on Mt. Dickey, Pete flew in and we caught a ride over to the Buckskin. A blue ribbon of ice flowed down the route. I could not have been more psyched to see it.

The temps at night were dropping to –20°F. I wore all my layers as we skied into a slight headwind and toward the face. The movement of skiing was methodical and calm. The weather was right. Every stride brought my dream closer to reality. We headed up the intro gully. The sun popped orange in the distance, and the ground dropped below us. After 1,500 feet of casual simul-soloing, we roped up and I led some stepped vertical s'nice. Our 70s came taut with only a few pieces between us. I pushed up to the base of the headwall with Pete as my moving belay. I put in a screw and clipped an old pin that I had left on rappel in 2010. I had lost sleep over the thought of this day. It was like reuniting with an old fling that had gone bad.

We switched leads. Tapley was out about 40 feet when he stopped, looked down, waved his ice tool, and yelled a few obscenities. His tool had broken off at the head! The disappointment was crushing, but there was nothing to do about it. We had to rap off.

Two days later we returned, making good time by soloing up to that old piton. The higher we climbed the better the ice got, as the line narrowed and steepened. We ditched our extra food and bivy gear at a belay stance, planning on a single push with light packs. Knowing the terrain ahead, and having rappelled it a couple of times, I felt comfortable going light.

We were in the blue ribbon and burning off pitches. As I neared the crux roof a grin split my face. I was sure it would go. A solid pillar, the width of a bear hug, was touching down. The pillar was fractured at its foot, but after a few rock moves, a handful of good screws, and some

[Previous page] The author checks his well-worn topo from *Alpinist* magazine. *Pete Tapley* **[This page]** Charging up NWS in 2013. The crux roof is visible in upper left. *Pete Tapley*

pumpy climbing, we had unlocked the door to the upper face.

The sun winked its last bit of warmth, and we climbed to a safe spot and stopped to brew up. After what seemed like hours of fiddling with a stubborn stove, we began to rehydrate. Pete stashed a warm packet of mac and cheese inside his coat before we ate, and then managed to dump much of it into the gloves he was drying on his chest. He had a look of disbelief like a kid on a hot summer day whose chocolate ice cream has just toppled onto the pavement. But we got some much-needed calories into us and headed up again.

We climbed on intuition through shrouded snow mushrooms until the sun splashed orange and showed us the way. We stretched the rope and simuled to find sheltered belays. The ice was bulletproof and our calves burned. At the overhanging cornice, we traversed a few feet and popped onto the top in the sun. We had climbed the 5,000-foot face in 27 hours, with no aid. We took off our boots to give our feet some fresh air and pondered the descent. The highest point of the massif was about 40 minutes away, along that corniced ridge Stover and I had wandered out 10 years earlier. I didn't feel the need to return.

The descent went as smoothly as the climbing had. We were like the marionettes in a dream I'd had many times—like we were just playing out a script that had already been written. My obsession was gone. We put in a blur of V-threads, and within six hours we were skiing back to camp. We called the route NWS, after a phrase coined by my climbing posse back in Utah, when we were all young: No weak shit. In all those tries on the east face, I had never given it a weak effort.

Editor's note: Two days after descending from NWS, the author began a three-day ascent of the new route Terror, on the left side of the face, with Chris Wright. (See Climbs and Expeditions.) This time they continued to the highest point of the Mooses Tooth.

SUMMARY

First ascent of NWS (1,500m, V WI6 M5) on the east face of the Mooses Tooth, April 13-14, 2013, by Scott Adamson and Pete Tapley. The route joined Arctic Rage (Gilmore-Mahoney, 2004) for the final three pitches and ended atop the east face. The two men climbed and descended the route in a 34.5-hour round trip.

ABOUT THE AUTHOR

Scott Adamson, 33, is based in Utah but says home is where he lays his head, "which is usually my 2002 Toyota Tacoma." In the fall of 2013, he did the first ascent of two peaks in Nepal, an expedition featured in an article by Chris Wright in this edition.

[Previous page] Pete Tapley leading on NWS. *Scott Adamson* **[This page]** The author airs his feet on top. *Pete Tapley*

KHUNYANG CHHISH EAST

THE FIRST ASCENT OF A KARAKORAM GIANT

HANSJÖRG AUER

A long line stood at the visa checkpoint in the Islamabad airport. Sleepy faces waited for the next person to inch forward. It was silent except at the front of the line, where five men with matching T-shirts were digging in their bags. A group of Romanians. The backs of their shirts said something like "Nanga Parbat Expedition," surrounded by sponsor logos.

Finally, Simon and I got through the checkpoint with the necessary stamps in our passports. We exchanged only a few words with the Romanians before our duffel bags slid down the baggage carousel. One of the guys was talking about the Rupal Face. In the arrival hall, Iqbal Asko from our trekking agency greeted us with a quick handshake. Soon Simon and I were sitting in a taxi amid the early morning chaos on the streets of Islamabad. We thought nothing more of the Romanians.

Crampons, ice axes, mountain boots, and heavy backpacks. This was the gear that shaped my life as a young climber. Although I started sport climbing at the age of 12, my first love was mountaineering. I was happiest coming home after a long day and feeling pain over my whole body and not just my fingertips. I did many classic mixed routes in the Alps, and I will never

[This page] Hansjörg Auer, above 7,000m, traversing toward the summit. *Simon Anthamatten*

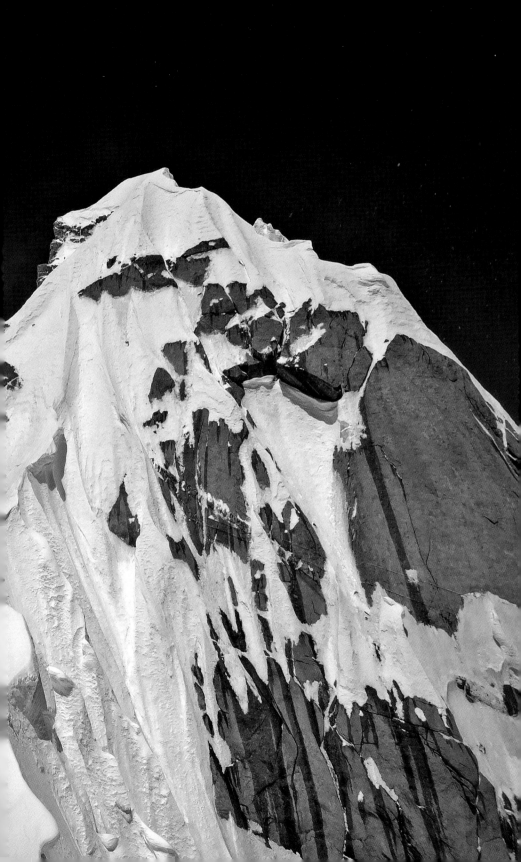

[This page] The team spent five nights on the face, with three at high camp. *Hansjörg Auer*

forget sitting on the summits and shaking hands with my brother Matthias. Which summits? This is not that important, and we stood on too many to list them.

I first got excited about pursuing sport climbing six years after my earliest climbs, mainly because I wanted to explore harder alpine terrain, but my rock climbing level didn't allow me to do so. For many years I tried to push my limits on rock, freed many hard multi-pitch routes, and made all those crazy free solos. [*Editor's note: Most famously, the author free-soloed Via Attraverso il Pesce (The Fish Route, 850m, 7b+) on the Marmolada in Italy in 2007, at age 22*]. I couldn't find the motivation to pick up my ice tools.

But over the last few years, I've rediscovered my old love. I still like the playing field of overhangs, tufas, and pumped forearms. But especially in the winter months, I enjoy doing ridge traverses, ice climbing, and winter mountaineering in general.

Simon Anthamatten and I became friends in Yosemite Valley in 2009. We spoke about doing a big trip together, but until 2013 we never found the right moment. When we finally began planning an expedition, Simon and I chose Khunyang Chhish East as our objective. An ambitious goal. I felt so happy when my brother Matthias agreed to join us. With three we would be much stronger.

Khunyang Chhish East (ca 7,400 meters) is a sub-peak of Khunyang Chhish in the Hispar Muztagh. The main summit, at 7,852 meters, is the 21st-highest peak in the world, and was first ascended by a Polish team led by Andrzej Zawada in 1971 (*AAJ 1972*). However, despite several attempts, the east peak remained unclimbed. The best attempt was by the American duo Vince Anderson and Steve House, who climbed to the top of the 2,700-meter southwest face in 2006 but were turned back by a steep rock step on the ridgeline, just 300 meters short of the summit.

Our expedition did not start according to plan. Initially we had problems with getting a permit, which delayed the expedition by a few days. Then, when Simon called from Bern to tell me that his passport issues had been resolved, Matthias called five minutes later with bad news. He was on his way to the hospital because he had severely injured his thumb. I sat down and tried to calm myself. We had invested so much time in this project, researching and training. It felt like a balloon had burst. But obstacles are part of life's tapestry, and Simon and I decided to go ahead. Matthias would come to Pakistan later, as long as his thumb healed well.

We first saw the mountain from a green terrace on the moraine of the Hispar Glacier, where the Pumari Chhish Glacier flows out from the base of Khunyang Chhish. I was in awe of its dimensions. I whispered to Simon, "I can't believe it. It's a monster!" The big amphitheater formed by the south, main, and east summits was one of the wildest places I'd ever seen. As we trekked toward base camp, Simon suddenly stopped. The clouds were lifting, and now we could see the whole southwest face leading up to the summit pyramid. We stared at each other, realizing that we had only seen half of Khunyang Chhish East earlier that day.

We began to acclimatize by climbing some ridges and little faces near base camp. As a final step we summited Ice Cake Peak, a summit along the south ridge of Khunyang Chhish, and slept on top at 6,400 meters. Serac danger and technical climbing made our life harder than expected during the first weeks of the expedition.

We learned about the tragedy at Nanga Parbat base camp during a weather check with Karl Gabl, back in Austria. Although we didn't know all the details, the news shocked us. Immediately we thought of the Romanians we'd met at the airport. Were they all dead? It seemed impossible that a massacre had just taken place so close to us. Simon and I were just finishing our final preparations for the southwest face, and we tried to push the entire situation out of our minds, vowing to dedicate any success to the victims of the Nanga Parbat massacre.

Meanwhile, Matthias had arrived at base camp, but with his injury and lack of acclimatization, it was not possible for him to join us, even for our ascent of Ice Cake Peak. That hit him hard, but there was no choice.

On June 25 Simon and I set off for our first attempt. Both of us felt really strong. In three days of climbing, we reached a small bivy site at 7,000 meters. The weather was starting to change and the wind was getting stronger. It was only 2 p.m., but the conditions wouldn't allow us to keep climbing. That night we just hoped we wouldn't be blown from that exposed

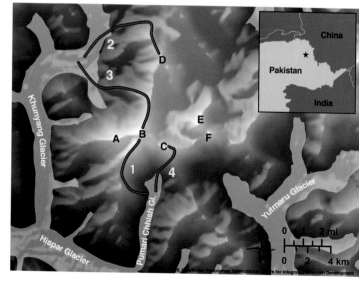

[This page] Khunyang Chhish and its satellite peaks have seen many attempts but only four ascents. (A) West peak (7,350m, unclimbed). (B) Khunyang Chhish (7,852m). (C) East peak (7,400m). (D) North peak (7,108m). (E) Pumari Chhish (7,492m). (F) Pumari Chhish South (7,350m). (1) South face to south ridge (Polish, 1971). (2) Khunyang Chhish North (Japanese, 1979). (3) Northwest spur to north ridge (U.K., 1988). (4) Khunyang Chhish East (Austrian-Swiss, 2013). Map by Anna Riling

bivy into the darkness of the Karakoram. The next morning it was even worse. Snow pressed through the zipper and into our tent. Normally I´m really good at suppressing my emotions during hard situations in the mountains. But at 8 a.m. I suddenly concluded that if we didn't react right away, the mountain would determine our fate. We packed and fought our way down. After 14 hours, cold, shattered, and emotionless, we reached the base of the wall. Matthias was happy to see us alive and helped carry our backpacks to base camp.

Four days later we made another try, but tons of fresh snow and many avalanches forced us to retreat at 5,600 meters. We had started too early to catch the forecast weather window. We were angry, but in the high mountains everything has to be perfect. The difference between failure and success is minute.

Although we had three more weeks in base camp, it was becoming clear that Simon and I had only one more attempt in us. The failures wear you out. We would need Matthias' enthusiasm for another go at the southwest face, but he was still not acclimatized adequately. Climbing alone, he could only reach 5,500 meters. Simon offered to go back up Ice Cake Peak with Matthias, and the two of them set off for a two-day climb while I chilled in base camp.

For the first time on any big climbing trip, I wrote very little in my diary. The mental stress was much greater than I'd ever experienced, and my mind was just too busy and full to be poetic. The weather was still perfect, and I wondered if Simon and I had blown our only chance with our second attempt. Would we have been successful if we'd started just one day later? There were strong winds on top, which maybe would have stopped us again, but the fact that we didn't get the chance to try was making me crazy.

For 10 days there wasn't much to do about it. Bad weather, high winds on top, and snowfall down to base camp tried our patience. But there was one positive: Matthias was now acclimatized and ready to join us on a potential third attempt, and that had us smiling again.

On the evening of July 13, Gabl gave us a promising forecast. Not the perfect window, but at least we would have clear, cold nights. Matthias was ready to go. On July 14 at 4 a.m., the team complete, we commenced the final try. The first two days went smoothly. After a spectacular bivy on a tiny snow mushroom, we climbed without problems up to 6,600 meters on the second day. Only some wind and spindrift on the last mixed pitches made the climbing uncomfortable. That night our little tent nearly collapsed from the weight of the spindrift. The morning was cold and gray. We tried to climb, but the conditions were too difficult. After only 200 meters, we found a little crevasse with a tunnel leading inside: a perfect shelter, where no wind or spindrift penetrated. Here we waited two days for the storm to subside.

Crammed into our tiny tent, we fought to suppress the rising feeling of futility and to keep the dim spark of determination glowing. Only rarely did one of us find the motivation to check the weather outside. As each hour passed we noticed how the altitude was draining our remaining strength. We had to make a decision. We couldn't wait any longer.

On the morning of July 18, the winds calmed and the clouds cleared. It seemed we would have our last chance. At 6 a.m., as the sun rose, we set off. The mixed climbing above our bivy was hard, our toes and fingers were freezing, and the long traverse out to the ridge on bare ice was exhausting. At 7,000 meters we took a small break and then aimed for the ridge, higher than the Americans had, and discovered that we could avoid the rock step that had stopped House and Anderson. The conditions worsened as we climbed the ridge, but we knew we would soon be on top. At 12:30 p.m. we stood on the summit, looking over a sea of fog, with only the highest peaks of the Karakoram poking through.

It was very windy and we only stayed at the summit for a short time. We climbed back along the ridge and then rappelled to the shoulder at 7,000 meters. After six more rappels we arrived at our tent, at 6,800 meters, just before nightfall. We immediately crawled into our sleeping bags. We had no food, but we were too tired to eat anyway. We dreamed of burgers, Coke, and potato chips. After a short night in our tunnel bivy, we started rappelling again under a starry night sky. The last hours of the descent, in the afternoon sun, were very dangerous. Rocks, ice blocks, and wet snow tumbled alongside us. But we had recognized the rhythm of the avalanches, and we used the short windows between slides to rappel, before hiding again behind rock buttresses. After 12 hours we crossed the bergschrund and literally sprinted over the remains of a fresh avalanche, down to the Pumari Chhish Glacier.

A few days later we were in Gilgit, waiting for a flight to Islamabad. No mountaineer wanted to travel the Karakoram Highway after the tragedy at Nanga Parbat. A tragedy that had cost many lives. What had happened to the Romanians? We had no idea. I was lost in thought when Simon's voice

[This page] Summit day. *Hansjörg Auer*

suddenly penetrated the silence. "There they are!" We could hardly believe it as the Romanians fell into our arms. Their faces looked gaunt—they were exhausted. Not only because they had climbed the Rupal Face, but also because the view down the other side of the mountain, into the empty Diamir base camp, had been etched into their minds forever. I was so happy to see them. It seemed to me that their successful ascent of Nanga Parbat had honored the spirit of those lost climbers in the best possible way.

SUMMARY

First ascent of Khunyang Chhish East (7,400m), by the ca 2,700m southwest face, by Simon Anthamatten (Switzerland), Hansjörg Auer, and Matthias Auer (both Austria), July 14–19, 2013.

ABOUT THE AUTHOR

Born in 1984, Hansjörg Auer lives in the Oetztal Valley, west of Innsbruck, Austria, and works as a professional climber and guide.

Parts of this story were translated from German by Simone Sturm.

LEARNING TO WALK

THE FIRST ASCENT OF K6 WEST IN PAKISTAN

RAPHAEL SLAWINSKI

Out of the shapeless mass that is the past, moments stand out like still photographs. I remember driving through the concrete canyons of Calgary's downtown one spring morning in 2005 and deciding that, yes, I'd go with Steve Swenson to Pakistan. Until then, I'd avoided expeditions to faraway, exotic mountain ranges, figuring I could do a lot more climbing if I stayed home in the Canadian Rockies. But that July, after 24 hours of continuous travel, I found myself blinking in the harsh sunlight as I stepped onto the tarmac of Skardu's airstrip.

That first trip to the Karakoram was also my first foray into the thickets of Pakistani bureaucracy, which denied us permission for both of the peaks Steve and I'd hoped to attempt. In the end, we settled for playing on the lower peaks of the Charakusa Valley. That trip also was my introduction to Asia's microbes. I vividly recall waking in the middle of the night in a stone guesthouse and making a desperate dash for the squat toilet. The following day, step by slow step, collapsing every few minutes among scrubby grasses, I took six excruciating hours to cover what's normally a two-hour walk.

All that was forgotten once we arrived at base camp, a green meadow surrounded by granite spires, icy couloirs, and hulking mountains. We acclimatized on the boulder-strewn hills and snowy peaks above camp, before a good forecast enticed us up the glacier. At the head of the valley stood the symmetric pyramid of unclimbed Hassin Peak (ca 6,300 meters). Climbing through intermittent flurries, we negotiated steep ice flows, granite grooves, and unconsolidated snow flutings to a spectacular bivouac on the crest of a sharp ridge. The following morning dawned cloudless. We set off for the summit, a mere 800 meters higher, with light packs.

By midafternoon we had ground to a halt 300 meters below the top. The snow, squeaky in the morning, had turned to mush in the fierce Karakoram sun. We gasped at thin air with open mouths. If only we'd taken bivy gear, even just a stove, we could have stopped, rested, and summited the following morning. As it was, throats burning from thirst and exertion, we drilled the first of many V-threads in the soft ice and slid down the ropes.

Walking out of the Charakusa 10 days later, I looked back one last time and thought of early starts under the arch of the Milky Way, curtains of chandeliered ice and verglassed granite

[This page] Ian Welsted heads into moderate mixed terrain, above the steepest climbing on the 1,800-meter northwest face of K6 West. *Raphael Slawinski*

corners. It almost didn't matter that the summits had eluded us. And I was secretly glad we'd been denied the permit for unclimbed K6 West, whose intimidating bulk and bands of seracs rose across the glacier from base camp. Yet I could not keep my eyes and camera off it. Is it any surprise that someday it would draw me back?

2006: Less than a year later I stepped off a plane in Islamabad, my T-shirt sticking to my back in the predawn heat. Ben Firth, Eamonn Walsh, Ian Welsted, and I were intent on unclimbed Khunyang Chhish East (ca 7,400 meters). Our gastrointestinal troubles started while we were still in Islamabad and never truly stopped. They punctuated the approach trek, during which, at one of the many switchbacks of the dusty trail, Ian didn't even have time to pull his pants down. They didn't relent during acclimatization, when I had to spend a night outside of the tent on all fours, the falling snow coating my back and the vomit on the ground. And they spelled the end of our attempt on Khunyang Chhish East, when, after two long days' climbing, we started rappelling in perfect weather, leaving behind bivouac ledges stained an ugly brown.

A couple of days before leaving base camp, Eamonn and I made the first ascent of one of the many nameless 6,000ers lining the Hispar Glacier in a 24-hour push. But once the satisfaction wore off, the frustration returned. Before I started going to Pakistan, I liked to quote Dave Cheesmond's saying about the Canadian Rockies: "If you can climb here, you can climb anywhere." I'd climbed rock, ice, and choss all over the Rockies, but this didn't seem to be helping much in the Karakoram.

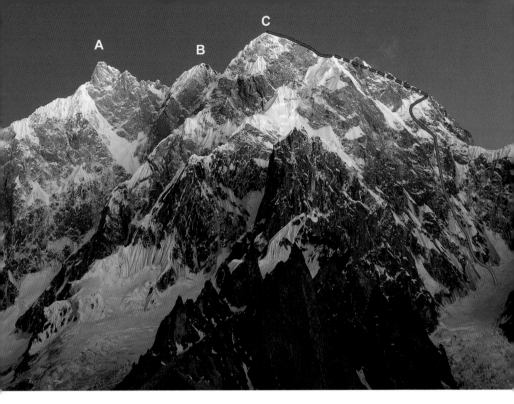

[This page] The K6 massif under moonlight, with less snow than the Canadians found a few days later. (A) K6, 7,281m. (B) K6 Middle, unclimbed. (C) K6 West, 7,040m. *Raphael Slawinski*

2009: This time Eamonn, Ian, and I had chosen yet another unclimbed bastion of granite and ice, Pumari Chhish East (ca 6,900 meters), one valley north of Khunyang Chhish. Thanks to the cooking of our friend Hajji Ghulam Rasool, we mostly avoided the gastrointestinal eruptions that had plagued our previous trip. But success—real success—continued to elude us. We climbed two smaller peaks in single-push efforts, but our attempt on the higher and harder Pumari Chhish East came to naught when, after an exhausting day of climbing, I threw up my dinner of undercooked freeze-dried chili and cheese. What would it take to finally find success on the great peaks of the Karakoram?

2013: As Ian and I stepped off the plane in Skardu, I experienced a comfortable feeling of familiarity: the car horns and clouds of exhaust along the main thoroughfare; the quiet, walled-in gardens of the back streets; Rasool's toothy smile when Ian and I walked out of the terminal building. But in other ways, everything was different.

Two nights earlier, armed men had stormed the Diamir base camp at the foot of Nanga Parbat and murdered 10 foreign climbers and a local cook. I came within a breath of saying I was going home. Jesse Huey, the third member of our team, did just that. But our objective, K6 West, lay deep inside traditionally peaceful Baltistan. By flying north we could bypass the troubled Nanga Parbat area. Cerebrally, I thought we'd be quite safe in Skardu and Hushe. And viscerally, I realized how much I still wanted to spend the summer in the Karakoram.

The last day of June dawned cool and showery as we walked beside the Charakusa Glacier, gray clouds hiding the big peaks at its head. Umbrella in hand, I skipped along the trail, chatting with porters one moment and enjoying solitude the next. After the surreal and yet all too real horror of the Nanga Parbat massacre, after all the subsequent hesitation, I was happy simply to be alive and in the mountains.

Even better, my engine wasn't smoking, to use Rasool's colorful phrase for diarrhea. Was it thanks to his scrupulously clean hands, so different from those of our cook in 2006? Or was my engine becoming used to running on Pakistani gasoline?

We started acclimatization the very next day by scrambling up the Flame, a 5,000-meter hill above base camp. Toward the top, postholing through isothermal snow, I was rudely reminded of what thin air felt like, as my lungs couldn't keep up with my legs. The Flame set the tone for the next few weeks. Every time we ventured above base camp we went a little higher, while trying as much as possible to avoid actual climbing. With sharp ridges and vertical faces all around, it felt strange to be seeking out snow slogs. Had we grown lazy? Or had we learned from earlier trips, when we'd proudly eschewed the easiest routes and failed to acclimatize as a result? What mattered at this stage was our red blood cell count. We'd find enough steep ice and granite on K6 West.

For our last acclimatization outing we planned a traverse of the triple-summited Farol (ca 6,300 meters). After two days of deep snow, corniced ridges, and steep couloirs, we pitched our little, yellow tent in a comfortable wind scoop just below the west peak. The following morning, with the sun lighting up the symmetrical pyramid of Chogolisa to the north, we started weaving between cornices toward the central peak. An hour later we were back, finding the sharp ridge to be more demanding than we'd expected or wanted. We spread our sleeping pads on the snow and settled in for a day of eating and reading. In 2006 we'd thought about spending a night on the summit of a 6,400-meter peak to acclimatize, but headaches made us seek the comforts of base camp instead. Now we knew there was no avoiding the dull rigors of acclimatization—we spent two nights on top of Farol West.

Back in base camp, we ate, read and waited for a favorable forecast. Every few days we'd receive SMS updates from Mohammad Hanif, an experienced meteorologist with the Pakistani weather office. They'd be couched in precise yet poetic prose: "Harsh weather next 3 days, be careful" or "5 day window

[This page] Raphael Slawinski starts the second pitch of "the gash," the climb's technical crux. *Ian Welsted*

opening in 2 days, don't worry." Hanif's latest forecast predicted a weeklong spell of good weather to begin in three days. I was glad of the enforced rest, for I feared K6 West almost as much as I desired it.

The choice of route had always been clear: an aesthetic ice line on the northwest face that appeared safe from the seracs that threaten most of the northern aspects of K6 and its neighbors. Unfortunately, we'd have to approach it up a broken icefall and through a narrow valley with huge mountainsides rising on three sides. More than once we'd witnessed avalanches sweep across nearly the entire width of the gorge. But there was no other way.

On July 25 we got up before dawn. A visibly moved Rasool made us milk tea and porridge. As we were about to shoulder our 20-kilo packs, he sprinkled flour on our heads. A traditional Balti farewell: May you come back safely and grow old and gray.

Two hours later we clicked into crampons at the base of the icefall. I was glad to be done with the anxious anticipation and to focus on simple, immediate actions: a burst of front-pointing up an ice wall, an end run around one crevasse, a face-in downclimb into another. As the midafternoon sun turned the snow into wet cotton candy, we dropped our packs inside a safe bergschrund. I breathed a sigh of relief. A vertical mile of icefields and rock walls rose overhead, but the random hazards of the approach were behind us.

In the morning, spindrift poured off the lip of the 'schrund as I swung repeatedly at the snow above it. Finally my picks bit into something substantial and I pulled onto the slope above the crevasse. We spent the day climbing seemingly endless 50- to 60-degree icefields interspersed with vertical pitches. These would've been easy enough in the Canadian Rockies. Here, at nearly 6,000 meters and with a heavy pack, my forearms and calves quickly filled with lactic acid. Nearing the top of a pitch, I'd rush tool placements and forego screws, intent on reaching lower-angled ice where I'd be able to drop my arms and stand flat-footed.

By late afternoon we reached the shelter of an overhanging rock wall. The ice below it swept up to near vertical, but after a couple of hours of work we'd fashioned a long foot ledge. Extended with a nylon tarp anchored to screws and filled with ice chunks, our makeshift ledge accepted two-thirds of the tent. Dinner was soup and mashed potatoes—after Pumari Chhish East, I would never again take chances with half-cooked freeze-dried meals at altitude. Sleep came easily.

The morning dawned blue and cold. Right above where we'd spent the night, a band of shattered granite reared up. The most promising option was a thinly iced, right-leaning gash. In spite of the cold, or perhaps because of it, I was eager to get moving and offered to lead the first few pitches. I balanced delicately up gritty slabs, tapped up a narrow ribbon of hollow ice, and, almost out of rope, squirmed into a nearly vertical gully. I anchored to stubbies in ice splatters on the left wall.

After an easier pitch the gully swept up past vertical. Icicles dripped from the overhanging rock. I didn't want to let doubt take root in my mind, and as soon as Ian arrived at the stance I grabbed the rack and started up. At least the gear was decent, if upside-down screws in snapped-off columns could be called that. Judging them to be solid, I relinquished control and committed to the knee-drops and lock-offs. Swinging desperately at thin ice, I expected to come off at any moment. But a pick draped over a rock fin stayed put, and I got my feet back under me. I'd gotten what I wanted: hard climbing above 6,000 meters.

Light and space flooded my senses as I ran out the ropes on the small icefield above. We still had a long way to go, but the steepest part of the wall was behind us. As we moved up and left to avoid a steep buttress, the summit ridge came into view. The thought of flat ground was alluring, and I almost suggested continuing into the night. Then I thought better of it: It wouldn't do to climb ourselves into a hole of exhaustion. We were finally grasping the immense scale of these mountains, and the patient effort it took to climb them. Stopping below a boulder in the middle of a steep slope, we chopped another ledge and crawled inside the tent long after dark.

In the morning it took us another few hours to reach a notch in the ridge. I peered down the south side. "It looks like good corn skiing," I joked, elated to see mellow ground ahead. After soup and mashed potatoes, we headed up an easy snow ridge. I hadn't forgotten the miscalculation on Hassin Peak, and we carried the tent, sleeping bags, and stove. For a while, as we trudged up the ridge, it seemed we might summit that very afternoon. Soon, though, the broad crest degenerated into a corniced knife-edge of smooth granite. Disappointed, we strode down sun-warmed snow to the notch where we'd first gained the ridge.

While we set up the tent again and made more mashed potatoes, we talked about what to do. We still had a couple of gas canisters; the weather held. Maybe we could drop down the south side of the ridge and outflank the knife-edge? It would mean losing height and make summit day much bigger, at an altitude unfamiliar to both of us. Success, seemingly so close a few hours earlier, now seemed like a long shot. But as the shadow of a rock pinnacle crept closer to the tent, we made up our minds to try again in the morning.

When we left the tent the sun was still below the horizon and the cold felt almost Alaskan. We frontpointed down a steep, icy slope, contoured below a rock wall, and, picking a likely line through crevasses and seracs, started kicking steps. This time luck was on our side: The snow was firm and we gained height slowly but steadily. After a couple of hours we regained the ridge above the knife-edge. In deep shade, at nearly 7,000 meters, we couldn't move fast enough to stay warm. The cloudless sky was the dark blue of high places, so different from the pale lowland sky that we might've been on an alien planet. Kick by deliberate kick, we switchbacked across an icy slope, a string of shallow tracks unrolling behind us in a thin crust of snow. Every few minutes we'd stop to swing blood back into our fingers.

Slowly, as the angle eased, we emerged into the sun. The summit was a gentle slope on the south side and a huge precipice on the north. Ignoring Ian's protestations at the other end of the rope, I edged toward the highest point, hoping for a glimpse of our distant base camp. To no avail. Perhaps if I'd been a raven I could have peered over the fragile edge. For a long time we sat in the sunshine: talking, sipping from our water bottles, and trying to hold on to this moment.

One V-thread, then another and another—we made close to 30 rappels down the northwest face the following day. Back in the 'schrund we waited all afternoon, looking longingly at the valley, while around us the mountains fell apart in the heat. When evening stilled the bombardment, we made a dash for base camp. We felt very small as we zigzagged between crevasses, with batteries of seracs and snow mushrooms ranged silently on three sides. Fortunately they stayed silent, and as night fell we took off our crampons, switched on our headlamps, and started hopping across the granite rubble covering the Charakusa Glacier.

A couple of hours later, we looked up to see lights waiting on the edge of the meadow above the glacier. It was Rasool and his helper, Iqbal, come to bring us milk tea and chapattis, and to take our packs. Farhan, our liaison officer, gave an impromptu speech about how we'd remember this moment all our lives. At the time I thought he was being bombastic. Now I think he may have been right.

SUMMARY

First ascent of K6 West (7,040m) by the northwest face and west ridge, by Raphael Slawinski and Ian Welsted, July 25–30, 2013. The two Canadians climbed alpine-style, bivouacking four nights during the ascent and once on the way down (1,800m, WI4+ M6+). Before their ascent, a Japanese trio made a spirited weeklong attempt on the same route, reaching 6,450m (*see Climbs and Expeditions*).

ABOUT THE AUTHOR
Raphael Slawinski, 47, lives in the shadow of the Canadian Rockies in Calgary, Alberta. During the week he's a professor of physics at Mount Royal University. Come the weekend, depending on the season, he morphs into a sport climber, ice climber, or alpinist.

[This page] Welsted nears the top. Behind him is the Nangma Valley. *Raphael Slawinski*

GAMLANG RAZI

A FIRST ASCENT IN MYANMAR'S MYSTERIOUS MOUNTAINS

ANDY TYSON

"Until one is committed there is hesitancy.... The moment one definitely commits oneself, then Providence moves too. All sorts of things occur to help one that would never otherwise have occurred." —W.H. Murray

Nineteen-thousand-foot glaciated peaks in a super-remote region of an exotic Southeast Asian country? Unsurprisingly, I was not alone in my interest in the northern reaches of Myanmar (Burma). I first thought of visiting the area back in the early 1990s. I was interested in "unexplored" mountains, and through that lens eastern India, southeastern Tibet, and northern Burma could not be overlooked.

In 1997 I read of the late Takashi Ozaki and Namar Jonsain's success on Hkakabo Razi, believed to be the highest mountain in Myanmar at ca 5,881 meters (*AAJ 1998 and 2003*). The mountain sounded mysterious and enticing, with immense difficulties even during the approach, requiring old-school Shipton and Tilman–style expedition tactics. In the following

years I journeyed and climbed in many remote regions of India, Tibet, and China, and now and then I revisited the idea of exploring northern Myanmar. But the difficulties of permits, politics, and geography kept pushing me away.

More recently, however, I read with interest about positive shifts in Myanmar's politics. The country held elections in 2010, and opposition party members were granted seats in the government. Due to the more open government, spending tourism dollars in Myanmar is no longer viewed as supporting an oppressive regime. Travel warnings and advisories have eased. In the spring of 2012 I recalled Ozaki's expedition and zoomed in to view the area around Hkakabo Razi on Google Earth. It felt a bit anticlimactic to sit in my living room and retrace Ozaki's journey with the latest 3D maps and satellite imagery. But, ironically, that day I discovered my own mystery of maps and geography.

On Google Earth, several peaks surrounding Hkakabo appeared to be similar to Hkakabo's height, if not higher. Answers about this part of the world don't come easily, so it took some time to identify one peak that was rapidly gaining my interest: Gamlang Razi. (Due to the local geography, the peak does not stand out prominently from any direction. The name likely came from a nearby river or pass, named Gamlang Wang and Gamlang La, respectively; Razi means "mountain" in the local Rawang language.) My research was just beginning. I

accessed maps and survey reports, and spent time in Harvard University's map library. A British survey in 1925, the first in the area, had presented Hkakbabo as the highest peak, and many subsequent sources maintained Gamlang Razi was lower, even after later surveys pegged Gamlang as the higher peak. "A bit of a mystery" was the eventual conclusion. This element of uncertainty and the improving political situation provided plenty of motivation to put together an expedition to attempt Gamlang and ascertain its actual height.

My wife, Molly Loomis Tyson, a couple of local friends, and I started discussing our dream trip, which would involve good friends and partnering with locals. Eventually, Eric Daft, Mark Fisher, and Chris Nance joined us as the team members from the United States.

MYANMAR PARTNERS

Exploring remote corners of the world requires venturing into politics, values, cultures, history, and relationships. Given the quickly evolving

[Previous page] The team climbed the glacier and west ridge (left skyline) of Gamlang Razi (left). *Mark Fisher* [This page] The author with Namar Jonsain, who joined Takashi Ozaki for the first ascent of Hkakabo Razi in 1997. *Mark Fisher (Fishercreative.com)*

political and social landscape in Myanmar, we did our best to make sure we were safe, informed, and that our choices and actions were contributing to a positive direction for the people and country.

The Technical Mountaineering Club of Myanmar (TCCM) was founded in 2010 with the help of Seattle climber Steve Davis, who spent four years working in Myanmar and teaching some of the locals how to rock climb in his spare time. TCCM is a loose club of young folk who had become disenchanted with the only historical option: the Myanmar Hiking and Mountaineering Federation (MHMF) and its university affiliates. Finding little support or inspiration for technical climbing in the MHMF, and with fewer government restrictions on interactions with climbers from other countries, this enthusiastic group formed a separate club. Now, providing guidance from back in Seattle, Steve saw an opportunity for TCCM members to be part of a Western expedition to their own high peaks, and thus gain technical mountaineering skills and experience.

Steve and TCCM approached the Htoo Foundation for support with permits and funding. This charitable organization, funded by a Burmese natural resources conglomerate, "assists in health, education, culture, regional development and preservation of national habitat." In our case the goal was to highlight opportunities in the Putao area of northern Myanmar for environmentally responsible tourism, while also providing health care to villagers and creating awareness about Hkakabo Razi National Park and its conservation efforts. Partnering with TCCM and Htoo cleared a path for traveling and climbing in the area.

In late March 2013, I flew to China, having volunteered to take nine TCCM members on a training climb of Haba Xue Shan (5,396m) in Yunnan Province. I then traveled to steamy Yangon, Myanmar, to work on expedition logistics with TCCM and the Htoo Foundation. Despite the 109°F temperatures and 80 percent humidity, we tried bouldering in nearby Hpa An. (There are better months than April for climbing in Myanmar!) In China

[This page] Gamlang Razi lies along Myanmar's northwestern frontier with Tibet. The approach from Machanbaw to base camp took 16 days. *Mike Clelland*

and Yangon, I climbed with Win Ko Ko and Pyae Phyo Aung, who would be the TCCM climbers on our team.

Despite the 17 years since Ozaki's expeditions, we heard constant remembrances of the Japanese climber's expedition to Hkakabo. At every turn we were advised to do something because that is what Ozaki did, or we'd meet someone who had been touched by his expedition. Every school kid learns the name of the highest peak in the country, Hkakabo Razi, and with that they learn the name of the persons who climbed it, making Namar and Ozaki the Tenzing and Hillary of Myanmar.

Namar Jonsain (a.k.a. Aung Tse or Nyima Gyaltsen), an ethnic Tibetan from northern Myanmar, was no less fit at 42 than he was when he climbed Hkakabo, and would host us in his village home and guide us to base camp and above. We also would be accompanied by Ko Thet Tun, regarded as the most experienced guide for journeys in northern Kachin state, where Gamlang and Hkakabo are located. He is a veteran of nine trips to the area and was one of the original members of Ozaki's Hkakabo team. We would be privileged to be following in Ozaki's steps, interacting with his friends and teammates, years after his journey but still very fresh in their minds.

INTO THE JUNGLE

We all arrived in Yangon by August 10. Though our instincts were to go later in the fall, our local contacts and a friend and meteorologist, Marc De Keyser (Weather4expeditions.com), had advised us that the end of August and beginning of September might, for a variety of reasons, be the best window for summit attempts. So we dove into the heart of the monsoon.

From Yangon we flew to Putao, the northernmost commercial airport in the country. A couple of days later, we drove 14 miles to the town of Machanbaw and started hiking. The trail distance from Machanbaw to Tahawndam is 150 miles. We planned to average just over 13 miles a day, taking 11 days to reach Tahawndam, the "Last Village" in Myanmar, and Namar's home. After the Last Village we would travel another four days to reach base camp. In all, we would spend 16 days just to get near our objective. We all were as excited about this part of the trip and the locals we would meet as we were about the climb itself.

As I stepped onto the Machanbaw bridge, I looked back on a gaggle of porters waiting to be chosen to carry a load and join our expedition. A line of team members trotted past me: seven climbers, ten on the Htoo support trekking team, the ten-person cook crew, and two

[This page] Nearing base camp. *Mark Fisher (Fishercreative.com)*

[This page] Unclimbed granite needles to the north. *Mark Fisher (Fishercreative.com)*

military escorts. Somehow this dream of mine, hatched in my living room 18 months earlier, had turned into an expedition of 70 people—more than I had ever imagined—heading into the remote northern tip of Myanmar.

Quickly the jungle took over, villages appearing like oases in the middle of overwhelming vegetation. The frightening novelty of the leeches wore off quickly, once we learned they did not hurt or itch much. The sand flies, bees, spiders, and mosquitos were much more annoying. The bug life at least kept us distracted from the potential consequences of an encounter with the vipers that occasionally crossed our path. The footpath was rugged, overgrown, and surprisingly difficult for being the only artery of connection between villages.

The travel was hot, wet, and dirty, but a bathing spot at the end of each day rejuvenated us. We were able to purge just enough heat, mud, itchiness, and stress at each swimming hole to wake up and do it again the next day. The villagers were a wonderful constant: welcoming and friendly, but not overly curious or solicitous. To them we were a passing curiosity, not an opportunity. They watched us come and watched us go, graciously inviting us to stay with them again on our return.

After 11 days and as many villages, the vegetation relaxed its grip slightly as we climbed to 7,000 feet, and we noticed an upswing in the crops, goods, and general health of the local people. The improved climate and foot trade with China gave the northernmost villages in Myanmar a somewhat stable and confident air, despite their exceptionally remote location.

After an amazing reception in Tahawndam, which we were told had not seen foreign visitors in seven years, we spent a day organizing our stuff and paying the porters that had traveled with us from Putao. From here we would employ local Tibetans (mostly), Rawang, and Taron for the last leg of the journey. After four more days, ascending to the edges of the jungle at 3,650 meters (ca 12,000'), we arrived at base camp, soaking wet and itching to climb—not to mention itching from incessant bug bites.

UP THE PEAK

The jungle journey had been like a multi-night train ride in India: long, uncomfortable, repetitive, yet full of adventure. Eventually you just need to get off the train, no matter where you are.

[This page] Molly Loomis Tyson high on the west ridge. *Mark Fisher (Fishercreative.com)*

In our case, base camp was not exactly where I'd expected, but it was close enough.

Hopes of comfortable camping on alpine vegetation were unmet. The jungle, while friendlier than below, was like the mid-elevation forests in the North Cascades of Washington: lots of tall, dripping vegetation and uneven ground. The bright side was we were close to our objective and finally on our own as a climbing team. With a summit still more than 2,000 meters above us, we needed to figure out which way we were going, acclimatize, and move gear.

Above base camp we ascended a super-steep rhododendron slope before finally gaining open, high-alpine vegetation around 4,600 meters. The exposed rock was poor-quality schist, which soured our interest in the ridge we had hoped to ascend. We refocused our energy toward a glacial snow and ice route. (Higher, at about 5,500 meters, the rock was nice granite.)

The weather was foggy and rainy much of the time, but in the morning we would get just enough of a view to keep us moving on a good path. A ridge, a pass, and three camps put us in position for a summit bid from our high camp at around 4,725 meters (ca 15,500'). Marc De Keyser texted a favorable forecast for September 7, adding that it would be the nicest weather we were going to get. We burned a day to rest and wait for the "better" weather.

On September 7, we rose at 3:30 a.m. It was lightly raining, but we suited up and started climbing. After traveling over bare and crevassed glacial ice, we transitioned onto the snow-covered glacier and the falling rain turned to snow. At the transition, Win Ko Ko, who had been moving slowly and having difficulty on the technical terrain, descended to high camp, while the rest of us continued. We still hoped to achieve a joint Myanmar-American ascent, and Pyae Phyo Aung seemed excited to continue, but he was a novice compared with the rest of the team. We hoped we'd find a route that would permit us to summit together.

Clouds swirled around us throughout the ascent, closing in and obscuring the route, then breaking just enough for us to push ahead. At one point the whiteout was so thick we tried three different paths before finding a good line. We used pickets on the steep slopes. The weather started improving and we could see the top ahead. At 2 p.m. six of us stood on the snowy summit. We hugged and shouted, relieving the stress that had built during the first 32 days of the expedition, not to mention the years of planning leading up to it. It truly felt like a Myanmar-American expedition from start to summit.

On top we used a Juniper Archer sub-meter GPS receiver to record position and elevation data for 30 minutes. After the trip, the data was processed and reviewed by Juniper Archer and Canada-based Effigis, and it showed the summit to be 19,258 feet (5,870m +/- 2m).

Pyae Phyo Aung was tired on the way down. He fell a number of times, requiring teammates to arrest him. The fifth time, due to the angle and soft snow, his team was unable to stop the fall. The rope team fell down the steep slope and across a bergschrund, eventually stopping on the glacier below, where the angle decreased. Luckily all were fine, and the descent continued uneventfully. Arriving in camp after dark, we met with Win Ko Ko. There was joy for our success and sadness that the whole team had not made it to the top.

So, could Gamlang be higher than Hkakabo? Maybe. Hkakabo has never been measured with an accurate recording instrument on the summit (as we did on Gamlang.) During the 1925 survey, the British/Indian team sighted the mountains from distant jungle ridges. Since that time, maps not based on the British survey have shown a wide variety for peak heights, mostly depicting Gamlang higher than Hkakabo. Current satellite-generated data also depicts Gamlang as higher. Our summit GPS record showed Gamlang Razi to be 11 meters (36') lower than the highest published height of Hkakabo Razi (the 1925 Survey of India height). But it's also possible that the British measurement of Hkakabo was too high. A summit measurement on Hkakabo should settle the question.

The mystery of Gamlang Razi's elevation, our international team, the villagers, the landscape, the mountains, and the jungle—all these elements fused into an unforgettable journey. Luckily for us, the mountains of Myanmar have been slow to reveal their secrets. There are plenty more yet to discover.

SUMMARY

First ascent of Gamlang Razi (5,870m) in northern Myanmar by the southwest glacier and west ridge, by Eric Daft, Mark Fisher, Chris Nance, Andy Tyson, Molly Loomis Tyson (all U.S.) and Pyae Phyo Aung (Myanmar), September 7, 2013.

ABOUT THE AUTHOR

Andy Tyson, 44 has been climbing, guiding, and adventuring around the world for more than 26 years. When not in the mountains, he manages Creative Energies, a solar company he founded 14 years ago. He lives in Victor, Idaho, with his wife, Molly.

TALUNG

A FAVORITE PARTNER, A FINAL SUMMIT

MAREK HOLECEK

It is no surprise that success comes only after years of gathering experience from previous failures. Nor is it any revelation that a suitable partner is crucial to climbing success. Since I have never been a focused climber—I love climbing of all kinds—I know that I have been very lucky to find the right partners and friends for each of my undertakings. Partners who aren't afraid of failure. Who can share the good and the bad.

Despite an age gap of nearly a generation between us, Zdenek ("Zdenda") Hruby was perhaps my greatest high-mountain climbing partner. He had vast experience on many 8,000ers, combined with truly unbelievable stamina and stubborn perseverance. However, our first attempts at big new routes were not successful. In 2009, on Gasherbrum I, we failed after reaching 7,500 meters in alpine style, when Zdenda was stricken with a ruptured ulcer. After the epic retreat, I managed to salvage some exciting memories of the mountain with a quick solo ascent of the Japanese Couloir, after all the other expeditions had gone home. Next followed an Andes expedition, but our proposed new line up the south face of Aconcagua turned out to be impossible due to extremely risky conditions on the face, and so Zdenda and I enjoyed pleasant rock climbing in Argentina.

In 2011 we spent another summer together, attempting our next great dream climb, a new route on the Rupal Face of Nanga Parbat. This time rockfall injured Zdenda´s hand and prevented him from climbing. I attempted a solo ascent but was stopped by a snowstorm at 7,300 meters. Our partnership seemed to have had little luck so far, but I knew we would get our chance.

In 2012 we returned to Nanga Parbat with a plan to pitch a tent below the summit on the Kinshofer Route, on the Diamir Face, where we would descend if we were successful with a Rupal ascent. We were quite surprised by the huge quantities of snow on the Diamir Face that season, and what was expected to be a mere warm-up turned into a desperate fight for every meter! Without previous acclimatization our progress was rather slow, and there was nobody else on the wall so we had to get through the deep snow ourselves. We had enough supplies, though, and after seven days of suffering we made an obvious choice right below the summit. We would skip the Rupal attempt and try to summit Nanga from where we stood at the moment. Despite the adverse conditions, we reached the summit on day nine of our alpine-style climb, returning to the green meadow below the Diamir Face after 11 days.

Finally Zdenda and I had achieved a great summit together, and this cemented our desire to try more climbs. We also agreed that it was time for another destination besides the Karakoram. I had two unfinished projects in Nepal. The first was Kyashar, a mountain whose

south face I had already attempted three times, and which was finally climbed in the fall of 2012 by a Japanese team, following nearly the exact line I had in mind (*AAJ 2013*). The other option was Talung.

My first encounter with the north-northwest ridge of Talung was back in 2004, with Tomas Rinn. Conditions on the mountain that fall were just fantastic. The rocky barrier at the start of the pillar was interlinked with steep ice gullies that led toward a sharp arête, which continued to an upper headwall. Our progress through the technically difficult lower section was very fast, and we reached nearly 5,900 meters on the first day, but an icy wind blowing harshly around the ridge caused severe frostbite in my toes at a hanging belay. We were forced back down after just one bivouac. In 2008 I planned to return to Talung, but there was not enough money after two previous expeditions that year. Despite these difficulties I knew I'd be back. I tend to return to unfinished projects, provided the line has not been climbed by someone else. In this way the project ripens.

Arriving in Talung base camp on May 1 was like rekindling an old love affair. At the head of this breathtaking amphitheater is the south face of Kangchenjunga, with the sublime Kumbhakarna (or Jannu) on one side and Talung on the other, its sharp ridge splitting the Yalung Glacier like a knifeblade. Truly an uplifting setting.

After acclimatizing on the original route on the west face (*AAJ 1965*) up to 6,700 meters, it soon became crystal clear that conditions on the north wall were totally different from those we'd seen nine years earlier. Now there was no ice on the lower rock wall. I walked up the glacier to the foot of the pillar with binoculars and watched for hours as the sun slowly circled around the mountain. At last I was able to piece together a line on the north face, to the left of the sharp north-northwest ridge. Steep, icy slopes in the lower part led to a rather unclear upper headwall, where narrow, twisted ice grooves might let us reach the summit slopes. I was so excited with the new line that it helped overcome the disappointment of not being able to finish the original project. It was true that the upper section had not revealed bivouac sites or emergency escapes from the climb, but these were just minor problems, impossible to be solved down on the glacier. The only way was to climb and see for ourselves.

On May 14 we loaded our packs with gear, food, and cooking stuff for eight days. The weather forecast seemed promising, with stronger wind gusts anticipated around May 18. This hinted at some wild moments up high, as this was just the time we planned to reach the headwall. We set out for advanced base camp at 5,400 meters, and dusk charmed us with a breathtaking show as the last sunshine touched the upper rocks of Kangchenjunga. There was scarcely any wind.

May 15 began with the roar of an avalanche at about 3 a.m. This didn't encourage us to leave our warm sleeping bags, but there was no choice—one shouldn't miss an opportunity in the mountains. The lower wall went quickly, and around 9 a.m. the real difficulties began as we bypassed several seracs on old, very steep water ice. We had to fight for each meter; each ice axe and crampon placement required at least five blows. After 14 hours of physical devastation, our day ended at a bivouac site at 5,900 meters.

After the strenuous efforts of the previous day, we got a later start the next morning. Though the ever-present hard ice continued, some lower-angle sections gave us the chance to sink our boots in snow and relieve our calf muscles a bit. We stopped around 4 p.m., finding a good tent site in a hole in a serac at 6,300 meters.

[This page] The northwest side of Talung (7,349m), seen from Kangchenjunga. (1) Thumba Party (Holecek-Hruby, 2013). The climbers descended to the west, near the right skyline, with one additional bivouac. (2) Attempt on the direct north-northwest ridge to 5,900m (Holecek-Rinn, 2004). *Billy Roos*

On May 17 we approached the upper headwall and were thrilled to discover that the tiny gullies I had seen through binoculars appeared to hold reasonable mixed climbing. The terrain was quite hard to protect, but the rock seemed relatively solid and our progression was not too slow. After 15 hours we dug a small platform for the tent at 6,700 meters. It was snowing lightly and spindrift poured down the wall. We had to get up twice during the night to clear off the tent.

All next day we followed narrow ice gullies through the headwall. While crossing a ledge, I accidentally kicked off a rock and watched it fall onto Zdenda and break his helmet into pieces. "Zdenda, are you OK?" I shouted. I could not hear his answer over the strong wind, but I could see him shake his fist at me. *Alright then, he is alive*, I noted with relief and continued climbing.

At 7,000 meters we struggled to pitch the tent behind a rocky spur in strong gusts of wind. My mouth was completely dry, and my whole body felt wasted. Zdenda fought relentlessly with the hard ice to level a platform. My few weak blows with the ice axe made only a modest contribution.

"I will help you, Zdenda, in a moment, just give me a little rest."

"No worries, you are leading the whole thing, take it easy," he responded. Though the rising hurricane carried his words into Sikkim, I felt a rush of love and gratitude for my friend. I was totally ruined. Inside the tent, our stiff bodies slowly warmed, with hot soup soothing our dry mouths. The wind bent the tent sideways, but it seemed to ease during the night.

When I finally managed to fall asleep, feverish dreams brought me back to the slopes of Mt. Meru in India (*AAJ 2007*). Honza Kreisinger and I were on the final slopes, where the snow was like a whipped frappé. Neither crampons nor axes could find solid placements, and it felt like we slipped backward with every move. It was our tenth day on the wall. Honza was suffering behind me, unable to help with a single move. In my dream, I thought, *We have to reach the summit today*. Right at this moment the slope turned into a sandy seabed. I sat and watched sunlight streaking through the water. Bubbles rose from my aqualung. I spat the mouthpiece out of my mouth, gasped, and woke abruptly.

Jesus, Talung! Unlike Meru, there was no way back down the face we'd just climbed. No matter what, we would have to climb over the summit the next day, and this night at 7,000 meters would have to be, by any definition, our "last bivouac."

The sun shone in the morning, and

[This page] Zdenek Hruby follows with the big pack. *Marek Holecek*

we could see beyond Jannu to the distant silhouette of Makalu in the west. We packed up and crossed the upper icefield toward the top of Talung. I led onto the sharp summit ridge, the other side falling to Sikkim. My nightmare of unstable snow did not come true, and we gained height quite rapidly on the hard-packed surface. Around noon I reached the summit and captured a few moments with my camera before thick fog completely covered the world. Zdenda arrived on top in dense, white darkness.

We could hardly see the tips of our noses as we began the descent. I rolled snowballs down the slope so their tracks would help us find the way through the diffuse light. Right before dusk, in what felt like a miracle, we rappelled from a serac to reach the bivouac site at 6,600 meters we had used during acclimatization. In the morning we continued down Talung's original route, avoiding seracs and crevasses all the way to the talus. Around 1 p.m. we reached base camp, where our porters were waiting. We packed the next day and, though very tired, happily started toward home.

Nobody could have foreseen that Talung would be our last summit together. Fate had been so generous to us, and then it took back what was given with no mercy. The first is so easy to accept automatically, but the second is very hard to cope with, and the memories leave deep scars that will never heal.

One month after our return from Nepal, Zdenda and I set out for another unfinished project: our new route on the southwest face of Gasherbrum I, which we had tried back in 2009. Everything went so smoothly at first. We warmed up on the normal route with a fast ascent to Camp 3 at 7,000 meters, where we deposited a tent for the planned descent. Then we moved over to the glacier below the southwest face. The five-day forecast was favorable enough, so we started climbing. The initial steep gully was nearly bare of snow this year, but the ice was good enough to enable fast progression. We reached the hanging serac at 6,800 meters and bivouacked right below it.

[This page] View over the fog-covered Talung Glacier to Jannu (7,710m). *Marek Holecek*

The following day, at a belay stance, Zdenda made a fateful mistake. Without a clear reason or a single word, he started to slide down the icy slope. He did not stop falling for a kilometer. Now my own life was at stake, as Zdenda had taken the rope and most of our climbing gear. I felt surges of shock and hysteria. The idea of downclimbing the whole face, moving backward like a crayfish, seemed like downright nonsense. But there was no choice. With one axe I hit the ice 40 centimeters below the belay stance, then kicked a foot to place a crampon, and then swung the second axe and kicked with my other crampon. Mechanically, amid a Russian roulette of falling rocks, I repeated these steps. After seven hours, it was finally possible to turn toward the valley and finish the last steps to Zdenda's body. There were no surprises. I had seen what was inevitable from the first moments of his fall.

These lines were written on board a tiny yacht bouncing through the stormy Drake Passage, en route to another adventure in Antarctica. Zdenda and I had planned this trip five years earlier, and ever since we'd looked forward to virgin peaks and new lines. Whatever ideas you have, fate sometimes has other plans in store. But no more sorrow—life goes on and we need to pursue our dreams. Zdenda would have done the same without hesitation.

SUMMARY

Alpine-style first ascent of the northwest wall of Talung (7,349m) in the Kangchenjunga Himal, Nepal, by Czech climbers Marek Holecek and Zdenek Hruby, May 15–19, 2013. The route gained about 1,900 vertical meters, with ca 2,500 meters of climbing distance (WI6 M6+). The two men descended to the south and west, mainly following the route of the 1964 first ascent, and returned to base camp on May 20. They named the route Thumba Party after the traditional Nepalese drink made from fermented millet.

ABOUT THE AUTHOR
Born in 1974, Marek Holecek has done big-wall and alpine first ascents in the Karakoram, Himalaya, and Andes. He lives in Prague.

Editor's note: Zdenek Hruby, age 57 at the time of his death, was president of the Czech Mountaineering Association, and was a distinguished figure in both his climbing and business lives. He had climbed eight 8,000-meter peaks as well as other summits throughout the world. Hruby had served on the boards of several of Czech's largest companies and as the nation's deputy minister of finance.

Translated from Czech by Zbysek Cesenek.

[This page] It's time for a Thumba party.
Holecek Collection

WILD SPORT

THE FUTURE OF AMERICAN ROCK CLIMBING LIES
FAR FROM THE HIGHWAY

JONATHAN SIEGRIST

I can't remember the first time I went climbing, but I do remember growing up outdoors. Long walks to Sundance Buttress and sinking my little feet in the sand around Gem Lake at Lumpy Ridge. Following my dad up Stettner's Ledges and the Diamond on Longs Peak. To go climbing was to have an adventure. You hiked. There was a thunderstorm. You got a little scared. At the beginning of the day you were uncertain; at the end of the day you were very tired.

When I was young, climbing essentially meant mountaineering. I aspired to do all the Colorado 14ers. After graduating high school, I did the NOLS Himalaya Mountaineering program in India. In the summer of 2004, at age 18, I went to the Cordillera Blanca in Peru with my dad. The snow conditions were terrible that year, so he dragged me up a 20-pitch rock route on La Esfinge, starting at well over 14,000 feet. For me, this 17-hour day was epic. I followed every single pitch, with what was surely a very tight top-rope. Afterward, wandering around base camp, I was wrecked. But something had clicked. Looking up toward the wall, I remember thinking, "Well, damn, that was incredible!"

For several years after returning to Colorado, I climbed six or seven days a week at the Boulder Rock Club. Gradually, as my strength and skills improved, my motivation shifted primarily to sport climbing. In the beginning I was mostly interested in the physical challenge, but as my climbing developed I also longed for adventure. At some of my favorite new sport crags, I've discovered both.

In American sport climbing, distinct from densely populated Europe and Asia, adventure will be a necessary part of the future, because the best undiscovered crags and hardest undone routes of the 21st century will likely be found well beyond the sight of paths or paved roads. Already, two of America's three 5.15 routes are around an hour's hike from dirt roads, following faint climbers' trails: Flex Luthor (Tommy Caldwell, 2003) at the Fortress of Solitude, Colorado, and Jumbo Love (Chris Sharma, 2007) at Clark Mountain, California. In recent years, almost all of the new crags I've explored and most of the hardest routes I've established have been pure sport routes in uniquely adventurous settings.

For me, adventure is a feeling of excited, optimistic uncertainty, whether you're facing an unknown landscape or a faint line of unchalked holds. Some adventures are grander than others, but for the characters involved, these experiences offer the ultimate growth, no matter the scale.

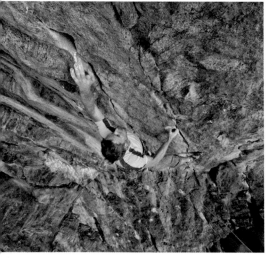

WIZARD'S GATE, COLORADO

In July 2009 I started hiking up to the obvious rocks beneath the Twin Sisters, across the road from Longs Peak. After 10 minutes I jumped off the main hiking trail and trudged steeply uphill, clambering over mossy rocks and slipping on the needles of larchpole pines. I reached the south end of the lowest cliff band after nearly an hour of hiking and trekked northward to see all of the possibilities.

I was by no means the first person to lay eyes on what would become the Wizard's Gate. A lone, low-angle trad route existed. When I saw the steep amphitheater, at first I was not that excited. It's easy to recognize rock climbs, but it's much harder to recognize *potential* rock climbs. Vision, like many things, takes time to develop. I skirted the whole mountainside and eventually got lost in a summer thunderstorm, surfacing at the road filthy, exhausted, and famished. In subsequent days of climbing, at other areas, I stared at established routes and wondered what they had looked like before bolts and chalk. Before long, I came to realize that this amphitheater near Longs Peak really might be something special.

I bought a drill. I asked friends and new-route pioneers: *How do I do this?* For the next month I practically lived at the Wizard's Gate. Sketching out above horrible gear and mossy stone to find a proper anchor. Hanging off hooks and dangling static lines, and knocking off loose blocks. Walking down the hill utterly exhausted each day. The whole experience was new to me. I contemplated ethics and access. Sometimes I pondered a bolt placement for 40 minutes before drilling. My dad, a few friends, and I put in more than 25 new routes, from 5.9 to 5.14, all in a beautiful alpine setting, with a cool breeze and shade even on the hottest Colorado days.

The following year, when 34 people arrive at Wizard's Gate on a bluebird summer day, the experience came full circle. Now there were people laughing and sending, using that same sequence I hoped they would, talking about the routes and having a good time. I *loved* that day.

THE FINS, IDAHO

As soon as it became known that I'd stepped into the realm of new-route development, this amazing community began to come forward. They had seen a cliff once; there was this

[This page] Tommy Caldwell climbing Black Magic (5.14a) at Wizard's Gate. *Andy Mann*

[This page, top] The author trying hard for the first ascent of Algorithm (5.14d) at the Fins in Idaho. *Keith Ladzinski* [This page, bottom] Fallout (5.13d) at the Fins. *Keith Ladzinski*

place down a dirt road somewhere.... I explored many options. Most of them were not obvious like Smith Rock or roadside like Rifle. These places were increasingly wild.

For years I had heard rumors about the Fins. "Such incredible limestone, with so much potential." But after having that beer-infused conversation enough times, you learn that not every messenger should be taken seriously. I don't ignore a lead from an old-schooler, though. They've been around, and they know quality when they see it. So when Dave Bingham, one of the main developers of the City of Rocks in Idaho, gave the Fins his thumbs up, I definitely paid attention.

In perhaps the most barren part of eastern Idaho, at the south end of the Lost River Range, a 30-minute jolting ride up a wildly steep, rocky road deposits you at a ribbon of limestone dancing down a wavy hillside—and in the middle of nowhere. Bolting new routes is really a one-person job, and when you're anywhere this remote the job feels extra lonely. I went

[This page] Siegrist on Spitting Venom (5.14c) at Wolf Point, Wyoming. *Caroline Treadway*

for days without seeing or hearing anyone. The nights were very quiet.

Walking along the top of the Fins for the first time was thrilling. The summit ridge is about the width of a sidewalk. To your left is a sheer 140-foot drop; to your right it's about 80 feet. With a drill, bolts, and other kit, and a 100-meter static line, I carefully downclimbed the rib, knocking off the occasional loose block with my foot, searching for a solid stance for an anchor. I battled sharp edges as I maneuvered to the lip. Beneath me was an ocean of white stone. What would I find? Excitement bubbled up when I spotted holds, and as I giddily followed them to the ground the stress dissolved and pure psych emerged. This is one of my favorite feelings in life.

There is a strong community of climbers in central and eastern Idaho, and they had done an exceptional job developing the Fins through the years. The likes of Dave Bingham, Marc Hanselman, Peter Heekin, and Matt TeNgaio, to name a few, all made significant contributions. But for someone like myself, searching for 5.14, the Fins were virtually untouched. Now, after two seasons, there are six new 5.14s (including a 5.14a trad climb, Enter the Dragon, and Idaho's hardest rock pitch, Algorithm, 5.14d) and well over a dozen new 5.13s. Although development has slowed, this face-climbing, foot-smearing, pocket-pulling super-crag still has open projects and even some unexplored walls.

WOLF POINT, WYOMING

In the summer of 2013 I spent several months exploring one of my favorite parts of the Lower 48: Wyoming. Rumors were swirling about a new spot in the foothills of the Wind Rivers, with enormous dolomite walls in a secluded landscape. On my first day in the Lander area, I followed some friends out to this crag in the making. The approach begins with an hour's drive, including 20 minutes on rough dirt roads, sometimes washed out, frequently evolving. The hike then takes about an hour, first losing over 1,000 feet in elevation, only to gain it again.

One day a grizzly cornered a good friend at the trailhead. He retreated to the roof of his van, brandishing a 9mm pistol in one hand and a can of bear spray in the other. The bear eventually wandered off, but the reality of its presence haunted our campfires for days. I stepped over more rattlers than I can remember. On two separate nights, returning from the crag, I was stalked by a mountain lion. Cat prints littered the campsite the next morning.

The climbs at Wolf Point are long, dirty, sandbagged, and savage. Storms whip overhead in no time. On a calm, sunny day, the main cave can feel tropically warm and sweaty, and then a breeze and shade will turn the day freezing cold. And yet you feel remarkably content, so far from everything. Wolf Point's curse is perhaps its salvation.

Locals had made a serious dent in the cliff, as characters like Steve Bechtel, Tom Rangitsch, Zach Rudy, B.J. Tilden, and Kyle Vassilopoulos equipped around 20 routes and many projects up to hard 5.14. Everyone had a little piece of the cliff to work on, and the psych was always high.

I started working on new routes during my second day there, lugging ropes and a bolting kit out to the cliff. Everyone else had left. I followed their directions to the top, crawling under old trees and ducking through rock passages. Skirting the abrupt lip, I found the spot I hoped was above my line and tossed my rope off the edge. CRACK! Too short. I tied two ropes together and used some slings to gain a few more feet. As I pushed off the very crest of the cave, a strong wind blew from below and suddenly I felt immense exposure. In this moment I felt very uncertain, but also wildly excited.

Literally *miles* of potential exists around Lander.

THE FUTURE

After so many miles of driving empty highways around the American West and hiking to endless cliff lines, I have no reason to believe that even half of this country's greatest cliffs have been climbed. Or even seen. Large states with small or condensed populations and remote cliffs offer the way forward. The Big Horns and Wind Rivers in Wyoming. The Mormon Mountains and Ely in Nevada. The west desert and southwest hills of Utah. Isolated pockets of California, Arizona, and deep into New Mexico.

The development of climbing in some remote settings will be limited by wilderness rules and access concerns. And it's important to understand a community and build a relationship with the local climbers before barging in to bolt new routes. Very few people are as blessed as I am with the ability to travel constantly. Locals usually want their own chance to develop their cliffs.

But there are lifetimes of possibility out there for those willing to get dirty and tired and scared. The next best cliff will probably require a sock-wrecking, bushwhacking nightmare of a hike. I bet you'll need a truck to get there. It will be a long drive from a grocery store or source of water. You'll see *wild* wildlife. Cell phones won't work. Injuries and mistakes may be costly. But the stars will be incredible, and the stories will be rich, and the adventures could be life-changing.

ABOUT THE AUTHOR

Jonathan Siegrist, 28, lives the nomadic life in his trusty pickup, with his dog, Zeke, as copilot. When he's not adventuring, you'll most likely catch him in Boulder, Las Vegas, or Wyoming.

PURGATION

EXPLORATION AND INTRIGUE IN NEPAL

CHRIS WRIGHT

Two thousand feet above the glacier, and moments before the screaming started, I felt the ice give way under my foot. I saw, as if from a distance, that my leg was swinging backward into space the way climbers' feet do in videos, with ropes clipped through draws connected to bolts. But my ropes were not clipped to anything for at least 20 feet, and below that not much more.

I remember the feeling of that foot cutting, and a sound like a war coming out of me. I remember stemming wider, my frontpoints searching desperately as the frozen rot fell away. I remember the weight of my body on my arms, the feel of the snow separating as my pick raked through what was not ice. I remember the moment of deciding that although I did not trust that anything would hold, I would have to trust, and that although I did not believe in any real way that I would get through, I would get through. I remember the feeling of pulling over, and of another scream, different this time. I remember thinking that I should place a screw, not because I was going to fall, but because I could. I remember keeping Scott's ropes tight as he climbed with both of our packs. And then when he reached the belay, and I saw my face reflected in his, I remember the feeling of snapping in two.

I had never cried on a mountain until that day. If, like all things, we are defined by our boundaries, there must be something universal about the desire to find them. And yet I suspect there may be something wrong with those of us who have to know exactly where they are. The story I came to tell was that by the time I realized I was committed I couldn't back off, but the truth is I had no intention of backing off. As the tears melted the spindrift on my wind-reddened cheeks, I knew that I had done a terrible thing, and yet I knew as well that I wouldn't regret it. I cried because I had found what I was looking for.

I HAD ONLY MET SCOTT ADAMSON once before last spring on Alaska's Buckskin Glacier. Friends in Talkeetna had said someone might be out there, and that the guy was alone and he might be crazy. As it turned out, Scott was not alone, and as far as I could tell he was not mad. Once my partner, Geoff Unger, had to pull out of our planned new route, after one attempt, thanks to an injured elbow, Scott and I got to know each other in a hurry as we clawed our way up the east face of the Mooses Tooth. [*See Climbs and Expeditions.*]

Though we knew we had shared something special, we parted ways with no plans to climb together again. With the support of a McNeill-Nott Award and a Mazamas Alpine Adventure Grant, I planned to return to Nepal that fall with Geoff. He and I had been partners for years, and in the fall of 2012 we'd made an attempt on a 6,589-meter peak in the Lunag

[This page] The author leads into the headwall on the northeast face of Pangbuk North. The crux pitch ascended the steep, rotten ice in upper left. *Scott Adamson*

Massif, a group of mostly untouched peaks northwest of the Khumbu. Unfortunately, in June, the same injury that had brought Scott and I together on the Mooses Tooth found Geoff pulling out of the trip. I knew that Scott already had plans for Pakistan, but after the tragedy at Nanga Parbat I thought it was worth a shot. I called him and got about as far as "Do you wanna come…" before he said yes and let me tell him where we were going.

We were hoping to try a line on Ripimo Shar, but agreed to stay flexible. While the peak that Geoff and I had attempted was on my radar, it was far from our first choice. We hadn't intended to try it in 2012 either, but with the dry conditions that autumn it had been the best thing going. After our attempt, I learned that the mountain had supposedly been climbed in 2009 by a party led by Swiss guide Stéphane Schaffter, and had been named after the expedition's sponsor. Those familiar with the area had serious doubts that this ascent had actually happened, but no real proof to the contrary.

After not having seen each other since the Buckskin, Scott and I met in late September and spent a few days packing gear. We were both aware that, despite having done one of the biggest climbs of our lives together, we had very little idea of who the other was. All we really knew was that when it got heavy we could count on each other, and that we saw eye to eye when it came to important things like spooning, booze, and coffee. On our way to the airport, I made a phone call and found out we were on the same flight as my friend David Gottlieb, who had been a mentor before my first trip to Nepal. We realized our itineraries lined up perfectly, and we decided to share a base camp with David and his partner, Chad Kellogg.

From Kathmandu, Chad and David headed for the Rolwaling while Scott and I caught a flight to Lukla. Our plan was to acclimatize in the Khumbu and meet at base camp, but

[This page] Scott Adamson and Chad Kellogg hike through the Hellplex toward advanced base camp. Pangbuk North is center left, and Lunag West is on the right. *Chris Wright*

unusually lousy weather kept the passes snowy and everything cold and wet, including us. After an abbreviated acclimatization trek, on October 10, Scott and I set camp at 5,050 meters near the confluence of the Nangpa La and Lunag glaciers. We still weren't sure of our plans, but we thought we'd start with one of the peaks that originally had drawn me to this area. There are a lot of bigger lines than the southeast face of Lunag West (6,507 meters), but there aren't many more obvious or prettier lines, with a couloir that splits the face from glacier to summit ridge.

With the sun shining and conditions looking prime, we packed up and set out across the four-and-a-half-mile mess of moraine and glacier that David and Chad had dubbed the Hellplex. The way was stacked with loose boulders separated by man-eating gaps, an undulating mess of rocks and tarns strewn across a moonscape of blue ice. We stashed gear for an advanced base camp under a giant boulder and headed back. David and Chad had arrived, and we got our first forecast of the trip: "heavy snow." During the next 72 hours, our camp was blanketed with more than four and a half feet. Since we had cached our only shovel at ABC, we spent our days digging out our tents with plates. On October 20, after days of digging and watching avalanches rake the walls around us, and after climbing a nearby 5,777-meter acclimatization peak, Scott and I cursed our way back through the Hellplex.

The line on Lunag West is like a giant hourglass, with mostly moderate climbing and what looked like a few hard pitches in the middle. It's the peak's only obvious weakness, but has the downside of being a garbage chute, with everything that falls off the sunny upper walls funneling straight into the choke. As we stumbled through the dark on the morning of October 22, the question looming in both of our minds was whether we'd find those hard pitches in good enough shape to climb. As we sped up the lower apron and into the amphitheater that forms the base of the hourglass, we saw with a mix of relief and trepidation that the streaks were ice but they did not look friendly. We were entering a potential shooting gallery as soon as we committed to the sinister black curtain, but we felt willing to climb and hope.

Scott dispatched the 100-meter flow in one long pitch, bringing us onto a snowfield below a second narrows. Our stomachs were in knots thanks to the gut-rot that comes of ramen, nerves, Cipro, altitude, and the occasional volleys of rock cascading down the couloir. Climbing as fast as we could, we raced through a few pitches of ice and mixed and managed to get as far from the sunny walls above as possible. I took a rock in the boot, and Scott took one in the arm, but both of us were just glad that they weren't bigger.

That evening and all through the night, if either of us had any questions about our partnership, they were answered. Although both of us had led hard pitches in Alaska, I came into the trip knowing that Scott was a far better climber than I was. I had given him the first hard lead of the route, certain he would be faster. Now, as I led toward a break in the flutings that guarded the summit ridge, stretching each pitch to make the most of the waning light and our meager rack, I was ready to hand over the lead again. But when Scott arrived at the belay, I could see that wasn't going to happen. I made sure he was clipped in properly, got out our headlamps, and took us to the ridge on one of those leads that are impossible to grade and embody the difference between the crag and mountains. We were met by a dim view into Tibet and a howling wind determined to blow us off the ridge or freeze us to it. Lurching toward the summit, we found a crevasse where we could get out of the wind and brew up.

All of a sudden it was my turn to need. As we sat on our packs, I shivered and struggled to eat and drink while Scott shouldered the work of melting snow and coaxing his partner back to life. We had no bivy gear, and we still needed to summit, reverse the ridge, and rappel through the night to avoid the morning's rockfall. By headlamp and moonlight, Scott led up to the top, which we reached at midnight, then led most of the rappels on the way down as I fought just to stay awake, clean the backups, lock my carabiners, and hold on. We stepped back onto the glacier just as the sun crept over the sleeping giants of Everest and Makalu, and staggered back to our boulder camp 26 hours after we'd left it.

AFTER A WEEK OF REST back in base camp, we again crossed the Hellplex, amazed that time had only made the trail worse. We were headed for the same route that Geoff and I had attempted a year earlier, the northeast face of the 6,589-meter peak that Schaffter called Jobo LeCoultre. We had reached a bivy at 6,150 meters, just below a headwall, before freezing toes sent us down. Knowing that our first day would

[This page] Scott Adamson nears the top of Lunag West. *Chris Wright*

[This page] Lunag West (6,507m), with the obvious line of Open Fire splitting the southeast face. The 1,000-meter route was climbed in a 26-hour round trip from ABC. *Chris Wright*

be our best, Scott and I planned to put in a big effort and try to get through the savage drips guarding the headwall and onto the upper mountain. If we could do that, we might be able to find a bivy at about 6,275 meters, leave the tent and sleeping bags on the ledge, summit, and make it back to the bivy again.

We left ABC on a cold Halloween morning, and despite howling winds the skies were clear and we felt good. We climbed over the 'schrund and through a few easy pitches, then battled snow until we could gain a rib below the upper face. In my orange belay jacket we joked that I had dressed as a pumpkin for the occasion. We took a break in the warm sun, and then I led straight up into the headwall.

Below the crux curtain, I placed two bad screws and downclimbed to the belay. The ice was completely rotten—it had only looked decent from below because the spindrift that had been pummeling us all day had also filled in the holes in the ice. I decided to hang my pack and try again. I headed back up and got sucked left toward a seam where I thought I might get gear and good hooks for my tools. It turned out I couldn't get either, and before long my leg was swinging, and then I was screaming, and pulling the lip, and building the belay, and keeping the ropes tight for Scott as he followed.

Scott took over and led up to a ledge where we hacked out a platform and set up the tent. In the morning I led one more hard pitch before the angle eased and took us into the snow flutings that converged on the summit. Scott took us up a runnel and then fought a section of steep, collapsing snow before he pulled onto the top. When I got there, I found him perched on a tiny rib with his pack hanging off one side as an anchor while he belayed me up the other.

We had only shaken hands on top of the Mooses Tooth, but now we hugged and laughed as the wind stung our faces. After another night at the bivy, we descended the following day. We called our route Purgation, a purification or cleansing, which might have referred to my episode on the crux, but in fact meant something else entirely.

WHEN I GOT BACK TO KATHMANDU, I confirmed that Peak 6,589m was at the center of an obscure controversy that began in 2008, when, after four years of effort to open the Lunag area to climbing, Stéphane Schaffter led a team to a virgin peak he called Jobo Rinjang. The plan was to "prepare" a new route on the mountain with fixed ropes in order to return the following year and shoot a film, in which luminary Nepali and Balti guides Apa Sherpa and "Little" Abdul Karim, together with a team of Europeans, would make the peak's first ascent. Schaffter had found a backer in the Swiss luxury watchmaker Jaeger-LeCoultre, which had put its considerable financial resources behind the project. Schaffter's team reached a high point of 6,000 meters on the south face, leaving with 1,000 meters of rope in place and plans to return the next fall. One can imagine his chagrin when, in the spring of 2009, his peak was climbed, in alpine style, by Joe Puryear and David Gottlieb.

In need of a new objective, Schaffter and company returned in the autumn of 2009 to attempt the southwest pillar of neighboring Lunag I instead. After nine days of effort from eight climbers, the team abandoned the wall, citing danger from rockfall. They turned their attention to Peak 6,589m, planning to ascend the left-hand snowfield on the northeast face to a notch in the southeast ridge, and then follow that complex line of snow flutings and mushrooms to the top. From October 19 to 21, a six-man team fixed 900 meters of rope up the moderate terrain of the lower mountain. On October 22, the team later reported, four of the men summited the mountain. But almost nobody believes this happened.

As reported by Lindsay Griffin in the April 2011 issue of Britain's Climb magazine, the principle point of suspicion has always been the team's photographs. Despite having both a professional photographer, Guillaume Vallot, and a videographer, Xavier Carrard, the team only released two images of the supposed summit. Now that Scott and I have been there, we can say with utmost certainty that these photos were not taken from or near the real summit. Since the peaks in the background are easily identifiable, it's clear that the camera is pointed southeast. In light of the claimed ascent from that direction, there should then be evidence of travel, but there is not. Knowing that the top of the mountain is a tiny point, it's also clear that the photographer would have to be levitating, as the photos are taken from the same level or higher than the purported summit. They're also pointed in a direction that avoids showing the upper mountain and the nearby peaks of the Lunag and Pangbuk glaciers, as those would provide reference to the actual location of the photographer. Carrard's video also has extensive footage of the ascent to the notch, but shows the same images of the "summit" curated to avoid the surrounding terrain. [This video can be viewed at the AAJ website.] Furthermore, in photos used in an advertisement seen at a shop in Kathmandu, there appears to be a bivouac platform on the alleged summit. All of this has led to the conclusion that the photos were taken in the vicinity of the notch on the southeast ridge, the team's likely high point. Wherever they were taken, it was not at the top.

The timeline of the ascent, as Schaffter reported it in AAJ 2010, is also implausible. It took a large team three days to cover relatively easy terrain and reach the ridge, while on the fourth day, Vallot supposedly joined them via the fixed ropes, climbed to the summit via

[This page] Pangbuk North (6,589m; 6,748m HMG-Finn map), with the line of the 2013 first ascent and bivouac site on the northeast face marked. The X marks the likely high point of the 2009 team, which attempted a line left of the 2013 route. In 2010, a French team attempted the leftmost ice sheet, continuing up the southeast ridge to the tower just left of the X. They described the ca 350 meters of terrain above this point on the southeast ridge as looking very difficult and tenuous, with huge snow mushrooms to pass. In the background: Pangbuk Ri (6,716m). *Chris Wright*

extremely difficult and insecure terrain, and took a few uninspiring and uninformative photographs. The team then descended all the way to the glacier, stripping ropes as they went, before returning to base camp on October 23 and summiting Peak 5,777m on the 24th. Both the difficulties and distances involved make this scenario unlikely.

With all of this swirling in my head, I thought I ought to give Schaffter and his partners a chance to defend their claim before publishing news of our climbs. I wrote to the four "summit climbers," as well as to Apa and Karim (who did not join the climb on Peak 6,589m). Somewhat to my surprise, I received e-mails from Jérôme Haeni and Schaffter himself, while the others never responded. Haeni's email was brief yet cordial, congratulating us on our climb and telling me to talk to Schaffter, who sent me a lengthy e-mail that ignored my questions and instead assailed Gottlieb and Puryear for climbing Jobo Rinjang before him, and for not giving him credit for opening the area for foreign climbers. Though he did not return my next e-mail pressing the point, one thing is worth noting: Neither he nor Haeni ever said they climbed it. [The AAJ requested comments on this story from Stéphane Schaffter. He replied with a brief note in French, saying, in part, "It is evident that the words Chris Wright uses confirm his wish to smear [me]. Personally, I respect his ethical values without respecting his retributive way of selling his exploits. In my response [to him] on 16 November, I explained that I really have no desire to participate or return to any controversy about this region, for which I have already committed enormous energy over several years."] The Nepal Mountaineering Association has suggested the names Pangbuk North and Lunag West for the mountains we climbed, and as they seem fitting, we have adopted them.

And, for now, that's where the story will have to end. I will forever remember this expedition not for any controversy but for a few brilliant moments, and as the only one I was lucky enough to share with Chad Kellogg. [Kellogg died just a few months later while descending from Fitz Roy.] I will miss Chad whenever I think about it, though I know his spirit is at peace in the Patagonian night.

X

SUMMARY

First ascent of Lunag West (formerly known as Little Lunag, 6,507m, Schneider map) via the southeast face, by Scott Adamson and Chris Wright, October 22–23, 2013. The route is called Open Fire (1,000m, V WI5 M3). First ascent of Pangbuk North (6,589m, Schneider map, formerly Jobo LeCoultre or Mt. Antoine LeCoultre), by Adamson and Wright, October 31–November 2, 2013. Their direct route up the northeast face is called Purgation (1,100m, VI WI6+ M6).

ABOUT THE AUTHOR

Chris Wright, 31, is an IFMGA mountain guide based in Bend, Oregon, and has climbed and guided all over the world (Nowclimbing.com).

MONTE SARMIENTO

AFTER 57 YEARS, TIERRA DEL FUEGO'S
SPELLBINDING PEAK GETS A SECOND ASCENT

CAMILO RADA

Dancing with the gusts of winter wind, Natalia Martinez and I inched onto the summit that had long been the focus of our dreams. It was 10:45 p.m. and pitch dark. More than simply the high point of a mountain, this peak was the validation of years of friendship, struggle, passion, and chance. No one had stood at this point in 57 years. Who knows how long it will be before climbers return?

In 1580, while chasing the notorious privateer Francis Drake through Patagonian fjords, Pedro Sarmiento de Gamboa spotted a "Volcán Nevado" (snowy volcano). Later cosmographers

pictured a mysterious smoking volcano in the unexplored interior of Tierra del Fuego, inhabited by sea monsters, giants, and tailed natives.

The mountain's twin peaks were a centerpiece of the writings of Robert Fitz Roy, who unveiled the geographical secrets of the southernmost end of America together with Phillip Parker King, during epic expeditions from 1826 to 1836 aboard the H.M.S. Beagle and Adventure. Among countless discoveries, they realized Sarmiento's Volcán Nevado was not a volcano, and they renamed it after its discoverer, even though that right should be given to the native people, the Yaghan and Kawésqar, who had arrived here 10,000 years earlier.

[This page] The north face of Monte Sarmiento. The first winter ascent climbed the ice face directly to the main summit (left). *Marcelo Arevalo* [Previous page] Monte Sarmiento rises more than 2,200 meters, directly above the sea. *Guy Wenborne*

In the 19th century, when steam-powered vessels made the Magellan Strait a popular oceanic passage—a golden age that lasted until the opening of the Panama Canal in 1914—thousands of travelers knew of this magnificent mountain, and the few who had the luck to see it spread the word about its surpassing beauty and colossal size. At the time it was perhaps the only place on Earth where a tourist could contemplate an ice wall rising vertically more than 2,000 meters just a few kilometers from the seashore. Many travelers enthusiastically lauded the sight, and even Jules Vernes drew upon it in his novel *Twenty Thousand Leagues Under the Sea*. In 1882, John Ball wrote, "I know of no other peak that impresses the mind so deeply with the sense of wonder and awe."

The climbing history of Mt. Sarmiento is one of the longest in the Americas, starting at a time when only a handful of major peaks had been climbed in the U.S. and Ecuador. The geologist Domenico Lovisato was first to attempt Sarmiento, in 1882. Later, at the twilight of the 19th century, after the first ascent of Illimani in Bolivia, the renowned British mountaineer Sir Martin Conway reached a point at 1,000 meters on the glacier that now bears his name.

With the 20th century came the indefatigable explorer Alberto De Agostini, who was spellbound by Mt. Sarmiento and attempted it twice between 1913 and 1914. Agostini's youthful dream became an obsession, and at the age of 73 he was back as the leader of a team of Italy's best alpinists, who, after nearly two months of attempts, launched a bold alpine push.

Carlo Mauri and Clemente Maffei, fighting with fog and wind, finally crowned Agostini's mythical "Esfinge de hielo" (Ice Sphinx) on March 7, 1956.

Since then many have attempted to follow their steps with no success, including the Italian Giuseppe Agnolotti. Lured by Sarmiento's spell, he organized expeditions in 1969, 1971, and 1972, and was deprived of the west summit by just a few meters. He would title his book *Sarmiento: White Hell.*

In 1986, thirty years after the first ascent, Maffei returned to score another victory with the Ragni di Lecco, making the first ascent of the west summit via its northeast face. [*Sarmiento's climbing accounts tend to be confusing due to its two independent summits, and the fact that some expeditions have had the secondary western summit as their main objective. The main summit is the east one, about 60 meters higher. Furthering the confusion is the fact that Mt. Sarmiento is not located in the Cordillera de Sarmiento, the mountain range that lies 200 miles to the northwest, and is covered in the Recon section on page 78.*] A star-filled expedition comprised of Charlie Porter, John Roskelley, Tim Macartney-Snape, Stephen Venables, and Jim Wickwire aimed to crown both summits in 1995. The team couldn't fulfill all their ambitions but achieved the second ascent of the west summit by a new route up the beautiful southeast face.

In 1999, another "spellbound" climber appeared, the German Ralf Gantzhorn, who, without giving up, returned in 2002, 2005, and 2010, in the last case alongside the prestigious climbers Robert Jasper and Jörn Heller. After aborting an attempt on the north ridge at a similar point to Agnolotti's 1972 expedition, the Germans made a bold traverse of the west peak's north face to join the 1986 Ragni route and complete the third ascent of the west summit.

More than ten other attempts were unsuccessful. [*See the online version of this story for a complete history of attempts.*] It was only in the austral winter of 2013 that the 57-year spell of mountaineering mischance on the main summit of Mt. Sarmiento would be at last broken, by a multidisciplinary expedition with a similar spirit to the historic 1956 one.

Our expedition, led by Gonzalo Campos and Gino Casassa, reached Mt. Sarmiento on board the sailboat Arco Iris, with mixed

[This page] A newspaper celebrates the "Italian victory in Tierra del Fuego" in 1956.

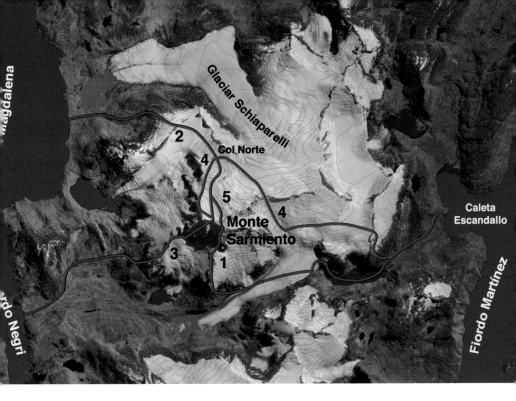

[This page] Monte Sarmiento or its west peak have been climbed only five times in 57 years. (1) First ascent of main summit (2,207m GPS), Mauri and Maffei, 1956. (2) First ascent of west summit (2,145m GPS), Ragni di Lecco, 1986. (3) Southwest face of west peak (Macartney-Snape–Roskelley–Venables, 1995). (4) North ridge to north face of west peak (Grantzhorn-Heller-Jasper, 2010. (5) North face of main peak, Martinez-Rada, 2013. *Uncharted Project*

objectives: dendrochronological studies, GPS and automatic weather station installation, photography and filmmaking, sea kayaking, and mountaineering.

The climbing team was divided in two. The reconnaissance team of Cristian Donoso, Mario Sepúlveda, and Uber Quirilao made an attempt on the west summit between July 21 and August 9, providing valuable reconnaissance. Natalia Martínez (Argentina), Inés Dussaillant, and I (Chile) targeted the main summit.

Our team set up base camp on August 19 on Bardonecchia Beach. We had received a forecast for a good weather window to arrive just four days later, and our logistics for a 30-day effort were quickly re-engineered in order to take advantage of that window, if it actually opened.

We followed a well-established trail through the forest, a legacy of Agnolotti's 1972 expedition, with its five tons of gear and the wooden "cube" hut that was used as high camp. We began using skis once well above the forest at about 300 meters. In the alpine we had to battle against bad visibility and constant winds, sometime gusting up to 140 kph (87 mph), forcing us to dig into an ice cave at Vittore Col. We were not able to set a high camp at the Col Norte (1,200 meters) until August 22.

The weather window did in fact start on August 23, and luckily it lasted to the 24th, when we were ready to tackle the climb, after ferrying all the necessary gear to high camp. Inés would wait at camp. Natalia and I left at 3:45 a.m. under dream conditions—

the wind nonexistent and the stars sharply defined in all directions, silhouetting the bold mountains around us. We skinned up Conway Glacier under strong moonlight to reach the bergschrund shortly before sunrise.

Four hundred meters directly below the summit, the bergschrund presented a five-meter overhang covered by more than 80 centimeters (two feet) of rime. After a brief attempt to free climb, I began to aid over the bergschrund, using a shovel to dig a trench diagonally upward.

Once we were above the 'schrund, the route unfolded elegantly to the summit, through a straight gully surrounded by lush rime cauliflowers, very sustained but rarely exceeding 75°. The ice conditions were excellent, although it was demanding to place protection. The rope quickly began to flow to the rhythm of the axes and the tinkling beat of ice screws. By the sixth pitch, twilight was already descending on this short winter day, and bitter cold brutally brought us back to reality, reminding us of the urgency. We knew these superb conditions would not last much longer—and might not be repeated for months. The wind began to blow and our infinite horizon was reduced to the square meter lit by our headlamps.

We had chosen our route on a bold bet, as the gully ended in a terrifying cirque of massive, overhanging ice mushrooms. A shadow we had seen in aerial

[This page, top] Approaching through a lenga forest. *Inés Dussaillant* [This page, bottom] The author deploys a shovel and a few aid moves to clear the bergschrund. *Natalia Martinez* [Next page] The climbers can be seen midway up the north face during the first ascent. *Inés Dussaillant*

photos led us to believe that one of the mushrooms on the left was disconnected from the main wall, opening a channel that might allow us to escape onto the gentle slopes leading to the summit.

As we neared the top of the face, my headlamp jumped nervously to the left with each step, probing for the exit. We began to fear this passageway had only been a figment of our imagination. Suddenly the beam penetrated deep between two colossal ice mushrooms. Powder snow lay waist-deep on the upper slopes, but we didn't care because the summit was at our fingertips.

During the long descent, small pieces of ice swept the face and rapped against our helmets to keep us awake. Once we were at the bergschrund, impenetrable fog swept in on the wind—everything was back to normal for Mt. Sarmiento. With one eye on the tips of our skis and the other on the GPS, we slowly made our way back to camp. At 10 a.m. we finally arrived, exhausted but with a deep feeling of fulfillment, after more than 30 hours on the move.

They say dreaming is necessary to digest one's experiences and set them to memory. If so, we still had a lot of work ahead.

SUMMARY:

First ascent of the north face of Monte Sarmiento's main summit (2,207m GPS) at the west end of Cordillera de Darwin, Tierra del Fuego, Chile, by Natalia Martinez and Camilo Rada, August 24–25, 2013. The new route, only the second summit route on Sarmiento in 57 years, was called Suerte de Sarmiento (400m, D+). [*See page 89 for information about the author.*]

RECON

UNEXPLORED & OVERLOOKED

TOWERS OF
WIND AND ICE
[p.80]

[p.90]
THE WHITNEY
MASSIF

[This page] Looking northeast from Canal Unión to Cordillera de Sarmiento. The highest peaks are (left to right) Dama Blanca, Trono, and Alas de Ángel (main and south peaks). Daniel Bruhin W.

TOWERS OF WIND AND ICE

THE CORDILLERA DE SARMIENTO OF SOUTHERN CHILE

CAMILO RADA & JACK MILLER

The word "remote" is no longer forbidding to mountaineers. Jet travel is relatively cheap and easy, and can quickly get you to any corner of the world. But getting close is one thing. Real accessibility is another story entirely.

Planes land in Puerto Natales, just 60 kilometers east of the Cordillera de Sarmiento in far southern Chile, and a well-used shipping lane passes a few kilometers from its southern tip. From there, sensational views of ice-covered towers may be had—but only perhaps three percent of the time. During the vast majority of any given year, these mountains are shrouded in clouds.

In the Cordillera de Sarmiento, accessibility has much more to do with climate than the logistics of covering distance. Even at the toe of your chosen peak, the biggest challenge is likely to be the atrocious weather rather than mere technical difficulty. Jack Miller, the first climber to explore this range, wrote, "After we arrived at the mountains, our first task was to see them."

Until the widespread availability of satellite photos, very few mountaineers had ever spotted these spectacular summits. Martin Conway saw them in 1902 from the deck of a steamer heading for Tierra del Fuego. H.W. "Bill" Tilman spied them in 1956 from his modest sloop, Mischief, sailing from England to Patagonia, where he would cross the Southern Patagonia Ice Cap.

In March 1973, when the indefatigable explorer Eric Shipton finally summited Mt. Burney, a volcano of 1,750 meters, on the third attempt, the Cordillera de Sarmiento was in clear view about 25 kilometers away. Marveling at the sight, he later wrote, "Northwards, across Union Channel, we looked up the narrow gorge of…[the] 'Canal of the Mountains,' flanked by the Cordillera Sarmiento, a splendid range of ice peaks as yet untouched."

[Next page] Unclimbed south and east faces of Cerro Trono (1,879m), second-highest peak in the area. It was first climbed in 2012, from the west. *Fernando Viveros, Onaspatagoni.com*

CORDILLERA DE SARMIENTO

The peninsula is about 65km long. (A) Cerro Dos Picos (1,250m). (B) Unclimbed Peak 1,706m. (C) Cerro Dama Blanca (1,941m, highest on the peninsula). (D) Glaciar Hermann. (E) Cerro Trono (1,879m). (F) Cerro Alas de Ángel (1,767m). (G) Cerro Tres Furias (1,314m). (H) Glaciar Bernal. (I) Cerro Cinco Amigos (1,401m). (J) Glaciar Zamudio. (K) Cerro Timonel (1,335m). *Uncharted Project, www.unchart.org*

MAP NOTE: The geographic nomenclature used for this article and map is the result of collaboration with all climbers who have named features in the range since the 1970s. The authors hope people will adopt these revised names. To get a highly detailed, digital copy of the 1:50,000 Cordillera de Sarmiento map, including all geographic names and climbing history, contact Natalia Martinez (natalia@unchart.org) or Camilo Rada (camilo@rada.cl).

GEOGRAPHY

WEST AND SOUTH OF THE TORRES DEL PAINE, the massive glaciers and rugged peaks of the Southern Patagonian Ice Cap extend into the Cordillera de Sarmiento, a mountainous peninsula about 65 km long and 15 km wide. The range centers about the 52° South line of latitude, west of Puerto Natales.

The main summits of the range are La Dama Blanca (1,941m), followed to the south by Cerro Trono (1,879m, a.k.a. Mt. Throne) and Alas de Ángel (1,767m, a.k.a. Angel Wings). Three more summits rise over 1,700 meters, and two of these are still unclimbed, as well as many other beautiful mountains above 1,200 meters. Many of the peaks are ice-covered towers or sharp rock spires, flanked by vertical walls.

On the official maps of the Chilean IGM (Instituto Geográfico Militar), not a single feature of the Cordillera de Sarmiento has been given a name, in part due to the total lack of human presence in the area. Nevertheless, over the years, explorers and climbers have named these bold summits, lakes,

glaciers, and rivers. That heritage is being rescued by the Uncharted project (unchart.org) through its maps and research, some of which is briefly presented here. [*Editor's note: Many of the peaks in the range originally were given English names, but the consensus now is that the Spanish names should be used. See "Map Note" on previous page.*]

With nearly 2,000 meters of jagged relief, the cordillera has a profile somewhat similar to the French Alps, but its glaciation is much more extensive, sending large glacier snouts into tidewater. In recent geological times the ice was thousands of feet thicker, bulldozing the long north-south fjords, rounding out basins in the main massif, and shaving smooth the neighboring ranges.

From the nearby sub-Antarctic waters, the persistent west winds—the Furious Fifties—pick up moist, cold air and plaster the peaks with thick frost. This forms the infamous "cauliflower ice" (a.k.a. "refrigerator ice"), similar to the rime that forms on peaks bordering the Patagonian Ice Cap, farther north, but much denser and more persistent.

Nearly all ascents, to date, have been on snow and ice. The rock, part of the rare Rocas Verdes formation, originated at the end of the Gondwana super-continent, when Patagonia started to break up and an oceanic basin was formed between the volcanic arc and the continent. The basin filled with large extrusions of basalts, sandstones, shales, and cherts. Still at depth, the rock was metamorphosed and then uplifted to roughly its present position. To all appearances the rock that underpins Sarmiento is solid. To the climber's hand, its gritty, olivaceous nature will provide real pleasure—if it is ever warm enough to climb without gloves.

[This page] American explorer Jack Miller during the 1992 National Geographic expedition that put these mountains on the map. *Gordon Wiltsie*

EARLY HISTORY

DISCOVERY IS A TRICKY WORD, given that the rugged lands surrounding these fjords were home of the Kaweshkar or Yamana people for thousands of years. Sadly, their names and tales were erased by the relentless and deadly European colonization process.

The range was first recorded in written history by Juan Ladrillero in 1558, but his tales were quickly forgotten as 58 of his 60 men died during that expedition, and the rest, including Ladrillero, died soon afterward. Twenty years later, Pedro Sarmiento de Gamboa followed in Ladrillero's wake and claimed for himself the discovery. Unfair as history often is, Sarmiento's name now is given to the fabulous mountain range he generically called "cordillera nevada" (snowy range).

Little further exploration was done in these waters for 250 years. In the 1830s, however, as Robert Fitz Roy and his crew explored the southern end of South America in the H.M.S. Beagle, they discovered the fjord that gives access to the eastern flanks of Cordillera de Sarmiento. This they called the Canal of the Mountains (now most commonly known as the Fiordo de las Montañas), "bordered on each side by a steep range of mountains, broken here and there by deep ravines, which were filled with frozen snow, and surmounted by extensive glaciers, whence huge avalanches were continually falling."

FIRST CLIMBS

IT WOULD BE NEARLY A CENTURY and a half before mountaineers ventured into this range. American Jack Miller first sighted the Sarmiento range from the summit of Gran Campo Nevado in the Skyring Sound area, southeast of the cordillera, in December 1974. His appetite whetted, Miller and Dan Asay assembled an inflatable boat, outboard motor, and foul-weather gear and left Puerto Natales in January 1976. Three days of sea travel got them into the Fiordo de las Montañas, and they set up camp on Peninsula Roca, just across from the huge, tidewater Bernal Glacier, to wait for a view of the range.

Aerial photos from the U.S. Air Force taken in 1944 had given them a general orientation

[This page] Climbing the north side of Jaco in 1992. The highest peak to the north is unclimbed Peak 1,706m. In the distance: the Southern Patagonia Ice Cap. *Gordon Wiltsie*

[This page] Cerro Cinco Amigos (1,401m) and Peak 1,429m (right) from the north. Only one secondary spire in this group has been climbed. *Camilo Rada*

to the landscape, but during their three weeks in the fjord they never sighted the spectacular summits. Nonetheless, they reconnoitered the full 58-kilometer length of the fjord. They climbed a prominent peak near the north end of the Peninsula Roca, where the gods applauded their effort with a horrendous electrical storm. On a day of quieter winds and lighter skies they crossed the fjord and followed the Bernal Glacier toward what they guessed (correctly) to be the highest group of mountains. Snow and high winds returned as they reached one of three prominent peaks of bare rock. The names they gave to the peaks they climbed, Rayos y Truenos (Thunder and Lightning) and Tres Furias (Three Furies), adequately describe the experience (*AAJ 1977*).

The pair then went to the Paine massif to dry out, and to attempt a route on the southwest face of Cuerno Principal that Miller had tried back in the 1960s. This time, Asay and Miller succeeded, together with Richard Smithers from South Africa. Along with their elation in reaching this summit, they enjoyed the irony and additional pleasure of seeing the Cordillera Sarmiento under clear skies, some 90 kilometers to the south.

In late 1988, a quartet of well-known climbers, Yvon Chouinard, Jim Donini, Rick Ridgeway, and Doug Tompkins, hired a fishing boat to drop them at the south end of the Peninsula Roca, just to the east of the Cordillera de Sarmiento. Although they only glimpsed the mountains briefly during weeks of stormy weather, Chouinard and Donini managed to climb the highest rock spire of the Grupo La Paz (1,190m), and then all four portaged across the peninsula and paddled five days in severe conditions to return to Puerto Natales.

Fourteen years after his first visit, Miller, now a confirmed Patagonian junkie, was driving the highway near Puerto Natales and was startled to see a completely clear Cordillera de Sarmiento. With no thoughts other than this exceptional opportunity, he dropped everything and found a plane and pilot to fly him at summit level along both sides of the entire range. This flight revealed mountains beyond his wildest imagination. To Miller, it was like seeing the French Alps or the Coast Mountains of southeast Alaska for the first time. The grandeur of the resulting photographs was enough to convince the National Geographic Society to support an expedition to explore and map the little-known range.

On this 1992 expedition, Miller and five friends—Pete Garber, Rob Hart, Phillip Lloyd, Tyler van Arsdell, and Gordon Wiltsie—completed the single most thorough ground survey to

[This page] Peaks above Glaciar Hermann (left to right): Cerro Trono, Cerro Tres Furias, Cerro Dama Blanca, and Peak 1,596m (unclimbed). *Fernando Viveros, Onaspatagonia.com*

date, exploring these mountains from both the Fiordo de las Montañas and the rarely visited Fiordo Taraba on the west side of the range (*AAJ 1993*). They climbed peaks in two of the main massifs, summiting and naming six mountains: Gremlin's Cap (now Gorro de Duende), Fickle Finger of Fate (Caprichoso), The South Face (Cara Sur, named for the peaks' prominent wall), Jaco (named after a legendary god of the area), Elephant Ears (Orejas de Elefante), and Taraba. In the process they created the first schematic map of the area.

The subsequent article in *National Geographic* magazine (April 1994) exposed the world to this range. And the expedition's failure to reach the main summit, La Dama Blanca, gave it sufficient notoriety to attract new expeditions—and new failures.

MODERN EXPEDITIONS

IN THE SUMMER 1994–'95, a British expedition led by David Hillebrandt, together with Keith Atkinson and Robin Earle, attempted La Dama Blanca. They were halted by persistent bad weather and an unexpected valley in their way. In spite of the tough conditions they reached the summit of Pico Anwa (*Alpine Journal 1996*).

Also in 1995, the first Chilean expedition ventured into these mountains, as Nicolás Boetsch, Christian Burachio, Alberto Gana, Giancarlo Giuglielmetti, Felipe Howard, and Pablo Osses accessed the area by kayak, traveling the full length of the Fiordo de las Montañas and eventually reaching the summit of Cerro Timonel (*AAJ 1998*).

At the end of 1997, Basque climbers climbed two peaks—Cerro Dos Picos and Cerro Cuatro Agujas—next to Miller and Asay's Rayos y Truenos, at the north end of Peninsula Roca.

Hillebrandt returned in January 1998, with Nick Banks, Chris Smith, and Nial Washington-Jones. They finally solved the riddle of accessing La Dama Blanca and reached a point 500 meters below the main summit, despite rain every single day of the 28 the British were there. Later the same year they returned, hoping to finish the route, but again were rejected by the merciless weather.

In 1999, a second Chilean expedition visited the area, comprised of Manuel Bugueño, Patricia Cuevas, Rodrigo Flores, Mauricio Ortiz, and Juan Antonio Villarroel. In spite of awful weather, they managed to climb one of the bold spires of Cerro Cinco Amigos as well as Punta Barlovento.

La Dama Blanca was still virgin, and at the end of 1999 an expedition backed by the Spanish TV program "Al Filo de lo Imposible" took up the challenge. In the team was the Basque climber Iñaki San Vicente, who had been part of the 1997 exploration. This new attempt failed, but just three weeks later San Vicente returned with Rafael Quesada for a second try. They finally reached the 1,941-meter summit of La Dama Blanca on February 8, 2000 (*AAJ 2000*).

That October the English climber Hillebrandt returned once again. Having missed his chance for the first ascent of La Dama Blanca, he decided to take on Alas de Ángel (1,767m), a more technical challenge. He and his partners reached a point at 1,100 meters, but a 14-day storm prevented a second try (*AAJ 2001*).

Since the highest summit of the cordillera had been reached, interest in the whole range soon fell off, even though prettier and more challenging peaks remained unclimbed. Almost

[This page, left] Unclimbed towers above Glaciar Zamudio. *Fernando Vivereo, Onaspatagonia.* **[This page, right]** Cerro Dama Blanca (1,941m), highest peak on the peninsula, and only climbed once. *Cristian Oyarzo, Fortalezapatagonia.com*

12 years passed before a new expedition visited the area. Natalia Martinez (Argentina) and Camilo Rada (Chile), while working on the Uncharted research and mapping project, were seduced by the charm of this remote corner of Patagonia and the many mountains that were still unexplored. With a light style similar to that of Miller and Asay in 1976, they made the first ascents of Cerro Alas de Ángel and Cerro Trono during the winter of 2012. [*See Climbs and Expeditions in this edition.*]

LOGISTICS AND WEATHER

GETTING TO THE CORDILLERA DE SARMIENTO by land is almost unthinkable and would require a major expedition by itself. However, the labyrinth of waterways on three sides of the range makes it accessible by boats—albeit ones that can withstand extremely rough seas. Puerto Natales, the gateway to Torres del Paine National Park, is also the seaport for the Cordillera de Sarmiento. During rare periods of calm weather, the 50 nautical miles can be traveled in four hours by a Zodiac inflatable or a bit longer by a fishing boat or private yacht. Kayaking will take several days, but portaging over strategic necks of land can shorten the distance to about 35 nautical miles. Indigenous boaters marked these shortcuts with rock paintings that are still found.

Once on land, the main foes remain water and moisture. Base camps must be positioned where they won't be submerged by heavy rain. Rubber boots are ideal approach footwear, and goggles are survival gear—spare goggles too. In the alpine, ice caves and igloos are good alternatives to tents, given the frequent gale-force winds, although warm summer rain can quickly ruin snowy shelters.

Some climbers prefer the winter months—May through August. Winds and storms are somewhat milder, on average, and there may be more days of clear sky. The trade-off is longer nights, but latter-day climbers have learned to move loads, establish high camps, and even climb during storms and in darkness. And winter can be a good ally by lowering the snow line within the wet forest and low-elevation alpine terrain.

Any expedition that waits for good weather to get out of the tent is almost certainly condemned to failure. Exploring, setting camps, and moving loads during foul weather is essential to success, requiring, in Shipton's words, "a certain amount of stoicism." Since many of the approaches will be "blind," due to storm and whiteouts, moving at night makes sense, putting the climbers in position to launch a summit push when a rare weather window opens. However, this tactic requires skillful use of all navigational resources. Maps have vastly improved since the early 1990s, and the miracle of GPS-aided route-finding has expanded the boundaries of Patagonian exploration as much as cams did for traditional rock climbing.

CLIMBING POSSIBILITIES

AFTER THE EXPEDITIONS BY NATIONAL GEOGRAPHIC in 1992 and "Al filo de lo Impossible" in 2001, many people thought the Cordillera de Sarmiento was climbed out. But during their research on the climbing history of the range, Martinez and Rada have realized there is still a long list of unclimbed peaks. Most of these rise above 1,500 meters and have steep walls or spires in the last hundred to few hundred meters. These are almost always covered in thick rime ice. Some may be reached on skis from the snow line, but most ascents will involve at least

[This page] High camp at 1,200m below the south face of Cerro Trono. *Camilo Rada*

few pitches of serious ice or mixed climbing.

Long glacier valleys are carved deeply into these mountains, offering some steep walls with 1,300 meters or more in vertical gain, including the north face of Cerro Trono and the southwest face of La Dama Blanca. The south faces sometimes support icefalls of a couple of hundred meters, clinging to vertical faces of dark rock. Some of the sub-massifs have never been explored, and many of the valleys have never been trodden. Real exploration is still to be done.

PRESERVATION

For centuries, isolation and a harsh climate kept the Cordillera de Sarmiento pristine. But in a world increasinlgy starved of natural resources, even in the remotest parts of Patagonia people will harvest old-growth dwarf cypress for fence posts or create salmon farms to grow the fish for North American and European tables. And though most climbers are scrupulous about keeping their camps clean, others have left heaps of trash or chopped down trees to build shelters.

The Reserva Nacional Alacalufes, created in 1969 and to date the largest Chilean national reserve, includes the Cordillera de Sarmiento. But the protection offered by this status is limited, and resources can be exploited if a sustainable management plan is presented to the government. Environmental enforcement is often deficient in Latin America, especially in remote areas like this. Climbers, therefore, carry significant responsibility, not only to leave no traces of their own time in these mountains, but also to keep an eye open for improper or illegal activities by other visitors, and, if necessary, inform the authorities.

About the Authors

Camilo Rada, 34, is a Chilean living in Whistler, British Columbia, while earning his Ph.D. in glaciology. He has done numerous first ascents in Patagonia and Antarctica. Jack Miller, 75, is a geographer and environmentalist living near Ridgway, Colorado. He first visited Patagonia in 1964 and was the first person to explore and climb in many of the wildest ranges of the region.

THE WHITNEY MASSIF

CLASSIC ROUTES, HOT NEW LINES, AND A BLANK CANVAS FOR THE FUTURE

DOUG ROBINSON, AMY NESS & MYLES MOSER

This is a story of people meeting terrain. It's a love story—this terrain is hot. The adventures are wild and timeless. The red lines are still being drawn. Many have fallen for this massif, seduced by the pleasure of dancing with its peaks.

From the barely 10,000-foot summits ringing Lake Tahoe, the Sierra Crest builds as it marches southward. Opposite Yosemite it climbs over 13,000 feet, and coming by Bishop it nearly grazes 14,000 with the distinctive chisel of Mt. Humphreys. Soon the Palisades Traverse links six peaks that top 14,000 feet. Farther south, massive Mt. Williamson soars as high over the Owens Valley as K2 rises above base camp.

Finally we arrive at the crescendo of the greatest granite range in the Lower 48, the Whitney Massif. Its heart stretches just two miles south to Mt. Muir, yet it is littered with buttresses, spires, ridges, and walls seemingly made for climbing. To the east, Lone Pine Peak stands guardian to walls that tear through the sky: Day Needle, Keeler Needle, the elegant spires of Mt. Russell, and Whitney itself, at 14,508 feet (4,422m) the highest summit in the continental United States.

The Sierra is a young range, and it's still having growth spurts. Take the night of March 26, 1872. It was a full moon. Mt. Whitney hadn't even seen its first ascent. At one in the morning, a slumbering fault ripped right under the tiny settlement of Lone Pine. Whitney lurched upward 20 feet. Twenty-seven of Lone Pine's inhabitants died as their adobe shacks collapsed on top of them. You can still see the scar from that night's slip fault right on the north edge of town.

And still it rises. Mt. Whitney is now 11 feet taller than when I began climbing it in the 1960s. After a series of quakes measuring 6.0 and more in the spring of 1980, it jumped seven feet. Living a mile from the epicenter on the East Side, I had a front-row seat. I was sitting on the ground in my front yard in Round Valley, watching rockfall tumble off the Wheeler Crest. A minute later a groundswell rolled toward me. It was a wave in the solid earth, maybe eight inches high. This land-wave rippled along at 20 miles an hour, bumped right under me, and disappeared beneath my house. Geologists told me such ripples had been reported before but never photographed. For several months after that my loaded camera sat just inside the front door.

These mountains are restless, alive. As I write this in Lone Pine I sit on top of 6,000 feet of debris, the sand and gravel and boulders that have tumbled off the Whitney Massif and then washed into the deepest valley in the country. Bedrock, more than a mile down, is below sea level. So, yeah, take your helmet up there. And know, too, that shift happens here on a scale that could make your helmet seem like a cruel joke.

SCHOOLED ON THE MASSIF

AMY: It was my first butt-kicker, on my first trip into the Sierra backcountry. During the hike in, we passed several unhappy hikers on their way out, cursing their partners and warning us of imminent storms. The air was frigid. The next day we got lost on Whitney's east buttress during a snowstorm, me in Norman Clyde-style leather boots. A day later we did Cardiovascular Seizure, up a buttress on the far right side of the east face. We knew it was going to rain. In fact, we started climbing in our rain jackets—the bright green and yellow made a good show for those hunkered down at base camp. Back at the tent, I was acting strangely. Myles forced me to eat, drink, and get warm. My $1 thrift-store rain jacket could have cost me my life.

But I was hooked. Bouldering, sport climbing, the multi-pitch trad routes of the Portal Buttress—all translated into training to go hard and fast in the alpine. Living a few seasons at the Portal allowed for continuous exploration of this granite playground. Soon the possibilities seemed endless, and year after year I'm more convinced they are. A day doesn't pass in Lone Pine when I don't look up and become intrigued by a new formation or a link-up that hasn't been done—lines hiding in plain sight!

CHAM I AM?

DOUG: Climbing writer Bruce Willey dubbed this region "America's Chamonix." Truly a charmed idea! Our local area likened to that quintessential alpine village, ringed by shining granite. Yet the first time I heard it, I thought, so close and yet…

The Mont Blanc Massif crowns Western Europe, with Chamonix nestled at its feet. Our Whitney Massif is the apex of the Lower 48, a seemingly infinite expanse of perfect rock rising above the huge Owens Valley—of course it's worthy! Not to mention we have way better weather and no annoying glaciers. Climbing in a desert range has its advantages, starting with approaching all that choice granite in T-shirts and sticky-soled tennies.

Maybe Lone Pine (pop. 2,035) lacks a bit of that sidewalk-café Euro ambiance, but in the evenings, after the heat of a desert day, people come out and stroll the main street. There are day-hikers, sore and proud from the marathon-length Whitney summit trail, and a scattering of thru-hikers down off the Pacific Crest Trail for resupply. Some stop into a restaurant or pub, but mostly they just want to be out and about and enjoy the air and look upward, where, two vertical miles above, alpenglow softens the edges of a white-granite skyline.

[This page] "Whitney Cirque" (annotated prints available at Jercollins.com). *Jeremy Collins*

[This page, top] The glorious east faces of the massif, with Mt. Whitney in center, Day and Keeler needles at left, and Mt. Russell far right. These two images were first published in *Above All* (2008), a photographic celebration of California's 14ers. *David Stark Wilson*

[This page, bottom] A striking view of Mt. Russell (left) and Mt. Whitney from the northwest. The southwest and south faces of Russell, on the right side of the peak, hold some of the finest climbs in the Sierra. *David Stark Wilson*

A rowdy group pours out of Elevation, the local climbing shop: a knot of sport climbers, yipping and clowning as they head back to a campfire in the Alabama Hills, a few minutes away. The 'Bamas have good bouldering, hundreds of sport climbs, and un-trafficked cracks. Those young climbers don't know it yet, but in all likelihood, during the next couple of years, most of them will be treated to a casual invitation that will sweep them up onto the Whitney Portal Buttresses. That day of multi-pitch cragging will forever expand their vision of climbing.

Above, along the skyline, are the airy arêtes and broad, white walls of the alpine zone: blockier granite with square-cut edges and well-defined cracks, a more raw and angular world, brightened by piercing light, with its shapes sculpted by the relentless forces of weather. Yes, we have bad weather too! Just not as much of it.

In Chamonix, the téléphérique station is the focus of the village as surely as cathedrals were in medieval times, offering a stairway to heaven. Riding to the 12,605-foot Aiguille du Midi, you not only risk instant altitude sickness but also can be treated to the odd moment of summiting a route by manteling onto the terrace of a bar, to the bemused glances of tourists sipping an apéritif. Thank goodness, you realize in a rush, for our particularly American concept of Wilderness, which guards our gleaming massif through the honest toil of uphill sweat. Our wilderness ideal keeps the huts away too—in return we get to sleep under the stars.

THE ALLURE OF SHINING GRANITE

Doug: John Muir was the first real climber to explore Whitney, even though it was hundreds of miles from his home base in Yosemite. He was Muir, after all, the ultimate mountain rambler and scrambler, and his first ascent of Cathedral Peak in Tuolumne a couple of years earlier had been solid 5.4—surely the hardest climb in the country in 1869. Just try to keep him away from

[This page] Key peaks of the Whitney region. *Anna Riling*

[This page, top] The airy east face of Mt. Whitney, first climbed in 1931. [This page, right] Star Trekkin' (5.10) on Mt. Russell's southwest face. *Both: PatitucciPhoto.com*

the apex of the Sierra. Besides, there was the small matter of a personal vendetta.

Back in 1864 a state geological survey team was roaming the southern Sierra, and during the first ascent of Mt. Tyndall they glimpsed the state's highest peak and named it for their boss and benefactor, Josiah Whitney, the state geologist. Whitney would later poo-poo John Muir's discovery of glacial polish in Tuolumne Meadows and his theory that rivers of ice had carved out Yosemite Valley. Whitney was sure the bottom somehow had dropped out of the Valley. He went so far as to call John Muir an ignorant shepherd. What might have been just a scientific disagreement over geological forces turned personal. Muir decided he would climb Mt. Whitney—a mountain his nemesis had never even laid eyes upon—and bag the first ascent.

Muir got to the mountain a little late. Local yokels—the Fishermen, as they have come to be known—had gone slip-sliding up a scree slope on the western flank of the peak in August 1873. But when Muir got to Lone Pine in October of that same year, it was overwhelmingly obvious to him that the shining eastern escarpment of Whitney was still untouched. The line he climbed, the Mountaineer's Route, is still by far the most popular of the actual climbing routes on the peak, and way worth doing. His line, which goes up the obvious gully just right of the sweeping east face, defines third class in a way that might be intimidating to many.

Now we know that Muir blew the timing in another way: After midsummer it's full of loose rock and sliding scree. It's way better earlier in the season, as a snow climb, with ice axe in hand, kicking steps in firm snow. At the notch a short, steep wall (a rope may be desirable) takes you onto the north face for 400 feet of easy scrambling, cutting a huge switchback off to the west across this broad face. But stay with me here for a fun alternative.

To the east of the scrambling route a shallow ridge shoots directly toward the summit. It only stands proud of the terrain by about 50 feet, but it's solid fourth class, so again you could want a rope. We probably have Norman Clyde to thank for this sportier variation to Muir's route—he did the first winter ascent in 1932. This ridgelet variation was passed on to me by Bob Swift and Smoke Blanchard, who were Clyde's successors as guides in the Sierra. When you consider that Clyde's first summer in the Sierra, 1914, was the year that John Muir died, it's an unbroken chain.

[This page] (A) Pinnacle Ridge. (B) Aiguille Extra. (C) Third Needle. (D) Crooks Peak (Day Needle). (1) Beckey Route. (2) BCB on the Prow. (E) Keeler Needle. (3) Harding Route. (4) Crimson Wall. (5) Australopithecus. (6) Blood of the Monkey. (7) Lowe Route. (G). Mt. Whitney. (8) Strassman Route. (9) Left Wing Extremist. (10) Direct East Face (11) Hairline (12) Great Book. (13) East Face (14) Sunshine-Peewee (East Buttress). (16) Mountaineer's Route. (17) Rotten Chimney. (18) Cardiovascular Seizure. Approximate lines; some routes not shown. *John Scurlock*

AFTER MUIR, BEFORE CROFT

DOUG: By 1926 all of California's 14,000-foot peaks had been climbed but two. Near the Whitney Massif, Norman Clyde had already picked off first ascents of Mt. LeConte, Mt. Carillon, and Peak 3,986. (The latter, as Amy and Myles would be quick to tell you, is the proud continuation of the south face of Lone Pine Peak.) Then he bagged the prize: the first ascent of Mt. Russell, by its east ridge. Even though it's "only" third class, Peter Croft considers it the finest third class in the entire Sierra.

Clyde also led the breakthrough climb of the era, Mt. Whitney's east face. It was 1931, the year the rope came to the Sierra, and this five-hour ascent (most climbers today can't repeat it that fast) was the crowning achievement of that summer. The party included Robert Underhill, a Harvard professor who passed on the proper belay techniques he'd learned in the Alps, and the hottest teenage climbers of the '30s, Glen Dawson and Jules Eichorn.

Then came the Mendenhalls, John and Ruth, who got engaged shortly after a cold night's bivy on Mt. Ritter. In 1941 they put up the second route on Whitney's east face. Ruth was a pioneering Sierra climber when it was shocking to see a woman roping up. (To read Ruth's story in her own words, see *Woman on the Rocks: The Mountaineering Letters of Ruth Dyar*

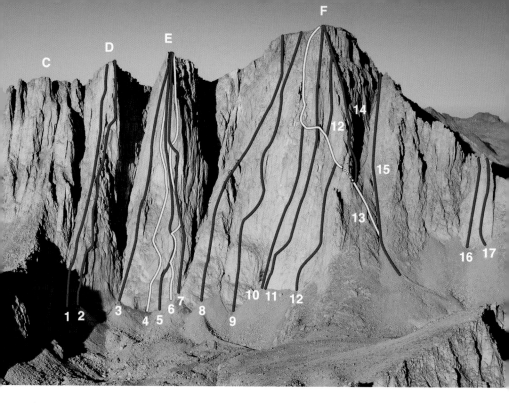

Mendenhall, edited by her daughter, the Sierra watercolorist Valerie Mendenhall Cohen.) Dawson, who had an eye for a great line, returned six years after his east face climb to do Whitney's east buttress, naming it the Sunshine-Peewee. It's got to be the best 5.7 in the massif.

Fast-forward past a couple of decades, during which remarkably little happened in the massif. When new development began again, it focused not on the skyline but down in the Portal. No one tells the story better than Peter Croft, in *Bishop Area Rock Climbs*: "The history of climbing in the Portal can pretty much be divided into Before Fred Beckey (B.F.) and after Fred (A.F.).... In the mid-'60s to the early '70s, Fred came and simply took what he wanted." Beckey roamed up the North Fork, too, climbing some smaller alpine towers and, in 1971, the northeast slabs of Mt. Russell. Hot on Fred's heels, as he so often was, came Galen Rowell, climbing Russell's west face a few days later.

In 1959, the direct east face of Mt. Whitney was climbed by Denis Rutovitz and Andrzel Ehrenfeucht. And then, in 1960, arguably the grand prize of the massif, Keeler Needle, got climbed by Warren Harding. In the 1970s, spiry Mt. Russell's walls exploded with activity, beginning with the elegant Fishhook Arête and Mithral Dihedral.

Tracking the climbs that have come hot and heavy ever since would take pages, but surely would include routes by such greats as Errett Allen, Alan Bartlett, Bob Bolton, Bill Cramer, Peter Croft, John Fischer, Bob Harrington, Darrell Hensel, Marty Lewis, Robs Muir, SP Parker, Allan Pietrasanta, Steve Plunkett, Kevin Powell, Galen Rowell, Steve Schneider, Gary Slate, Mike Waugh, and Jonny Woodward. Not to mention Myles Moser and Amy Ness.

THE PORTAL

MYLES: Let's head up the mountain, sampling the climbing along the way. Turn at the one stoplight in Lone Pine to go west on Whitney Portal Road, which dead-ends at 8,365 feet.

There are rules here, so listen up. A permit is required to go past the first lake; the only exception is hiking up to the Portal buttresses. Permits can be surprisingly hard to get. Start at the Interagency Visitor Center, one mile south of town, or by visiting www.recreation.gov. There is also a lottery held every day at 11 a.m. for permits. Make sure to allow an extra day for your trip if you're counting on your lucky number to be drawn.

Stop into the Whitney Portal Store for whatever you forgot. Peter Croft highly recommends the burgers and fries, and the cooler is well-stocked with beer. Don't miss your personal opportunity to be heckled by the one and only "Sandbag Senior," Doug Thompson, a wealth of backcountry info.

Just downhill from the store is the main trail to Whitney, which switchbacks right below the Whitney Portal Buttress. Many don't even notice as they trudge by, but the buttress has some of the best climbing any of us have ever experienced. Nearly 2,000 feet high, the wall hosts about 13 routes, ranging from eight to twelve pitches. Only two routes are regularly done: Ghostrider and No Country for Old Men. Both go at 5.10c.

There are far more adventures to be had. For instance, the Womack Route (established in 1989, now 5.11 A0), had likely never seen a second ascent until Amy and I did it five years ago. This route climbs fingertip seams to reach a 13-foot, dead-horizontal roof. Trivial Pursuit (5.12) also sees very few ascents. Put up by the slab masters Darrell Hensel, Kevin Powell, and Jonny Woodward, it will test any aficionado. Gangway (5.12 or 5.11 A0), put up by Croft, has one of the best liebacks in the Sierra. Or take the 20-minute walk to the Never Ending Story

[This page, left] Endless granite west of Whitney Portal, as seen from the Candlelight Wall. The Cleaver is in upper left. Many of the other formations have no known climbs. *Jeff Mahoney* [This page, right] The Altisimo Arena, high over Whitney Portal. (1) Tycho, 5. 10c. (2) Moon Walker, 5.12 A0. (3) Corpus Christi Buttress, 5.9 (4) Apollo 13, 5.10d. (5) Sombra de la Luna, 5.11. (6) Pillar Altisimo, 5.11. (7) Altisimo Arête, 5.10c. (8) El Segundo, Beckey Route, 5.9 (9) Premier Buttress, The Premier Route, 5.8 A0. Routes 5 through 7 are new (*AAJ 2013*). Some shorter routes not shown. *John Svenson*

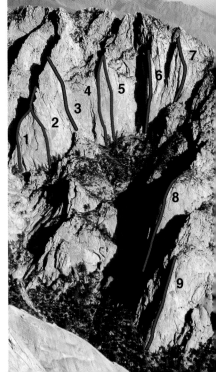

[This page] Myles Moser leads the fifth pitch of Never Ending Story (V 5.12), a new route on Whitney Portal Buttress. *Amy Ness*

(V 5.12), which Amy and I established just a couple of years ago. Although several strong climbers have gone up to pitch five, no one has repeated all 12 pitches of this burly route. What about trying to free the Beckey-Callis route? A crumbly roof appears to be the crux, and the spinning, quarter-inch button heads don't instill much confidence—but what an adventure!

Take a walk back down the main road to find Premier Buttress and El Segundo, home to the Beckey Routes (5.8 A0/5.10c and 5.9, respectively), which will make any climber beam ear to ear. Look south across the canyon, where the "Eiger of the Portal," Candlelight Wall, rockets skyward with thousands of feet of unexplored alpine terrain. Green in color, bomber in quality, and riddled with cracks, it awaits dozens of new adventure routes.

From the summit of El Segundo, turn your eyes uphill to the north. The Altisimo Arena, facing hot south, is a jewel all its own. The cracks here are more fractured than those on the rounded walls below and much steeper. This entire region of the Portal—with, it's true, a longish approach—was untouched before Phil Bircheff, Amy, and I began staring up this way with the scope. We soon discovered that Hensel and Woodward had begun work close by—and then found them promptly returning to finish the job after an email notified them of our presence! We put up several routes in the Arena, and along with the now-finished slab routes, there are plenty of second ascents to be had. Altisimo's neighbor, Moonstone Buttress, a sharkfin blade, features the route Tycho, a great 5.10c climb that will have you dancing along a massive swirling dike and ending on one of the most exposed arêtes in the Portal.

To the west of the Portal Buttress are steep, clean cliffs abundant with black knobs and dikes—many of these walls wait to be traveled. Did you know there is an unclimbed dome above the Portal? Did you know there is a 2,500-foot Royal Arches of the Portal, complete with a pendulum? (Ummagumma, IV 5.7 A0; see Climbs and Expeditions.)

UP THE TRAILS

AMY: About 3.5 miles up the main hiking trail toward Mt. Whitney is Thor Peak. With its numerous cracks and serene setting by Mirror Lake, this 12,306-foot peak will make any climber ponder. Myles and I have a slight obsession with one of the routes on Thor: Stemwinder (5.4). We use it as a cardio-training romp before work, with a 4,000-foot gain from the Portal, a few technical cruxes, and mostly easy scrambling to the low shoulder.

Six more miles will bring you to Consultation Lake, or "Trail Camp," the base for many of those hiking up Whitney. The view from this camp is seldom seen by rock climbers, who are usually up in the North Fork. Too bad. They might notice the east buttress of Mt. Muir (Mendenhall-Nies, 1935) or the massive expanse of spires rolling out to the north, the Whitney Aiguilles. How many towers are there? R. J. Secor's encyclopedic and authoritative guidebook, *The High Sierra: Peaks, Passes, and Trails,* lists five between Day Needle and Mt. Muir. But that is an understatement that merely follows what's been climbed and recorded, mostly by Scott Ayers and Mike Strassman. A long, lingering look will reveal plenty of new-route potential.

The North Fork, splitting off to the right just a mile up the main hiking trail, is your access to Mt. Carillon, Mt. Russell, and the entire 2,500-foot east wall of the Whitney Massif. Good route-finding on this sometimes-rough climber trail is essential—many first-timers find themselves cliffed out. Camping near Upper Boy Scout Lake, at 11,600 feet, allows for acclimatization and offers plenty of distraction. Just last year, Myles and I pulled our friend Phil Bircheff out of retirement, and the three of us hiked to the southeast face of Mt. Russell and put up a straightforward, five-pitch 5.9 in only a few hours. Much of this face and its beautiful ridgelines are seldom seen, much less climbed.

From Upper Boy Scout Lake, the trail continues toward Iceberg Lake. Now the massif's needles—Keeler, Day, and the Aiguilles—soar above, sporting enough open, unexplored space to keep you busy for years. Besides the venerable Harding Route, Keeler Needle has several lines that haven't seen a second ascent. Only three routes are known on Day Needle (officially

[This page] Amy Ness explores Tycho (5.10c) on the Moonstone Buttress. *Myles Moser*

[This page, top] Just a pretty face to hikers intent on Whitney's summit, Thor Peak has about nine routes on its broad south face. *Richard Piotrowski* [This page, bottom] The east buttress of 14,015-foot Mt. Muir (center) is a classic Sierra "fourth class" challenge. On the south face is a possible new route that's easily seen from the "99 Switchbacks" section of the Mt. Whitney Trail. Doug Robinson got a third of the way up it one winter, only to discover that his client couldn't climb 5.7 in his ski boots. It remains unfinished. *Richard Piotrowski*

known as Crooks Peak), and we have never heard of any being repeated. Many of the seldom-climbed routes on Whitney's broad east face await free ascents.

Most climbers we meet in the North Fork have the same list of objectives: the east face or east butt of Whitney; Fishhook and Mithral Dihedral, or maybe Western Front, on Russell; perhaps the Harding Route on Keeler. But not many even notice such gems as Cardiovascular Seizure. This route lies just to the north of the Mountaineer's Route and provides eight pitches of steep and sustained 5.10 climbing.

But let's face it, the classics are popular for a reason. We recommend the Sunshine-Peewee Route (a.k.a., the east buttress) as a far more interesting alternative to the east face, which meanders and has a lot of third class. It's an appealing line up the sun-shadow arête. Skirt the looming block of the Peewee to its right on incut holds, and then weave your way through more blockiness to the summit. Start early—this climb is longer than it looks.

The Harding Route on Keeler Needle is considered one of the gems of the Sierra for location, aesthetics, and difficulty. It's got up to 16 pitches (although we recommend linking some with a 70-meter rope) and cruxes up to 5.10c—you'd better like offwidths!

The Fishhook Arête (5.9) and Mithral Dihedral (5.10) are justifiably popular routes of about six to eight pitches on Russell's south side. Since they're practically side by side, Myles and I decided to climb them back to back, on a summer day when the wind was so strong it kept blowing the stacked ropes into my face at belays. On the Mithral Dihedral, I took Myles' advice—"you have small feet!"—and kept my approach shoes on. They jammed into the cracks perfectly. Myles said he will never forget watching me bite off my gloves one at a time and shove them into my bra for the 5.10 lieback crux, then immediately put them back on. When we got back to the base, ice had formed on our backpack from a leaking bottle.

LOST AMONG THE RANGES

DOUG: The backside of the Whitney Massif, a huge wild playground, is both a problem and an opportunity. The problem is getting permits to do the approaches up those super-popular hiking trails. The opportunity is a virtually unknown realm of pristine camping, no waiting in line for routes, and first ascents to be done everywhere.

Every climber coming down the trail from Whitney's summit has a full view of the north face of Mt. Hitchcock for over an hour. It's hard to miss: a mile wide, with a good dozen major ridges and buttresses, ranging from 800 to 1,200 feet. Yet it wasn't until 2011 before the first route went up. Mt. Chamberlain is a virtually identical story. Climbing there began earlier, but it too has recently seen some fine, hard new lines.

Even the backside of Whitney itself has new routes going begging. Michael Thomas and I climbed the very first line on its southwest quadrant in 2006. It took us two days to approach up the North Fork trail, pop over Whitney-Russell Col, and wander down the pristine Alpine Lakes valley, where only four sets of footprints from that entire summer wandered among gleaming, untouched walls.

We'll skip over the mini-epic of having our tarp shelter blown apart by the sudden blizzard that night and losing a day drying out our sleeping bags. When we finally got onto our ridge it greeted us with classic 5.7 climbing, then off-camber 5.9 to regain the ridge and

[This page] The east buttress Mt. Irvine, said to be the best grade V in the Sierra. *Amy Ness*

[This page, top] The north face of Mt. Hitchcock near the "backside" of Mt. Whitney. The face has only three known routes, all of which were put up after 2010. *Richard Piotrowski*
[This page, right] Doug Robinson looking like he knows the way on Lost, a 20-pitch 5.9+ established in 2006 on Mt. Whitney's southwest side. *Michael Thomas*

an inspiring 5.6 arête. Darkness caught us after nine pitches, and we bailed into the gully. But this fine route drew us back the next year, and we completed it with 20 pitches up to 5.9+, not unroping until 2:30 the next morning.

In early September 2012, a neighboring ridge got climbed by SP Parker and Urmas Franosch. In what Parker called a "classic Sierra four-day excursion," they climbed a possible new route on the Arctic Lakes Wall, a 5.10 direct start to the Left Arête on Russell's southeast face, and a 1,200-foot route to the left of our route Lost. Of course it was named Found. Many other possibilities await.

LONE PINE PEAK

Amy: From below, this labyrinth of a mountain appears so massive that many tourists mistake it for Mt. Whitney, snapping pictures for their scrapbooks. At first glance, you can't help but fixate on the north, northeast, and east ridges, each gaining 7,000 feet from the desert floor, casting their shadows over one another. The ridges vary from 5.5 to 5.7, with lengths up to three miles. Depending on the climber's skill, speed, and preferred season of ascent, these ridge lines can be a quick solo on a summer day or a multi-day ascent of snow and ice, with some of the best bivy views one could ask for.

Below the ridges are some of the best and biggest "crags" in the region. The north ridge floats over Bastille Buttress, where the Beckey Route (V 5.11 A0) has 15 pitches of the most pristine climbing on the mountain. The fifth-pitch bolt ladder, a monument to determination (with Beckey relics intact), leads to a crack that must have been split by Zeus himself.

Around to the east, the Three Arrows look a bit small, but they're perched at 10,000 feet with 1,200-foot walls. These climbs are all in sight from the road, yet the long, scree-filled approaches and little access to water keep most climbers from ever joying in their presence.

And finally there is the south face of Lone Pine Peak: thousands of feet high and wide. This terraced, baking granite wall has routes up to 22 pitches shooting up its flanks, with aid climbs and free routes alike to explore in this "Land of Little Rain" (V 5.10c). Recently, the active Pullharder group from San Diego led the way, once again, out of the obvious crack lines and onto the open faces, where they climbed a superb 500-foot dike, the Michael Strassman Memorial Route (6 pitches, 5.11). Repeating it, Doug let fly some of Mike's ashes from the summit.

THE ENCHAINMENTS

DOUG: Now the Lone Ranger makes his appearance. And we're not talking about the Western movie sets frequently appearing down in the Alabama Hills. Marty Hornick is a climber's climber, and he can hike too. Between acting as our government-sanctioned safety net up on the Whitney trail, shoveling tourists the official dogma, Marty got strong and stayed acclimatized. On days off he didn't necessarily feel like descending to Lone Pine. A grand scheme began to form—a dream he dubbed the Lone Ranger Traverse. He started up the north ridge of Lone Pine Peak, a long Grade IV. Then over Mallory and Irvine (incidentally, check out the Grade V east buttress on that one!). Next came Mt. Muir and the spiky crest of all the Whitney Aiguilles. Keeler, Day, the Big W, and Russell. And then, for good measure, even Mt Carillon. Whew!

An equally astounding enchainment began far to the north and way down in the desert at Manzanar, the WWII Japanese internment camp. Peter Mayfield climbed the northeast ridge of Mt. Williamson, longest in the Sierra, then hopped on down the crest past Tyndall, Barnard, and Carl Heller, over Mt. Russell, and clear on down the spiky Aiguilles to Mt. Muir.

Peter Croft once hiked up the North Fork, climbed the east face and east buttress of Whitney, scooted over to Russell to hit Fishhook Arête and Mithral Dihedral, and then ran over to do the east ridge of Carl Heller—in a day! Jason Lackey performed a similar feat a few years ago, but instead of heading to Carl Heller he fired off Keeler Needle. And Myles hit up

[This page] Winter view of the vast south face of Lone Pine Peak, with routes up to 22 pitches. During climbing season, thirst is a bigger issue than snow. *Richard Piotrowski*

two Grade V's consecutively: Fred
Becky's Direct South Face of Lone
Pine Peak and the East Buttress of
Mt. Irvine. With so many route
options in close proximity, the
ante is always being upped.

WHAT'S OLD IS NEW

AMY: In the last five years, Myles
and I have repeated several old
lines but in new ways. With a few
variations, we freed Windhorse
on Lone Pine Peak at 5.11. Our
new free route on Keeler Needle,
Blood of the Monkey, combined

several existing routes to get us to where we needed to start our own variation. Some of the
direct lines on Whitney could still see a free ascent, if a motivated party gets the inclination.
On Keeler Needle the Jeff Lowe possibly could go free. It's the idea of seeing something in a
new light, and not being afraid of what was A2 or A3 in the past.

There's still so much new route potential here it's ridiculous—for 5.6 and 5.14 alike. We
each have our secret stash of new lines. Once a possibility becomes a gleam in your eye, it starts
to look so obvious that you begin to assume everyone else sees it too. And you get a bit cagey.
Over beers, though, sometimes the idea comes spilling out, and suddenly there it hovers in the
twilight: challenging, unknown, waiting.

ABOUT THE AUTHORS

*Since the 1960s, Doug Robinson has been one of the foremost climbers, ski mountaineers, guides,
and writers of the Sierra Nevada. His cabin is up Rock Creek Canyon, northwest of Bishop.*

*In a "shameless co-author rave," Robinson writes: "I met Myles Moser six years ago in the
Alabama Hills, when he was living in a ratty Volkswagen Bug. Fast-forward to Joshua Tree, where
a band of boy boulderers encountered a band of girl boulderers that included Amy Ness, a North
Dakota climber fresh out of college. Soon Myles was admiring Amy's 'style' so much that he missed
a spot and she broke an ankle. Their first kiss was in the ER. Fast-forward again to Patagonia's
Torres del Paine. Now they are 2,000 feet up a new route on the North Tower and marooned in a
single-person portaledge through an eight-day blizzard. No big deal—they'd learned perseverance
in the Whitney Massif, putting up a 10-day Grade VI 5.12 on Keeler Needle and another Grade
VI (5.11 A0), among a slew of other new routes. I am honored to call this badass team my friends."*

*Moser and Ness live at Tuttle Creek Campground, less than half an hour's drive below
Whitney Portal.*

*Special thanks to Dr. Joel Matta, elite hip surgeon, who flew us on a recon flight over the
massif.*

[This page] Lone Pine Peak's north ridges gain 7,000 feet from the valley. *John Svenson*

CLIMBS & EXPEDITIONS

2018

UNITED STATES — LOWER 48

WASHINGTON

CASCADES

North Hozomeen, west face, Zorro Face. Both the north and south summits of Hozomeen Mountain (8,012') bear a great mystique, and an ascent from any direction has long daunted mountaineers (see the "Battle for Hozomeen" in Fred Beckey's *Challenge of the North Cascades*). In the early 2000s, John Scurlock's aerial photography of the foreboding west face of North Hozomeen, the "Zorro Face," stirred—perhaps haunted—the imagination of many Cascades alpinists. Its zigzagging ledge systems and few apparent weaknesses only added to its evil reputation. Rumored attempts surfaced: seasoned hard men were spurned before even attaining the base of this great, unclimbed wall.

Rolf Larson and I were just another two moths attracted to the ill light of this wall. The opening passage of Jack Kerouac's *Desolation Angels* speaks volumes about the dark attraction of the mountain: "Hozomeen, Hozomeen, most mournful mountain I ever seen…vertical furrows and bumps and Boo! crevasses, boom, sheer magnificent Prudential mountain, nobody's even heard of it, and it's only 8,000 feet high, but what a horror when I first saw that void…"

Established routes on the north side of the peak reputedly held difficult-to-protect rock, loose and devoid of cracks. Colin Haley's account of his attempt seemed to confirm this was also true of the Zorro Face: "The face is very large, much steeper than we expected, the rock is friable, and most importantly, there are almost no protection cracks, even for thin pitons. I think that the north face of South Hozomeen and the west face of North Hozomeen are perhaps the two most difficult walls in the Lower 48. The significance of an ascent with bolts will all depend on how many are placed." (adapted from Colinhaley.com). These words compelled us to wait for the right combination of weather, fitness, and appetite to make an attempt that would honor the style of Cascade alpinism. Leading up to our climb we trained for expected runouts on this wild wall.

Everything harmonized at the end of August. On day one a long hike brought us to a bivouac. On day two, we downclimbed a loose gully and then crossed several precipitous rocky ribs to our

[Previous spread] Luka Lindic attempting the east pillar of Phola Gangchen (7,703m) in Tibet. *Marko Prezelj*

[This page] One of the photos that inspired it all: the Zorro Face in winter. The line climbed by Rolf Larson and Eric Wehrly mostly follows the left-facing corner system leading directly to the summit. They bivied just 100m below the summit where a snow patch is visible. *John Scurlock*

targeted launch point below the face. The stuff called "rock" on this peak is metamorphosed basalt—also called Hozomeen chert—and was valued by the native Salish for making knives and arrowheads (Hozomeen is Salish for "sharp"). What it lacked in solidity and protection, it somewhat made up for with a plethora of in-cut features—good for climbing when solid.

Rolf won the first lead. On the second, I found the only evidence of human visitation on the wall: a quarter-inch bolt and a bail biner. The next pitches led up friable, vegetated, wet, and mostly welded-shut rock. The well-featured rock and sparse pro engendered a methodical rhythm of movement. The hook was set. On the third pitch Rolf's expletives drifted down to my belay. On the fourth I traced one of Hozomeen's tiger-stripe ledges left to avoid an overhanging headwall, revealing an avenue toward left-facing corners above. The fifth lead fired down rock missiles, more curses, and words—*I wanna go home*—in the wind. But we were drawn to the dark promise of corners above. Pitches 6 to 10 were rope-stretchers, mostly following the corner system. Atop pitch 10, I placed a single, crappy pin to augment the anchor. Above, Rolf raced the sunset to a ledge, where we would shiver through an exposed bivy.

At dawn I pieced together a long, winding pitch 12 on worsening rock to the summit ridge. From here it was a casual stroll for 100' to the summit, with incomparable views of the North Cascades. We had placed and removed one shallow pin, placed no bolts, and stretched the rope for 12 pitches on this unmatched and uniquely Hozomeen adventure: the Zorro Face (IV 5.9). 🔲

Eric Wehrly

Southwest Bonanza Peak, northwest buttress, Oregonian Route. In early September, Erik Bonnett and I climbed a mostly independent route on the northwest buttress of Bonanza Peak, reaching its

southwest summit (9,320'). This route begins on the prominent buttress a few hundred yards left of the Soviet Route (AAJ 1976), the only other route on this wall. Prior to our climb we had seen beautiful photos from the Soviet Route, and both of us, independently, came up with the idea to try the new line. Also, having never climbed in the Washington Cascades, we figured it was a good place to start.

Our route climbs 1,600' of independent terrain before joining the Soviet Route on the west buttress for 600' to the final summit block. The climbing is mostly sustained 5.6–5.8, punctuated with moves up to 5.9+, with a few ramp and ledge systems. Much of the rock is loose, and it was noticeably cleaner on the upper portion of the Soviet Route. We made our ascent in 30 hours, including one bivouac: the Oregonian Route (2,200', V 5.9+).

A 32-mile one-way approach (including 10 miles of biking) due to ferry and road closures, a terrifying electrical storm, and wet climbing added interesting aspects to our experience. Overall, we feel we made the very most of our five-day trip. 📷

SETH KEENA

Goat's Beard, second ascent and first free ascent. On January 12, 2013, Vern Nelson Jr. and I made the second known ascent and first known free ascent of Goat's Beard (IV WI5), an approximately 350m ice climb up the center of the Goat Wall in Mazama. The route was pioneered in 1991 by Tom Kimbrell and Jack Lewis, and originally graded V WI5+ 5.9 A2.

After two weeks of waiting and close monitoring, we found the climb in chance-of-a-lifetime conditions. The route consisted of six pitches up the longest and best quality ice we have ever encountered in Washington; this thought was seconded by John Frieh and Wayne Wallace, who repeated the climb the following day. There was significant and unavoidable objective hazard caused by falling ice. Later parties described this hazard as "multiple assassination attempts."

We rappelled the route, though later climbers may have found safer descents via neighboring, bolted rock routes, avoiding the objective dangers. At least three parties, including ours, experienced severely stuck ropes high on the route while descending. 📷

CRAIG GYSELINCK

[This page] A 32-mile one-way approach leads to Southwest Bonanza Peak: Oregonian Route (left) and Soviet Route (right). *Steph Abegg*

CALIFORNIA

YOSEMITE NATIONAL PARK

Liberty Cap, southwest face, Mahtah. On May 31, Lucho Rivera and I began climbing the southwest face of Liberty Cap, ground-up, and succeeded in making the first free ascent of the formation. Our new route Mahtah (1,100', 16 pitches, 5.12+/5.13-), named for the Ahwahneechee word for Liberty Cap, is a long linkup that travels between three existing aid lines, as well as a bit of new ground.

We started climbing on the first two pitches of the Original Southwest Face (Faint-Harding-Rowell, *AAJ 1970*), then traversed right via a short bit of new ground to reach Bad Moon Rising (Allee-Boque-Mucci, *AAJ 2013*). (Mucci's report on Bad Moon Rising had been our inspiration for checking out the free-climbing potential on this face.) We then followed Bad Moon Rising for four difficult and sustained pitches up a corner comprised of immaculate stone. From there, we moved over to a wild and heinously pumpy roof pitch on the Direct Southwest Face (Braun-Cashner, *AAJ 1983*). We then left that route, climbing dead left for 50' to reach the 130-foot, horizontal "Crack of God" pitch on Bad Moon Rising. The Crack of God brought us back to the Original Southwest Face route, which we mostly followed, save for a couple small variations, to the top.

This is by far the best first ascent I have ever done, and I think it ranks as one of the best free routes in Yosemite Valley—a harder hardman's Astroman! Every pitch is spectacular, sustained, and improbable. There are five 5.12 pitches in a row once reaching Bad Moon Rising, and they are all very physical, with the final three in the upper end of 5.12. From there, you traverse the Crack of God—picture campusing sideways for nearly a rope length, with Nevada Falls booming below. After that pitch, the hard climbing is done but it's not *over*.

As for the grade of the climb, we are going to leave it open-ended and let repeaters give it a definitive grade—let's say it's somewhere between 1980s 5.12b and modern 5.13a. The real difficulty isn't in any particular pitch but in climbing it all back-to-back without your forearms exploding.

CEDAR WRIGHT

Liberty Cap, southwest face, Scarface, first free ascent. While perusing the 2013 *AAJ* I stumbled upon a line from Josh Mucci about the first ascent of Bad Moon Rising, "We have…had free climbing in mind while new-routing on Liberty Cap, as the lines are damn near built for classic free climbing." I reached out to Josh for direction before I settled on the route Scarface [*AAJ 2011*], and thus began the series of guessing games: *Would it all go?*

I fixed ropes, trundled loose rock, cleaned dirt, and worked on the pitches with various partners between February and March. Each contributed to the route, helping figure out sequences and push the route a pitch or two higher. Eventually, I redpointed six of the first seven pitches.

When I returned in April there was still prep work to do. I spent consecutive weekends drilling a few more bolts and working out the beta for the upper pitches. The southwest face of Liberty Cap is an oven, and the sun was starting to be a problem. James Ritt and I hiked up early in the morning on the last weekend of April and swung leads up the route. Despite my previous successes, I was unable to send either of the crux pitches. James saved the day when he followed the eighth pitch clean and proved Scarface would go free.

My fitness peaked again the first weekend in October, but the government had other plans, locking me out of Yosemite. On the last weekend of October I headed up for another round on

Scarface. My friend Ben Steel was keen to help finish my dream. We split the difficulties with Ben leading the first crux (pitch 5, 5.12), and I the second (pitch 8, 5.12). We both fell off on our first attempts but redpointed them second-try, allowing us to top out on my yearlong project. [*The free version of Scarface mostly follows the original aid line; however, significant variations to the original route were used on pitches 1–2 and 9–11.*]

LUKE STEFURAK

Schultz's Ridge, Psycho Bitch, first free ascent. I rolled into Yosemite Valley in customary fashion—no plan and no partner. I soon repeated a few neoclassic routes, including Border Country (Collins-Drummond-Schaefer, *AAJ 2010*) and the Final Frontier (Berry-Lucas, *AAJ 2014*), but then became restless. I needed a project. A Mikey Schaefer route on the far left (east) side of Schultz's Ridge, below El Capitan, came to mind: Mikey had added a new free pitch above an old Dale Bard route called Aint That a Bitch (5.12b), which he called the Dividing Line (5.13b), and he believed the line could continue to the top of the cliff via the old aid route Psycho Bitch (A3+, Kevin Andrews, solo). This lies a few crack systems left of the well-known route Moratorium.

I first hiked up to the base of the climb and then spent seven days aiding and French-freeing the climb, solo, leaving the pitches fixed as I went. After aiding each pitch, I would rappel down and Mini Traxion the pitches. As I climbed higher on the route, the climbing became steeper. The penultimate pitch followed an unbelievable arching crack with wild, three-dimensional movement. The character of the rock varied as well: The first three pitches ascended classic Yosemite granite, while the second half comprised much darker and highly featured diorite. There was no more than five combined feet of choss on the whole route.

After another week alone on my fixed ropes, working out the moves, I felt ready to give the route a proper try. Spring, unfortunately, was dead and gone, and the forecasted temps for the next week were 95°F and higher. I decided to wait it out. Two weeks later, the highs had reached 100°F. I was tired of waiting, so I called my buddy Cruise, and he agreed to give me a belay.

We hiked to the base on the afternoon of July 24. Before starting up, we drenched ourselves in water—a technique acquired from the legendary Surfer Bob. I slipped and fell on the first pitch,

[This page] Schultz's Ridge, showing the now-free line of Psycho Bitch. *Mason Earle*

the easiest one on the route. Annoyed, I pulled the rope and climbed it clean. I managed to climb the crux second pitch (The Dividing Line) first try. Relieved, we continued upward. I didn't fall again, despite getting apocalyptically pumped a couple of times, and even tearing my right hamstring on the last hard move of the last pitch. We topped out just as darkness began to fall. I was elated. Hiking down the Zodiac talus in the dark, it was only now just cool enough to put on a shirt.

This is my first real contribution to Yosemite climbing, and while I free-climbed the route in an odd style—ground-up, headpoint—it was the best style in which I could achieve a free ascent. The six-pitch free version of Psycho Bitch is sustained at 5.12: It goes at 12b, 13b, 12b, 12c, 12d, 12d. In October, Alex Honnold and Will Stanhope made the route's second ascent. 🔲

MASON EARLE

Fifi Buttress, Final Frontier, first free ascent. While climbing on Romulan Warbird (AAJ 2013) on Fifi Buttress with Lucho Rivera, I noticed another aid line on the wall: Final Frontier (V 5.7 C3, Black-Griffith-McDevitt-McDevit, 1999), which follows a series of steep, thin cracks. A local aid climber had fixed ropes through the steepest part of the 900' buttress, and I jumared the route to inspect it for the possibility of free climbing. "It's going to be hard," I thought.

Final Frontier appeared attainable with a psyched, strong partner: Nik Berry. So, in early Spring, Nik and I jumared up, brushed the thin cracks, and swung around on the steep face to find the crimps that would link larger features. Though the aid route had seen only a handful of aid ascents, fixed gear still covered the rock. I decided to buff the route, yarding out the heads, pins, and fixed mank. I replaced the bad gear with bolts: Dan McDevitt wanted the route to see traffic and approved of the bolts, and I wanted other climbers to try the line. On route, the rock was immaculate, the climbing was steep and sustained, and the hike from the Bridalveil parking lot consumed a mere 24 minutes. Half of climbing on El Capitan is time-consuming, blue-collar work: hauling bags, jumaring, and toiling on the wall; Fifi Buttress offered a quiet location and more climbing than working.

Soon after inspecting the climb, Nik attempted a redpoint but fell off the 5.13b crux, the California Girls Corner. I attempted the pitch but ripped off a chunk of rock and gouged my arm. We headed down and rested. A few days later, in late April, Nik redpointed up to the corner and fell again. This time, he pulled the rope and then sent the pitch next try. He fired the subsequent difficult pitch, another hard arching crack, then led to the summit. I had followed Nik on the route but fell on the harder pitches.

After Nik left the Valley, I returned to the route. I had figured out the difficult first corner, managed to piece together a 5.13 traverse, but had difficulty with a high-step move on an upper 5.12 corner and the boulder problem on the California Girls Corner. In May, a month after Nik's ascent, I attempted to redpoint the route again: I fell dynoing to a hold on the California Girls Corner. I came down. I rested. I hiked in Tuolumne. I slept at 10,000'. I wanted to hit that hold, and I hoped sleeping at a higher altitude would help.

Katie Lambert joined me for my second redpoint attempt. I felt strong and dispatched the initial 5.12+ corner, then the 5.13 face traverse, but I fell on the California Girls Corner yet again. "You just have to let yourself do it," Katie said. My second try, the corner felt easier. I hit the end of the crux and climbed to the anchor. The next hard pitch went smoothly, and I fired the rest of the route. Katie climbed without falling, flashing the route on top-rope. Final Frontier has now seen a number of attempts and been repeated four times. 🔲 🔍 📄

JAMES LUCAS

[This page, left] Cadence Reed following the crux 5.10 overhang on Four Gables. *Dave Nettle*
[This page, right] The east face of Four Gables, showing the Nettle-Reed Direct. The route may share terrain down low with the Rowell-Neale route (not shown). *Dave Nettle*

SIERRA NEVADA

Four Gables, east face, Nettle-Reed Direct. Just a few miles west of the world-famous Buttermilk Boulders, the Horton Lake trail leads into a valley of spectacular scenery and mining history, and to the dramatic east face of Four Gables (12,720'). On August 15, 2012, Cadence Reed and I ascended a direct line up the main east face of the peak that is probably a mostly new route: the Nettle-Reed Direct (10 pitches, 5.10+).

The route begins in a right-trending crack system in the center of the face, aiming for the massive left-facing dihedral leading to the summit. After two pitches of clean corners and flakes (5.7), two rope-lengths of easy terrain lead to a steep headwall. At this point it's likely the Rowell-Neale route (*AAJ 1973*) angles right, following cracks and chimneys (5.8) around the right side of the massive summit buttress. Our direct line continues up and left on steep flakes and cracks (5.10-) to the base of a huge, left-facing corner system. This corner contains two pitches of sustained climbing (5.10) through a tiered roof and delicate stemming around some blocks. After that, you tunnel through a wild chimney (5.5) then exit to a final pitch with a clean offwidth slot (5.7).

A furious wind-driven hailstorm greeted us at the top of the chimney, where we were able to hunker down under a chockstone until it let up just long enough to dash for the top. We topped out as the storm rolled back in full force, adding a very alpine feel to the adventure. After a long, roundabout descent in soggy clothes we arrived at our camp at upper Horton Lake. 📷 🔍

DAVE NETTLE

Pine Creek Canyon, Brownstone Mine, summary. I first noticed the cliffs adjacent to the Brownstone Mine while hiking to Merriam Peak some years ago, thinking there might be good routes to do on the clean, featured granite. In the summer of 2009 my wife and I hiked over Italy Pass and down into Pine Creek Canyon, and on this trip I stopped to take a closer look: We spotted line after line of potentially excellent climbing.

So it began. The next summer Tai Devore and I started doing the one-hour hike up the steep two-mile trail and establishing routes. Our first explorations yielded five- and six-pitch trad routes, which made us familiar with the terrain. Over time we filled in the gaps with mostly mixed climbs, but also some sport routes. Today the tally stands at over 30 routes. Many of the routes are single-pitch climbs, but a number of them are multi-pitch—up to eight pitches long. The climbing is varied and interesting, and the fine-grained, gray and white granite is as good as any in Pine Creek. Much of the climbing is on featured faces reminiscent of Lover's Leap or the Needles of California. There also are splitter cracks in flint-hard golden granite among the many dikes and edges. The routes range from 5.8 to 5.12b, with most in the 5.10 to 5.11 range.

The cliff faces north-northwest and is at ca 10,000', making it an ideal midsummer destination. Clean water is available a short distance below and above the crag, along the well-maintained Pine Creek Pass Trail. In addition to Tai and myself, SP Parker, Darrel Hensel, Jeremy Freeman, Shayd Forest Otis, Hunter Sibbald, and Steve Bullock have contributed to route development. This area and many more will be covered in an upcoming guidebook, *Climber's Guide to Pine Creek*, by Tai Devore. 🖸

URMAS FRANOSCH

Bishop Pass to Piute Pass, Evolution Crest Traverse (previously unreported). During the summer of 2008, Kyle Sox and I completed a new traverse in the Evolution region of the Sierra Nevada: the Evolution Crest Traverse (VI 5.9). This consists of a complete traverse of the Sierra Crest from Bishop Pass to Piute Pass, a distance of approximately 16 miles.

Between Bishop Pass to the south (12,000') and Piute Pass to the north (11,400') is a continuously high ridge, unbroken by any major gap and uncrossed by any established trail. The traverse ascends 10 major peaks and a dozen additional summits, crosses five technical notches, and traverses over six of the high summit plateaus that give this section of the Sierra a unique character. The elevation hovers near 13,000' and includes peaks such as Mt. Goode, Mt. Gilbert, Mt. Thompson, Mt. Powell, Mt. Haeckel, Mt. Darwin, and Mt. Lamarck.

Traversing the Evolution Crest offers a surprising mix of challenges, including approximately five miles of class 2-3 ridge scrambling (much of it good, some of it excellent); four miles of class 3-4 ridge climbing (much of it excellent, some of it superb); three miles of class 4-5 notch and tower traversing (none of it easy, some of it dangerous); and, finally, four miles of simple hiking across broad summit plateaus. To the best of our knowledge, a complete traverse of this ridge had never been attempted, primarily, we surmise, due to its length.

We approached the traverse with something akin to an expeditionary mindset, as my experience on a similar climb, the Palisade Traverse, had demonstrated how frequently storms could occur. We therefore came prepared to remain on the crest twice as long as we estimated it would require. Even with excellent weather, it took us eight days to complete the climb (June 24–July 1, 2008). We first portaged and cached food, fuel, and other supplies above several different drainages so we could sustain a single, uninterrupted push. After we started climbing, our plan was simple:

Reach the next cache before our supplies ran out. The route we followed strayed no more than a rope length from the crest throughout the traverse. For the nearly 200 hours we spent on that magnificent granite spine, the Sierra Crest was our home, workplace, and playground.

[*Editor's note: This traverse of the Evolution Crest is not to be confused with Peter Croft's historic eight-mile traverse of the peaks around the Evolution Basin, known as the Evolution Traverse (VI 5.9). Croft's Evolution Basin Traverse and the Evolution Crest Traverse share only 2.5 miles of terrain: the section between Mt. Wallace and Mt. Darwin, which is the only stretch of Croft's traverse that is actually on the Sierra Crest.*]

SCOTT MCCOOK

Mt. Whitney, southwest face, Found. After talking with Doug Robinson and getting his account of the first ascent of the southwest face of Mt. Whitney via Lost (*AAJ 2007*), Urmas Franosch and I decided to take a look. Being a local guide has its advantages, and we sent our equipment in with a pack-supported trip in early September 2012. This allowed us to hike in over the Whitney-Russell Col with just daypacks, meeting our gear at Guitar Lake.

The southwest face is a complex array of arêtes and ridges that only get more confusing from below. Doug had already got the best line, so we climbed the next best one to the east. We soloed the majority of the route, finishing on the summit plateau, and called our route Found (1,200', 5.9).

The following day we headed to the Arctic Lake Wall and climbed a prominent 5.10 arête on the main wall, left of where we believe the Rowell and Nettle routes to be. We then sent the majority of our gear out with another pack-supported trip. On the hike back over the Whitney-Russell Col, we added a direct start to Left Arête (Cleary-Fuller, 1984) on the southeast face of Mt. Russell, via a perfect straight-in crack (5.10b), ending a classic four-day Sierra excursion.

SP PARKER

[This page] The Arctic Lake Wall on Peak 3,940m. There are at least five routes on this southeast-facing cliff, but their exact position is not known. The supply of cracks and corners for new-routing appears practically endless. *SP Parker*

[This page, top] The southwest side of Mt. Whitney showing the general locations of Lost (left) and Found (right). There are no other known routes on this side of Whitney. *SP Parker*

Whitney Portal slabs to Wrinkled Lady, Ummagumma. One step from the sliding-glass door of the Whitney Portal Store kitchen shows it all: the looming pyramid of the south-facing Wrinkled Lady, slashed with dihedrals, rising to 10,900'; below it, a system of slabs, terraces, dikes, and tunnels that make up its foundation.

Over three years, from 2010 until 2013, I carried rocks while climbing this feature to stack cairns in strange places for future followers. I down-soloed, taking wrong turns, battling foliage, and building monastery-like steps. Friends would join in the effort of perfecting this adventure big wall with me. We would get lost together in the unknown.

Once I had done the first ascent, solo, I often found myself racing the clock to be at work by noon (usually late), pushing up the final 500' dihedral, then charging down the scree decent. I would show up sweaty and torn to the restaurant kitchen, just in time.

The 2,500' "Royal Arches of the Portal" begins by romping up a polished gully to the left of the Whitney Portal Buttress for 2,000', then joins the 500' south face of the Wrinkled Lady. Only one route had been done prior on the Wrinkled Lady, the central dihedral

[This page, bottom] The south-facing side of Whitney Portal, showing the new line Ummagumma, which starts just left of Whitney Portal Buttress and finishes up Wrinkled Lady, where the original Beckey-Brown line is shown in yellow. *Richard Piotrowski*

(Beckey-Brown, *AAJ 1972*). Of that route, Fred Becky said, "Rough un-glaciated rock surface and very deep cracks conspired to scrape hands and knees and to tear clothes in serious struggles with cracks." But don't worry, this new route takes on a corner to the left, following a system of easier, and *pleasant*, cracks. A chimney caps the 500' corner, allowing you to look down and catch all the exposure. From the top, a descent down the west ridge of the Wrinkled Lady leads to a fourth-class gully back to the valley.

The route is Ummagumma (2,500', III/IV, 5.7 A0 or 5.9). One definition provides that the word is, "A slang term for having sex. And of course Rock and Roll was originally slang for having sex." So, if you look at it that way, the word Ummagumma could simply mean "Rock and Roll!"

I can fire the route bottom to top in about two hours, if not faster; the descent takes about an hour. But I have everything dialed. For the average team, it could take much longer with all the route-finding [*see online report for all the details*]. Neil Woodruff has been working on a similar route just right of this one for a few years, but no other known routes exist in this area.

MYLES MOSER

Moonstone Buttress, Moonwalker. The Moonstone Buttress stands out like a shark fin, peeling away from the rest of the buttresses in Whitney Portal. It's speckled with dikes, black knobs, and sometimes is utterly blank. After a solid attempt on the wall early in the summer with Chris Orozco, I watched our little haulbag and portaledge dangle from the wall for nearly a month, awaiting our return, as thunderstorms pounded the area. We finished up the difficult six-pitch route in late summer, over two days, first reclimbing the initial pitches, then finishing the final three.

Out of all the lines that I have put up in Whitney Portal, this was by far the hardest to equip. From the massive whippers to ripping hooks, the airtime logged was astronomical. A thank-you to Chris for hanging in there and being willing to catch winger after winger. The six rope-stretching pitches went almost entirely free. It's still waiting for a ground-up free ascent, and a short section of A0 midway up will require an all-points-off dyno. The route is full value and a clean, direct line bottom to top. We called it Moonwalker (IV 5.12 A0), in reference to the wild climbing along a small handrail just above a massive crescent-shaped roof.

MYLES MOSER

Angel Wings, southwest face, Val Kilmer. "An alpine El Capitan," as Galen Rowell described it, Angel Wings is neither as tall nor as steep as El Capitan, but it is impressive in its own right. Angel Wings twists roguishly from the ground, like the horns of a wild beast guarding the cirque of Valhalla.

Jonathan Schaffer and I hoped to discover unclimbed lines on the southwest face, but after being shut down by numerous dead ends, we settled on starting up Valkyrie (V 5.12, Croft-Nettle-Thau, *AAJ 2013*), looking to split left low on that route toward the central pillar of the formation. Over the following weeks, we continued weaving our way up Angel Wings, returning each night to our camp. The healing waters of Hamilton Lake provided vital rejuvenation, allowing us to push our route higher each day.

Intricate routefinding on the wall and mangled toes from the arduous approach meant we had barely reached the midway point after two weeks, and our food stores were nearly exhausted. Racking up one final time, we knew this would be our last chance to do the route in a one-day push and hoped to make our way through the wide crack system splitting the upper headwall. Rather

[This page, top] "An alpine El Capitan," the massive south-southeast side of Angel Wings, showing approximate locations of: (1) Wings Over Sequoia (Beckey-Lahr-Neifeld-Martinson, 1977). (2) The Lorax (Bland-White, 1996). (3) Just a Rock in the Park (Felton-Joe-Leversee, 1996). (4) Val Kilmer (Gibson-Schaffer, 2013). (5) South face, right side (Long-Steck-Wilson-Wilson, 1967), which climbs terrain in the general vicinity of Valkyrie. (6) Valkyrie (Croft-Nettle-Thau, 2012). (7) The Devil Made Me Do It (Franosch-Mayfield, 2000). (8) Hell on Wings (not to summit, Grandfield-Joe-Leversee, 1989),.(9) South Arête (Jones-Rowell, 1971). (10) Right Wing (LaBounty-Thau, 2005). *Timothy Gibson* [This page, right] Jonathan Schaffer pinches an arête high on Val Kilmer, a mostly new, 15-pitch route on Angel Wings. *Timothy Gibson*

than slimming down our hefty rack, which included a hand drill, four bolts, six pins, and big cams, we opted to pare our food and water.

Our new route, Val Kilmer (V 5.11+) begins on the first four pitches of Valkyrie before cutting left to a left-facing corner, which leads to a candy-striped roof. A short traverse out this roof leads to a portion of deteriorating rock just before an offwidth/chimney. By this point in our trip we had the first seven pitches of our 15-pitch route dialed, so we were able to focus on the wild and wonderful climbing higher up.

To gain the flared chimney and offwidth

system on pitch 8, one must first bear-hug, knee-bar and head-scum up a massive tooth of granite hanging from a roof. Above, steep climbing up wide cracks is interspersed with kneebars and pinches, involving more chicken-wings than a KFC giveaway in Mobile, Alabama. The remaining pitches are very high quality, including a steep hand-to-finger splitter on pitch 13.

We found ourselves at the summit as the sky became indigo, dappled with sweet potato-colored clouds. The excitement of topping out was immense, but quickly overshadowed by thoughts of the convoluted descent. After some hours of wandering down gullies and across slabs, my balance deteriorated and I noticed the foul taste of hypoglycemia in my mouth. Within moments of suggesting we settle in for the night, Jonathan and I were cuddling in our Mylar bag, on the floor of a sandy cave. I tracked the coming of dawn by the full moon's progress across the sky, and was nearly lulled to sleep by mice chewing on our gear.

As the sun rose, we found the proper gully and we lumbered back to camp by midmorning. To our surprise, some kind hikers had left us a stash of tasty, organic snacks their mom made, so we spent the remainder of the day eating in our sleeping bags in a state of exhausted bliss. We rode this high all the way down the trail and back through the giant sequoia forest of the lowland. 🔲 📄

TIMOTHY GIBSON

Castle Rock Spire, east face. After two failed attempts, Tom Ruddy and I completed a new route on the east face of Castle Rock Spire in July. The route shares part of the first pitch with the Regular Route (Bettler-Long-Siri-Steck-Wilson, *AAJ 1951*) before it goes left and ascends an obvious crack system up the center of the east face for a total of five beautiful, steep pitches (5.9 C1) [*Other routes ascend the spire, including Spike Hairdoo, the West Face, and Cinco de Mayo. See AAJ 2003.*]

Our route could be free-climbed by strong crack climbers, but we aided through the crux sections to beat the sunset. John Salathé and Jim Wilson first attempted this line in 1949, before anyone had climbed Castle Rock Spire, but they turned back after a large block fell. We found a couple of Salathé-era pitons and some homemade hangers at their high point on our second pitch. The route can be rappelled with one 70m rope, removing the need to carry two ropes on the legendary (long) approach to Castle Rock Spire. 🔲 🔍

DANIEL JEFFCOACH

ARIZONA

Sedona, new routes. In Sedona, Zach Harrison and Jack Snyder climbed one new route and free-climbed another. In April 2013, they free climbed the aid route Justice of the Peace (550', A2, McDonald-Shaffer,) on Courthouse Butte. The route climbs the northwest aspect of the tower and contains six pitches of free climbing up to 5.11+. They added bolts to a variation on pitch 5, but otherwise followed the original line.

In March 2014, they established Southern Revival (560', 5.12-) on Oak Creek Spire, after five days of effort. The route climbs a prominent corner system on the south face of the tower. They found old hardware from a previous, unknown attempt on the first two pitches, but this likely marks the first complete ascent of the line and first free ascent. The duo replaced some of the old bolts and added some others but the line is primarily gear protected.

From reports on Mountainproject.com

[This page] The 800' freestanding Cathedral Tower, which was unclimbed until 2013. The west face is shown. *Mark Richey*

Cathedral Tower, west face. On March 20, Mark Wilford and I made the first ascent of a spectacular freestanding tower, which we named Cathedral Tower, as it is part of a large formation known as Cathedral Rock. This formation is located in Cave Creek Canyon in the Chiricahua Mountains of southeast Arizona, just a few miles south of the town of Portal. [*Editor's note: Cathedral Tower is located on USFS land and not located within Chiricahua National Monument, where climbing is currently banned. Future parties should be mindful of this access issue.*]

The climb starts just left of a large, overhanging alcove of gray rock on the west face of the tower and passes three very spaced-out bolts placed by a previous party. The bolts end at a two-bolt anchor with rap slings about 100' off the ground. Just before the anchors we traversed right and into a chimney/ramp system that led to a steep, clean face of reddish-colored rock and then the summit.

Although the welded rhyolite tuff can be friable and loose in places, the rock on our route was quite solid and featured, with short cracks and deep holes that would accept natural gear and was fun to climb—though it was a little run-out in places. After about six hours of climbing we reached the true summit and spent time exploring the top. We found no evidence of previous ascents. We descended our route (800', 7 pitches, 5.10) and also circumnavigated the entire base of the formation, concluding that our route is probably the easiest and first way to the top.

We are both quite amazed that a rock formation this big and prominent in the Lower 48 had not been climbed. The area has seen very limited activity but does hold significant potential, with many other freestanding towers and big faces within easy access of the park roads. It is also a popular birding destination. 📷

MARK RICHEY

IDAHO

BITTERROOT MOUNTAINS

Mystery Dome, southwest arête. I had been searching for this rock for roughly 20 years, having first heard of it from a wilderness outfitter, who said it was somewhere in the southern Bitterroot Wilderness and was one of the biggest walls in the range. My searching brought about many other great ascents in this remote area (*AAJ 1993, 1994, 2001, and 2003*). Over time, after many wild goose chases, I began referring to the unknown rock as Mystery Dome.

In 2010, I gazed at a telephoto image taken from the Bitterroots' El Capitan: 15 to 20 miles west I noticed a big dome. Paul Weese helped me match the photo to what I saw on a satellite map. The dome's southwest aspect appeared bigger than Fairview Dome in Tuolumne, suggesting

[This page] Mystery Dome is ca 20 miles from the road. The immense and unclimbed south face is shown, and the southwest arête climbs the left skyline. *Steve Porcella*

a worthy prize. It appeared to be near or part of Cuneo Point (8,285'), a massive mountain. But research suggested Mystery Dome was unnoticed, unnamed, and unclimbed.

In early June 2012, on a recon trip, I departed from Paradise, Idaho, which lies at the end of the Magruder Corridor Road. I failed to get more than 10 miles up White Cap Creek Trail due to rain and mud. Three weeks later, with drier trails, Devin Bartle, Paul Madeen, Craig Weese, Paul Weese, and I made it 14 miles up the trail in one day. Hiking four more miles the next day, I finally glimpsed the formation, and at the 20-mile mark we found a great base camp area below it in a grassy meadow. From the meadow, a 1,500' vertical approach brought us to the base. I took many photos to study later. Our friend Chinook Swindle volunteered to help haul in the heavy climbing gear with his horse and two mules.

On July 3, Jimmy Pinjuv, Phil Wesseler, and I, along with Chinook and his stock, gathered at Paradise to stage our climb. By July 6 all of our gear was at the meadow. Chinook would meet us again on July 9 to help us out. We carried 80-pound packs to the base up the steep, bush-choked gully. A spring below the wall was dry, but we found water in a gully to the east. We dug a bivy site and were quickly overwhelmed by clouds of mosquitos.

At 5 a.m. on July 7, the three of us began climbing up the southwest arête of the formation. The opening pitches were all 60m on good granite, consisting of friction climbing up to 5.9+, often run-out, with seams for tied-off pitons or micro-cams. We found decent belays. Moderate terrain continued until pitch six, where the rock became suddenly blank. We found a way up a shallow corner and thin seam; up higher, a roof led to a corner with a good crack in the back (A3). This tough pitch consumed two hours. The seventh pitch offered more of the same: seams in leaning corners, bolt and pecker required. At 9:45 p.m. we reached the start of pitch eight, which looked blank for at least 70' with a roof above. We were down to one quart of water between us and knew it would be a scorcher the next day. We had only our clothing for bivy gear.

I have done many cruxy night leads over my 40-year climbing career, and I don't starve for those sections like I used to. I suggested Phil take the lead while I coached him on how to rivet. The tap, tap, tap of the hammer was endless and rhythmic. Occasionally he would hit a discontinuous seam and give the hammer a rest. Higher up he was forced to place a couple of quarter-inch bolts, which allowed him to nap in his aiders. By 3 a.m., Jimmy and I had begun shivering. I used the movement of the constellations to track time and progress. Gradually, a faint hint of light appeared on the horizon. By the end, Phil had placed eight rivets and two quarter-inch bolts on his unrelenting, all-night lead (A3).

The climbing on the next pitch was easier (5.8). Then a falling block on pitch 10 core-shot our lead rope. We tied a knot and continued. Pitch 11 offered more thin seams and a traverse leading to an alcove with no apparent way out. A marginal belay off half-driven pins and a quarter-inch bolt, along with incoming lightning, caused me to dub it the "Alcove of Despair." Above the alcove, another hard lead up a seam gained a ledge with another marginal two-pin anchor. The rock above relented, and the summit seemed close. Free-climbable terrain (5.10) through shallow corners, with the best cracks that we had seen on route, led us to a notch on the skyline. There was no sign of prior ascent, and we left a register in a water bottle. We descended an alder-choked gully that felt like a highway to us, and after 2,000' reached our bivy and some water. Totally dehydrated, with full-body cramps, we continued down to the White Cap Creek Trail and passed out. At 6 a.m. the following morning we grabbed our 80-pound packs and met Chinook farther down trail, finishing the hike out the following day.

Our ascent of the Mystery Dome via the southwest arête (13 pitches, V 5.10 A3) required 34 hours of continuous climbing and is one of the finest first ascents I have done. Only two pitches were shorter than 180'. We placed a total of eight rivets and four quarter-inch bolts. I won't lie—it was a suffer-fest.

The steep west face and unclimbed terrain on the south face of Mystery Dome await hardy, adventurous souls looking for a big wall in a truly remote, challenging wilderness. In honor of Chinook, we named a small, black satellite spire on the southeast shoulder Chinook Spire. I still wonder if this was the rock the outfitter told me about 20 years ago. I think it healthy to suggest not, and continue to wonder: *What if?* 📷 🔍

STEVE PORCELLA

LOST RIVER RANGE

Mt. Borah, east face, various routes; Sacajawea Peak, north face. Until 2011 very little development had occurred on the steeper rock faces in central Idaho's Lost River Range. But now that the door has been opened, several very fine routes have been established. These are big limestone and dolomite walls, 1,500' to 3,000' tall, where the anchors are few, rockfall is an ever-present danger,

[This page] The 13-pitch southwest arête route on Mystery Dome, splitting the west and south faces. This is the first known route on this big wilderness wall. *Steve Porcella*

[This page, top] A foreshortened view of the east face of Mt. Borah: (1) East Face Direct (Collins-Hansen, 2011). (2) Dirty Traverse (Collins, 2011). (3) East face/north ridge (Boyles-Florence, 2012). *Bob Boyles* [This page, bottom] The north face of Sacajawea Peak, showing the new 13-pitch route climbed by Wes Collins and Kevin Hansen on the left and Broken Wings (Dickerson-Mordicai-Lords, 2006) on the right. *Bob Boyles*

and in some places the rock is just crap. No bolts or fixed anchors have been placed on these routes, and all were climbed ground-up and onsight.

Idaho has nine summits that reach over 12,000' and all but two lie within the Lost River Range. The tallest is Borah Peak (12,647') which holds classic snow and ice climbing. Borah offers several hidden gems on its north face, including the recent and difficult route Psycho Therapy (Lords-Wood, *AAJ 2004*). In spite of all the traffic, the remote east face of Borah remained unclimbed until the summer of 2011.

I first visited the eastern side of the mountain from the Pahsimeroi Valley in 1972 and spotted a line that followed some water streaks in a nearly straight path to the summit. I described this face as "Idaho's Eiger" to potential partners, but at the time the range had no technical rock routes, and the state has so much fine granite it was hard to justify a trip to the Lost Rivers. In the fall of 1975, Mike Weber and I approached the face from the west fork of the Pahsimeroi River. On that trip, a brutal rockfall almost killed us below the face, and then rain caused flash flooding. In the following decades, my climbing partners and I continued to explore and put up routes in the range, but we never made it back to Borah's east face. I grew to think of it as a very dangerous place, and the risk no longer appealed to me.

In the spring of 2011, however, Wes

Collins, a local climber and native of the area, immediately became interested when I told him about it. Wes couldn't wait to see the face up close, so he took off on an exploratory trip with his wife and dog in July 2011. What started as a recon turned into a solo first ascent of the east face, via the Dirty Traverse (III 5.4). This somewhat contrived route climbs a few steeper sections and makes use of ledge systems to gain the summit of Borah. Wes returned with Kevin Hansen in September of the same year and climbed the East Face Direct (1,800', III 5.9). In July 2012, I finally made my way back to the face, and with Frank Florence climbed another route, which starts up the east face to the right of the Dirty Traverse, and then gains the north ridge (III 5.6 WI2).

On the same day, following our climb, Wes Collins and Kevin Hansen also climbed the north face of Sacajawea Peak by a new 13-pitch route (III 5.8). [*Editor's note: The Collins-Hansen route on the north face of Sacajawea Peak climbs left of the ice/mixed route Broken Wings (not to summit, Dickerson-Mordicai-Lords,* AAJ 2006*), taking a direct line to the summit.*] ◙

BOB BOYLES

UTAH

Bridger Jack Butte, Sucker Punch. In October 2012, Mary Harlan and I began work on some new routes on the northwest corner of the Bridger Jack butte in Indian Creek, just outside of Canyonlands. The routes are just around the buttress as you hike toward the climb Rimshot. I returned in spring of 2013 with Jack Jefferies to finish one of these routes to the summit, and then it took one more trip with Lizzy Scully to get the free ascent. I called it Sucker Punch (5 pitches, 5.12). The route's highlights are an overhanging, zigzagging splitter crack on pitch two and an overhanging and leaning four-inch crack on pitch three, which begins with a dramatic roof. I'm working on an additional route to the right that will likely check in at 5.11/5.11+. 🔍

JASON NELSON

FISHER TOWERS

Titan, east face, Jade Gate (not to summit); Cottontail Tower, east face, Free Gaza. In winter 2014, Jim Beyer soloed two new routes in the Fisher Towers. He reported that he did not place any heads on the climbs, a technique for which he has been criticized on some of his other Fisher Towers routes (*AAJ 2013*).

In January, Beyer climbed a new line on the east face of the Titan, which he called Jade Gate (VI A4). The five-pitch route lies approximately 200' right of World's End, climbing to the Finger of Fate. Beyer did not summit because of ice above the Finger. He reported over 120 beak placements on the route, with up to 29 placements in a row. He drilled two short ladders with buttonhead bolts on pitches three and four, and placed standard bolts at the belays.

In February, Beyer climbed a line on the east face of Cottontail Tower, which he called Free Gaza (VI A4+ R). The six-pitch route lies 100' right of his earlier first ascent Intifada [*originally graded A6 but subsequently down-graded to A4/A5*] and climbs to the summit. He took about 50 beaks on the route and reported 44 placements in a row on pitch three. A number of buttonhead bolts were placed on lead in addition to bolted belays.

Information from Mountainproject.com

Kingfisher, Return of Mudzilla. Over three trips in March and April 2013, Jeremy Aslaksen and I established a new route on the north face of the Kingfisher, between the climbs Dead Again and Hazing. We had spied the line on a rest day the prior year when we established Beak to the Future on the Oracle (*AAJ 2013*).

At the end of March I made a solo recon trip and carried a bunch of gear and water to the base of the Kingfisher. We then made two more trips to fix pitches on the climb before tagging the summit on a picture-perfect day, April 21. The climb marked our sixth new route in the Fishers in just over three years.

The Return of Mudzilla (V A3) follows thin features connected by a short rivet ladder to a money crack system that shoots uninterrupted toward the capstone. A short traverse and small roof lead over the capstone to typical wide climbing, which ends just right of the start of the last pitch on the normal route (Colorado Northeast Ridge). A short but loose independent pitch reaches the top. As with all of our routes, be prepared with 45 to 50 Peckers and Spectres.

PAUL GAGNER

MONTANA

ABSAROKA-BEARTOOTH WILDERNESS

Pisce Wall, The Great Bear. In August, Patrick Kingsbury, Patrick Odenbeck, and I set off into the Absaroka-Beartooth Wilderness, returning to a wall I first saw in 2009. This remote wall is located above Lake Pisce, in a high cirque north of the Two Sisters and slightly detached from Two Sisters West. It is approximately 1,100' tall and was previously unclimbed, with the only known attempts failing to even reach the wall.

Starting on August 15, we made the approximately 20-mile approach via Lake Plateau, dropping into the top of Flood Creek. The trail down this drainage is unmaintained, and there is no trail to the wall. The hiking is steep and overgrown, with numerous areas of deadfall and sections of talus to negotiate. The alternate approach from Stillwater River, heading in at Cathedral Point and

[This page] Jeremy Aslaksen is just visible, midway up the Return of Mudzilla on Kingfisher in the Fisher Towers. *Paul Gagner*

[This page] The very remote Pisce Wall, showing the 11-pitch route called The Great Bear, the only known route on the formation. *Tom Kingsbury*

lower Flood Creek is considered even worse and is not advised. We set up our camp between Needle Lake and Comet Lake, about 40 minutes below the wall.

On August 18 we established the Great Bear (IV 5.11c R) in a 13-hour, tent-to-tent push. We led every pitch onsight and placed no fixed gear. The route comprises 11 pitches and follows an obvious corner system on the tallest portion of the formation. The climbing was varied and very clean overall, with only a few loose sections. There were many highlights, including pitch three, which we dubbed the Bear Flare, a strenuous, bottoming crack and the physical crux of the route (5.11c). Pitch five was the mental crux, featuring a 35' run-out traverse to the belay (5.10 R). We dubbed pitch 10 the Golden Pitch, as it features an immaculate 5.8 splitter that leaves the corner system and climbs the headwall directly, making for a spectacular position high on the route.

We walked off the backside. Although this looked improbable at points, a slow, thoughtful pace through the steep talus brought us down to Avalanche Lake, and eventually back to our tents. Though our time-window only allowed for the one ascent, there are plenty of worthy objectives for future parties in this hard-to-reach cirque. 📷

TOM KINGSBURY

East Rosebud Canyon, Lower Doublet, Line of Constant Sorrow. There are many impressive walls in East Rosebud Canyon, but few are as proud and spectacular looking as the Doublets. The Upper Doublet is a monster at approximately 2,000', perched high on the west side of the canyon; the Lower Doublet, at 1,500', rises just to the left and is just as impressive.

The Doublets host a few imposing lines, both free and aid, but the history is vague and somewhat hidden, like most Beartooths climbing. The Lower Doublet has seen a lot of attempts but very few successes. While shorter than the Upper Doublet, it's steeper and slightly cleaner, but with seemingly few options for routes. Large parts of the southwest side—the side you see from Snow Creek Trail—have rather poor rock. The west face has better rock but is steeper and more compact.

[This page] From left to right: (A) Ice Box Tower. (B) Lower Doublet. (C) Upper Doublet. (1) The line climbed by Jack Tackle and Doug Randal in 1979 (1,200', IV 5.10). Tackle and Gary Skaar did the second ascent of the same line in 1982. Another line exists right of their route: Fear Factor Five (V 5.9 A2), climbed by Lou Wendt and Rick Anderson in 1975; it's likely the route did not reach the summit. (2) Line of Constant Sorrow (V 5.12 C1, Bechdel-Cavanaugh-Goodhart, 2013). (3) Southwest face (IV 5.10, Burson-Willis), which starts on the west face but finishes out of view on the southwest face. (4) The first ascent of the formation by Jack Tackle and Rick Hoven in 1981 (V 5.10+ A1). Tackle notes that the 12- to 14-pitch route went all free except for a few short sections of aid (perhaps 30' total). Additionally, it's rumored that Pat Callis and Meg Hall attempted a line just left of Constant Sorrow on the prominent arête, but it was never finished. It's also possible that Mike Abbey and Kevin Hutchson completed a route on the Lower Doublet, but the exact line is unknown. (5) The approximate location of the Northwest Buttress of Upper Doublet (13 pitches, 5.11, Abbey-Schock, 1999). (6) The first ascent of the wall by Hank Abroms, Pat Callis, Brian Leo, and Gray Thompson, in 1972, which they called Time Trip (VI 5.8 A4/5). In 1999, Meg Hall freed Time Trip at 5.11 by a slight variation; Callis, Mike Carey, and Rand Swanson joined her for the climb. Additionally, Frank Annighofer and Bill Davey completed a direct start to Time Trip, farther right, in 2010. (7) The second ascent of the wall by Jim Emmerson and Craig Zaspel in 1975, E-Z Route (20 pitches, VI 5.9 A3). The line was repeated by Tackle and Zaspel in 1980. *Ian Cavanaugh*

My first attempt at this wall, with Max Bechdel, left us at the top of pitch one, exhausted, humbled, and craving a second chance. After many nights poring over photos, we found a weakness in the center of the west face—a single crack system that ran practically straight up the center-left side.

After many attempts, often cut short by storms, Artley Goodhart joined Max Bechdel and I to see our project though. Max and I amassed six attempts spread out over three years, vying for a first ascent. With Artley, we finally succeeded on our seventh trip, reaching the top of the Lower Doublet on June 15 after a two-day push employing a portaledge, and thus put an end to the Line of Constant Sorrow (1,500', 12 pitches, V 5.12 C1). We freed all but the fifth pitch (proposed 5.12d). We rappelled the route, drilling bolted rappel anchors on our way down to encourage repeat ascents. 📷

IAN CAVANAUGH, *with additional information from Max Bechdel and route line assistance from Pat Callis, Jack Tackle, Frank Annighofer, and Ron Brunckhorst*

WYOMING

CLARKS FORK

Clarks Fork, Sunlight Creek, Battered by the Devil. In June, Kevin Volkening and I established a new route in the Sunlight Creek tributary to the Clarks Fork, a relatively remote climbing area just outside of Yellowstone in Wyoming.

Day one was spent scouting the area's massive potential in the rain. After identifying a promising-looking line from the north side of the canyon, we crossed to the south side and bushwhacked to the top of the buttress. As luck would have it, we found an improbable descent down the buttress' side that dropped us right at the base of our line (which lies approximately a mile-and-a-half east of Highway 296). The psych level was high on the 'shwack back to the car through pouring rain.

We spent the next two days establishing the five-pitch climb, with a mix of free and aid climbing. We named the route Battered by the Devil (5 pitches, 5.8 A2), which is a play on the Southern phrase "the devil's beating his wife," which means that it's raining yet blue-skied and sunny—describing a majority of the weather during our climb. With some cleaning and fixed gear, much of the route would likely go free. Our plans to go back for a free attempt were tragically derailed when Kevin passed away in a climbing accident in Clarks Fork over Labor Day weekend.

[This page] Max Bechdel leading high on the Line of Constant Sorrow, a new, nearly free route on Lower Doublet. *Ian Cavanaugh*

There are no other routes on this buttress (we asked the Bozeman crew who've put up most of the stuff in Clarks Fork), and the only other evidence of climbing we saw in this canyon was an anchor one pitch up on a completely different buttress.

IAN DORKO

TETONS

Rock Springs Buttress, Knockin' on the Sky. Of Jackson Hole's cragging opportunities, Rock Springs Buttress is by far the best overall. The climbing here would be of high caliber anywhere in the country. The approach can be long, taking around two hours if unable to ride the Jackson Hole Aerial Tram. Many routes have been climbed on the buttress since the 1970s. However, over the last few seasons, the Rock Springs Buttress has seen a tremendous amount of development; the vast majority of these new routes have managed to stay off the local climbing radar. This is unfortunate because many are well deserving of attention, and a handful are likely to be deemed classics.

In addition to three new routes established by Greg Collins and various partners (from 5.11c to 5.12b/c), Toby Stegman and I established Knockin' on the Sky (4 pitches, 5.12a) in October 2012, which offers a good combination of length and difficulty. The climbing is a mixture of well-protected sport climbing with intermittent sections of moderate cracks protected by gear. This line charges up feature-rich granite on the far right side of the east buttress, with overhanging flakes and two sections of wildly exposed arête-slapping fun. The crux second pitch is the prize.

WESLEY GOOCH

WIND RIVER RANGE

Fremont Peak (not to summit), west face, Marmot's Tooth; Cirque of the Sun, Thunder Child. In August, Eva Christ and Jake Tipton climbed a new route on the west aspect of Fremont Peak in Titcomb Basin, summiting a sub-spire they called the Marmot's Tooth. The spire lies just left (north) of the West Face Spire. They called the 12-pitch route Beginner's Mind (1,600', IV 5.11-) and rappelled the line of ascent from atop the spire.

In September, Jayci Ferrimani and Brady Nuemann climbed a new route, Thunder Child

[This page] Neighboring walls viewed from the approach to the route Battered by the Devil above Sunlight Creek, Wyoming. The walls shown are 600–800' tall. *Ian Dorko*

(700', III 5.11), in a small cirque south of the Monolith (on the east side of Big Sandy Mountain, southeast of the well-known Cirque of the Towers). The cirque lies off the North Fork Trail from Dickinson Park, out of Lander; a permit is required to cross an Indian reservation. They dubbed the area the "Cirque of the Sun" and the wall the "Resolute Buttress." The route ascends a prominent crack system on the west end of the wall for seven pitches.

Information from Mountainproject.com

China Wall, Left Handed Compliment. In August, Jared Spaulding and I put up a new route in the northern Wind River Range, near New Fork Park, on the 800-1,200' China Wall. We started on good rock on the leftmost part of the main wall, which required several points of aid through a steep section off the ground. We then followed cracks up and right for five pitches (5.9–5.10, with some points of aid) to a large ledge. From the ledge we moved right over a large chockstone to a 5.9 hand crack that joins the last pitch of China Wall Left (5.10). We followed the existing route's 5.8 finish to the top. We called our route Left Handed Compliment (III 5.10 C1). The rock was generally good, with some lichen and grassy cracks. The line likely would go free, with a first-pitch crux in the 5.11c/d range.

The potential for new routes on this wall is high and, being only five miles from the trailhead, it could become a modern Wind River crag with some cleaning and possibly some fixed gear. We simply followed the obvious path of weakness up an unclimbed section of the wall. 📷

MATT HARTMAN

Mt. Hooker, north face, new free linkup. David Allfrey, Mason Earle and I went to Mt. Hooker from August 8–24. After hiking in from Dickenson Park, we began scoping the cliff and found what we believed was the most continuously blank and steep part of the wall. Over the next few days we aided and free-climbed sections of the first 600'. Dave did most of the aiding, since it required A4 beaking and Dave is a boss aid climber. We brought 15 beaks in total, and Dave needed all of them on each pitch. Initially, we believed we were on a new line, but after finding many old bolts we used our phone-a-friend card: We were on Sendero Luminoso (VI 5.10 A4, Quinlan, 1980). Bummed, but with great free climbing, we were very happy to continue up the line.

We bolted a two-pitch variation to the aid line on the third and fourth pitches. Dave led the third pitch at 5.12d, and I led the fourth at 5.12c. This led to a beautiful 5.11c corner. After the corner, Dave aided a breathtaking seam, which we dubbed the A3 Beauty (5.14a). Mason and I spent many days rehearsing this steep, thin pitch, and only with a perfect weather window was I able to send. The pitch above the crux involved a 5.13a seam that Mason led with many equalized beaks and a few cam placements as protection. Above these two difficult pitches, we traversed right (5.12) into the flake system comprising the existing route Shady Lady (VI 5.11 A4, Bradshaw-Dockery, 1978). Getting somewhat lost, we took a very convoluted way to the top, but we continued all-free.

Later in our trip we aided the remaining seven upper pitches of Sendero Luminoso (possibly making the second ascent of the route). We hoped to free these pitches but ran of time and are hoping to return. [*Editor's note: In all, the team freed the first seven pitches of Sendero Luminoso before linking up with terrain near Shady Lady. This linkup is currently the hardest alpine free climb in Wyoming. In 1990, Paul Piana, Galen Rowell, Todd Skinner, and Tim Toula did the first free ascent of Mt. Hooker's north face, at 5.12a, via a long variation to Shady Lady/Original*

Route, which they called Jaded Lady.]

Steve Quinlan's solo first ascent of Sendero Luminoso is incredible: It is a perfect line and his vision was extraordinary. The rock would be great rock anywhere. In our experience, Hooker was not as cold as people say—and anyway for hard granite you want it to be shady and cold. The wall is in the shade pretty much all day, so it offers perfect temperatures for sending.

NIK BERRY

Mt. Hooker, Jaded Lady, first one-day, all-free ascent. Josh Wharton and I, along with photographer John Dickey, made a 10-day horse-packing trip to Mt. Hooker, starting from Big Sandy. We first attempted a new route on the east face of Hooker, a sub-wall on the left shoulder; however, we bailed at a seemingly unprotectable headwall, which would have required hard aid and bolts.

Shifting gears, on August 26 we started climbing at first light up Jaded Lady in "rope, rack, shirt on your back" style. [In 1990, Paul Piana, Galen Rowell, Todd Skinner, and Tim Toula did the first free ascent of Mt. Hooker's north face, at 5.12a, via a long variation to Shady Lady/Original Route, which they called Jaded Lady.] We topped out that afternoon in a misty rain, having met our goal to do the first one-day ascent with leader and follower freeing every pitch. Jaded Lady is one of the best alpine/big-wall free routes I have ever climbed, with marble-like rock and varied climbing.

It's worth noting that on the third pitch, a green 5.11 arête protected by bolts, all the bolts are old and rusty, and some are totally worthless. Thankfully, someone had added a new 3/8-inch bolt to the anchor. (There were some other bad bolts on the route, but nothing as bad as the third pitch.) We feel there are five or so pitches in the 5.10 to 5.12 range that warrant an R rating. We climbed the route in 13 pitches; the topo shows 16.

WHIT MAGRO

Trepidation Tower, Trepidation; Bottle, north face; Squaretop, northwest face. August found Oliver Deshler and I once again back in the Winds with dreams much bigger than our abilities. Hiking

[This page] An early start for Josh Wharton as he begins the first one-day free ascent of Jaded Lady on Mt. Hooker. John Dickey

[This page, left] The north face of the Bottle, showing the new eight-pitch route climbed by Mark Jenkins and Oliver Deshler. *Mark Jenkins* [This page, right] Trepidation Tower, showing the route Trepidation. *Mark Jenkins*

beneath lumpen packs, we came in from the north, forded the Green River twice, and then bashed our way through steep, trailless deadfall into the Marten Lake drainage. We established camp three-quarters of a mile northwest of Marten Lake, squeezed between the west face of Squaretop and a looming, unnamed rock tower due west.

The next morning, despite trepidation, we managed a new nine-pitch 5.9 up the prow of the unnamed tower. The rock was dubious and a second ascent unwarranted. We named the tower and the route Trepidation. The following day we put up a new eight-pitch 5.9 on the north face of the Bottle, following a clean cleavage directly up the left side of the wall. Early afternoon lightning storms almost blew us off the mountain. On the morning of our fourth day, we ascended a 10-pitch 5.10+ crack line up a prominent left-facing corner system on the northwest face of Squaretop. The hardest climbing consisted of several pitches of perfect eight-inch offwidth, inside of which we discovered a single ancient carabiner, proving once again Joe Kelsey's wry dictum that, "In the Winds it's common for climbers to find evidence of previous ascents on the first ascent."

Out of food, our stove broken, but our spirits soaring, we hiked out the next day. 📷

MARK JENKINS

Wolfshead, south face, Red Cloud. The south face of Wolfshead is the sunniest and cleanest wall in the Cirque of Towers. Armed with the experience of opening earlier routes on this wall, Brandon Gust and I packed a single rope, four steel and three nylon brushes, and the requisite load of hardware. A

September storm with hail and snow was forecast, but after a long summer we thought the cloud cover might just cool us down, and we launched anyway. The storm blew up as we hiked toward the Continental Divide from Big Sandy Opening. Tentless, we were forced to seek shelter in the spacious Boulder Room in North Creek. In his usual minimalist style, Brandon, with a pack full of gear, did not include a sleeping bag. He made the best of it at 0°C.

We finished the approach the next morning, hiking directly to the project. Reconnaissance photos showed a beautiful, red-colored, spear-tip-shaped corner linked by thin cracks in the middle of Wolfshead's steepest facet. This was our mission. We began by climbing a nice warm-up groove, then headed out right toward the spear. Here, we onsighted a clean, crackless, heady, and thin flake, the Broken Treaties (5.10 R). Next was the Red Spear, an overhanging tips corner. Lichen and hard climbing ended the onsight, and we spent the rest of the day scrubbing the corner for a redpoint. We sent the corner with difficulty the next morning (5.12-).

Above, lichen forced us to grab gear on a roof with a curious white spot, the Wasichu Roof, and then on a steep, red crack, Red Cloud (A1). Moderate free climbing led us to the east ridge. We descended the ascent line, drilling a bolt at each belay and exhausting the bristles on all of our brushes in hope of a future free burn on this incredible climb: Red Cloud (IV 5.12 A1).

GREG COLLINS

Haystack Mountain, Lowe Route, mostly free ascent. In mid-August, Justin Griffin and Kyle Dempster went into the Deep Lake area to explore Haystack Mountain and work on free climbing the upper part of an old Jeff Lowe aid line at the southern end of the wall. Steve Bechtel had previously tried to free the bottom of the climb. After a week of work, including placing a few bolts, they found a great line weaving in and out of the aid route, and were confident their line would go free.

In the beginning of September they invited me to come and try the route with them. We horse-packed into Deep Lake and spent a week climbing on the route and trying the crux pitches. On September 6 we tried the route from the ground up. The weather was perfect—almost too hot. We succeeded in climbing the 11-pitch route to the top, free climbing up to 5.13b, but were unable to free the fourth pitch, which currently stands at 5.13 A0. The climbing includes everything from steep roofs and offwidths to very delicate slab climbing. We tentatively called the route the Lowe Spark.

HAYDEN KENNEDY

[This page] Looking up at the Wasichu Roof on the route Red Cloud. *Greg Collins*

COLORADO

SAN JUAN MOUNTAINS

Camp Bird Road, new routes. Steve House and various partners established two new routes on Camp Bird Road during the 2013-2014 winter season. The first route, Goodnight Irene (900', IV M5/6 PG13), was climbed by House and Ian Yurdin in November. The five-pitch route was established ground-up and climbs the gully system just right of Snowblind Fiend/Walk the Line (Jeff Lowe, 1978) and left of Desperado and is easily identified by a large chockstone high on the first pitch.

In January 2014, House and Steven Van Sickle established another route, Rusty Cage (800', III M7 PG13), completing the line ground-up over five days, bolting on lead with both hand and power drill from free stances; they added additional protection and belay bolts on rappel and from fixed ropes to make the line safer. The route lies just left of the Ribbon and right of Desperado and climbs a steep orange-colored groove for five pitches [*the location of this new route was incorrectly identified as Walk the Line in previous guidebooks*]. A couple fixed pins help protect the route in addition to about 25 bolts; however, a full rack including short ice screws is mandatory.

Additionally, in mid-January, House and Josh Wharton climbed variations to two other routes in the area. First, they added a two-pitch direct start to the Demon, a route that lies just left of the Talisman, which they called Hairy Devil (M6-7). They then climbed a two-pitch alternate start and became the first to top out the previously unreported route True GRIT (Nance-Vilhauer, 2006), which lies a half-mile right of Sapphire Bullets of Pure Blue Ice, in Telluride.

Information provided by STEVE HOUSE

BLACK CANYON OF THE GUNNISON

Summary. In July, Bill Grasse, Ben Kiessel, and Matt Pickren established Black in Action (8 pitches, III 5.10+ R) on a prominent pillar below the Cross Fissures Overlook, which is located along the South Rim of the canyon. Six pitches gain the top of the pillar, which they called Echo Canyon Tower, and some rappelling/downclimbing plus a couple of additional pitches regain the rim proper. They climbed the route ground-up without bolts.

Topos and information on other new climbs that are currently unpublished can be found at the North Rim ranger station.

From information at Mountainproject.com

ROCKY MOUNTAINS

Mt. Evans massif, Black Wall, High Variance. During a warm weather window in early October, I completed the first ground-up free ascent of a new eight-pitch route on the Black Wall. Prior to the ascent, I had cleaned the route from the top down and worked the pitches with a Mini Traxion. High Variance (700', IV 5.12b) follows a bunch of cool features on the far right side of the wall, in an area that often seems to be dry. The style is varied, involving steep face climbing and knee bars, though it requires a significant amount of pure crack climbing. The gear on the route is good most of the way, with very few mandatory runouts, and the three 5.12 pitches are well protected. A total of three bolts were added for protection on the crux pitches, in addition to a couple of two-bolt belays. As is standard on the Black Wall, the rock is fairly scaly in parts, but most of this eventually comes off, leaving behind perfect granite. As this route sees more traffic, I think it could become a classic.

MATT WILDER, *from a report on Mountainproject.com*

Mt. Evans massif, Black Wall ice climbs. Most people who climb on the Black Wall in summer can't help but notice the seeps that prevent good rock climbing between the route Roofer Madness and the standard rappel route. The problem with climbing these seeps when they are frozen is that the road up Mt. Evans, which provides quick access to the Black Wall, is closed from October into late May.

One option, exercised by the late, great Mike Bearzi in 1988, was to make the long hike in from the Chicago Lakes. Unfortunately, the details of his explorations were not recorded. Another option is to try dashing in immediately after the road opens around Memorial Day. This approach was used by Chris Sheridan and Dave Wolf in June 2013 to climb the main, obvious gully feature,

but it is not conducive to climbing the smears that form on either side of the gully, most likely in the fall. In October 2013, I had the good fortune of being contacted by Taylor Brown, who had figured out that one could approach the top of the Black Wall from the Bierstadt Lake trailhead at the top of Guanella Pass. It took about two hours—much quicker than the Chicago Lakes approach.

After doing the committing rappels into the Black Wall, we climbed a line of iced-up grooves leading to an obvious smear on the right wall of the gully. We called this line Black and White (III WI4/5 M5/6). While on this route, we noticed two really enticing features on the left wall. The first was a series of thin smears heading up the steep wall immediately left of where the rappel line ends; the second, a series of hanging daggers and a steep crack on the left wall of the gully, starting about 200' above the bottom of the rappel line.

[This page] Scott Bennett leading while Doug Shepherd belays on the first ascent of Monochrome, adjacent to the Black Wall on the Mt. Evans massif. *Daniel Gambino*

Scott Bennett and Doug Shepherd climbed the first of these two routes, calling it Monochrome (III WI4 M5). I told Will Mayo about the second line and suggested he give it a go. Somehow, I'm the one who found myself hiking in with him. A short, easy pitch gained the feature. Belaying the next lead, I stood witness to an impressive display of strength and tenacity as Will onsighted the crux second pitch (WI6+ M9). Thankfully, the third pitch was a good bit easier at WI5+. We called the route Silhouette (3 pitches, WI6+ M9) and climbed the route entirely on gear. 📷

BENJAMIN COLLETT

Rocky Mountain National Park, summary. In August, Tommy Caldwell and Joe Mills redpointed the first 5.14 route on the Diamond on Longs Peak (14,259'), free-climbing the complete *Dunn-Westbay* (1972). After a number of days of work, Caldwell led the route free on August 21 in four rope-stretching pitches, and Mills followed all of the pitches free. The four pitches, all above 13,000', were climbed ledge to ledge without hanging belays, and went at 5.10+, 5.14a (80m), 5.13a (70m), and 5.12b. The duo did not place any bolts. In 2011, Josh Wharton free-climbed the *Dunn-Westbay* at 5.13b but with substantial variations to the original route.

A number of notable mixed climbs were established during 2012-'13. In the winter of 2012, Josh Wharton climbed Two Dragons (400', III M7), on the northeast face of Dragontail Spire (ca 12,000'). The route begins on Dragon Slayer (III 5.11) and then takes a variation up and right for two pitches before joining the towers' south ridge. (Wharton did not climb to the summit.) In March 2013, Erik Rieger and Jonathan Merritt climbed a new route on the southeast face of Flattop Mountain (12,324'). Steep is Flat (500', III M5/6) ascends a previously climbed couloir and then tackles four steep pitches up a prominent corner and chimney system on the upper mountain. In April 2013, Wharton and Jesse Huey completed the Production (IV M7) on the south face of Otis Peak (12,486'), following the first part of Brain Freeze (IV M5+) before breaking up and left on a steep wall for three sustained pitches. Also in April, talented mixed climbers Aaron Montgomery and Ryan Vachon climbed a new route on the southwest face of Sharkstooth, tackling a large, tiered roof system. They called their route Circling Sharks (III M8+).

In October 2013, Kevin Cooper and Topher Donahue made what is believed to be the first ascent of an ephemeral and spectacular ice smear high on the east face of Longs Peak: Window Pain (WI5+/WI6). This single, long pitch is particularly significant given the difficult "approach"—for Cooper and Donahue, and repeat ascents, this required first hiking five miles, then climbing Field's Chimney (III WI5 M6), crossing Broadway, and, finally climbing a majority of the Window (IV WI4 M4), all before reaching the climb. Cooper and Donahue and subsequent parties rappelled from atop the smear.

From reports on Mountainproject.com and Climbing.com

The Stilleto, new routes; Seldom Seen Wall, new routes. When Jacob Neathawk and I climbed a new start to the southwest corner on the Petit Grepon in Rocky Mountain National Park in September 2012, I realized that there was plenty of untapped terrain farther up the Sky Pond basin. So, in June 2013, Josh Finkelstein and I wandered up the valley, intent on exploring the Seldom Seen Wall.

On our first trip we got a little distracted by a lovely tower to the west of Sharkstooth: the Stilleto. We climbed a steep line on the left side of the tower: Misericorde (III 5.11- R). We also saw a great-looking line on the right side of the tower and felt compelled to return the following weekend

[This page, left] Josh Finkelstein leading the third pitch of Shoe Fetish on the Stilleto. *Ben Chapman*
[This page, right] Erik Wellborn following the third pitch of Ol' #6 on the Corinthian Column, Pikes Peak. *Phil Wortmann*

to complete Shoe Fetish (III 5.11-). Both of these routes involve steep, featured climbing.

Finally, in July, Doug Haller and I made it to the Seldom Seen Wall and explored the steep buttress to the left of the Route That Kor Forgot (Grauch-Sheridan, 2010), thinking that the continuous, steep terrain might provide some good climbing. We climbed a prominent dihedral system high on the wall: Peekaboo Dihedral (III 5.10-). A few weeks later, Josh and I returned with the hope of climbing a steep dihedral to the left, but stormy and cold weather made us opt for the buttress to the right, and we climbed the Relusive Buttress (III 5.9 R). We later returned and climbed that steep diehdral left of the Peekaboo Dihedral. The resulting route, Outta Sight (III 5.10+), was as steep as we'd anticipated, with our tag line hanging free for the final three pitches. 🞑

BENJAMIN COLLETT

Pikes Peak, new mixed climbs. There are few places anywhere in the world where you can approach multi-pitch alpine ice and mixed climbs with just 20 minutes' walking. For better or worse, the Pikes Peak toll road delivers just that. Most of the classic rock and ice routes on the mountain were climbed by the legendary Colorado Springs hard men in the '70s and '80s. However, modern mixed climbing on the mountain has rejuvenated the game.

In October 2012, I climbed two new mixed routes and one new variation with Erik Wellborn. Early in the month, while approaching Total Abandon, Erik spotted a promising-looking pitch of ice on the right side of the Corinthian Column, left of Total Abandon. We fired the four-pitch line the next weekend, climbing to the top of the buttress, and called the route Toga Party (420', 5.8 WI3 M5). The following weekend we added a three-pitch variation to Blind Assumption, on the left side of the Corinthian Column, starting on that line and then tackling a steep roof and corner system. We called the variation Blind Luck (400', WI3 M7+).

At the top of the Corinthian Column, on the right side, is a horizontal roof that arcs out to the right for 30' or so. For years I've looked up at it with fear, but after a closer look we saw that a nice hand crack traversed the entire length of the roof, and we decided to give it a go. After climbing the first ice pitch of Toga Party, we found sustained and engaging dry tooling up corners (M5/6). Micro-edges beneath the roof were just big enough for front-points, forcing us to look straight down 400' while skating for footing. As I belayed Erik to the top of the last pitch, I felt we'd really done something important, finding big adventure close to home, which seems rare these days. We named it *Ol' #6* (450', 5.10+ WI3 M6+) from a great line in *Blazing Saddles*.

In the spring of 2013, on a wall below the Corinthian Column, Doug Shepherd and I found a new, thin ice line that we called Lost and Found (270', WI5 M6), due to the fact that we were actually trying to climb the route Wet and Wild. A perfect melt-freeze scenario created three great pitches of thin ice pasted into corners and cracks. We found many sections to be very committing, on questionable gear, but not scary enough to bail. Most of the ice was thin enough that the second was forced to do a lot of dry tooling.

That autumn, Matt McKinley and I explored a dark chimney in Pikes Peak's southeast cirque, finding an interesting and likely unclimbed route. The route started with a steep pitch of thin ice (WI5). We then followed icy crack systems (5.8 M6) to the top of the buttress for three more pitches. We called the climb Southern Circus (400', 5.8 WI5 M6).

PHIL WORTMANN

Big Rock Candy Mountain, new routes. During the summer and fall of 2013, Greg Miller and I ferreted out two new lines on Big Rock Candy Mountain in the South Platte. In June we established Nicaraguan Nut Butter (1,300', 11 pitches, 5.9); in September, the White Whale (900', 5.10c), on the northwest corner of the rock. Both routes were climbed ground up and onsight, in a day.

JASON HAAS

NEW MEXICO

Minerva's Temple, new routes; Organ Needle, new routes (previously unreported). The Organ Mountains are about 60 miles north of El Paso, Texas in southern New Mexico. Sugarloaf is perhaps the most prominent peak in the range, and it was from that summit that I became intrigued with the "The Great East Faces," as guidebook author Dr. Ingraham described the east face of the Organ Needle and its adjacent walls. I spent hours studying a prominent buttress in the background of my Organ Needle summit photos taken in the 1980s: Minerva's Temple. The formation became an obsession: From June 2000 to May 2007, I completed three new routes on the east face of Minerva's Temple and one on the east face of Organ Needle. The routes range from IV 5.10 to V 5.12b. [*See AAJ online for the full report.*]

JOHN HYMER

ALASKA

REVELATION MOUNTAINS

The Angel, east buttress. In July, Graham Zimmerman and I spent 10 days in the remote Revelation Mountains, at the far southwest end of the Alaska Range. This sub-range has seen a recent surge of activity in the spring season, and climbers have returned with stories of huge mixed lines and perfect white granite. We found almost no information on summertime rock climbing activity in the range, so we were excited to make a reconnaissance mission and see what these mountains could offer.

We flew in by helicopter due to lack of snow for a ski plane. This was Talkeetna Air Taxi's first helicopter insertion for a climbing trip. (Landing a helicopter in Denali National Park is illegal, but the Revelations are outside of the park.) The hour-and-a-half ride into the range gave us a visceral feel for the scale and isolation of this area. Once the drone of the chopper had faded, and Graham and I were left on the glacier with our gear, we were the rulers and sole inhabitants of our own mountain kingdom. We set up camp directly underneath the most enticing objective: the east buttress of the Angel (9,265').

We began climbing on July 13, starting up a beautiful granite wall with quality cracks and corners aplenty. We climbed for 600m, with difficulties up to 5.10, before finding a perfect bivy spot on the ridge, where we could take shelter from a passing squall. After a few hours of rest under the pale midnight sun we began climbing again, surrounded by blue skies. Another 500m of classic ridge terrain separated us from the summit, and we occasionally donned crampons to navigate snow and ice while simul-climbing. Higher up, we joined the southeast buttress route (Collins-Walter, 1985) and reached the summit midday.

We descended to the north and then rappelled 600m down the eastern aspect of the north ridge to a hanging glacier, down which we mostly walked to the main Revelation Glacier, reaching camp again on July 14. Following our climb, our options became extremely limited due to multiple core shots in our ropes and terrible weather, so we left the range on July 21.

[This page] Graham Zimmerman approaching the Terror Towers, named during the first ascent of the southeast buttress. It was less chossy than it appears, and they found easy passage. *Scott Bennett*

[Editor's note: The Angel was first climbed in May 1985 by Greg Collins and Tom Walter, who succeeded after four attempts by climbing the left flank of the east buttress and gaining the east ridge, which then led to the summit (AAJ 1988). There are unconfirmed tales that a second team climbed this same route, thinking they were making the Angel's first ascent. Rumors say they found a rappel sling high on the route and were more than a little displeased. Further details are lacking—such is the mystique of the Revelation Mountains. In April 2012, Clint Helander and Ben Trocki climbed the south ridge, which was famously attempted numerous times by David Roberts and teammates in 1967. For a more comprehensive look at the Revelations, see Helander's article "Recon: Revelations" in AAJ 2013.*]*

SCOTT BENNETT

Apocalypse, west face, A Cold Day in Hell. In early April, I spent ten frustrating days waiting in town, hoping to fly into the Revelation Mountains. Nothing was going our way. First the weather was bad and pilots were available; then the weather was good, but our pilots couldn't fly in. One partner had to drop out, and another ran out of time. In a last-ditch effort of desperation, I started calling friends of friends, looking for an available partner: Jason Stuckey answered the call and flew into the range.

After first retreating from another unclimbed mountain, Pyramid Peak, Jason and I set our sights on the Revelations' tallest unclimbed peak, Apocalypse (9,345'). Named by David Roberts in 1967, the peak had been tried several times in the early 1980s, but had thwarted every attempt. Apocalypse's 4,400' west face is one of the most continuously steep, Kichatna-like walls in all of the Revelations. Numerous walls comprise the expansive west aspect and tower over the narrow Revelation Glacier. In between the two largest walls is a narrow cut in the face. From the ground we could easily see huge amounts of ice choking the serpentine gully. [*Clint Helander's* AAJ 2013 *article "Recon: Revelations" briefly covers prior attempts on Apocalypse.*]

Jason and I spent two days and two nights climbing the wall, encountering over 2,000' of ice climbing up to AI5. The summit ridge felt wildly exposed and committing, and with only two pickets we were forced to use seated belays and simul-climb with no protection between us. On the summit, we could see all the way to Denali. We carefully downclimbed and rappelled the route, A Cold Day in Hell (4,400', AI5), leaving only a few pieces of gear and V-threads. When we hit the glacier, we realized we had been climbing in a massive inversion. Our base camp thermometer bottomed out at –25°F.

CLINT HELANDER

[This page] The Angel, showing the east buttress route climbed by Bennett and Zimmerman. The south ridge comprises the left skyline; the Collins-Walter line lies in between. *Scott Bennett*

[This page, left] Jess Roskelley leading the crux ice pitch of Hypa Zypa Couloir. *Kristoffer Szilas* [This page, right] East face of the Citadel, showing (1) Hypa Zypa Couloir and (2) Supa Dupa Couloir. The north ridge comprises the right skyline. *Kristoffer Szilas*

KICHATNA MOUNTAINS

Citadel, east face, Hypa Zypa Couloir. During April 5-7, Jess Roskelley, Kris Szilas, and I established a new line on the east face of the Citadel (8,250') above the Shadows Glacier. We encountered sparse protection, vertical rotten snow, quality ice, and mixed and aid climbing on poor rock.

We began by climbing fantastic, steep ice runnels up the major couloir system left of Supa Dupa Couloir (McAleese-Turner, AAJ 2004). After many pitches, we chopped a bivy ledge in the ice. After resting, more ice and mixed climbing brought us to an intersection with the south ridge, where we switched to full rock mode and used a mix of free and aid, climbing in double boots on poor-quality, run-out rock. We then continued up a moderate snow ridge, rappelled 60m off the west face, and continued up a 200m snow ramp to the summit.

Descending the line was not an option, and so we downclimbed and rappelled the involved north ridge, arriving in camp after a 70-hour round trip. We named the line the Hypa Zypa Couloir (1300m, VI 5.10R AI5+ M6+ A3) in humorous respect to the line next to it. 📷

BEN ERDMANN

CENTRAL ALASKA RANGE

Peak 13,100' (Reality Peak), east face, The Reality Face. Jared Vilhauer and I spent all day skiing up and down the West Fork of the Ruth Glacier and looking for an inspiring, safe line to give our all. Our original objective was sporting a new look—its summit snow slopes had cracked open to reveal a hanging serac that might, just might, sweep our route clean were it to cut loose. Surprised and a bit bummed, we kept scoping for something that wasn't so threatened. Jared's little black book led us up another fork of the glacier and under the 4,000' east face of what we would later nickname Reality

Peak. [*Reality Peak is a ca 13,100' satellite peak of Denali, located on its southeast spur, rising above the West Fork of the Ruth Glacier to the north of Mt. Huntington and northwest of Peak 11,300'.*] One "safe" line existed in an otherwise chaotic landscape of ice cliffs, snow mushrooms, and soaring granite walls. After a few pictures we glided back to camp to meet our friend Seth Timpano, who was due to fly in that evening.

We gathered in the rapidly chilling evening. "What do you guys want to climb?" said Seth. Jared explained what we had seen that day and put in his two cents. I fidgeted as we broke down the details. "I think the route on Reality Peak has a fair amount of danger, but no more than what we've already accepted by coming to climb big routes in the Alaska Range," Jared said. He was right. High fives sealed the pact before an icy, down-glacier breeze sent us crawling into the tents.

The next afternoon we donned crampons and stashed skis as shade crept over Reality Peak's east face. "I can get us started," Jared said, already clipping gear to the loops on his harness. The following 17 hours were filled with ecstasy and torment. Crisp snow, flowing ice runnels, and one-swing sticks were balanced with dehydration and exhaustion. A cramped and foggy bivy stalled us at ca 12,000' for nearly a full day. When the clouds parted we attacked the final 1,100' to the summit. Of course, the ridge climbing was steeper, longer, and scarier than expected. The exposure, although camouflaged with misty clouds, made the ridge feel like a monster swaying just below our boots.

Three days earlier I had been indecisive and fearful. At the top, peace filled me. I had made my choice and was living with the beautiful consequences. After downclimbing the ridge,

[This page] The southeast-east aspect of Denali, showing (A) Reality Peak and (1) The Reality Face. (B) Reality Ridge. (S) Thayer Basin. (C) Southeast spur. (D) Denali, main summit. (E) South buttress and (2) Isis Face. (F) Ridge of No Return. *Jared Vilhauer*

we brewed, ate, and then broke down our high camp and started 4,000' of rappels. A powerful sun caught us while rappelling. Snow mushrooms clung inexplicably to the granite walls above, and ice chunks tinkled down the grooves in the steep couloir we were descending. If something fell from above there was no place to hide.

Once past the 'schrund, I pulled the ropes and heel-plunged down one last slope. Within moments of clicking into our skis, Reality Peak fell far behind.

[*Editor's note: The Reality Face (5,300', AI5, Holsten-Timpano-Vilhauer, 2013) topped out on 13,100' "Reality Peak" on the southeast spur. Two earlier routes had reached this satellite summit and followed the southeast spur to Denali's south buttress, then continued up by the 1954 route: the Southeast Spur (Cochrane-Everett, 1962) and Reality Ridge (AK Grade 4+, 5.5 A2, Florschutz-Metcalf-Stoller-Thuermer, 1975). The 2013 team descended their route from the satellite summit.*]

JENS HOLSTEN

Mt. Frances, south face. In April, two Japanese climbers, Daizo Watanabe and Tani Takeshi, reported a possible new route on the south face of Mt. Frances, right above the Kahiltna base camp. Their route climbs one of several obvious, large gullies on the south aspect of the peak. Most of the route consisted of moderate snow and ice terrain; a steeper rock gully up high had reported difficulties up to M5. The duo called their climb Jumping Jack Flash (AI4 M5).

Given the many unreported team and solo ascents on this aspect of Mt. Frances throughout the years, it's suspected that much of the Japanese route had been climbed previously but not reported. It should also be noted that typically this route is highly hazardous later in the season, turning into one of the biggest garbage chutes in the range and unleashing spectacular rockfall.

From information provided by MARK WESTMAN *and* COLEY GENTZEL, *Denali National Park*

Mt. Laurens, northeast buttress. Mark Allen and I had an excellent and fruitful expedition into the Central Alaska Range in May, making the probable second ascent of Mt. Laurens (10,042') via a

[This page] Seth Timpano entering the goods midway up the Reality Face. The route contained numerous sections of well-formed and steep waterfall ice before gaining the ridge. *Jared Vilhauer*

new route on its northeast buttress (4,650', V AI4 M7 A1).

Mt. Laurens is a prominent peak located along a ridgeline that runs south from the Fin (ca 13,300'), between the Yentna and Lacuna glaciers. Mark and I sighted the very impressive east face of Mt. Laurens during our first ascent of Voyager Peak (ca 12,213', *AAJ 2012*) in 2011, dubbing it the "Mastodon Face." Other peaks in the area include the Bat's Ears (ca 11,044', Wilkinson-Turgeon-Gilmore, *AAJ 2009*) and another unclimbed peak (ca 10,020').

Paul Roderick alerted us to a prior ascent of Laurens by Austrian climber Thomas Bubendorfer, who

he flew into the Yentna Glacier in 1997. [*Bubendorfer reportedly spent 16 days alone in the area and soloed the peak by the north face and west ridge in an 11-hour push. He named the peak for his son. In 1983, Bubendorfer set a speed climbing record for the north face of the Eiger that stood for 20 years, among other impressive climbs and solos.*]

In early May, Paul flew us to a new landing strip in the Ramparts, located between the Lacuna and Kahiltna glaciers. We then approached for two days on skis up the Lacuna Glacier to the confluence with its southwest fork (ca 14km). Between May 9–15, Mark and I made two attempts on the very precipitous east buttress of Laurens, getting turned around both times after 1,500' of climbing, due to blank, overhanging walls and very dangerous climbing on an unformed ice hose.

On the evening of May 20 we started up the northeast buttress instead. The first half of the route comprised difficult mixed climbing, separated by long sections of excellent, steep ice and snow climbing. After this initial section we bivied on a beautiful prow. The second half of the route gained a steep snow arête that we ascended to the confluence with the north ridge. We continued up this ridge to a short second bivy. This bivy site was superb, affording excellent views of the Alaska Range, including Foraker and Hunter. The entire ridge provided wild, unprotected climbing on steep snow, both over and around huge gargoyle cornices, and eventually led us to the summit plateau.

On the summit we were caught in a very cold windstorm that forced us to hunker down for three uncomfortable hours in our tent. With the coming of the sun the wind died, and we were able to climb one final pitch of 70° snow to the summit. Our GPS and altimeter showed the summit elevation at 10,042'.

We descended along the southern end of the east face, following a series of couloirs. We made 12 total rappels on ice, snow, and rock, and were then able to downclimb steep snow for

[This page] The northeast buttress of Mt. Laurens as climbed by Allen and Zimmerman from the Lacuna Glacier. The line reported by Bubendorfer on the north face lies on the other side of the peak, starting from the Yentna Glacier. The attempted east buttress lies left of the line shown. *Mark Allen* another 2,000' to the glacier. The route took us a total of 67 hours—59 hours up and eight hours down. We rested for a day and a half before skiing back to the landing strip. A combination of an adventurous approach, exploratory alpinism, marvelous position, and challenging climbing gave the trip a fabulous flavor. 🔲

GRAHAM ZIMMERMAN

BUCKSKIN GLACIER

Mooses Tooth, east face, Bird of Prey. After the first ascent of the east face of the Mooses Tooth in 1982, Jim Bridwell wrote of his return to base camp: "The cards were played and we had drawn aces. Finally I collapsed into prone paralysis. Just before unconsciousness, the memorable words of the French climber Jean Afanassieff came to mind. 'This is the fucking life! No?'" [*AAJ 1982*].

With their first ascent of the Dance of the Woo-Li Masters, Bridwell and Mugs Stump drew a line up the east face in impeccable style. Virtually no gear was left on the face, leaving a clear message on a cold and remote wall—one that would impact the approach to alpine big walls for decades to come.

Now, I am up on this wall. The morning sun is burning on my back, and still it's brutally cold. For more than an hour, Dani Arnold has been fighting his way up an icy crack. I'm holding the ropes at my belay device with my right hand while I knead the fingers on my left hand to get the blood flowing again. I suddenly hear my Swiss friend yell from above: "You think we'll get up this thing?" For a few seconds I have doubts as well. We have chosen a bold line, for sure. Still, I have the feeling that, like Bridwell and Stump, we can successfully put our ideas to the test on this wall. We'll just have to stand on our toes, stretch, and grow with the difficulties.

Only a few clouds had veiled the mountains as we flew toward the Buckskin Glacier on April 10. That same evening, the fog disappeared and we saw the compact and steep heart of rock on the east face for the first time. So far, no one had managed to pull off a line through the center of the east face's headwall. The next day, using a sled, we dragged our equipment to the bottom of the wall and analyzed our intended route with binoculars. The route, to be our first climb in Alaska, would climb a face notorious for Alaskan eccentricities, including huge snow mushrooms and enormous amounts of spindrift. On the other hand, we hoped our impartiality could provide the boldness that is always necessary for walls of this size. We planned to start the climb the following morning, April 12. [*Editor's note: Arnold and Lama's route begins on Arctic Rage (Gilmore-Mahoney, AAJ 2005), which shares the same start as Dance of the Woo-Li Masters. The duo followed Arctic Rage to below the headwall, then branched left and climbed 17 pitches of new terrain, reaching a subsidiary summit atop the wall.*]

"We certainly won't turn around on the first day!" I yell back to Dani. After another half-hour he finds a suitable anchor. Dani continues leading. It's definitely not getting easier. With pendulums, vertical and extremely thin ice, and tricky mixed terrain, the climbing demands our full concentration. After two pitches, Dani is done and I take over the lead again. I'm tired from leading the first part of the route, but we still have to climb a couple more pitches if we're to stand a reasonable chance of reaching the summit the next day.

At dusk, we put up our tent. More than half of it sticks out over the void, but it protects us from the icy wind and the annoying spindrift. The next morning greets us again with perfect weather. According to our forecast, it is not going to last long. We decide to leave our bivy gear

[This page] Dani Arnold seconding steep mixed terrain high on the east face of the Mooses Tooth. The Austrian-Swiss route was the first to breach the central headwall on the face. *David Lama*

behind. Like Bridwell, we hope to draw aces. After three pitches, we reach a large roof. Dani has led until here, but he can't get past the huge snow mushrooms suspended menacingly above us. I lower him and we switch ends of the rope. With two pendulums, I manage to bypass the roof. We traverse rightward and can almost feel the icefields leading to the top. Between them and us is another roof.

Navigating difficult mixed terrain, I climb up until I'm under a big snow mushroom and then make a rightward traverse for two or three meters. The snow formation looks extremely fragile. I'm almost above it when I finally get in good gear, which I hold onto as I place my ice tool on a small hold. As I weight the hold, part of it breaks. I immediately catch myself with my left hand but still touch the snow mushroom. It collapses and hundreds of kilograms of snow fall onto the ropes. The gear holds and Dani is fine too, even though a pin pulled from his anchor. Once Dani rehammers the pin, I climb on. Two more pitches bring us to the icefields leading to the top.

At 6 p.m., we both stand at the top of the wall on the upper plateau, hardly believing that we managed such a dreamy line so quickly. A couple of days earlier we'd been at home in Europe, and now we stand on top of this impressive face. A long descent with many rappels over our route ensues. Because we mostly use ice threads for anchors, we leave almost no gear on the face. It's 48 hours after starting when we finally arrive back in base camp, done, very much done. I can't help but think our new route Bird of Prey (1,500m, 6a A2 M7+ 90°) may be worthy of the idea Bridwell and Stump first had about climbing this wall. *This is indeed the fucking life, Jim!* 📷

DAVID LAMA, *Austria*

Mooses Tooth, east face, NWS. In mid-April, Scott Adamson and Pete Tapley established NWS (1,400m, V WI6 M5), the east face's first completely free route, over two days. The route takes an independent line just right of Arctic Rage (Gilmore-Mahoney, *AAJ 2005*) before joining that route for the last several pitches. The two men topped out the east face but did not continue to the summit of the Mooses Tooth. A few weeks after the climb, Jared Vilhauer and Tim Dittman repeated NWS, reporting great climbing with one bivy en route. [*Scott Adamson's feature article on his many attempts to complete this route can be found earlier in this edition.*]

Mooses Tooth, east face, Terror. After leaving a balmy spring in the Oregon desert, Geoff Unger and I headed for the east face of the Mooses Tooth. We shared the flight with David Lama and Dani Arnold, who were gunning for a line up the middle of the face, while Geoff and I were after a drip out to the right. When we landed on the Buckskin and found Scott Adamson and Pete Tapley already there, we were more than a little bummed to hear that our drip was actually a longtime project of Scott's. Geoff and I began looking for something else to climb: A thinly iced corner system on the left side of the face was the next best thing. With David and Dani set to launch up the middle, and Scott and Pete set to launch up the right, we got set to launch up the left.

On the morning of April 12 we set out for the wall. We were held up by a tricky 'schrund crossing before gaining the face's lower slopes. We then moved slowly on funky snow before reaching what we called the Racing Stripes: parallel lines of 75–90° névé that link the lower snowfield to the upper headwall. We weren't able to find belays or gear on the steep, at times insecure névé. It took us all day to reach the corner system at the start of the headwall, and we bivied below the first hard pitch. After trying the pitch the next morning, we decided to bail. We had moved far too slowly, and Geoff was suffering from an elbow injury.

With the perfect blue skies gnawing at me every minute I spent sitting in camp, I was keen to go back; coming to terms with an injury, Geoff was not. After a few days of rest, I managed to

[Previous page] The impressive east face of the Mooses Tooth: (1) Southeast face [approximate location, Gilmore-House-Mahoney, 2000]. (2) The Beast Pillar [direct start to Dance of the Woo Li Masters. Bridwell-Pfinsten, 2001]. (3) Dance of the Woo Li Masters [Bridwell, Stump, 1981]. (4) Terror [Adamson-Wright, 2013]. (5) Bird of Prey [Arnold-Lama, 2013]. (6) Arctic Rage [Gilmore-Mahoney, 2004]. (7) NWS [Adamson-Tapley, 2013]. (8) There's a Moose Loose About This Hoose [Bracey-Helliker, 2008, not to summit]. (9) Magic Mushrooms [Bonniot-Dall'Agnol-Moulin-Revest, 2012]. *Chris Wright* **[This page]** Chris Wright starts up the first pitch of the crux corner system on his initial attempt on Terror. *Geoff Unger*

convince Scott Adamson, who I barely knew, to have a go with me instead. Having just completed the first ascent of NWS [*see feature article in this edition*] in a single push, Scott was excited to get some more climbing in before flying out.

We left camp at 3 a.m. on the morning of April 18, and planned to go as fast and light as possible. Where Geoff and I had bivied below the upper corners, Scott and I decided to try and climb through them and gain the large snow patch on the peak's southeast shoulder, about halfway up the headwall. We were happy to find that this time the snow conditions had improved, and we gained the Racing Stripes by about 6 a.m. Knowing that they were unprotectable, we decided to keep soloing until we reached the headwall. We roped up there, and Scott led one long pitch of ice until we could simul-climb on easier ground. We arrived at our previous bivy ledge around 8:30 a.m., fired up the stove, drank some water, and set off up the corners.

Six pitches and 14 hours later, we reached a big snow patch in the dark. A biting wind and serious fatigue had us both feeling completely shattered. All of the corner's pitches had been difficult, sustained, and hard to protect, with each pitch somewhere in the M6/7 and WI5/6 range, with the occasional short section of aid. By the time we climbed another pitch to the top of the snow shoulder, we were both as strung-out as either of us could remember.

After a 2:30 a.m. bedtime and a night of strategic lying down, we coaxed ourselves awake around 8 a.m. We downclimbed a short pitch before moving rightward, and after one of the few easy pitches on the route we again encountered hard, steep climbing with marginal pro. Five more pitches, which included Scott's impressive lead of a hard, dry pitch on rotten rock, as well as a funky ice and mushroom traverse, found us at an airy bivy on a snow rib near the top of the headwall.

After another 2 a.m. bedtime and a much more comfortable night at the Dr. Seuss Bivy, we traversed left to gain a weakness, and then climbed straight up on fun mixed terrain for two pitches toward the top of the face. One more pitch led around some monster cornices and onto the ridge, and a short walk led to the summit plateau, where we ditched our packs and set out for the top. A very Alaskan traverse on the corniced summit ridge brought us to what we thought was the top at around 3 p.m. Fearing that the next point on the ridge might be higher, we continued the traverse, only to find ourselves cursing as we looked back and realized we had already summited. After a few words and a few pictures, we retraced our steps to the top of the face.

We rappelled using anchors that Scott had just installed during his descent from NWS. After traversing and downclimbing toward the 'schrund, one more rap brought us back to the glacier. The descent had taken only four and a half hours. Exhausted, we rifled through the food that Geoff and I had cached before our attempt. At 10:30 p.m. on April 20 we arrived back at camp to whiskey and a warm dinner, coming in at a total round trip of about 67 hours. I estimate we climbed about 22 belayed pitches, with most being harder than WI4 or M5. Our new route, Terror (1,500m, VI WI6 M7 R/X A2), was without doubt the hardest, scariest climb of my life, but I wouldn't change anything—except maybe just a few more pieces of gear. 🔘

CHRIS WRIGHT

COFFEE GLACIER

Broken Tooth, west ridge, Haeussler-Rowe variation. On May 31, Peter Haeussler and I, both from Anchorage, reached the summit of Broken Tooth (9,050') via a major variation to the west ridge route (Bauman-Lewis, *AAJ* 1988). [*Cody Arnold, Peter Haeussler, and Jay Rowe first completed the lower part of this variation in 2009 (AAJ 2010); however, they were forced down from their bivy site due to a large storm and were unable to complete the climb to the summit by the west ridge.*]

Starting on May 30, we climbed three long ice pitches (WI4+ M6+) in the left of two parallel ice chimneys on a buttress approximately 200m north of the original route. The crux came on the third pitch, where warm temperatures had turned the ice to slush and I took a 20' leader fall. Above the chimney, we climbed three pitches of 60–70° snow with mixed rock and ice sections. (A considerable wet avalanche released on this slope while I followed Peter. Thankfully, I was roped.) This led to the crest of the west ridge, where we excavated a tent site and slept for five hours before continuing to the summit via the ridge.

From our bivy, we avoided a rock step by climbing out onto the north face, where good alpine ice led to the final obstacle, a 60m rock tower. This was overcome by a short 5.9 section, followed by the best pitch of the entire climb: a steep, shoulder-width runnel of ice in a left-facing corner. Above that we climbed to the summit in four low-angle pitches on kitty-litter granite. The round trip back to our bivy took 23 hours, with warm temperatures and deep, wet snow persisting. Back at our bivy, we waited 12 hours for cooler temperatures before finishing the descent.

This ascent of Broken Tooth represents the completion of a longstanding project for me. My first attempt on Broken Tooth was in 1993, and was then followed by 10 additional attempts over the next 20 years. I had tried this mountain from every aspect and been turned back by everything imaginable, but this time the pieces fell into place. 📷

JAY ROWE

RUTH GORGE

Gargoyle, Beauty and the Beast; Tooth Traverse, second ascent. When Alex Bluemel and I (both Austrians) arrived in the Ruth Gorge on May 19 it was wintertime. However, things began to change immediately as an extraordinary weather window lasting more than a month established itself. The

[This page] View of the west ridge of the Broken Tooth showing (1) the west ridge route by Bauman and Lewis and (2) the new variation by Rowe and Haeussler. The bivy site is marked where the two routes join. Not shown: the south face (Stump-Quinlan, *AAJ 1988*); the southeast ridge (Haire-Plumb, *AAJ 1983*); the east face (Root Canal, Walsh-Westman, *AAJ 2007*, not to summit); the northwest face (Before the Dawn, Ichimura-Satoh-Yamada, *AAJ 2007*). Numerous other attempts have been made on various aspects. *Jay Rowe*

mountains started to shake off their winter jacket.

We were alone the first week. It was quite a tough time, as we had no information about conditions. Several of our attempts were forced down by icefall and avalanches. "Winter is definitely over here!" we thought. But the rock was far from dry. Having investigated the area in detail, we discovered that other Austrian alpinists had played a big role in the history of Ruth Gorge climbing. Andi Orgler left big routes on almost every important summit in the Great Gorge, including the Wine Bottle on Mt. Dickey and the Pearl on Mt. Bradley. Previously unknown to us, he seems almost forgotten over in Europe. We hoped to leave our own mark.

Our first target for a new route was a big system of cracks and corner systems on the Gargoyle, supposedly unclimbed. After being driven off the climb, we gathered motivation and gear again and forged a new line on May 29 with one bivy sitting in the middle of the wall and one on the summit (to give the snow time to freeze for the descent). Two days later we returned to free three remaining aid pitches. Afterward, only one aid pitch remained because of chossy rock, overhanging snow, and running water combined with very poor protection (A3). In such conditions this 30m pitch was a tough, psycho fight, and we agreed it would provide hardly any more pleasure if dry.

The name Beauty and the Beast (650m, 7a+ A3) was easy to decide. "The Beauty" was found lower on the route in the form of finger cracks, roofs, and flakes, all on perfectly solid rock; "The Beast," well, you can guess. For the record, we placed one bolt on the aid pitch and left a few pitons in situ.

After two weeks of high pressure, the amazing weather window was interrupted by a few bad weather days, affording us time for socializing with our neighbors Freddie Wilkinson, Renan Ozturk, and Alex Honnold. Sitting in the tent with the American climbers, we got more and more psyched on trying the Tooth Traverse, which was only completed last year after a few attempts by Freddie and Renan. We decided it was ridge season, as the time for couloirs and ice

[This page] The south-southwest aspect of the Gargoyle, which is located just west of the Mooses Tooth massif at the north end of the Ruth Gorge, showing (1) Beauty and the Beast and approximate lines of (2) New Mother Nature (Medara-Spaulding, 1996) and (3) Electric View (Holden-Kalland-Lund-Mjaavatn, 2004). See *AAJ 2006* for another view of these earlier climbs from the southeast. *Gerhard Fiegl*

was long over and it was still too early to rock climb.

When the high pressure returned we set off on June 6 at 10 p.m. toward the Sugar Tooth and reached the summit around lunchtime the next day. After a nap we continued to the Eye Tooth, following the Talkeetna Standard up the south ridge. Following a 24-hour climbing day, we were happy to establish a bivy below the summit of Eye Tooth. From there, a 12-hour day brought us to the Bear Tooth, where we bivied for the night. The third full day was a long one again. We rappelled the White Russian (*AAJ 2005*) from the Bear Tooth and climbed the Swamp Donkey Express up the Mooses Tooth, taking about 14 hours. However, the day was not over. A long descent down the west ridge of the Mooses Tooth proved tricky at times, with cornices waiting in the dim light.

We were so happy to realize the Tooth Traverse for the second ascent, just one year after the first ascent. We reached our base camp at 9 a.m. on June 10, 83 hours after setting off. Special thanks to Renan and Freddie for the inspiration and good beta. 📷

GERHARD FIEGL, *Austria*

Mt. Johnson, point 7,500', Twisted Stair. From April 20–21, Silas Rossi and I established a new climb on a ca 7,500' satellite peak of Mt. Johnson (8,460'): Twisted Stair (2,300', V WI6 R/X M6+).

We flew into the Ruth Gorge on April 10 with the goal of climbing something and not sacrificing too many fingers and toes. Still in the grasp of winter, day- and night-time temperatures were frigid, ranging from 0°F to –35°F during our first week. We maintained our psych by skiing and scheming, while waiting for a bump in the mercury. We eventually attempted routes on Mt. Bradley and Mt. Dickey, with excellent climbing and good weather, but weren't able to finish either climb due to mega–snow mushrooms or other objective hazards. Ten days into our trip, we headed for a line we'd spied the previous season.

Twisted Stair climbs a clean and obvious line directly to Pt. 7,500', at the back of an east-facing amphitheater between Mt. Johnson and Mt. Wake, on the far right end of Johnson's west ridge. We started in the

[This page] The line of Twisted Stair on the right, topping out at Pt. 7,500'; the approximate line of the Ladder Tube to the left. The Elevator Shaft lies one chimney system left of the Ladder Tube [see AAJ 2008 *for photo of these routes*]. Both the Ladder Tube and the Elevator Shaft followed Johnson's west ridge to the summit (out of view, left). *Peter Doucette*

[This page] Peter Doucette gets committed on the crux WI6 ice smear of Twisted Stair. *Silas Rossi*

same chimney system as the Ladder Tube (Ichimura-Sato-Yamada, *AAJ 2008*), splitting right from its first pitch to climb what we believe is entirely new ground. Reaching the toe of the route requires broken, arduous glacier travel and affords an unflinching perspective on Mt. Johnson's north face. The sight instills a feeling of equal parts awe and intimidation, and includes a rare close-up view of the Elevator Shaft (Chabot-Tackle, *AAJ 1996*).

We started climbing on April 20, completing the climb and descent over two days, with one snow-cave bivy below the crux ice smear. We were inspired by the quality and sustained nature of the climbing, finding many physical and committing "blue collar" Alaskan pitches—one right after the other. Bergschrund to summit cornice, there was little reprieve as we navigated steep s'nice, mixed terrain, and a dizzying and delicate WI6 R/X ice smear at two-thirds height.

We rappelled—with a few variations to our line of ascent—from many V-threads and nuts under a clear night sky and moon shadow. The ski back to our camp below Mt. Dickey ended at Hour 49 on April 22. We left Alaska grateful, with more projects in mind for next season and the same number of functional fingers and toes with which we started. 📷

PETER DOUCETTE

Mt. Johnson, east face, Fire Escape. In May, Todd Tumolo and I completed a new route on Mt. Johnson (8,460'). We first saw the new line, the Fire Escape (4,000', V 5.6 AI4 65°), while scouting conditions in the lower gorge.

We began on May 6 at 5:30 a.m., climbing up a 70m smear of low-angle ice on the east face. The smear led to the broad snow bowl that eventually funnels into the Escalator (Shaw-Wagner, *AAJ 2001*) a route that is growing in popularity. Where this snow bowl narrowed, instead of continuing up the Escalator, we cut right and ascended an enjoyable 70m pitch of alpine ice. This proved to be the crux of the route. From atop the crux, Todd led up, zigzagging through steep snow and short ice steps. When the rope came tight, I began simul-climbing and eventually met

Todd at an anchor about three rope-lengths higher.

From there, I led out on a steep snow traverse that led to a long couloir we dubbed the Fire Hose. The Fire Hose lies adjacent to the infamous east buttress, and finding adequate protection in this area is challenging at best. We simul-climbed about 350m of 45–65° snow, finding only about five pieces of questionable protection. Near the top of the Fire Hose, Todd took over the lead and ascended an ice smear plastered into a tight corner, which exited onto the upper snow slopes. Here, snow conditions deteriorated into bottomless facets, and our pace slowed considerably as Todd swam his way upward toward a steep, rocky ridge that looked like it might hold protection. The climbing on the ridge was very enjoyable, with short steps of fun 5.6 climbing. From the top of the rocks, Todd led the last 70m toward the top over dangerous and unprotectable, wind-loaded snow. We dubbed this the Emergency Exit due to the tenuous conditions. The exit brought us to the summit of Mt. Johnson at 8:45 p.m., after about 15 hours of climbing.

There was little to no information about the descent other than: Follow the ridge down to the Johnson-Grosvenor col. This summit ridge is very narrow and heavily corniced to the east. There is occasional protection in the rocks that jut from the west side. We continued along to where the ridge splits and steepens, and downclimbed about 10 feet in the middle of the split into a rocky gully system. From there we slung a block and made one 70m rappel into a broad snow bowl, which we descended to the Johnson-Grosvenor col. The objective hazards in the descent couloir below the col are very high due to the near perfect avalanche angle and looming seracs. We chose to wait and descend in the coldest part of the night, and from the col we downclimbed until reaching some ice on climber's right. At the ice we made four 70m rappels to mellower snow slopes. Below, we downclimbed and negotiated two bergschrunds to the exit. It was only a short walk back to the base of the route, where we had left our skis. Our total time on the mountain, including descent, was 22 hours, and we were back in camp around 24 hours after starting.

JOSH HOESCHEN

Mt, Bradley, northwest face, Névé Ruse. I flew into the central Alaska Range on April 23 to meet Dusty Eroh in the Ruth Gorge, where he was camped between Mt. Dickey and Mt. Bradley. The next three days consisted of condition-scouting trips to the base of a line we eventually climbed: Névé Ruse (4,000', V AI5 R/X 60°), on the western end of Mt. Bradley's north face.

[This page] The upper east face of Mt. Johnson showing the Escalator on the left and the significant new variation, the Fire Escape, to the right. The Johnson-Grosvenor col is the obvious saddle left of Mt. Johnson. *Josh Hoeschen*

From the ground, the line appeared to be "in," and the névé slabs that comprise the first four rope lengths seemed to be thicker then I had ever seen them. We decided to go for it on April 26, leaving at 3 a.m.

The route began with a steep snow slope up to the base of the névé slabs. The névé was enjoyable, most of it being 70° and thick enough for full pick penetration, with only a few steps of steeper, 80–85° climbing. There was essentially no protection on this part of the route, and we were forced to simul-climb, finding only marginal anchors to belay from. We anticipated this for these lower pitches on the route, but we expected the protection to improve once we gained a large corner system that angles up and right after the névé slabs. Unfortunately, the unprotectable nature of the route would continue to its end.

The entrance into the corner system proved to be the crux, with an over-vertical step of alpine ice. The pitch took no worthwhile protection besides a Pecker up high in the runnel above the steep climbing. After this pitch we realized that the climbing was all going to be heady and run-out. The névé continued and brought us to another crux step; it soon became overhanging as I began tunneling through endless s'nice. After tunneling up the s'nice for about one and a half hours, my tool broke through into a chasm about 50' deep and three feet wide; I was able to chimney up to the top of this and burrow another hole back out to the surface and find some good névé.

Atop this pitch, the angle of the climbing eased back a little for two rope lengths. Higher up, we climbed two steps of really enjoyable alpine ice (AI4) plastered in a right-facing corner. One more pitch of thin névé (80–85°) brought us to the upper snow slopes. It was getting late, so we found a spot to chop a bivy ledge. We spent about six hours at the bivy, between chopping and sleeping, and were on the move again around 8 a.m. The terrain on the summit ridge was generally 45–50° snow with one short step of 60° ice. Eight to ten rope lengths of climbing from our bivy site brought us to the summit around 12:30 p.m. on April 27.

We descended the west ridge to the Bradley-Wake col. The descent was straightforward in the conditions we had, and we only made two rappels, one on the ridge and one over the cornice at the

[This page] The northwest flanks of Mt, Bradley, showing the line of Névé Ruse. Spice Factory lies just out of frame around the left skyline to the east. Further to the east: Welcome to Alaska, Heavy Mettle, and the East Buttress. *Todd Tumolo*

col. After this we were able to downclimb and jump over the filled-in bergschrund. We then picked up an old ski track through the icefall back to camp. We made it to camp 39 hours after leaving.

TODD TUMOLO

Mt. Barrill, Cobra Pillar; Mt. Bradley, south face, The Pearl; Mt. Dickey, southeast face; repeats and speed ascents. Renan Ozturk, Alex Honnold, and I rendezvoused in Anchorage the third week in May. Our goal this year was to climb on the west side of the gorge, feeling more inspired to repeat routes than try any remaining untouched line. We flew to a base camp below Mt. Dickey on May 23.

First up was a 19-hour ascent of Mt. Barrill's Cobra Pillar (2,600', 5.10 A1). [*Zack Smith and Ozturk made a 12-hour ascent and 20-hour round-trip climb of the Cobra Pillar in 2009. The first ascent by Jim Donini and Jack Tackle took five days total (with two and a half days stormbound) in 1991. Mt. Barrill is often misspelled as Barrille. The peak was namd for Edward N. Barrill, who accompanied Dr. Frederick Cook in the Ruth Gorge in 1906.*]

Next was a 40-hour round-trip ascent of the Pearl (4,000', 5.12 A0) on the south face of Mt. Bradley, for the second ascent. Alex sent the route's A3 crux pitch in something more akin to 5.12 A0 R. [*The first ascent of the Pearl (Neswadba-Orgler-Wutscher, AAJ 1996) on Bradley's south face took five days in alpine style.*]

And, lastly, we did a 19-hour ascent of Mt. Dickey's southeast face (5,100', 5.10c A0). It is to our knowledge the first time one of the big, technical routes on Dickey has been climbed in a day. [*The first ascent of the southeast face of Dickey, a.k.a. the 1974 route (Roberts-Rowell-Ward,* AAJ *1975) took six days round trip.*]

FREDDIE WILKINSON

Peak 7,400', north face, Gangster's Paradise (no summit); Thunder Peak, north face, Kearney-Mascioli variation. On April 25, Eitan Green and I flew into the Ruth Gorge with a good forecast and three weeks to get something done. Our first five days in the range were productive: We set up camp in the Root Canal, knocking off Shaken Not Stirred and Ham and Eggs on back-to-back days. After a rest, we finished with the Japanese Couloir on Mt. Barille. These climbs afforded us perspective on other objectives in the region, and we decided to set our sights on the north race of Peak 7,400', where

[This page] The north face of Peak 7,400' showing Gangster's Paradise on the left and the Optimist on the right; the Bibler-Klewin route climbs just left of the latter. See *AAJ 2011* for another photo of the right-side lines. *Sam Hennessey*

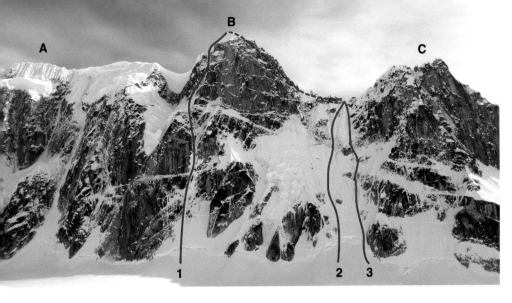

[This page] The north side of the "Thunder Mountain" massif, showing (A) "Thunder Mountain" (a.k.a. Peak 10,920'), (B) "Thunder Peak" (a.k.a. Peak 10,600'), and (C) an unnamed peak. "Thunder Peak" was first climbed in 1983 by Kearney and Mascioli, who ascended a line (2) to the prominent col, then up the west ridge (right skyline) to the summit; they did not climb "Thunder Mountain." The summit of "Thunder Peak" was reached again from the north by Tackle and Smith via a new route, Tangled Up In Blue (1), in 2009. Green and Hennessey completed a new variation to the right of the Kearney-Mascioli route leading to the prominent col (3), then repeated the first-ascent route up the west ridge to the summit. "Thunder Mountain" has never been climbed from the north side but has seen a number of ascents and attempts from the south. It was first climbed by Barlow and Hornby (*AAJ 1994*) from a couloir on the south side [*see AAJ 2001 for a detailed route line photo of the south face*]. Peak (C) has been mistaken for Peak 9,070', which lies further west; Peak 9,070' was also climbed by Barlow and Hornby from the northwest (*AAJ 1994*). *Sam Hennessey*

several enticing ice smears seemed to link snowfields and steep rock. [*Editor's note: Peak 7,400' is an unnamed summit located on the east side of the Ruth Gorge, across from Mt. Bradley.*]

A storm then dropped two feet of snow, delaying our plans for several days. Eventually, we started up the left side of the north face of Peak 7,400', enduring one scary spindrift incident and constantly questioning our decision to continue. The first half of the route contained moderate climbing, but soon we were committed, as the compact rock made anchor-building difficult and the ice smears that had excited us days earlier turned out to be unprotected névé.

In the upper third of the route, awkward climbing around a snow mushroom led to a pendulum to overcome steep, blank rock and reach another corner system. Night fell and four more pitches of challenging mixed climbing, aid up overhanging corners, and an exciting finish up unconsolidated snow mushrooms and cornices brought us to the summit ridge. A shovel and pickets were critical for forward progress on the final pitch. Shivering, we were happy to find the morning sun at the top of the face, and we elected to immediately descend toward the Coffee Glacier rather than complete the route to the summit. We slogged over Cavity Gap and back to our skis, returning to camp after about 30 hours on the move. We named the route Gangster's Paradise (V AI4 M6 A2). [*Editor's note: Two other routes ascend terrain on the northwest and west aspects of Peak 7,400': the Bibler-Klewin (1989), which climbs the prow formed by the north and west faces, and the Optimist (Amano-Masumoto-Nagato, 2010), which climbs the west face, possibly sharing some terrain with the earlier route near the exit.*]

The next morning saw us frantically packing up camp and dragging it a half-mile to the airstrip to meet Paul Roderick, who flew us to a small fork below the north side of Thunder Mountain on the Kahiltna Glacier for our final week in the range. It immediately lived up to its name, as we saw numerous, enormous serac avalanches, including several that seemed to threaten our intended line on Mt. Providence. We settled for our Plan B, which turned out to be a very enjoyable climb up the far right side of Thunder Peak's north face, leading to a prominent col, and then up snow slopes on the peak's west ridge to the summit.

We climbed the first part of the route to the col in 14 pitches with some moderate mixed climbing through rock bands (AI4 M5). After a comfortable bivy at the col on the ridge, a traverse toward Thunder Peak led to 50° snow slopes and roughly 1,800' of elevation gain to the summit. We chose to downclimb and rappel the route, which was straightforward and deposited us back at camp after 30 hours away.

[*Editor's note: The route climbed by Green and Hennessey on "Thunder Peak" ascends a line just right of the Kearney-Mascioli (1983), then joins that route on the west ridge to the summit. It should be noted that "Thunder Peak" (Peak 10,600') is a seperate summit from the slightly taller "Thunder Mountain" (Peak 10,920'). The two names have been used synonymously and incorrectly in the past. See photo caption at left for further clarification.*]

SAM HENNESSEY

LITTLE SWITZERLAND

Red Dragon Wall, Green Couch. After enduring the fury of a 10-day Alaskan storm, we were rewarded with one six-hour period of sunshine during which we established a new four-pitch route on a small, unclimbed wall in Little Switzerland. Green Couch (III 5.10a) was a fun and high-quality consolation prize after getting completely skunked on our main objective, a traverse of the Dragon's Spine, a long, unclimbed ridgeline. [*The Dragon's Spine lies a few miles down glacier (northwest) from the Trolls and other formations.*] We named the cliff the Red Dragon Wall because of its red-varnished face; it is located just southeast of the Dragon's Spine, right where the Pika Glacier meets the granite. The climb consists of mostly splitter hand and finger cracks up to 5.9, with a 5.10a move through a small roof. There is an additional pitch through very moderate terrain to top out and walk off the wall. Overall, the rock and climbing are very high quality. 📷

ZACH CLANTON

[This page] The Dragon's Spine formation, which rises up from the Pika Glacier in Little Switzerland.
Zach Clanton

[This page, top] Chad Diesinger on the summit of Peak 9,400'. McGinnis Peak is the prominent peak in the distance. The northeast ridge comprises the right skyline; the Cutthroat Couloir climbs the prominent couloir down and right of the summit before joining the northeast ridge at a notch. *Jason Stuckey* [This page, bottom] The northwest face of Peak 9,400'. Don't Wake The Snake climbs the marked couloir then angles right toward the top to gain the summit. *Jason Stuckey*

HAYES RANGE

McGinnis Peak, northeast ridge, attempt; Peak 9,400', northwest face, Don't Wake the Snake. In March, Chad Diesinger, Andy Ducomb, and I made our fourth trip to McGinnis Peak, the easternmost peak in the Hayes Range. A 14-mile approach brought the three us to the east face and provided easy access to a col on the northeast ridge, our objective. Once gaining the col, we dug in for the night and continued up in the morning. After a few blocks of simul-climbing along the knife-edge ridge, Andy arrived at the belay and told me he was feeling pretty worked. I turned and looked at the long section of ridgeline remaining to the summit—almost a mile. I know we could have made it to the summit, but the descent back down the knife-edge ridge was worrisome. We headed down.

As we downclimbed under bluebird skies, I struggled with disappointment. During all of my previous trips here the weather had been horrendous. However, as we descended through the

icefall, a likely unclimbed, S-shaped couloir on the northwest face of Peak 9,400' caught my eye. Chad and I decided to give it a go the next day while Andy rested in the tent. [*Peak 9,400' is located approximately three miles east of McGinnis Peak, directly across the McGinnis Glacier.*]

We started up the couloir around 9 a.m. The snow was a bit deep at the bottom, where the couloir pinched down, but conditions improved above. The angle was around 45°, steepening to 60° on the upper part of the face. Simul-soloing, we topped out 20m from the summit just before 1 p.m. The face had been in the shade the entire morning, and a strong wind had begun to blow about halfway up. But the summit was warm, sunny, and sheltered from the wind. It was glorious. I usually don't like to waste too much time on a summit, but we stayed for almost an hour, eating and taking in the incredible views. An hour and a half of downclimbing brought us back to our skis, and the next day we skied out to the car.

We named our route Don't Wake the Snake (3,400', 60°) due to the shape of the couloir and the problems that would arise if anything slid, and also in honor of Will Ferrell and his tight pants. Peak 9,400' had been climbed before by the north ridge, southeast ridge, and east face. But the northwest face had not been climbed.

JASON STUCKEY

Mt. Hayes, southeast face, variation and solo ascent. In April, Samuel Johnson soloed the southeast face of Mt. Hayes (6,500', AI3 M3) in 18 hours round-trip from a base camp on the Trident Glacier. He and Ryan Johnson (unrelated) had hoped to attempt a more north-facing line on Hayes' east side, but when brutally cold temperatures quashed that plan and his partner came down with a cough, Samuel Johnson decided to solo a sunnier aspect of the wall. He climbed directly below the summit for the first third of the climb, then veered up and right for the middle portion (to avoid a steep rock band and stay clear of the cornices near the summit), and then continued directly up to reach the east ridge, which he followed to the 13,832' summit. He descended the heavily crevassed east ridge.

For about two-thirds of his ascent, Johnson generally followed the line climbed by John Bauman and Tom Walter (*AAJ 1989*) for the first ascent of the face. In the upper third, he climbed directly up where Bauman and Walter traversed rightward toward the east ridge. This was possibly only the second ascent of the face and the first solo ascent of Mt. Hayes, though there are many undocumented climbs in this range.

DOUGALD MACDONALD, *from information supplied by Samuel Johnson*

[This page] The southern aspect of Ultima Thule Peak. The southwest ridge ascends the ridge on the left skyline (this photo only shows the upper portion). The first-ascent route is believed to go more or less straight down from the summit on the center-left side of the broad south face. *Arturo Polo Ena*

ALASKA ST. ELIAS MOUNTAINS

Ultima Thule Peak, southwest ridge. The 2013 climbing season in the University Range proved to be challenging. Dangerous snow conditions and temperamental weather brought close calls, false starts, and more failures than successes—and just plain tough climbing.

However, on April 20, persistence paid off, and Jay Claus and I were able to make the second ascent of Ultima Thule Peak (10,950'). We chose the long, prominent, unclimbed southwest ridge. [*Editor's note: Paul Claus, Ruedi Homberger, and Reto Reuesh made the first ascent of the then-unnamed Ultima Thule Peak (then estimated to be ca 10,500') in 1996 via the south face, joining the upper southwest ridge to the summit (AAJ 1997). The complete southwest ridge lies left of the south face. The peak is located at the head of Canyon Creek, in the University Range.*] The 16 hours of climbing under blue sky was fantastic, the climbing varied. Mixed climbing wove around and over stone gendarmes; there were long, exposed corniced ridges; and steep snow culminated in a truly classic and steep Alaskan ridge traverse to the top.

We stood one at a time, as close as we dared, on the overhanging summit, and then chose a fairly direct descent to the left of the south face first-ascent route to avoid having to reverse the slow, horizontal mixed pitches. We celebrated with fireworks in base camp. 📷 🔍

KEVIN DITZLER

Bear Glacier, many first ascents. On May 19, our group of five—Greg Encelewski, Galen Flint, Hannah North, Ben Still, and I—flew to the Ultima Thule Lodge with pilot Paul Claus. The next morning Paul dropped us at a ca 8,500' base camp on the northeast fork of the Bear Glacier. This remote part of the Alaska St. Elias Mountains is overshadowed by the larger peaks of Mt. Natazhat (13,435') 10 miles to the north, Mt. Bear (14,831') seven miles to the south, and Mt. Bona (16,421') 19 miles to the west. We could find no record of any previous climbs in this valley. This was my 31st expedition into the Wrangell-St. Elias Mountains and my 25th flying with Paul.

Over 10 days, our group summited eight peaks and attempted a ninth. All of these climbs were first known ascents, between AK Grade I and II in difficulty: The Cub (10,540'), southeast ridge; Panda Peak (11,425'), west ridge; Polar Peak (11,350'), east ridge; Bruin Peak (12,150'), southwest face; Lesser Panda (10,850'), east ridge; Sow Peak (11,875'), north face; Oso Peak (10,390') east ridge; Kuma Peak (10,450'), southwest ridge; and Canbear Peak (10,750'), west ridge, attempt.

Highlights from the trip include 10 days of glorious sunshine, a group ski descent from the summit of Sow Peak, and beautiful powder skiing in the Polar-Panda bowl. 📷 🔍 🗐

DAVE HART

CHUGACH MOUNTAINS

Heritage Point, Boiled Goose. In the first week of March, John Kelley and Ben Trocki established another new route on the Heritage Wall, a seldom-climbed, 3,900', Scottish-like wall located outside of Anchorage [*see* AAJ 2005 *and* AAJ 2013 *for more information*]. The new route, Boiled Goose (3,500', VI WI6 M6 A2), was climbed in 58 hours roundtrip from a bivy at the base of the wall and included two bivouacs en route.

From information posted by JOHN KELLEY *at Supertopo.com*

COAST MOUNTAINS

West Mendenhall Tower, south face, Balancing Act. A lot of things had to come together to get Ryan Johnson, Gabe Hayden, and I all on the tarmac at the same time on a sunny autumn afternoon in Juneau. I had been in town for almost two weeks, testing my short-lived Coloradan patience for waiting out wet, drizzly weather, and was also rapidly running out of time. I had already postponed my trip twice due to having a regular, salary-earning lifestyle that's not conducive to training or Alaskan climbing trips. Gabe and Ryan, Juneau locals, merely lined up a few days off work last-minute to take advantage of a rare forecast for September sunshine.

We were dropped off by helicopter at the base of the Mendenhall Towers on September 13, with two days of decent weather in the forecast. After a short reconnaissance, we set our sights on

[This page] The south face of the West Mendenhall Tower, showing the new 1,400' route, Balancing Act. *Jason Nelson*

[This page] The south side of the Mendenhall Towers, showing the seven summits from left to right (including minor summits, which are hard to see): West Tower, Second Tower ("Midget"), Main Tower, Fourth Tower, Fifth Tower, Sixth Tower, Seventh Tower. *Painting by John Svenson*

the unclimbed south face of West Mendenhall Tower, with its alluring, steep, steel-gray upper headwall. Setting up camp, we had the horrible realization that half of our food and all of our beer had been left in the car back at the airport. The emaciated Gabe and my gargantuan self worried about our slim rations; Ryan, with a hobbit-like physique, is uniquely prepared for situations such as these, so he was not overly concerned.

After a meager breakfast, we launched the next morning. The climbing began with two fun and engaging pitches of steep rock, highlighted by a 5.10 offwidth. We then followed an easier ramp for several hundred feet to the headwall. From the top of the ramp, we climbed five more steep, sustained, engaging pitches to the summit ridge, with difficulties up to 5.11c. The climbing was generally on clean splitter cracks with great friction. Another easy pitch along the mossy summit ridge led us to a short walk to the summit. Far below we could trace the contours of the Mendenhall Glacier all the way to Juneau, almost spotting the airport where our car was parked with its load of food and beer; beyond, the channels of the inside passage and mountainous islands stretched across the horizon. An uneventful rappel back down our line got us to our tent just before sunset.

Our original plan had been to climb for two days and then walk out. However, the forecast took a turn for the worst the next day, so we hiked out a day early, on September 15. This hike is a chore in *good* conditions. This year, an unusually hot and sunny summer had shredded the glacier; it was almost to the point of being impassable. After about 11 hours of pushing hard, we made it back to the trailhead. Three hours later the rain began to fall. We dubbed our route Balancing Act (1,400', 5.11c) due to the logistics and sacrifices we dealt with in order to climb together.

JASON NELSON

Mt. Emmerich Cirque, Point 4,700', Dysentery Chute; Upper Dewey Lake, "Ships Prow," northwest ridge. In May, David Hertel and I flew into the Mt. Emmerich Cirque, located outside of Haines in the Takhinsha Mountains, to attempt new routes. We first did some recon climbs: Dave cruised up the Crypt (4,850'), and I went up a couloir on the northeast side of Mt. Emmerich (6,405'), which is adjacent to the route climbed by Beckey, Tackle, and Zaspel (*AAJ 1977*). In the following days the temperature rose substantially and the cirque began to fall apart.

Once things cooled off, we decided to check out a route that we had spotted earlier—a cool-looking runnel of ice on a spire-shaped summit. We left the tent at 3 a.m., snowshoeing northward across the cirque until reaching steep snow leading to the base of a rocky spire. After 45 minutes of snow climbing, we reached the base of a rock band. There was ice on the technical pitch above, but none solid or thick enough for protection (M5 R). A couple more pitches of loose rock climbing took us to the tiny 4,700' summit, where only one person could fit at a time. After two rappels and some reverse slogging, we were able to find a reasonable descent in the obvious couloir left of the spire. We called our route the Dysentery Chute.

After this worthwhile climb, temperatures continued to increase, ending our climbing plans. Additionally, our planned walk out became threatened by cornices; fortunately our pilot, Drake Olson, stuck his neck out and flew in to keep us out of hazardous terrain.

From Haines, we headed to Skagway to attempt another formation Dave called the "Ships Prow," above and due east of Upper Dewey Lake, a few miles above town. From town, we hiked up to an awesome and free, hiker-maintained cabin by the lake to stage our attempt. We left before dawn, punched up a steep couloir, and began climbing the prominent northwest ridge of the formation, the highest point overlooking Upper Dewey Lake. As predicted, the climbing was very loose but fun and in an awesome position, with the Sawtooth Range in one direction and the sea in the other. Five or six short pitches with a lot of traversing back and forth between the north and west faces took us to the summit (5.9 WI3). To descend, we made two 60m rappels back into the couloir we started in and downclimbed to the base. 📷 🗒

KURT ROSS

Cats Ears Spire, south face. Zach Hoyt (U.S.) and his partner "Shaz" (AUS) established a possible new route on the south face of Cats Ears Spire, to the left of the Least Snowed Up Route (900m, IV 5.10+, Edwards-Millar, *AAJ 2003*), which climbs just right of the southeast arête to the spire's east summit. It's possible that the new route may share pitches with the former near the top; however, details and a topo for the climb are currently lacking (900m, 5.10/5.11).

There are only two other known routes on this spire: the east face (Culbert-Douglas-Starr, 1972), and the northwest face (Elias-McMullen, 1996), which also both reached the east summit. The west summit has since been gained from the Cat's Brow (the notch between the two ears, via the Elias-McMullen); few people—perhaps fewer than 15 total—have reached either summit.

From information supplied by DIETER KLOSE

CANADA

ST. ELIAS RANGE

Mt. Eaton, east ridge and epic. On May 7, pilot Paul Swanstrom flew Derek Buckle and me from Haines to ca 3,700' on the lower Seward Glacier close to the Yukon border. The week prior, storms had broken precipitation records for much of neighboring southeast Alaska. Our objective was the complete east ridge of Mt. Augusta (14,070'). I had tried accessing this ridge in 1993 via a spur from the north, reaching ca 10,500' on the spur (*AAJ 1994*). Our plan was to make a long traverse over the east ridge of unclimbed Mt. Eaton continuing along the unclimbed ridge to Mt. Augusta.

Several sources misrepresent the location of Mt. Eaton and incorrectly state that it was previously climbed. Canadian and USGS maps correctly show the summit directly overlooking the lower Seward Glacier, the main corridor between the icefields and the coast. The only known previous attempt was by our team in 1993. After starting the climb, we realized we could not complete the traverse to Mt. Augusta in a short weather window, so we stashed surplus supplies and shifted our aims to the summit of Mt. Eaton only.

On May 10, from our high camp on an exposed foresummit at ca 8,700', we took a little over five hours to cover the 3km to the main summit of Eaton, as we climbed over false summits, huge mushroom-domes, and undulating corniced ridge. On top, the GPS read 10,946' (3,336m), which corresponds well with the 3,320m contour on the Canadian map. Ahead, the 5km or so to Mt. Augusta looked similarly straightforward, although undoubtedly foreshortened. Conditions were clear but windy. As we started our descent, clouds descended with us. By the time we reached our foresummit highcamp, Derek was too tired to go further. I consoled myself with the forecasted day of additional good weather. However, during the night, wind-blown snow half-buried our tent. We packed and began to descend, but found ourselves groping in almost total whiteout—untenable in the crevassed and corniced terrain. We climbed back up to the foresummit and re-pitched the tent.

We had one day of spare food, but in the ensuing nightmare we became trapped for the next eight days. During that time, 20' or more of snow fell at our camp. We had to keep the tent mostly sealed from weather, so could not safely use the stove and relied on melting water in our sleeping bags. We tried a snow cave, but found the speed of burial even more alarming. We made a second attempt to descend on May 15, which served only to demonstrate the thigh-deep snow and our weakened ability to cope. We concluded our only prudent option was to raise an emergency with Kluane National Park. An impressive effort was launched on our behalf, but to little avail.

Late on May 16 I listened intently as Craig McKinnon in the park office set out the grim forecast. We mentally prepared ourselves for a hungrier and more wearing round of blizzards and burials—a definitive clearance was potentially another five days away. After our eighth stormy night, on May 19, the morning dawned clear and calm. At around 6:45 a.m., rescuers Dion Parker and Scott Stewart landed a helicopter next to us, and some edgy navigation around rapidly building clouds brought us to Haines Junction and the greeting, "Are you the back-from-the-dead climbers?". It was several more days before the weather settled and our base camp could be retrieved. 🔲

PAUL KNOTT, *New Zealand*

[This page, top] Looking down the east ridge of Mt. Augusta toward Mt. Eaton, as seen from the north ridge of Mt. Augusta. (A) Mt. Foresta. (B) Mt. Seattle. (C) Mt. Cook. (S) the ca 8,700' foresummit leading to the summit of (D) Mt. Eaton [the summit above the clouds between Mt. Augusta and Mt. Cook]. (E) Mt. Owen. (F) Point 3,440m [unnamed subsidary summit on Augusta's east ridge]. (G) North spur of Mt. Augusta [Knott's ca 10,500 highpoint on this ridge lies just out of view, left]. *Paul Knott* [This page, bottom] Mt. Augusta (A) and Mt. Eaton (B) from the lower Seward Glacier. On Mt. Augusta, the east ridge faces the camera and sweeps to the right behind Mt. Eaton. On Mt. Eaton, the south/southwest ridge is visible on the left; the east ridge on the right lies out of frame. *Paul Knott*

[This page, left] The south face of Lowell Peak showing the line of ascent. *Peter Dronkers* [This page, right] The north ridge of Alverstone NE5. *Peter Dronkers*

Lowell Peak, south face; Alverstone NE5, north ridge. In early April, Jonathan Crabtree, Charles Parr, Eli Sturm, and I explored a portion of Canada's St. Elias Range, located within Kluane National Park. Our primary objective was the south face of Lowell Peak (11,910', known as Pinnacle W4 on some maps). This mountain had been climbed twice before, by the east face to north ridge (Stainier-Rodden, *AAJ 1994*) and by the west ridge (Hesleden-Richardson, *AAJ 2008*)—when an attempt was also made on the unclimbed south face.

Landing on the Upper Dusty Glacier we established base camp hastily to take advantage of good weather. [*This east-west glacier is called Lowell Glacier on some maps and is bordered by prominent peaks on all sides. The team established their base camp on this glacier approximately four miles north of Mt. Kennedy (13,905). Of the two peaks climbed, Lowell Peak is located along the northern side of this glacier and Alverstone NE5 is located along the southern side.*] The plan was for Eli and Charles to climb Lowell's west ridge while Jonathan and I climbed the south face; they would leave wands in place to help aid our descent.

Jonathan and I left camp the next morning with two days of food and fuel and light bivy gear. Eli and Charles left shortly after. We navigated an icefall, climbing serac walls along the way, before arriving at a small plateau beneath the face. The bergschrund crossing was straightforward, and from here we climbed a short gully to the top of a rock outcropping where we cached most of our protection and one of the ropes. The rock quality was terrible and there was no ice to be found; we realized that the climb would be entirely on steep snow and névé. We crested the summit ridge a few hundred yards from the top, which we reached by early evening; however, there was no sign of Eli and Charles. We decided to downclimb our ascent route unroped that same day, despite being somewhat knackered, and arrived at base camp 14 hours after leaving. Minutes later Parr and Sturm returned from their attempt, reporting a high point about halfway up the mountain.

Two days later, Jonathan and I attempted a subsidary peak east of Mt. Lowell, but we were defeated a couple of hundred meters short of the summit due to high winds, tedious and loose rock, and not having a rope.

A few days later Jon and I made an ascent of a peak approximately three miles northeast of Mt. Alverstone (14,565') called Alverstone NE5. We climbed the peak's stunning north ridge, encountering steep snow fluting, a short ice pitch, and an exposed ridge traverse that made the route more technical—but probably less dangerous—than Lowell. We downclimbed the route, placing protection, and arrived at base camp 12 hours after leaving. From our research, this is likely the first ascent of the peak. Our team thanks the American Alpine Club and the Alaska Alpine Club for grant funding which made this expedition possible. 📷 🔍

PETE DRONKERS, USA

COAST MOUNTAINS

Southwestern British Columbia, summary. After a couple of slow years, there seems to be an upswing of interest in new routes in southwestern B.C., including several new winter lines.

In late February 2013, Bruce Kay and Damien Kelly climbed Fire Ball (500m, WI5 M5) on the west face of Mt. Athelstan, north of the established summer climbs. The mountain is located 50km northwest of Pemberton and required an extensive approach as the roads were buried under deep snow, leading to a 45km snowmobile approach plus 1,000m of steep skinning through forest to reach the base of the climb.

A new gondola provided renewed interest in the Sky Pilot group near Squamish. New routes included Escape Velocity (7 pitches, 5.9) on Mt. Habrich by Jeremy Frimer and Matt Parker, and a new summer route (5 pitches, 5.10a) and winter route (300m, WI3) on the north face of Sky Pilot Mountain, both established solo by Marc-Andre Leclerc. The summer line was climbed as part of a massive solo-in-a-day enchainment that Leclerc began by onsighting the Wonderful Thing About Tiggers (7 pitches, 5.11a) on the Fluffy Kitten Wall below Mt. Habrich's north face.

Across the Squamish River, in the Tantalus Range, Marc-Andre Leclerc soloed a new route on the east face of Lydia Mountain under early-winter conditions in late October (300m, M4/5). Later in the winter, Carl Kohnstamm and Martin Schuster did the first winter ascent of the northeast ridge of Niobe Peak. Further up the Squamish River, in mid-winter, Conny Amelunxen and Tennessee Trent took advantage of a window of stable conditions and high snow levels to climb a long gully route on the southeast face of Icecap Peak (1,300m, WI4 M4).

In the Joffre Group near Pemberton, in mid-summer 2013, Alistair Davis and Jason Ammerlaan climbed the new route Native Copper (250m, D+ 5.10+) on the north face of Mt. Joffre. This route took on the previously unclimbed rock pillar between the Joffre Couloir and the Central Couloir. Joffre's north face has a reputation for loose blocks, but the climbers reported mostly solid rock.

In July, Marc-Andre Leclerc completed a solo, in-a-day linkup of the North Rib and Northeast Buttress on Mt. Slesse (a.k.a. Slesse Mountain), for a total of about 6,000' of climbing. Both routes have been soloed many times before, but this is the first time Slesse had been soloed by two routes in a day. Leclerc climbed both routes earlier to familiarize himself with the terrain. Guy Edwards and John Millar had previously completed a large linkup by simul-soloing the east ridge of Mt. Rexford (across the valley from Slesse), descending to Nesakwatch Creek, and then soloing the Northeast Buttress of Slesse. This involved significantly more total distance on the ground but much less technical climbing.

On Vancouver Island, two new winter routes were established: the northwest face of Rugged

Mountain (700m, WI3), by Henrik Hinkkala and Hunter Lee, and Third Time's A Charm (1,000m, WI3) on the east face of Mt. Colonel Foster, by Patrick Parker and Ryan van Horne. Both climbs were multiday undertakings during a long cold, clear spell in January–February 2014. During the same cold snap, Lee and Mike Shives made what was probably only the third ascent of Directissima (1,000m, WI4 M4/5, Bajan-Nichol, 1978), also on Mt. Colonel Foster.

Finally, in mid-February Will Gadd and partners John Freeman, Sarah Huenkiken, and Katie Bono established the longest and most sustained route yet at Helmcken Falls, a large cave located in Wells Gray Provincial Park. Gadd called the route Overhead Hazard (200m, 7 pitches, M11/M13+)

DREW BRAYSHAW, *Canada, with additional information from reports at Gripped.com*

WADDINGTON RANGE

Mt. Bute, west face, Foweraker-Serl, first free ascent. I first became aware of Mt. Bute several years ago, when a team of three climbers from Squamish succeeded in establishing a monstrous 50-pitch ridge climb: School of Rock (Kay-Martinello-Sinnes, AAJ 2010). After their trip they noted the free-climbing possibilities on the west face.

The west face was first climbed in 1986 by Greg Foweraker and Don Serl; it received a second ascent three days later by Fred Beckey, Kit Lewis, and Jim Nelson. Since then, the line had seen one repeat, in 2010 by a Canadian team, who tried to free the line but were thwarted by a wet July snowstorm; nevertheless, they described the west face as better than Half Dome or Lotus Flower Tower. [*Most recently, in 2011, Jim Martinello and Dean Potter, along with Mikey Schaefer, free-climbed the west face during a National Geographic–funded expedition, following a line that starts on the Foweraker-Serl route and then continues further to the left.*]

Inspired by these efforts, Madaleine Sorkin and I flew into Mt. Bute in mid-August, landing on a tiny spot in the glacial moraine below the west face. After scoping the route and deciding to bring ice axes and puffy jackets, but no stove or bivy gear, we set alarms for early the following morning. After a short glacial crossing, Madaleine led the first block, which featured some run-out corners and poorly protected, closed-off seams, linked by unlikely face traverses that prevented several near dead-ends. I then took us up a major corner system in the middle of the route, climbing world-class granite, with good protection, and enough wide climbing to keep us warm as the weather began to deteriorate. After climbing three-quarters of the route, we had yet to see pitons or slings from the pendulums used by prior teams.

Madaleine took the lead again below a steep, thin corner, which we hoped was the original line. She onsighted the pitch (5.11+/5.12-), and then I swung through and led up more steep 5.11 terrain, finding amazing face holds up an overhang between the two corner systems where other teams had previously pendulumed to switch corners; higher up, I clipped an old piton from a previous ascent. A couple more pitches got us to the summit via excellent 5.10 terrain, and we topped out amid rapidly deteriorating conditions.

Despite having ice axes, we opted to forego the unknown glacial descent in the dark and building cloud layer, and rappelled the route instead. We spent that night in a perfect bivy cave on the face that had been used by the first ascent team. It began raining as soon as we tossed our rappel ropes the following morning, and it proceeded to rain for the better part of the next week.

After enduring many tent-bound days, we hiked out the Galleon Creek drainage to the west, aiming for saltwater at the head of Bute Inlet. (Don Serl calls this a "legendary bushwhack.") After

[This page, left] The west face of Mt. Bute, showing the Foweraker-Serl route, which was free-climbed by Blake Herrington and Madaleine Sorkin at 5.11+/5.12-. The Martinello-Potter route climbs a line left of the one shown. *Blake Herrington* [This page, right] Madaleine Sorkin following a pitch high on Mt. Bute. *Blake Herrington*

two days we stumbled onto a trail that led us to Homathko Camp, an outpost at the mouth of the Homathko River, where we were fed and hosted by homesteaders Chuck and Sheron Burchhill. They radioed for a floatplane, and we were back in Campbell River by noon. 📷

BLAKE HERRINGTON, *USA*

Mt. Waddington, McNerthney Pillar, second ascent; Bicuspid Tower, west face, On a Recky. In July, Ben Kunz, Tim Halder, and I enjoyed nine days of impeccable weather in the Waddington Range. Our primary objective was the McNerthney Pillar (McNerthney-McNerthney,1986) on the northern flanks of Mt. Waddington.

Our pilot, Mike King, allowed us to drop all our base camp gear at Sunny Knob first, then fly up to the Waddington-Combatant Col with our climbing gear. This highly recommended maneuver saved us a full day of approaching via the Tiedemann Icefall, where seracs pose an objective hazard.

At the base of the McNerthney Pillar we were excited and humbled by the 700m climb: The pillar would offer climbing similar to the Alaska Range, with complexities involving rock, snow, and ice. We were lucky to find ledges for bivouacs and reached the northwest summit of Waddington in two and half days. After a flat bivy up high, we descended the northeast face to the Bravo Glacier to our base camp on the fourth day.

Following our climb, Ben and I went up the Stiletto Glacier to get a closer look at potential new lines on Dentiform. This exploratory mission took a big shift as I started mapping out a series of cracks and corners on the bone-white west face of Bicuspid Tower. We soon ditched our tools and boots at the base of the tower and climbed six pitches of flawless cracks, establishing a new line to the right of existing routes: On a Recky (240m, IV 5.11). The second and sixth pitches proved to be the cruxes, requiring tricky sequences up thin cracks and seams, while the third pitch offered

[This page, left] A foreshortened view of the 800' west face of Bicuspid Tower, showing: (1) Routine Brain Surgery [Cassels-Menitove, 2004]. (2) Life in the Fast Lane [Nicholson-O'Connell, 2007]. (3) On a Recky [Kunz-Sambataro, 2013]. *Joe Sambataro* [This page, right] The northern aspect of Mt Waddington. The McNerthney Pillar ascends the obvious rock pillar. *Joe Sambataro*

exhilarating splitter jamming. After reaching the south summit of this twin-topped tower, we rapped down and reached camp just after dark. Other potential lines exist on the face, which makes a stellar single-day outing from Sunny Knob.

After sleeping in the next day, we scrambled up to the Plummer Hut for a look at the climbing above the Upper Tellot Glacier. We enjoyed simul-climbing moderate terrain to the top of Serra One. Satiated, we returned to Sunny Knob later that day and packed up to fly out on the ninth day of perfect weather, just before a storm came in the following week. 📷 🔍

JOE SAMBATARO, *USA*

REVELSTOKE

Victor Lake Wall, new routes. The steep, 365m-high, south-facing wall directly above Victor Lake, 15km west of Revelstoke, B.C., got its first route in 2007, when Dean Flick from Revelstoke completed the Mission after nearly 10 years of work. Since then the

[This page] Alex Geary following the exposed pitch 11 of Mystery, a new route on the Victor Lake Wall. *Ruedi Beglinger*

featured quartzite wall has sprouted nine routes up to 13 pitches long. Two recently established routes, Mystery and Grand Finale, are some of the best on the wall, and Mystery is among the hardest multi-pitch sport climbs in British Columbia.

Jonas Gessler and I did the first complete ascent of Mystery (13 pitches, 5.12c) in September. The name came from pushing the new route ground up, bolting on lead, unsure of what we'd find. Mystery is the most sustained route in Revelstoke, with five pitches in the 5.11 range and two in the upper 5.12 range. It's a pure sport route, linking a natural line up steep, compact rock, and offers incredible climbing.

The newest addition is the 11-pitch Grande Finale (5.12d), which Alex Geary and I established in October. The name came from the final two pitches, which lead directly over a large overhang at the top of the wall. Grand Finale is sustained in the 5.10 to 5.11 range, with a section of hard 5.11 climbing and a short section of hard 5.12. Most of the route is bolted, but gear placements are needed. 🔲 🔍

RUEDI BEGLINGER, *Canada*

PURCELL MOUNTAINS

Hall Peak, east face, Upper Ramp. In August 2013, Evan Reimondo and I spent seven days in the remote Leaning Tower group in the southern Purcell Mountains. [*The Leaning Tower group is located south of the Bugaboos and is home to impressive granite walls on Hall Peak (a.k.a. Leaning Tower), The Pulpit, Block Tower, Wall Tower, and others*]. After a three-day approach lengthened by road washouts, we finally set up a base camp beneath Hall Peak's east face.

The first day, we climbed the central north face of Hall Peak (II 5.6 80°) and descended the north ridge. The next day, we climbed a new route on Hall Peak's east face via the upper of two large ramps that cut the face: Upper Ramp (1,700', IV 5.9 A1). We started climbing a dirty chimney (5.7) to access several pitches of easy climbing across a large bowl at the base of the face. Above this, four or five pitches of fun, well-protected climbing in an arching corner system (5.7–5.9) gained the base of the upper ramp. (Lichen and dirt-filled cracks caused us to aid two short portions up high, but the route would likely go free at 5.9 with a little cleaning.) Three more pitches of slab climbing

[This page] The east face of Hall Peak (a.k.a. Leaning Tower) showing the approximate line of the first ascent (McComb-Myers-Twomey, 1975) on the left and the new route Upper Ramp on the right. The prominent summit to the left is the Pulpit. *Ryan Leary*

(5.7–5.9) on the ramp led to Hall Peak's east buttress, and then two more easy pitches gained the summit ridge.

This is the second documented route on Hall Peak's east face [*see Canadian Alpine Journal 59 for the other*]. There is enormous potential for new routes in this area. Special thanks to the AAC's Mountaineering Fellowship Grant for helping to make this trip possible.

RYAN LEARY, *USA*

BUGABOOS

Snowpatch Spire, east face, East Columbian. A system to the right of Hobo's Haven on Snowpatch Spire's Tom Egan Wall had long been eyed from Applebee Camp. Cody Lank and I succeeded in climbing this new line in 2012: East Columbian (4 pitches, 5.12).

The blank first pitch was the key to unlocking this aesthetic line. After two days of hand-drilling on lead, we had placed six bolts on the 5.10 slab, which granted access to the beautiful overhanging hand crack above. This second pitch went onsight at 5.11+. The pitch above was more complex, as the hand-sized crack tapered to nothing. Where it blanked out, some edges out right looked inviting and eventually led us to a steep hand crack and the end of the pitch (5.12). (We came back later and hand-drilled another bolt to facilitate the crack switch.) After a short section of 5.8 we joined Hobo's Haven and finished on the Power of Lard.

CHRIS BRAZEAU, *Canada*

Snowpatch Spire, north face, the Dark Prince. In the summer of 2008 Paul McSorley casually mentioned a line he had scoped on the north face of Snowpatch Spire, starting about 40m right of Sunshine Crack. [*The un-freed Hell or Highwater (8 pitches 5.11 A2, Langsford-Moorhead, 2007) climbs between these two lines.*] Since it was just a short stroll from Applebee Camp, I was easily convinced to have a closer look. A good effort on our first attempt that year got us to the top of the crux sixth pitch (5.12-). We had two pitches and plenty of light left, but there were friends back in camp, and it was happy hour, so down we went.

Five years later I finally climbed the final two pitches and scrubbed the route for the send,

[This page] Paul McSorley starting up the fourth-pitch splitter crack of the Dark Prince on Snowpatch Spire. *Chris Brazeau*

climbing it with Jon Simms. Many different partners had helped bring the line to fruition: the Dark Prince (8 pitches, 5.12-).

Chris Brazeau, *Canada*

Snowpatch Spire, west face, Wile Flowers. "Wile: devious or cunning stratagems employed in manipulating or persuading someone to do what one wants." To an outside observer, it would seem that Chris Brazeau was using powers of persuasion in lining up our rock climbing adventure for the day. The truth is, both of us were equally intrigued by the prospect of a new line, and one should blame the events of my first day in the Bugaboos on the cosmic forces of the gleaming granite and a bluebird August day, not on the wily Canadian.

From below, it was obvious that a prominent, unclimbed dihedral system sliced the west face of Snowpatch Spire, just to the left of the Great Chimney. Chris was certain this system had never been climbed.

Up, up, and away! We blasted off from the snow onto a glorious gray-granite finger splitter. This entry pitch was not new, having been established by Topher Donahue and Patience Gribble (Tower Arête, 5.11). The next pitch approached the dihedral via wandering through ledges, blocks, and flowers (5.8). I stopped 50m up, beneath a gleaming right-facing corner, the bait that had lured us here. Slammed shut. I might have sworn. I might have giggled. Just another one of the many cracks and dihedral systems that *look* like they will provide when viewed through my wily camera's zoom.

I waited for Chris to arrive, handed him the rack, and gave him a pat on the back. "I think it will go." Or maybe I said, "*I think it will go?*" He headed up for a closer look: no bueno. Not wanting to spoil the fun or momentum, we started looking around. Chris headed right, from below the blank corner, reaching an overlap with some flakey holds on a pillar. It looked spicy but provided the just-good-enough edge or two, finishing with a granite hueco. I led the next pitch, gardening my way up a beautiful left-facing, widening hand crack that paralleled the dihedral system.

Chris took the next wide hands and fists splitter, a burly and radical pitch, with a thoughtful finish stepping left. This landed us back into the dihedral system to our left. The final pitch was mine, and I must admit: I wanted out. I headed up a short ways, but the flaring crack was too intimidating, so I veered sharp right, foot-traversing up a sketchy layback flake. With ridiculous rope drag, I stepped onto moderate terrain above the flake, taking the route to the summit ridge.

It was fun climbing but far from direct, a wily climb but not a wild climb, not what we expected but exactly what we were looking for: Wile Flowers (IV 5.12).

Quinn Brett, *USA*

[This page] The line of Wile Flowers on the west face of Snowpatch Spire. *Quinn Brett*

CANADIAN ROCKIES

Canadian Rockies, summary. In early September, Sonnie Trotter climbed a new route Castles in the Sky (5 pitches, 5.14a) on Castle Mountain. The route, which he established with Sam Eastman, took 10 days to redpoint and ascends an overhanging prow on the lower limestone band of the mountain, topping out on the large, flat shelf called the Goat Plateau.

In November, Maurice Perreault and Colin Bissonnette climbed a moderate new mixed route on the north face of Mt. Hurd, located in the Ottertail Valley, outside of Field, BC. Lost in the Mountain (9 pitches, WI3 M3) climbs up an icy gully just right of the only other route on this face, Playboy Bunny, established by Perreault in 2011

In the final week of November, Raphael Slawinski and Ian Welsted climbed a new route on the northeast aspect of Mt. Kidd, which they called Bigg Kidd (150m, WI5 M7+). The route ascends a steep and discontinuous ribbon of ice on Kidd's highest rock band and involves a sustained section of steep drytooling.

In early March 2014, Jay Mills and Steve Holeczi established a new mixed climb on Loder Peak that they called Coire Dubious (600m, M5). The line climbs just left of Doors of Perception (600m, M6), and was established ground up with no bolts or fixed protection.

Compiled from information provided by Raphael Slawinski and reports from Gripped.com

Twins Tower, Blanchard-Cheesmond, second ascent. Fewer than a handful of people I know have expressed interest in climbing Twins Tower. Not wanting to miss good conditions, thanks to a low snow year and hot summer, I went out on a limb and asked Josh Wharton. I was surprised when he said yes and immediately bought a plane ticket from Denver to Calgary. A high-pressure system settled into place as he stepped off the plane.

The next morning, September 9, we headed up the Icefield Parkway and hiked over Woolley Shoulder with light packs. We expected to find the food and fuel cache that Josh had left at the Lloyd McKay Hut in 2011. A friend had confirmed it was looking good two weeks earlier; tragically, though, the latest entry in the hut logbook, dated September 1, read, "Thanks for the grub, Josh." Only slim pickings remained. As Josh's note said he'd be back in 2012, we could hardly blame anybody but ourselves, and we accepted the fact that light and fast had just gotten lighter and faster! Our remaining food totaled 5,000 calories apiece.

We left the hut at 5 a.m. on Sep 10, and by 10:30 a.m. we were on the first pitch of the Blanchard-Cheesmond route on the North Pillar (*AAJ 1986*). By the second pitch, Josh wasn't sure if he was psyched anymore. A lot of the climbing was chossy and the gear marginal, with just enough to keep us pushing upward. For the remainder of the climb we would be on the edge of our risk-tolerance levels. At 9 p.m. we found a bivy site on "Ice Ledge," just below the headwall. The headwall turned out to be impressively steep, and we began to haul the packs more than climb with them the following day. Fortunately the rock quality improved. Continuous crack systems, often connected by gymnastic face moves, led through vertical to overhanging terrain for 12 pitches before we bivied one pitch from the top of the wall.

The morning of Sep 12, we dispatched the final headwall pitch via a wild climax. Only 15m below the lower-angled summit ridge, we were forced to aid 4m up a knifeblade seam above a ledge (the only aid on the route for us, and possibly free at 5.12-). This gained a run-out jug traverse across the lip of an overhang. The rest of the route was fairly straightforward, and after traversing some cornices we reached the summit around 4 p.m. on September 13. We crossed the Columbia Icefield toward the Cromwell-Stutfield Col and bivied. On September 14 we rappelled and downclimbed for six hours, continued hiking, and reached the car at 3:30 p.m.

In hindsight, climbing Twins Tower was a great and satisfying experience for both of us. It would be hard to recommend to anyone unless you're looking for a huge physical and mental adventure. The conditions we found were absolutely perfect. Visibility was unlimited, freezing levels stayed above 3,500m the entire time, and there was virtually no natural rockfall. We found the rock generally dry. *[Editor's note: Only three parties previously had climbed the 1,500m north side of Twins Tower: in 1974, 1985, and the winter of 2004. The first ascent of the North Pillar was made by Barry Blanchard and David Cheesmond in 1985 at a difficulty of 5.10 A2. Walsh and Wharton upped the ante by adding a variation start to the right of the original route and freeing all but a 4m section of the route and proposed a grade of 5.11b R/X A1.]*

JON WALSH, *Canada*

BAFFIN ISLAND

AUYUITTUQ NATIONAL PARK

Gauntlet Peak, Violett's Rige; Mt. Turnweather, north buttress, Butter Knife Ridge and south buttress attempt. During a trip to Mt. Asgard in 2012, my brother Joshua Lavigne noticed the imposing 900m north face of Mt. Turnweather. After seeing photos of the route Dry Line (Condon-Prohaska, *AAJ 1999*), we decided to make a return trip with the intentions of free climbing the route.

Joshua and I made a quick trip to Auyuittuq National Park from July 16 to August 2. We first ferried our gear to the base of Turnweather, then set up camp on the glacier below. We quickly realized that the wall would need more time to dry after a snowy and cool spring. In unsettled weather, we managed to climb a short and aesthetic new line on nearby Gauntlet Peak: Violett's Ridge (400m, 5.9).

In the coming weeks, Dry Line never fully dried. Refocusing our attention, we first tried the south buttress. We climbed 600m of new terrain ground-up, with free climbing up to 5.12 R,

[This page] Jon Walsh leading typical mixed terrain on Twins Tower. *Josh Wharton*

but retreated before an incoming storm. Fifteen hours of rain and warmer temperatures saturated the wall, making free climbing unlikely.

With a week's worth of food remaining we decided to try establishing a first ascent on the northwest aspect of Mt. Turnweather. During our ascent of an unknown peak on the north end of Turnweather Glacier, we had spied a reasonably accessible route to the summit of Turnweather on what we deemed the "north buttress." We hoped to climb about 500m of snow and ice up a couloir to reach a 400m granite headwall above; however, during our 16-hour ascent, we were forced out of the couloir and onto a broken face left of the north buttress in order to safely avoid a shooting gallery of falling rocks.

The first half dozen pitches ascended wet and broken terrain up to 5.8. Higher up, we gained a prominent ridge leading to the imposing upper headwall. This provided us with all that one would hope for in a first ascent: exposure, solid granite, long pitches, good belays, and free climbing up to 5.12: The Butter Knife Ridge (900m, 5.12 AI3). From the top, we made a relatively easy descent down a couloir, using a handful of rap stations left behind by a recent Italian ascent. 📷

DELANO LAVIGNE, *Canada*

Mt. Asgard, south face, Scott-Hennek route; Mt. Loki, southeast ridge. In March, Rueben Shelton and I shipped 200 pounds of food and climbing gear to our outfitter Peter Kilabuk in Pangnirtung, which he snowmobiled to a cache near Summit Lake prior to our arrival. Rueben and I arrived in Pangnirtung on July 3, and Kilabuk motored us up the fjord to the drop-off point with one backpack each. Our light and fast program was in full swing.

Over the next two days we backpacked up the Weasel Valley. By midday on July 5 we reached the shelter at Summit Lake and breathed a sigh of relief to find our five boxes of essentials intact. Three days later, on July 9, we set off from camp at 4 a.m. with daypacks and a few snacks, and by 9 a.m. we were at the base of the south side of Mt. Asgard, hoping to repeat the Scott-Hennek route.

[This page, left] Gauntlet Peak, showing the new route Violett's Ridge. *Delano Lavigne* [This page, right] Mt. Turnweather's northern aspect showing the line of the Butter Knife Ridge on the left skyline of the tower. The approach to the ridge is shown by the dashed line. *Delano Lavigne*

Mark Synnott calls this "one of the most classic long free routes on the planet," and as we stood on the summit at 5:30 p.m., after 20-plus pitches of splendid free climbing, we had to agree. We rappelled the route and arrived back at base camp after 26 hours on the go.

After some poor weather, we left camp again on July 16, intent on a new route on Mt. Loki. Our day began at 3 a.m. with thigh-deep wading across the frigid, churning creek near camp to reach the Turner Glacier. At 9 a.m. we set off up a nice crack system just left of the very toe of the southeast ridge. The climbing was fantastic. After a few opening pitches we veered to the crest of the ridge, following it for the remainder of the route. The first section of the climb followed a steep, clean, and dry right-facing corner system, with continuous 5.8–5.10 jams and laybacks for about 800'. This section was capped by a sandy ledge and a short section of tricky 5.10 climbing, which led to easier ground.

From this point we gazed up at an orange false summit and also got a clear view of the south buttress route to our left. The single rope-length of climbing on the orange wall would define our route: a perfect 5.10 crack, narrowing from chimney-size to fingers. Easier ground brought us to the summit of Mt. Loki at 5:30 p.m. (20+ pitches, 5.10+).

We made eight rappels off the north side, aiming for a snowy col and ramp system on the east side of the peak. However, what we'd hoped would be an "easy ramp" turned into many hours of sketchy, character-building downclimbing to return to the Turner Glacier. We arrived back at camp after 27 hours away.

DAVE NETTLE, *USA*

[This page, left] Rueben Shelton ascends clean splitter cracks on Loki's southeast ridge below the prominent orange headwall. *Dave Nettle* [This page, right] Mt. Loki from the Turner Glacier, showing the approximate location of the south buttress route on the left and the new route on the southeast ridge [Nettle-Shelton, 2013] on the right. Dave Nettle and Rueben Shelton descended the right skyline to the snowy ramp system. *Dave Nettle*

GREENLAND

WEST GREENLAND

Ummannaq region, The Horn, Cosmic Rave and Choss, The Universe, and Everything; Ummannaq, Islands in the Sky; Ivnarssuaq Great Wall, The Incredible Orange; various other routes. From June into August, the Oxford West Greenland Expedition combined a major sailing voyage with adventurous climbing in the Ummannaq area, putting up five big new routes and a number of minor routes, including first ascents of two previously unclimbed faces. Peter Hill, Angela Lilienthal, Clive Woodman, and I sailed from Montreal to Greenland in five weeks, and met Ian Faulkner and Jacob Cook in Aasiaat.

The team achieved a double success on its first objective, the Horn, a striking coastal headland on the northeast spur of Upernivik Island. First, Peter and I climbed Choss, The Universe, and Everything (1,200m, E2/XS 5c) in a 42-hour single-push round trip. We climbed the right-hand lower face and discovered secret (and occasionally loose!) ways around the main difficulties of the upper headwall. After 24 hours of climbing we bagged part of the summit ridge before descending the route.

A few days later, Ian and Jacob made the first ascent of the main headwall with Cosmic Rave (1,000m, E6 6b), an uncompromisingly direct line that followed a previous attempt by Matt

Burdekin and George Ullrich (*AAJ 2011*). Ian and Jacob fixed to 300m, placing one bolt, before pushing to the top and descending via Choss, The Universe, and Everything.

The team then endured a storm in base camp, as our yacht, Cosmic Dancer, struggled with engine problems. The storm caused massive rockfall, which chopped every one of our fixed ropes and sent rocks bounding past the tents into the sea.

In Ummannaq, we managed to buy a couple of ropes from a departing Irish expedition. Unfortunately, they stank of semi-digested fish, after being

[This page] The Horn on Upernavik Island. (1) Cosmic Rave. (2) Choss, The Universe, and Everything. *Tom Codrington*

[This page, left] Ian Faulkner about 1,100m up Cosmic Rave on the Horn. *Jacob Cook* [This page, right] The Incredible Orange on Ivnarssuaq Great Wall. The climbers walked off via the plateau to the left. *Tom Codrington*

thoroughly soaked in fulmar vomit during one of their climbs. After a rest we set about the second ascent of Ummannaq Northwest via a new route. [*The summit was reached in 2010 by Burdekin and Ulrich.*] Ian and I climbed the lower tier before rain forced us to retreat down a scree gully. Two days later, Jacob, Peter, and I returned up the scree gully to extend the line to the summit. Islands in the Sky (810m, E4 6a) was named for a stunning cloud inversion.

We next investigated an area around Ikerasak, southeast of Ummannaq. There, Ian and I spotted a line on Ivnarssuaq Great Wall, a plumb-vertical face rising straight out of the sea, opposite Ikerasak on the Nugssuaq peninsula. The Incredible Orange (800m, E3 5c) provided extremely steep and sustained climbing. We opted for a pure alpine approach, bivouacking twice on the route. The wall turned out to be a huge pillar, connected to the mainland by a rickety natural bridge.

Meanwhile, Jacob and Peter had a terrible time on Umanatsiaq Mountain, above Ikerasak, due to loose rock. Their first attempt saw Jacob accompanying a foothold as it parted ways with the cliff on pitch two, injuring his ankle. A few days later they completed Flake or Death (200m, XS 5b), with the rock quality varying from loose to extremely loose.

Just before returning to Aasiaat and laying up the boat for the winter, Peter, Jacob, and Ian established That Sinking Feeling (300m, E5 5c), up a striking knifeblade feature on the Nugssuaq peninsula, east of Ivnarssuaq. The route offered good climbing but little protection. It was also connected to the mainland via an exciting bridge.

The expedition was a huge success, thanks in large part to generous financial support from the Irvine Fund, BMC, MEF, Gino Watkins Memorial Fund, Alpine Club, Arctic Club, and the Andrew Croft Memorial Fund. 🔘

Tom Codrington, *U.K.*

EAST GREENLAND

LIVERPOOL LAND

Storefjord region, various ascents. With research indicating there had been no ascents of peaks immediately north and south of the Storefjord, seven members of the Eagle Ski Club visited this area, northeast of the commercial airport at Constable Pynt, in April. Using local agent Nanu Travel, Phillipa Cockman, Stuart Gallagher, Adele Long, Declan Phelan, Howard Pollitt, John Russell, and Dave Wynne-Jones (leader) snowmobiled from Constable Pynt to the ice-covered Storefjord, and then north up a side fjord to a small, wooden hut alongside thermal springs. Polar bears are a threat in the area, and the team took not only a rifle but also a sled dog to act as an alarm.

Although the team included veterans of Denali and Logan, everyone felt the cold more than on any previous trip, despite recorded temperatures never falling below –20°C. For this reason, technical climbing proved out of the question, but soaking cold-damaged feet in the hot springs gave some compensation. The main mountains north of the fjord were steep and rocky, and the spires of the main peak, Kirken (1,209m), would offer challenging rock and mixed climbing at a warmer time of year. The team climbed four modest peaks in this region, enjoying fine ski descents.

The group then moved south across the fjord to the Himmerland Peninsula, and together with the dog reached an 815m summit to the west of the access valley, only to find a small cairn on the top. This was disappointing, as it was the dog's first ascent of the trip.

Unfortunately, they were unable to penetrate a major glacier system to reach the highest summit, Doppeltoppen (1,040m), so decided to move south of Himmerland to the Mariager Fjord and explore its surrounding peaks. Three of the team climbed a fine unnamed 1,100m peak in rather marginal conditions, after which the group made a spectacular journey by snowmobile down the east coast sea ice and back along Scoresby Sund to Constable Pynt. 📷 🔍

LINDSAY GRIFFIN, *MountainINFO, with information from Dave Wynne-Jones, U.K.*

SOUTH GREENLAND

Torssuqatoq Spires, various ascents. On June 24, John Dickey, Prairie Kearney, Lizzy Scully, and I arrived by small powerboat in Torssuqatoq Fjord. The surrounding scenery remained illusive, socked in, but the rain eased as we shuffled loads up the steep, tufty slope to base camp. This beautiful valley lies directly west across iceberg-filled waters from the famous Baron and Baronet, and fits more into alpine than big-wall category.

After a day of snow, the gang headed up valley, finally catching a glimpse of the beautiful walls we had ogled in photos the previous winter. The left ridge of the cirque (running north-south) began with a 550m buttress and culminated with a beautiful knife-edge ridge and a tower, Breakfast Spire, named by a British party in 2000. The right side of the valley was a granite sea of walls and ridges: A Half Dome–esque peak (called the Whale's Back), another peak named Flattop, and yet another, the Great White Spire, extended ca 600m above us. Most of the sheer faces were untouched.

On the fourth day, Prairie, Lizzy, and I blasted off to attempt a new route on the left side of the 550m buttress. The peaks were still spattered with snow—our hope was that the perfect, bluebird day would provide us with mostly dry rock.

Our line, Plenty for Everyone (550m, 5.10+/11-) ascends the southeast arête of Barnes Wall,

[This page] Looking northwest at (A) Barnes Wall, with the American route and the ridge leading north toward Breakfast Spire. (B) El Katxalote (2013 Basque-Spanish route is on opposite side). (C) Navianarpoq and the route Nunatak (Basque-Spanish, 2013). *Quinn Brett*

both names in the spirit of an amazing soul, Andrew Barnes, who died climbing in the Black Canyon while we were on this extravagant journey. It was a classic adventure with a little bit of everything: hand-sized splitters, tiny smears and face holds, loose blocks, a clean right-facing dihedral, and a little wet choss before the summit mantel. We hooted and giggled with elation. First try, we'd succeeded on an unclimbed wall. How cool is that! We made it safely back to base camp about 14 hours after starting. We later discovered that this summit had been reached in 2012 by a large French group, via moderate climbing and scrambling up the south ridge.

After one rest day we set off for the south ridge of Breakfast Spire. The scrambling up the steep, slabby slope to gain the ridge was moderate, while the view of neighboring Shepton Spire was jaw-dropping. We flirted with the gradually steeping south ridge for two long pitches before zagging right onto a ramp. This gained a long and clean 5.7 chimney. From here the climbing zigged back over to the left side of the ridge, where it would remain until the summit-block wrestle. Our eight-pitch route contained two stellar 5.11 stem-box corners, one with an offwidth start and the second opening up into a gorgeous hand crack. If in Colorado, Morning Luxury (420m, 5.11-) would surely be a favorite climb. We rappelled the steep east face of the spire, noting its potential.

Our progress during the rest of our stay was not as successful, as news of Andrew's death had us leaving nine days early. We established two shorter routes on Submarine Wall, a north-facing ridge that tempted us from advanced base. Mind Your Ps and Qs and Four Quickies were both 120m and 5.10. We also failed on a big-wall attempt farther left on Submarine Wall after four beautiful left-trending pitches. We never got another opportunity to finish these lines, but I hope to return to this magical place. So many peaks to ascend! 📷

Quinn Brett, *AAC*

Narsarmijit Valley and Torssuqatoq Spires, various routes; Semersoq Island, Punta Alborán. During July and August, the three-member Spanish-Basque team of Txemari Andrés, Vicente Castro, and Kepa Escribano added five new rock routes in the region of the Torssuqatoq Spires. Andrés and Escribano flew to Narsarsuaq, where they met Castro in his own yacht. From here all three sailed to

[This page] Half Dome/Punta Alborán from the east, showing the only existing route. *Kepa Escribano*

the coastal settlement of Narsarmijit (formerly Frederiksdal), and then made a four-hour walk north up the Narsarmijit Valley to a base camp at ca500m on the west side of the final lake. The very next day, July 30, all three reached the foot of the south-southwest face of Breakfast Spire [*climbed earlier in the season by an American team*] and climbed it in five hours to the west top. There was excellent crack climbing, with the main difficulties in the middle section of the wall. The 375m route, named Marmitako, was graded 6c A1. They descended ledges east of their ascent, then made eight rappels to the foot of the face.

The following morning, the three opted for an easily accessible spire on the ridge between Tikaguta (1,350m) and Navianarpoq. They climbed a 270m route up the east face in five hours,

reaching a tower they dubbed Moskito Spire, and naming their route La Cuadrilla Pika Pika (6b+).

Their next objective was the big southeast face of Navianarpoq (reported by previous parties to be Greenlandic for "dangerous"). The mountain was first climbed in 1996 from the north (AD), and in the following year a British expedition added Steel Drum Idolatry (600m, E3 5c, Benson-Benson) and the Colour of Magic (750m, E2/3 5c, Cool-Powell) to the north face. The Spanish-Basque team started their climb at 6 a.m. on August 4, piecing

[This page] El Diablo leading to Pt. Aiarpoq. *Kepa Escribano* together a line that was often wet in the lower section. They were caught by darkness one pitch below the summit, and spent a long, chilly night on a good ledge, before moving slowly to the top the following morning. They then made a complex descent of the previously unclimbed south ridge. The route was 735m long, completed in 35 hours camp-to-camp, and named Nunatak (7a A1).

On August 7 the three completed their next objective, a peak on the watershed ridge south of Breakfast Spire. The central section of the west face looked steep and hard, so in keeping with their "clean, fast, and no bolts" philosophy, they opted for a prominent slanting line on the right flank. Unexpected difficulties in the upper section of the face slowed progress, but they reached the summit after 10 hours, completing Urrezko Balea (515m of climbing, 6c+ A1). They named the summit El Katxalote. (Some summits on this ridge have been ascended in the past.)

On the 9th, Andrés and Escribano set off for a new route on the wall to the left of Shepton Spire. Following a right-to-left-slanting line, they climbed for nine hours up the southeast face to reach the ridge at a summit, 150m higher than Shepton Spire, that they named Aiarpoq. They rappelled the route through the night, arriving tired and late at camp. The 545m line, which took 15 hours round-trip from the tents, was named El Diablo (6c).

On the 10th all three were back in the harbor. After sailing via Nanortalik, they reached the northern shores of Semersoq Island on August 15. Clearly visible north of Nanortalik, Semersoq has been well explored in the past, though only a few technical routes exist. The team established camp alongside a large glacier lake north of Half Dome (1,060m). In 2003 a six-person British expedition had attempted the north ridge. There is no record of it being climbed since. [*For a condensed history of climbing on this island see AAJ 2004.*]

On the 17th, Andrés and Escribano climbed a continuous crack system directly to the summit in seven cold hours, naming their line Fisuras en la Niebla (300m, 7a). They returned to camp 13 hours after leaving. The British party that first named Half Dome did not make much progress on their attempt, so the Spanish felt justified in giving it a new name: Punta Alborán, after Castro's yacht.

Returning to Nanortalik, Castro sailed back to Europe single-handed, while the other two took the more conventional flight home. 🔲

LINDSAY GRIFFIN, *MountainINFO, from information provided by Kepa Escribano*

A brief history of the Torssuqatoq Spires. The mountains immediately west of Torssuqatoq Sound were not explored until 1975, when a large and productive British expedition from St. Andrews University, led by Phil Gribbin, invaded the area. Its achievements should not be underestimated: Members climbed around 42 new peaks and made a total of 47 new routes up to TD and UIAA V. Activity focused on the area of bigger peaks immediately north of the Torssuqatoq Spires (the latter referred to as the Land of the Towers), making first ascents of summits such as Agdierussakasit (1,763m) and Maujit Qaqarsuassiaq (1,560m; the eastern, seaward side of this peak holds the huge sea cliff sometimes called the Thumbnail). Their furthest foray south was to a summit in the Magic Arrow group, west of Maujit Lake and immediately north of Breakfast Spire.

The spires themselves were not visited until 1996, when Simon Inger's four-man British team placed a base camp at the head of the Narssap Sarqa Fjord immediately west, and climbed a number of peaks, including Navianarpoq (1,550m, AD) and Magic Arrow (1,200m, TD- V+).

The huge potential for hard rock climbing encouraged a second British team to visit in 1997. Andy and Pete Benson, Kenton Cool, and Al Powell made 18 ascents, some of which were major climbs, with technical difficulties of British E3 6a and E4 5c. They noted several fine objectives to the east, notably the southwest ridge of Whaleback (ca 1,200m) but could not access them from their valley. These would have to wait until 2000 and the visit of an eight-member British expedition, which was based in the same valley visited by the Americans in 2013. Several shorter routes were climbed on the south flank of Breakfast Spire's east ridge, before Jon Bracey and Ian Renshaw attempted the impressive 800m east face. A few pitches short of the top, Renshaw fell and broke an ankle. The pair managed to traverse to the east ridge and rappel the shorter north face, and then Renshaw crawled back over a col and eventually was evacuated by helicopter.

In 2010 Bob Shepton anchored in Torssuqatoq Sound, dropping Ben Ditto, Nico and Olivier Favresse, and Sean Villanueva at the mouth of the same valley leading up to Breakfast Spire. Lost in the mist, the four found themselves in the Narsarmijit Valley immediately west, below the unclimbed peak between Navianarpoq and Breakfast Spire. They climbed the south face of this peak by two independent parallel lines, naming the summit Shepton Spire after the skipper, then traversed the long ridge east (D/TD) to Breakfast Spire (*AAJ 2011*).

The summit area of Breakfast Spire has several mini-spires. The one reached by the Americans this year (the south block) and its close neighbor (the north block, most likely the top reached in 2010) are the highest.

LINDSAY GRIFFIN, *MountainINFO*

Torssuqatoq Fjord, Marlulissat (903m), Two Hobbits from the Moon; Qaqaq Eqqamanngilara (ca 950m), Polish Route. In 2007, operating mostly alone and moving around in kayaks, Eliza Kubarska and I climbed a new route, Golden Lunacy, on Maujit Qaqarsuassiaq (*AAJ 2008*). In July 2009 we returned with a film crew to record documentary footage. During that time we climbed three pitches at the foot of a peak named Marlulissat, above Appillattoq village. On August 5 and 6, after the film crew had departed, we completed this climb. The first 250–300m follows slabs and dihedrals on solid rock. We made a bivouac several pitches above the huge terrace crossing the face and watched rain clouds gather on the horizon. With no bivouac sacks or bolt kit, and with friction slabs above, our best option early next morning was to finish the route as fast as possible. We traversed left through a very loose system of rock columns, and topped out at 4 p.m. We named the climb Two Hobbits from the Moon (23 pitches, UIAA VII+, two bolts on the initial section).

[Previous page] David Kaszlikowski in one of the giant chimneys in the upper part of Qaqaq Eqqamanngilara. *Eliza Kubarska* [This page] (1) Polish Route on Qaqaq Eqqamanngilara. (2) Golden Lunacy on Maujit Qaqarsuassiaq; upper part of route and summit are off picture. *David Kaszlikowski*

After a prolonged period of bad weather, we set out on August 17 for an unclimbed summit south of Maujit Qaqarsuassiaq. Our objective, the seaward face, is only accessible by boat. We asked an Inuit friend to drop us and come back in three days. Scrambling through "vertical blueberries," with several roped rock pitches along the way, led for 700m to a large ledge and bivouac under a huge boulder. Next morning we awoke surrounded by clouds, and we were forced to wait before we could see a way up the final 380m wall. Leaving our bivouac equipment, we began climbing toward huge chimneys. Some were over three meters wide, forcing us to climb the side walls. Others were full of large, loose chockstones. Around 200m below the top it began to rain, but we summited at 9 p.m., after climbing 10 pitches that day.

We left a small cairn and began rappelling through the night, placing two bolts for anchors. The Inuit told us the mountain was unnamed, so we decided to call it Forgotten Peak, which translates as Qaqaq Eqqamanngilara. The Polish Route has nearly 1,200m of climbing, with difficulties of VII+ R.

After a controversy in Poland provoked by a book covering our climbs, the Polish Mountaineering Association (PMA) organized an expedition in 2012 to re-climb Golden Lunacy and Two Hobbits from the Moon. After repeating these routes (*AAJ 2013*), the PMA report stated that Golden Lunacy was "seriously overgraded" and Two Hobbits was a "nice route on good rock, though again with several overgraded pitches." [*The original ascents of Two Hobbits and the Polish Route were not reported in the AAJ, hence the details here.*] I accepted this at first, but eventually was able to see their topos. They climbed our crux pitch on Golden Lunacy (VIII+/7a+, with one rest point, as we reported; downgraded to VII+/6c), but it is also clear they didn't climb many of our pitches; in some cases they were as much as 40m from our line. The grade of Golden Lunacy is VIII- (top pitch of our line), or VII+ by the 2012 variants. They also did not follow the exact line of Two Hobbits, especially in the upper section, and "downgraded" sections of virgin rock. In our opinion the verification process was biased. 🖻

DAVID KASZLIKOWSKI, *Poland*

MEXICO

EL POTRERO CHICO

El Sendero Luminoso, solo free ascent. In January 2014, Alex Honnold free-soloed El Sendero Luminoso (V 5.12d), on El Toro, which was established by Jeff Jackson and Kurt Smith in 1994. Eleven of the route's 15 pitches are rated 5.12, making the climb perhaps the most sustained free solo yet completed. Honnold climbed the route in just three hours after rehearsing the line four times with a rope. ▶

Compiled from various sources

PARQUE NACIONAL CASCADA DE BASASEACHIC

The Cascade Wall, Arista de Cascada. Clemens Pischel and I traveled to the Cascada de Basaseachic (Basaseachic Falls) in the beginning of January 2014. Once there, we were absolutely overwhelmed by the fantastic rock walls, forming a natural amphitheater around the 246m waterfall, with almost endless potential for first ascents. [*Several long, hard routes exist on the Cascade Wall, with at least three to the left of the falls and a couple of others to the right, as well as shorter sport routes at the base. Search the AAJ website more info.*]

The ridge to the southeast (right) of the falls rises from the valley floor and diagonals up and left to a small high point above the top of the waterfall. We spent some effort establishing a long free route ground-up on this ridge (up to 5.11b, with a number of easy pitches). We completed the fully bolted line on January 12: Arista de Cascada (16 pitches, 5.11b). Two shorter, bolted routes (about 100m in length), established by Alex Catlin and partners, begin to the left of the start of our route and intersect the ridge we climbed. See Oriol Anglada's *Mexican Rock Climbing Guidebook* for more info. 📷 ▶

KAI MALUCK, *Germany*

[This page] The 246m Basaseachic Falls. Arista de Cascada (16 pitches, 5.11b) climbs the prominent ridge line on the far right side, topping out on the pinnacle above and right of the falls. *Kai Maluck*

El Gigante, Tehué. The initial plan was to go ice climbing in Chile, but just four days before the flight my partner Marta Alejandre seriously injured her knee. I suddenly found myself searching for something to do with my motivation and time.

I decided to go to El Gigante, outside of Chihuahua, since it's adventurous, easy to get to, and I know it well. In 1998 I was lucky enough to make the first ascent of the wall with Luis Carlos Garcia Ayala, establishing Simuchi (1,000m, VI 6c A4), and a year later we returned to establish the wall's second route, Yawira

Batú (750m, VI 6b A4+). [*See AAJ 2003 for Garcia's feature article about the climbing history of El Gigante and elsewhere in the Parque Nacional Cascada de Basaseachic, as well as companion articles in the same edition about other climbs and controversial rappel bolting on the formation.*]

Carlos couldn't come this time around, so I teamed up with 24-year-old Tiny Almada, a strong climber from Chihuahua. Once in Basaseachic, Oscar Cisneros and a couple of others helped us with logistics and carrying equipment to the wall.

Starting on October 8, we fixed the first three pitches of the route, then set off with 12 days of food and water. On day six we were hit by a large rainstorm and forced to stay in our portaledge for the next three days. We stood by and watched as the river below and the nearby waterfall swelled; it was beautiful to feel the strength of nature and witness the transformation of a canyon that feels as if it belongs to another era.

When the storm ended we started climbing again. Above, we found the best pitches of the route. We topped out after 11 days on the wall on October 18. We called the route Tehué (700m, 21 pitches, VI 7a A3).

The route takes a line up the center-left side of the wall and climbs the first pitch of my route Yawira Batú. Additionally, it shares seven pitches with another unknown route that appears to have been established recently. The bottom section of the climb was dirty and contained loose rock, requiring slow aid climbing. The upper section, on the other hand, breaches clean, high-quality rock. We used a variety of clean gear, bolts, and pitons on the climb. 🖸

CECILIA BUIL, *Spain*

[This page] Cecilia Buil running it out, high on Tehué (700m, VI 7a A3). *Tiny Almada*

COLOMBIA

SIERRA NEVADA DEL COCUY

Pan de Azúcar, Corredor Tropical. In January 2013, Santiago Zuluaga and I achieved the first ascent of the remarkable hanging glacier on the northeastern aspect of Pan de Azúcar (ca 5,120m). This route is easily visible from the lake of La Plaza and had seen a couple of previous attempts.

We reached the base of the mountain late on January 26 after a lengthy trek, and after resting briefly we set off at midnight to begin our climb. Low on the route we encountered an ice ramp followed by a large, vertical rocky band (5.9). Gaining the hanging glacier proved difficult, but we managed to surmount it by sunrise. After this we climbed moderate but sustained snow and ice fields, with some vertical sections (AI4). We reached the broad and relatively flat upper glacier by climbing through a band of seracs. The sun began to set as we climbed the last meters up the ramp leading to the summit of Pan de Azúcar. After summiting we headed west down easy glacial terrain to complete a traverse of the mountain.

The total effort lasted 45 hours round-trip, including 18 hours on the wall. We named our route Corredor Tropical (450m, TD 5.9 AI4). The climb is unique for Colombia as it presents a multi-pitch, very steep ice climb in a tropical mountain area, where the attention is usually centered on ascending rock walls. 🅾

JULIO BERMÚDEZ, *Colombia*

[This page] The Sierra Nevada del Cocuy from the northeast. (A) Pico el Diamante. (1) Licantropos (350m, 5.10a, Gomez-Pardo). (B) Pico Campanillas Blanco. (2) Operación Oriente (350m, 5.10c, Hilarion-Macias-Liebert, partially shown). (C) Pan de Azúcar. (3) Five routes ascend this part of the wall, see detail on p. 192. (4) Para Que Te Enamores (450m, 5.11d, Guarderas-Morales-Navarrete. (5) Corredor Tropical (450m, TD 5.9 AI4, Bermúdez-Zuluaga, to main summit). (D) Pico el Toti. (6) Chikara (400m, 5.10b, Bravo-Torres). (7) Aun Queda el Alma (400m, 5.12d A0, Guarderas-Morales-Navarrete). *Luis Pardo*

[This page] Climbing steep terrain on the southeast face of Cóncavo. *Roberto Morales*

Pan de Azúcar, Para Que Te Enamores; Toti, Aun Queda el Alma; Cóncavo, Conspiración Ecuatoriana.
In January 2014, Felipe Guarderas, Nicolas Navarrete, and I put up three new routes in the Cordillera del Cocuy. The park service had closed the east side of the range, forcing us to camp on the west, so we had to do long approaches to most of the walls.

The east face of Pan de Azúcar (ca 5,120m) was our first objective. The wall appeared to have lots of face climbing, but without a power drill any new line might be contrived. After analyzing our options we chose the right side, following nice cracks for the most part, with some runouts. After a day and a half we had completed the route, freeing all the pitches and fixing anchors at every belay. We named it Para Que Te Enamores (450m, V 5.11d). The 10-pitch route is to the right of the previously established routes La Sonrisa (550m, 5.10d), Matando Bacterias (450m 5.10d), and others.

Not wanting to repeat the long approach, we decided to bivy at the base and try free climbing Guerreros de Terracota the next day. We were still tired from the day before, and starting to climb at ca 4,000m on 5.12b, 5.12d, and 5.13b pitches was not easy. After the first three pitches, the sun started to warm up the wall and we were able to move more efficiently. We reached the summit at sunset. Many rappels and a long hike back to base camp kept us busy for the next few hours.

After a couple of days' rest, we focused on the northeast face of Pico el Toti (4,875m). When we got to the base after the long approach from the west, we knew we were in trouble. Huge roofs and a long blank section loomed. Our hand drill and handful of bolts did not seem enough for this objective. We decided to go for an adventure nonetheless and took off on the first pitch.

We found discontinuous cracks through big roofs for the first third of the face. The middle

section was a beautiful face with intermittent horizontal cracks. Felipe had to place a bolt on lead on one of the pitches, but managed to free it after a long struggle. On the last section the roofs continued but cracks also showed up, allowing us to enjoy really hard pitches with good protection.

After a few hundred feet of scrambling we reached the summit in the dark. In all we placed one lead bolt and some at anchors to encourage repeat ascents. We called the 10-pitch route Aun Queda el Alma ("There's Still the Soul Left," 400m, V 5.12d A0) because our single rope had three core shots, but with tape it remained intact. We freed every pitch but one.

After this climb we took many rest days eating and enjoying the sun. Fully recovered, we decided to try one more climb. This time it was the southeast face of Cóncavo. The wall was not as high as our previous climbs but very aesthetic and vertical the whole way. We climbed a mostly independent and free variation to Conspiración Cósmica (200m, IV 5.12b, Gonzalez-Wilke), first climbing left of the previous route, then crossing it three-quarters of the way up and climbing right of that line, directly to the summit.

The first pitch was the hardest, a long and vertical face protected by bolts and pins (5.13a); the second one was easier, with a beautiful dihedral that crossed the previous route high up. The last two pitches climbed slightly overhanging cracks directly to the summit. (5.12+). We called the route Conspiración Ecuatoriana (200m, IV 5.13a). [*Editor's note: Also in January, climber Sebastián Muñoz climbed a 40m variation to the final pitch of Conspiración Cósmica. It ascends a line directly between the two routes mentioned above.*]

Exploration, remote big walls, no other climbers, and lots of uncertainty made this trip a unique adventure. 📷 🔍

ROBERTO MORALES, *Ecuador*

[This page] The east side of Pan de Azúcar. (1) South by Southeast (250m, 5.10a, Curletto-McCalley-Restrepo. (2) Cinco Dias de Soledad (450m, 5.10c, Anderson-Guzman. (3) Guerreros de Terracota (450m, 5.12d A2, Contreras-Cortes-Rodriquez). (4) Matando Bacterias (450m, 5.10d, Arias-Bernal-Moreno-Wilke). (5) La Sonrisa (450m, 5.10c, Morales-Vallejo). (6) Para Que Te Enamores (450m, 5.11d, Guarderas-Morales-Navarrete). *Roberto Morales*

VENEZUELA

Acopan Tepui, east face, Gravity Inversion. In late December 2013, Luis Cisneros, Blake McCord, Joel Unema, and I traveled to the friendly Pemon village of Yunek. From there we hoped to establish a new route on the east face of the Acopan Tepui. Analyzing the formation, we found a weakness on the gently overhanging, red-colored, 2,000' wall a few hundred feet right of Pizza, Chocolate y Cerveza. This was Luis and my second trip to the Tepui, after established Araguato King [*AAJ 2009*].

Starting on December 30 we spent ten days establishing Gravity Inversion (VI 5.12d R). We found some vertical crack systems on the first half of the route. The second half challenged us with horizontal crack systems reminiscent of the Gunks, making for committing, athletic, and often run-out leads. Thankfully, the crux 5.12d pitch allowed passage via a stunning, continuous finger crack that weaved its way through three roofs. Despite an occasional downpour, we stayed dry thanks to the overhanging nature of the climb. Four pitches clocked in at 5.10, eight at 5.11, and six at 5.12. Some belays were reinforced with a bolt, while almost all of the climbing is naturally protected (one fixed piton).

Problems with our stoves led us to add firewood to our haulbags, and we cooked dinners on small ledges along the way. A couple of the upper pitches presented difficult jungle climbing, and a machete was an important part of our lead rack. From the bivouacs our view was dominated by the massive south-facing wall of Churi Tepui, which is many miles long, up to 2,000' tall, and, to the best of our knowledge, unclimbed. Four 1,000' waterfalls pour down Churi, and that number doubled after storms. Other unclimbed walls can be found northwest of the Acopan Tepui in the U-shaped valley connecting Acopan Tepui to Churi Tepui. We encourage future teams to be respectful of the locals' wishes in Yunek, as access to climbing can be granted or withheld by the villagers. Paying for guides and porters is required. 📷

ERIC DESCHAMPS, *USA*

[This page] Climbing out the crux roof on Gravity Inversion. Almost all of the climbing is protected by natural gear, unlike many hard climbs on Acopan Tepui that are mostly bolt-protected. *Blake McCord*

Acopan Tepui, east face, Escalador Selvático. At the end of January 2014, Rolando Larcher, Luca Giupponi, and I began climbing a route in between the newly established route Gravity Inversion and Pizza, Chocolate y Cerveza. The route contained fantastic climbing in a unique environment, and it was very continuous all the way to the summit. The beautiful, ultra-overhanging rock surpassed all our expectations, except for the final meters which we breached "Tarzan" style. We reached the summit on February 6 after seven days of climbing. While mostly free, a few pitches remained to be redpointed.

Two days after our climb, on February 8, Rolando and Luca made the route's first redpoint ascent. After an intense 14 hours on the face, they finished climbing by the light of their headlamps. We called the climb Escalador Selvático (630m, 18 pitches, 7c+). The face overhangs at least 50m, making the abseils complicated; gear needs to be clipped during the descent to remain close enough to the rock. All told, we placed 36 bolts on the climb, including belays. 🔍

MAURIZIO OVIGLIA, *Italy*

ECUADOR

El Obispo, north face, second ascent and first free ascent. El Altar (a.k.a. Kapak Urku) is a large, extinct stratovolcano located on the western side of Sangay National Park in central Ecuador, 170km south of Quito. Comprising the massif of El Altar are nine major peaks that rise over 5,000m and form a horseshoe-shaped ridge about 3km long, surrounding a lake located in the volcano's crater, known as Laguna Collanes (ca 4,200m, a.k.a. Laguna Amarilla). The north face of El Obispo (5,319m), the highest peak in the Altar massif, is located at the southern end of this lake.

[This page] Acopan Tepui, showing (1) Mundo Perdido (Madinabeitia-Vacampenhoud, 2010), (2) Pizza, Chocolate y Cerveza (Arran-Arran-Rangel, 2003), (3) Escalador Selvático (Giupponi-Larcher-Oviglia, 2014), (4) Gravity Inversion (Cisneros-Deschamps-McCord-Unema, 2014), (5) Purgatory (Albert-Calderón-Glowacz-Heuber, 2007). (6) Dempster-Libecki (2007). *Blake McCord*

This incredible but dangerous wall was first climbed in 1984 by the Franco-Ecuadorian team of Guilles de Latillade and Oswaldo Morales (*AAJ 1986*). After failing on two attempts, they managed to reach the summit in an epic multi-day battle up the left-hand side of the face. Thirty years later, after many attempts by numerous climbers, Felipe Guarderas and I made the second ascent of the wall and the first free ascent in January 2013. Despite the conditions, we followed the original line for the most part, doing some variations here and there (800m, VI 5.10d M4). We're sure the route is much drier now—less snow and ice, more loose rock.

From our car, we reached the mountain in one day, using burros for the approach. We left camp at 5 a.m. the following morning. This was my second attempt, and we reached the upper headwall by noon. Here we encountered face climbing with poor protection, for which I put on my climbing shoes, leaving my heavy boots behind. After a total of 15 pitches of climbing, Felipe continued with a long and exposed traverse to the right, where he encountered scary sections of icy rock before reaching the summit ridge. A short hike brought us to the summit by 3:30 p.m. It was a dream to be up there after climbing such a wall and knowing we could take the normal route down. After a long descent down the Italian route and a couple of hours of sleep, we reached our car the next day.

[*Editor's note: El Obispo was first climbed in 1963 from the south (outside the caldera) and has since seen numerous ascents from that aspect. A new route was reported on the north face in AAJ 1991, but this is incorrect; the Culberson-Culberson is on the south face and believed to climb ground right of Arista del Calvario and share terrain with another route, Galeria de Tiro.*]

ROBERTO MORALES

[**This page, left**] Ecuador's "nordwand"? The north face of El Obispo showing the only known route. *Roberto Morales* [**This page, right**] Run-out rock climbing on the upper headwall. *Roberto Morales*

PERU

CORDILLERA BLANCA

Ishinca, northwest face variation, Carlito's Way; Ranrapalca, north face, Learning of our Weaknesses. Carlos Solé and I met in Huaraz in late May. On our way up to a bivouac at the Ishinca-Ranrapalca col, a possible new route caught my eye on the northwest face of Ishinca (5,529m), leading directly to its summit. I suggested to Carlos we climb it the next morning.

We began climbing on June 5 at 5:45 a.m. at ca 5,050m, directly in line with the summit. From there we climbed 40° snow for 190m to reach a prominent rock band. [*Editor's note: At this point, the route intersects the start of Celjska Smer (Gracner-Gracner, 2009), which diagonals left under the rock band to the southeast ridge, and the Cosley-Houston (2003), which climbs a prominent snow and rock ramp on the right side of the rock band. Pineda and Solé's variation, Carlito's Way, ascends a line up the center-right of the rock band, just left of the Cosley-Houston, joining that route again on the final snow slopes.*] We climbed two pitches of steeper mixed ground directly through the rock band, left of the Cosley-Houston, and then three more pitches of 60-80° snow. A short final pitch of easier snow climbing led us to the summit by 11:15 a.m: Carlito's Way (480m, D+ M5 60-80°). From the summit we descended the north-northwest slopes, reaching our bivouac two hours later.

From the summit of Ishinca I had scouted the north face of Ranrapalca (6,162m) and its central, unclimbed couloir. [*This is the major couloir right of the normal route on the northeast face and left of the many other north face routes, and long thought too dangerous to climb.*] On the morning of June 7 we climbed Ishinca again to better acclimatize, and then rested in the afternoon, trying to calculate the best time to start up the couloir and avoid the rock and ice avalanches we had witnessed each day and night.

We left our bivouac at 12:30 a.m. on June 8, walking up to the huge debris cone at the couloir's base. We climbed this on its right side and simul-climbed into the couloir, hoping to get out of the most exposed part before sunrise. Passing the first crux, a pitch of thin ice and mixed on an almost vertical slab, and having been hit by some showers of powder, we found our first protected belay just

[This page] Carlos Solé following a section of loose rock, halfway up the new route Learning of our Weaknesses. *Carlos Esteban Pineda Beyer*

protected belay just before 6 a.m. From there we navigated our way up, avoiding the danger of the main channel in the couloir while watching large amounts of ice and rock go through it. We climbed for some time on the central rock pillar in the gully, comprised of rotten and loose rock. Just before sunset we reached the upper couloir, which is divided by three channels. We took the left one, which contained a series of vertical waterfall ice steps.

When we reached ca 5,700m, the sun set and the temperature plummeted to -20°C. We fought to stay warm by rubbing our hands over our knees, taking short rests, and continuing to climb through the night. Just before midnight, we encountered the last waterfall ice, just below the summit plateau. The last pitch required us to break through an unstable cornice to reach the glacier and ramp leading to the summit.

We reached the top at 11:30 a.m. on June 9, under strong winds, with snow freezing on our faces and a very little visibility. We descended the normal route down the northeast face. Dehydrated, tired, and walking incoherently, we reached our bivouac at 7:30 p.m., after 43 hours on the go. No matter how much we suffered, we loved it: Learning of our Weaknesses (960m, ED M6 5.10+ 70-90°).

Carlos Esteban Pineda Beyer, *Venezuela*

Nevado Shaqsha, west face, Würmligrübler (no summit). After climbing Karma de Los Cóndores (300m, 5.11+, *AAJ 2005*) in the Ishinca Valley, Swiss climbers David Hefti, Marcel Probst, Mathias Schick, and Florian Zwahlen, set up their tents at the foot of Nevado Shaqsha (5,703m).

After a day of reconnaissance, they located a promising crack system through the steep rock wall on the west face. On July 23 at 4 a.m., the Swiss team departed their base camp (ca 4,500m). After passing a small lake and the bergschrund, the team started the difficult climbing at ca 5,350m, where they climbed two pitches, 5c (35m) and 6c+ (65m) before gaining a big dihedral. The route continued up the corner at 6b (30m). Above the corner, an easy ramp brought them to the most difficult part of the route, two hard pitches of 7a+ (40m) and 7a (35m), which ended with a final pitch in a chimney. After six total pitches, the team topped out the wall. Above, they climbed 60m of 60° snow and ice, reaching a highpoint of ca 5,600m on the summit ridge. [*This high point is a small top adjacent to Shaqsha's southwestern summit (point 5,697m)*]. They did four rappels down their route and downclimbed over the bergschrund. The climbers returned to base camp at 8 p.m., calling their route Würmligrübler (240m, 7a+ 60°). Much of the route consists of clean, finger and hand-sized cracks.

Sergio Ramírez Carrascal, *Peru, with information from David Hefti*

[This page] The west face of Shaqsha showing the mostly rock route Würmligrübler, which stops below the peak's southwestern summit (5,697m). The main summit (5,703m) lies to the left. *Mathias Schick*

Vallunaraju, east face. In early August, Mexican climbers Franco Gualdi and Daniel Navarro climbed a possible new route on east face of Vallunaraju (5,686m). They began climbing on August 5, at 2 a.m, from a camp on the moraine between Ocshapalca and Vallunaraju. Gualdi and Navarro first climbing an easy ramp of rock and névé without a rope. Above, they climbed harder mixed terrain, often run-out, for a few hundred meters. Midway up the face they were hit by a large storm, and they climbed the remainder of the day under significant snowfall. They found a bivy about four pitches below the summit, where they spent a cold night. They set off the following morning up steep rock (55m, 5.10), which was followed by one pitch of ice and two pitches of soft snow leading to the main summit (500m, MD 5.10a 60-70º). They descended by the normal route down the north ridge. *[Editor's note: It's unknown if this route is completely independent from previous lines on the face (see AAJ 1983 and 1988).]* 🖻 🔍

SERGIO RAMÍREZ CARRASCAL, *Peru, with information from Daniel Navarro*

CORDILLERA HUAYHUASH

Puscanturpa Este, southeast face, Qiumplirgun Swerminganta; Trapecio, southeast face, Los Viejos Roqueros Nunca Mueren, second ascent. Masarau Noda and I (both from Japan) climbed two routes in the Cordillera Huayhuash in June, achieving a first and second ascent.

We first acclimatized in the Cordillera Blanca, climbing Pirámide de Garcilaso (5,885m) by the southwest face (Renshaw-Wilkinson, 1979, 800m, TD+ WI5 AI4+). The climb took us 18 hours round-trip from the bottom of the face. We returned to Huaraz and took the fastest approach to Puscanturpa and Trapecio, at the southern end of the Cordillera Huayhuash, starting from the village of Cajatambo.

On June 15 and 16 we opened a new route up Puscanturpa Este (5,410m), via the southeast face, in lightweight style. The steeper lower part of the climb began with excellent rock; however, the upper snowfields transgressed into steep sugar snow and loose rock. This time-consuming effort caused us to endure a cold sitting bivy at ca 5,300m. On the second day we finished climbing the easy-angled upper slopes and the upper headwall, reaching the summit midmorning. We called our route Qiumplirgun Swerminganta (700m, ED+ VII M5+ A1), which means "dreams come true" in the local Quechuan language. *[This is likely the fourth ascent of the peak, following ascents of the north ridge (1986), the east face (AAJ 2008), and the north face (AAJ 2013).]*

We then made a base camp at the lake (ca 4,750m) below Trapecio (5,644m). On June 24 we

[This page] The southeast face of Puscanturpa Este, showing the new route Qiumplirgun Swerminganta. The difficult 700m route was climbed over two days. *Yasushi Yamanoi*

climbed Trapecio's southeast face, via the rightmost couloir, right of the Slovenian route (Ivanek-Kozjek-Lamprecht-Monasterio, *AAJ 2004*), believing it to be a new line. We later learned it had been climbed previously (Fernandez-Pita, *AAJ 2008, see Editor's Note online for the full history of this face*). We encountered 50–70° snow and ice slopes in the lower part, with a crux section of steep ice and loose mixed climbing near the top of the face (AI6 M5+). We reached the summit in 14 hours and bivied on the descent at ca 5,200m, concerned we'd rappel the wrong route in the dark. We resumed our descent in the warmth of the sun the next morning.

I had lost 10 fingers and toes during an alpine-style ascent of the north face of Gyachung Kang (7,952m) in 2002, so I'm happy for these successes. 📷 🔍 📄

YASUSHI YAMANOI, *with additional information from Sevi Bohoroquez and Miguel Pita*

CORDILLERA URUBAMBA

Nevado Capacsaya, east face. Peruvian climbers Jorge "Coqui" Gálvez, Dominique Riva Roveda, and Manolo Urquizo made the first ascent of the east face of Nevado Capacsaya (5,044m). They entered the range from the southwest, from Capacsaya, traveling past the Pumahuanca Valley, the village of Sutoc (ca 3,750m), and Laguna Manalyosec (ca 4,050m). Once past the lake, they established high camp on the glacier beneath the east face, part of large cirque of numerous steep walls.

On October 1 at 7 a.m. they began climbing 100m of easy mixed terrain (60°) up a left-trending ramp, finding bad conditions. Steeper climbing was bypassed via chimneys interspersed with snow climbing. Upon reaching a large ledge system, they traversed right to reach a prominent right-facing dihedral, the crux of the route (70m, 6c+ A1). Above, four easier pitches (250m) and some scrambling along the upper ridge brought the team to the central summit by late morning. They descended the same route (450m, 6C+ A1). 📷

SERGIO RAMÍREZ CARRASCAL, *Peru, with information from Jorge Gálvez*

[This page, top] The east face of Nevado Capacsaya showing the line of ascent. *Jorge Gálvez* [This page, bottom] Jorge Gálvez leading the crux dihedral. *Manolo Urquizo*

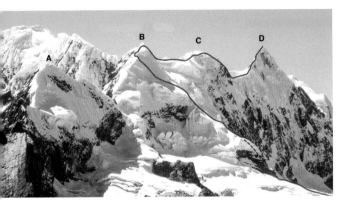

CORDILLERA VILCANOTA

Nevado Caracol, Concha de Caracol, Puca Punta, traverse. Puca Punta (5,740m) is an intimidating, steep pyramid of ice and rock. It stands like a sentinel over Jampa Pass, guarding entrance to the inner Cordillera Vilcanota. With other partners, I had already tried climbing it twice, via a chute on the left side of the southwest face. Both times we only made it to the west ridge leading to the summit. On the second climb we had a serious accident when an avalanche caused us to fall 120m into a crevasse. I had been thoroughly defeated by the mountain, but this time my approach would be different: Tom Ryan (U.S.), Luis Crispín (Peru), and I hoped to enchain Nevado Caracol (5,625m), Concha de Caracol (5,640m), and Puca Punta (5,740m) via the long ridge connecting the mountains. We hoped to finish with the unclimbed northwest ridge of Puca Punta.

On May 31 we reached a base camp at ca 4,900m below Jampa Pass on the Ausangate Circuit Trek, below the chain of peaks leading to Puca Punta. We left the tent at 1 a.m. on June 1 to start our climb up the west face of Nevado Caracol. I led the first crux, a 15m section of hard ice (80°). Then Luis took the lead, breaking trail through knee-deep snow up a 45° slope. Higher up we passed a bergschrund and joined the north ridge to the summit of Caracol, passing another short crux of snow and ice (80°). From the pointy summit we walked to the south, dropping 50m to a col, and then walked up easy terrain to the rounded summit of Concha de Caracol. It had taken us four-and-a-half hours to arrive here.

The steep summit of Puca Punta loomed over us just to the southeast. It was now 6 a.m., and Luis and I decided to go for it while Tom waited on the summit of Concha de Caracol. We first descended 100m to the col and then began the intimidating northwest ridge. We found much rotten

[This page, top] The peaks of (A) Tinki (B), Nevado Caracol, (C) Concha de Caracol, and (D) Puca Punta as viewed from Jampa Pass. The line of the 2013 traverse is shown. *Nathan Heald* [This page, bottom] Luis Crispin winds up the corniced ridgeline toward the summit of Puca Punta. *Nathan Heald*

ce and only a little hard snow. Several sections were vertical, and we barely spoke while delicately passing the cornices that hung over the west face. As we arrived at the top, I saw that the actual summit was just a large flake of ice, about the size of a car, balanced on top. It was too dangerous to stand on it, so I just touched the top with my hand. It took us four hours to climb the final ridge, and we went back the same way we'd come, with Luis down-leading and me cleaning. We reversed the rest of our route, by downclimbing and rappelling, then walked out to Pacchanta that night (200m, TD, AI2).

From my research, the south face of Nevado Caracol has been climbed twice: by an Austrian team in 1957 and Yugoslavs in 1979; Concha de Caracol had been climbed by the south face by a German team in 1972, and in 1966 a German team traversed from Tinki to Caracol to Concha de Caracol. [*Puca Punta, also called Choquetecarpo, was first summited by Harvard University climbers in 1957 from the east (approaching from Laguna Ticllacocha); it was climbed again by a Swiss expedition (AAJ 1960). It has also been climbed by the technical east ridge: first in 1962 by a New Zealand team, and again in 2003 by Canadians Amelunxen and Easton (AAJ 2004). As with the all reports from the Vilcanota/Vilcabamba, note that the government-issued maps have many errors and some peaks have been known by numerous names throughout the years.*] 📷 ▶

NATHAN HEALD, *Peru*

CORDILLERA VILCABAMBA

Nevado Ausangate, northwest face, variation (no summit). On July 6-8, Edwin Espinoza Sotelo, Luis Crispín, and I climbed the northwest face of Nevado Ausangate by a variation to the Dueber-Nave-Zebrowski [*AAJ 1984*]. We took two days to approach—first camping at Laguna Azulcocha in the valley formed by the neighboring Cerro Percocaya, then at the base of the northwest face. We climbed and descended the peak in a day on July 8. [*Editor's note: The route taken by Crispín, Heal, and Sotelo mostly follows the line of Deuber-Nave-Zebrowski (AAJ 1983), a route which was possibly climbed by an Italian team in 1982, but not to the summit (AAJ 1985). Heald and team made significant variations at the many bergschrunds to negotiate significantly altered terrain, which often involved steep ice and mixed climbing. Although they only reached the upper ridgeline, their ascent was much faster than the previous ones, which required bivouacs en route.*] 📷 🗎

NATHAN HEALD, *Peru*

Nevado Salcantay (6,279m GPS), northeast ridge, rare ascent. With various partners, I made several attempts on Nevado Salcantay (also spelled Salkantay) in 2011 and 2012 before succeeding twice in 2013.

On June 16, 2013, Luis Crispin, Thomas Ryan, and I placed a high camp at 5,900m on the northeast ridge. We left the tent at 1 a.m. and after nine hours we finally stood on the east summit of Salcantay. We took an elevation reading of 6,279m with our GPS. It took another five hours to get back down to the high camp, downclimbing the entire way. I climbed the route again in late July with James Lissy and Edwin Espinoza.

Nevado Salcantay is a very difficult mountain for many reasons. The approach requires a 22km hike over two passes (5,100m and 4,700m). The climb up to high camp is relatively technical while carrying a large pack. There are places where the avalanche danger is significant. Also, since

the mountain is directly above the cloud forests of Machu Picchu and the Amazon, clouds often reduce visibility to a minimum, and it is difficult to continue if you do not know the route well.

[*Editor's note: The last reported ascent of Salcantay was in 1995. The mountain has two summits, west and east, separated by about 1km. When Salcantay was first climbed, by an American-French team in 1952, the western summit was ca 30m higher. But a portion of the peak collapsed in the 1970s, leaving the two summits roughly equal in height. In early season, Nathan Heald reports, the east summit is the highest because of accumulated snow, but by July and August the western top often is higher.*]

NATHAN HEALD, *Peru*

Cerro Soray, southeast ridge, north face. In September 2012, Luis Crispín and I decided to explore a peak labeled Cerro Soray (5,428m) on the Peruvian IGN 2344 map, four kilometers west of Soray Pampa, hoping to find a climb similar to that of Vallunaraju in the Cordillera Blanca.

On September 7 we reached a camp beneath the southeast face of the peak (ca 4,813m). We found puma footprints in the soft dirt around the campsite, and a deer trail went up to the col between Cerro Soray and a rock peak marked as Cerro Yanajaja (5,093m). On the other side of the col there was a steep face of broken rock.

We left the tent at 3 a.m. to start our climb up the southeast ridge. We walked un-roped, stepping over a few minor crevasses on the way up. Higher up, the southeast ridge converges with another ridge rising from the south. From this juncture, the rest of the ridge appeared difficult and dangerous. I looked at Luis to see what he was thinking; he basically said, "I'm ready when you are."

[This page, top] The north aspect of Nevado Salcantay showing (1) east ridge, (2) northeast ridge, (3) northeast face, (4) north face [to east summit], (5) north face [to west summit], and (6) north ridge. *Nathan Heald* [This page, bottom] The east-southeast aspect of Nevado Salcantay showing (1) northeast ridge, (2) east ridge, (3) southeast buttress [1973], (4) southeast face [1978], (5) southeast ridge [1968], (6) south face [1986, approximate], and (7) south face attempt [1970, approximate]. *Kerly Salamanca*

We roped up and simul-climbed the ridge; however, we had not brought any rock protection, believing it would be easier, and did the best we could using only slings. There were spots of ice, so we kept our crampons on. The last bit involved an exposed hand traverse along the ridge, capped by a short and loose crux to the summit. We reached the top around 9:30 a.m. (my GPS read 5,446m), and then downclimbed the route to our camp (200m, D).

On October 23, 2012, Edwin Espinoza Sotelo and I climbed the north side of the peak after finding the south side much too hard for any novice climber. We discovered a route up the north face and ridge the next day. The route is quite easy but does require some good routefinding (F/PD). Since then, we have brought many people up this route, an enjoyable climb for every skill level.

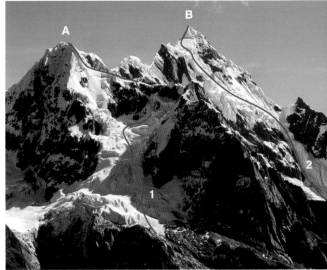

[*Editor's note: It should be noted that Cerro Soray is an easier, shorter, and separate peak from the nearby, taller, and more difficult Tucarhuay (also called Tucarway and Humantay), which has been called Soray by some past expeditions. Nevado Tucarhuay (5,910m) was first climbed via the north face by Lionel Terray and party (AAJ 1957), then via the south ridge by a Japanese team (AAJ 1969). It's also probable that Piero Ghiglione and party reached the subsidiary east summit (5,700m) of Nevado Tucarhuay via the north face and ridge (AAJ 1954). Nathan Heald and Edwin Espinoza Sotelo repeated this route to the east summit in September 2013, verifying the rough summit elevation by GPS. Additionally, a Japanese Alpine Club party attempted the unclimbed west face of Nevado Tucarhuay in 1980; however, they only reached a highpoint of 5,100m. That face remains unclimbed. The peaks north of Nevado Tucarhuay and west of Nevado Salcantay, called "Nevados Humantay" on the Peruvian IGN map, are possibly unclimbed and appear to be very technical.*]*

NATHAN HEALD, *Peru*

[This page, top] The north aspect of Cerro Soray. The route climbs the general line of weakness up the snowy ridge on the right side. The more difficult southeast ridge climbs the other side of the peak. *Nathan Heald* [This page, bottom] The northern aspect of Nevado Tucarhuay. (A) East summit and (1) north face/ridge. (B) Main summit and (2) north face. *Nathan Heald*

BOLIVIA

Overview. The mountains of Bolivia have seen a resurgence in new routing, largely due to the emergence of a strong cadre of local mountain guides, as well as a number of talented, enthusiastic foreign climbers resident in La Paz. A team of local guides reportedly made the second ascent of one of the hard Slovenian routes, Nada Mañana (ED1), on the northwest face of Illampu, while another has made the complete traverse of the Illimani massif in a single push of 18 hours. Although the traditional season has been the austral winter (June–September), climbs are now being made at all times of year, as locals snatch ephemeral lines whenever conditions allow.

Of note, at a less technical level, are the mountaineering exploits of the Frenchwoman Anne Bialek. By climbing Pomerape (6,282m) in 2013, the La Paz resident became the first known female to summit all 13 of the 6,000m peaks in Bolivia. She first visited the country in 2005 and climbed Huayna Potosí, but it wasn't until 2008–'09, when she relocated from France to La Paz, that she formulated plans to collect Bolivia's highest peaks. On her way she made several important female ascents: In 2011 she climbed the 900m west face of Huayna Potosí, a route that has become harder over the years (D+/TD, 80°), and in 2012 was likely the first woman to do the integral traverse of Illimani.

Visiting climbers may find the increasing number of Bolivian sport crags beneficial for acclimatization. The La Paz Sport Climbing Association is responsible for developing the sport climbs near Lago Zongo, and also maintaining the routes at the Aranjuez area of La Paz. (*See Zongo Pass report below.*) Members can usually be found on Saturdays at La Galleta (Aranjuez area). The group also has worked with local authorities to keep El Peñón, a small but very popular venue, open for climbing. The club holds an annual bouldering event—the Bloqueando—in Chalkupunku, a massive boulder field near Sajama.

LINDSAY GRIFFIN, *Mountain INFO*

[This page] The last slope before the summit of Cololo on day six of the Apolobamba traverse. *Vincent Kronental*

CORDILLERA APOLOBAMBA

South to north traverse. The international expedition called A Cada Uno Su Thaki (To Each Their Own Trail) was conceived by Anne Bialek (France) and Sergio Condori (Bolivia). Whereas traditional treks in the Apolobamba region tend to follow the Caminata de los Medicos Kallawayas, they envisioned a route that followed the glaciers, and an expedition that would bring together the country's high-mountain guiding community, without clients or commercial purposes. From Google Earth, a south-to-north trek along the glaciers seemed realistic.

The expedition comprised six UIAGM guides (Hugo Ayaviri Quispe, Julio Choque Alana, Sergio Condori Vallejo, Ignacio Pacajes Silvestre, Nolberto Soliz Mamani, and Rolando Tarqui Choque), Anne Bialek, a videographer/photographer (Vincent Kronental), and support crew. The team began at Laguna Chuchuja (4,230m), at the southern end of the range, on May 17, and finished on May 28 after climbing Chaupi Orco. The route stayed largely west of the main chain, but moved into it to climb and/or traverse five major peaks: Huelancalloc (which Bolivians refer to as Ullakaya, 5,836m); Iscacucho (referred to as Condorini, 5,650m); Cololo (5,915m); Huanacuni (5,790m), and Chaupi Orco Sur, 6,044m.

Returning to a small village at 4,685m on the west side of the range, the team was evacuated by 4X4. In total the journey was ca 147km, and the team GPS recorded 9,955m of ascent and 8,950m of descent. Although none of the peaks or routes climbed appears to be new, this was most likely the first traverse of its kind in the range. A complete record of the traverse, with GPS coordinates on Google Earth maps, is available at the AAJ website. 📷 ☰ 🔍

AIMEE VERDISCO, *Bolivia*

CORDILLERA REAL

Pico del Norte (6,050m), northwest face, Ñeq'e Ñeq'e. On July 12, Argentinians Gabriel Fava and Carlitos Molina put up a new route on Pico del Norte, the rarely climbed northern outlier of Illampu (6,368m) at the north end of the Cordillera Real. Leaving the mining town of Ancohuma (a.k.a. Ancoma), they walked to the foot of the small but contorted glacier that bars access to the northwest face and pitched a tent at 4,900m. Leaving at 7 a.m. the following day, they quickly reached the bottom of the northwest buttress. Some sources describe a route up this buttress at a grade of TD+ AI4 UIAA III, but first-

[This page] Carlitos Molina on the fourth pitch of Ñeq'e Ñeq'e. *Gabriel Fava*

ascent records are unclear (possibly German, possibly 1984). This buttress lies to the left of the original line on the west face, the 1964 Slovenian Route (Golob-Mihelic-Savenc).

The Argentinians chose an unclimbed line up the left flank of the buttress, starting via a pronounced corner system. Three 60m pitches in the corner (11a, 10c, and 10b) led to a large snow terrace. The granite proved to be of surprisingly good quality, and above the terrace another excellent rock pitch (10d) led to an area of easier ground where the two could move together. To reach the upper mixed terrain, they climbed another steep rock wall via an enjoyable thin crack. Above, they moved together again, this time for around three rope lengths, to reach the sharp north spur, which forms the left edge of the face. Here, one and a half pitches of 5.9 led to easier ground and the summit dome. They reached the highest point at 5 p.m. and subsequently named the route Ñeq'e Ñeq'e (1,000m, 5.11a 60°); Ñeq'e is an Aymara word meaning "motivation."

Fava and Molina downclimbed the northwest ridge (first ascent unknown), running into darkness near the base. They made four 60m rappels down the west flank before contouring along moraine northeast to regain their tent at 10 p.m. 📷

LINDSAY GRIFFIN, *from information provided by Gabriel Fava, Andeslimite.net, Argentina*

[This page] Pico del Norte (6,050m) from the north-northwest, as seen when approaching from Ancohuma. (1) Northeast ridge (Hein-Horeschowsky-Hortangel-Pfann, 1928). (2) North spur. (3) Ñeq'e Ñeq'e (2013). (4) West face (Slovenian route, 1964). (5) Northwest ridge. *Carlitos Molina*

Pico Italia (ca 5,750m), east face, Arthritis; Milluni peaks, complete traverse. At 4 a.m. on August 10, Gregg Beisly and I set off to add another route to Pico Italia's east face, of which we made the first ascent in 2012 (*AAJ 2013*). We were keen to find an easier line leading directly to the summit. After wading two hours through waist-deep snow, we started climbing 800m north of our previous route.

In fact the new route proved to be harder and longer than our 2012 line. Although the hardest pitch was only about F6a, the route was generally steeper and more complicated, and we didn't fix any pitches. The climbing was superb, absorbing, and with generally good protection, but challenged by navigational difficulties around a series of false summits and overhanging sections. We completed the 600m route in 12 sustained pitches and 17 hours, thankfully finding a straightforward descent along the ridge to the col between Huayna Potosí and Pico Italia, then down the glacier. We christened the route Arthritis, as I struggled with a significant flare-up of a longstanding arthritis condition affecting my right hand, which added considerably to the challenge and burden of the climb. The overall grade is TD+/ED-.

Prior to this, on August 5, we made what was possibly the first complete traverse of the three Milluni peaks (highest summit 5,500m) in seven hours—a classic traverse with nothing desperate.

ERIK MONASTERIO, *New Zealand*

Charquini Group, Wila Manquilizani (5,324m), west face (not to summit), Los Llokallas. On August 13, Alex von Ungern (Swiss) and I established a route we believe was previously unclimbed on Wila Manquilizani, a summit between the Cumbre (the ca 4,650m pass on the main road over to the Yungas) and Chacaltaya. The route is best approached from Pampalarama, about an hour's drive from La Paz. Park at the end of the road, at Albergue (Eco Lodge), and walk several hours up the broad valley, well to the left of the obvious main glacier of Wila Manquilizani, which faces the Eco Lodge. Before reaching the glacier at the head of the valley, the route is visible on the right.

We first climbed a fun thin strip of snow and ice for ca 200m to a hanging bowl. Above, we followed broken rock to a highpoint on the west ridge (total of 500m). We descended the way we came with several rappels, until it was possible to traverse from the bowl onto gentler slopes on descender's right.

The name of the route, Los Llokallas (AD), means "young men who refuse to take on the responsibilities of adulthood." It was intended as a bit of a joke, because Alex recently became a father and my first child just graduated from university. We made the climb in a day from La Paz.

CHRIS CLARKE, *Bolivia*

[This page, top] East face of Pico Italia with (1) east face buttress (2012) and (2) Arthritis (2013). *Erik Monasterio* [This page, bottom] (1) Los Llokallas on the west face of Wila Manquilizani. From the top, the route was rappelled to the snow bowl, from which the first ascensionists traversed off (2). *Chris Clarke*

Zongo Pass rock climbing. Many worthwhile rock climbs are found on the granite cliffs above Zongo Lake. Located at ca 4,800m, these can form part of an acclimatization program or provide relaxing days before or after a climb of Huayna Potosi. There are around 30 older, trad-protected routes and many new sport climbs. Fun sport routes can be found in the immediate vicinity of the memorial plaque on the aqueduct leading from Zongo Lake to Charquini, 10 minutes' walk from the start of the aqueduct at Casa Verde. Routes are 6a to 6c+ on good granite. There are also a dozen single-pitch sport routes below the dam (6a–7a+). Descend the rickety metal ladders and look for bolts.

Longer routes lie on the large buttress rising from the dirt road between the Casa Blanca and Casa Verde refugios at Zongo Pass. In August, Chris Clarke and Robert Rauch completed a three-pitch route they called California Dreaming (6b+). The bolted first pitch starts at the left edge of a prominent low roof, while the second either follows a beautiful dihedral (6a+, some trad gear required) or the bolted arête on the left (6b+). The third pitch is also bolted. Other routes lie farther to the right.

Information supplied by CHRIS CLARKE *and* ROBERT RAUCH, *Bolivia*

Hampaturi Group, Serkhe Khollu (5,546m), southwest face, Los Sospechosos de Siempre. On October 18, Gregg Beisly, Robert Rauch, and I headed to the southwest face of Serkhe Khollu with the intention of climbing steep ice right of Tiers of Pachamama (*AAJ 2012*). We found somewhat less ice than expected, and so decided instead to follow an obvious thin line of ice to the left. This resulted

in a five-pitch mixed route that we called Los Sospechosos de Siempre (The Usual Suspects, WI4 M5). It was a fun route, without any real rockfall, with an interesting exit pitch that was mostly rock.

Gregg went to the summit following non-technical snow and ice, while Robert and I descended from the ridge via the normal route. We were back in the car before dark, after leaving La Paz around 6 a.m. This route is just another example of the great potential for mixed climbing at a decent elevation within a day of La Paz.

Although the right side of the broad southwest face always seems to have some snow and ice, it appears the left side only ices from late August through October. We climbed Tiers of Pachamama in early September of 2011, and we noticed that in mid-October 2013, while climbing Los Sospechosos, the crux pitch of Pachamama had already gone. ⬚

CHRIS CLARKE, *Bolivia*

[This page] Gregg Beisly in the narrow ice runnel of Los Sospechosos de Siempre. *Chris Clarke*

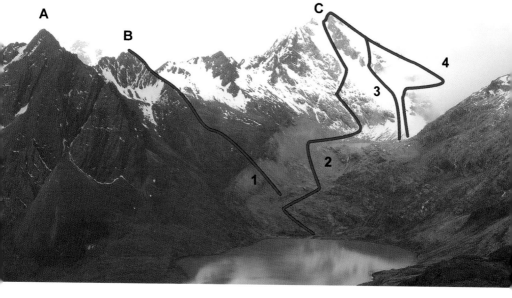

[This page, above] (A) Cerro Tigra Killa, (B) Unnamed, and (C) Jati Khollu from the southwest. (1) Southeast ridge (AD), climbed in 2012 by Gregg and Sal Beisly. (2) South face gully (AD, Beisly-Clarke-Meehan, 2013). (3) South face and southeast ridge (AD+, Brain-Davis, 1995, now probably no longer practical due to glacial recession). (4) Southeast ridge (PD/AD, Heung-Rauch, 2012). *Gregg Beisly* [This page, right] Chris Clarke beginning an attempt on one of the attractive granite spires to the east of Jati Khollu in the Hampaturi Group. These ca 250m towers, rising above 5,000m, were still unclimbed at the end of the 2013 season. *Eduardo Unzueta*

Hampaturi Group, Jati Khollu (5,421m), south face. On July 8, Gregg Beisly (NZ), Paul Meehan (USA), and I left La Paz at around 6 a.m. with the intention of climbing water ice in the valley containing Laguna Jachcha Khasiri, the same valley used to access the regular route (southeast ridge) on Jati Khollu (*see AAJ 2012*). After the water ice failed to materialize, we climbed what we believe to be a new route on Jati Khollu's ca 400m south face. This follows a gully several hundred meters to the left of the other routes. After a few hundred meters of moderate snow, ice, and mixed ground, the route joins the large snowfield that leads to a col just north of the summit. A loose pitch of rock gained the top. The overall grade was AD.

Chris Clarke, *Bolivia*

Mururata (5,775m), south face, Guias AGMTB. On April 21–22, a group of UIAGM guides and aspirants, led by Sergio Condori (head of the

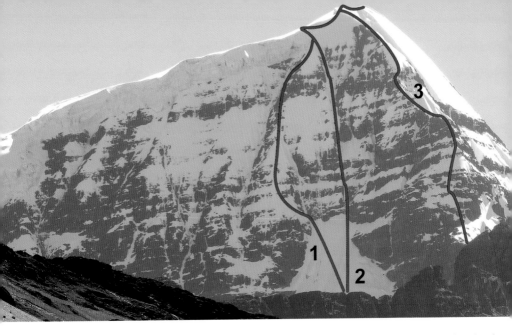

[This page] South face of Mururata. As with many Bolivian peaks, the history of its exploration is confused, with second (and third) first ascents reported. (1) Guias AGMTB. (2) Goulotte Marie, most likely first climbed by Slovenians in 1987. (3) Southeast ridge. Although claimed by parties in 1972 (French) and 1974 (French-Italian), this was most likely climbed first in 1970 by John Hudson, Roman Laba, and Roger Whewell. *Sergio Condori*

Bolivia Guides Association), opened a new route on the south face of Mururata. Departing at 1 a.m. from Lake Arkhata, they arrived at the foot of the face at 5:30. The 700m route begins at the same point as Goulotte Marie [a route most likely first climbed in June 1987 by Slovenians Filip Bertoncelj, Bojan Pockar, Bojan Pograjc, and Jernej Stritih, who quote 540m, with two pitches of 90°], then slants left to climb a snowy buttress before moving back right at the top. The climb was sustained, with the overall angle 55-65° and technical difficulties of WI4/5 M4/5.

The traditional route up flat-peaked Mururata (the summit was first reached in 1915) involves an endless glacier traverse, more suitable for skiing than alpinism. The south face is highly exposed and technically challenging, but threatened for much of its length by seracs. According to Andean mythology, the god Mururata was constantly mouthing off to Illimani and Illampu. After he tried to claim the title of highest peak, Illimani chopped off his head, leaving a large summit plateau. His decapitated head was thrown in the direction of the Chilean border to become Sajama, the highest of all Bolivian peaks.

CHRIS CLARKE, *Bolivia*

Mururata Massif, Unnamed Peak (ca 5,400m), south face, Itsy Bitsy Spider. On August 30, Gregg Beisly (NZ), Robert Rauch (German/Bolivian), and I climbed an 800m ice line on an unnamed 5,400m peak above Totoral Pampa, near the south face of Mururata (5,864m). We left La Paz mid-morning on the 29th and, other than passing a corpse on the road, had an uneventful 2.5-hour drive to Totoral Pampa, from which we hiked for a few hours to a pleasant base camp by a small lake.

Snow beat on the tents at our appointed 3 a.m. start time, so we slept for a few more hours. Eventually, Gregg convinced us to go to the base of the route and see how it looked. We climbed most of the route unroped to save time, but did make five belayed pitches. Fortunately, we experienced almost no rockfall.

On the descent, we reversed our line for ca 150m, until it was possible to cross the ridge to descender's right and drop into a subsidiary valley. This led back to the main valley, where we had camped. We packed out that evening, and after a few hours wandering along llama trails in the dark, we found our car. We reached La Paz just before midnight. We have named the route Itsy Bitsy Spider (800m, WI4 M4), because Robert thought the upper snowfield looked like the Eiger's White Spider.

CHRIS CLARKE, *Bolivia*

Illimani (6,439m), south face, Jach'a Kuntur Ajayu. Of all Illimani's aspects, the south face is perhaps the most beautiful and impressive. This huge wall offers lines of high technical difficulty, through vertical ice runnels and rock. Hidden from general view, it seems inaccessible, but it is not.

A four- to five-hour drive from La Paz in 4WD, followed by a four-hour trek along an abandoned road, leads to Mesa Khala mine (4,695m), where you can make camp or stay overnight in the mine. A 3.5-hour trek up the glacier leads to a possible high camp beneath the south face at ca 5,000m. With my brothers Juvenal and Vidal, I followed this approach, but established high camp at 4,700m, one hour from the foot of the face. On this section we passed the wreckage of an Eastern Airlines Boeing 727, which crashed on New Year's Eve 1985. It was really impressive to see the snakeskin luggage, clothes, engine parts, turbines, and cables that have not yet disintegrated. We looked, with respect for the fallen, and with curiosity.

We had needed to wait a long time until we were granted the right to climb the south face of Achachila Illimani ("Grandfather Illimani"), because for my grandparents this mountain was considered a sacred ancestor and a source of power. Knowing it would be useless to use courage and strength without wisdom, we waited until we felt the signs were positive from Illimani.

At 3 a.m. on December 1, Juvenal and I left high camp. Above the bergschrund, which we crossed by a 2m ice wall, the slope was well-packed snow of 55-65°. At the top, this slope changed to 75-90°, the rock became variable—sometimes rotten, at other times fairly reliable—and we were forced to climb pitches of delicate snow and ice. These six long pitches were very intricate and time-consuming. There was rockfall, and on more than three occasions our hair stood on end from fright.

At 12:45 p.m. we finished the mixed section. There was a sense of relief that no more rocks would fall. However, the face's belligerence had not diminished—rather, it had just begun. We now sunk into wet, loose snow and it became very difficult to break trail. It was precarious, and a moment of negligence would prove fatal. Screws would not hold in this terrain, though deadmen buried one meter deep were secure. There was nowhere to stop and wait for a refreeze, so we had to continue. Finally I arrived on the summit ridge at 8:10 p.m. and saw the lights of La Paz. I waited for Juvenal with much excitement, and when he arrived I shouted with joy, *Salimossss!*

We shook hands and ate a little, but also talked about the fact that we were not done yet and should not do anything in a hurry. We finally reached the summit of Illimani at 1:25 a.m. and descended the normal route through the night, meeting Vidal and the 4WD in Pinaya, and arriving back in La Paz mid-morning on the 2nd.

We named the route Jach'a Kuntur Ajayu (Spirit of the Giant Condor), which is the way I saw the mountain from my grandparents' home near Lake Titicaca. We climbed the 1,200m route and descended to Pinaya in a continuous 27-hour push. Difficulties were TD VI WI4 X 5+ M5. [*See the AAJ website for an updated photo of all routes on this face.*]

SERGIO CONDORI, *Bolivia, translated and adapted by Chris Clarke*

QUIMSA CRUZ

Cerro Taruca Umana (4,852m), southeast face, partial new route. In May, Camilo Lopez and I visited the northern Taruca Umana Valley, and on the 21st completed a route on the southeast face of Cerro Taruca Umana, climbing new ground in the upper section. We found excellent granite, though sometimes covered with slippery moss. The crux pitch was 60m of run-out face at 6b R. Four hundred meters of climbing led to a sub-summit, from which we fourth-classed to the final wall. We simul-climbed the final 100m via 5+ crack systems. We were able to scramble down from the summit, so no rappel anchors or fixed gear were left on the mountain.

We named the route Esta Es Para Ti, but on returning home found that this wall had been climbed extensively in the past (see below). Our route climbed Gales Crack (British HVS 4c) to the first terrace, then a similar line to Valley Boys (British E2 5b) to the sub-summit. Above, we climbed new ground on the wall right of Continuation Cracks (British HS).

[*Editor's note: At least 20 routes have been climbed on or near the southeast face of Cerro Taruca Umana, dating back to 1991. The full version of this report at the AAJ website includes a brief history of climbing in this area, as well as photos detailing the routes described above and many others.*]

ANNA PFAFF, *USA*

Solo ascents, including first ascent of Llegada del Bourne on Gran Muralla. The three most significant summits in the well-known Kuchu Mocoya valley of the Northern Araca are Saturno (ca 5,340m), Gran Muralla (ca 5,100m), and Cuernos del Diablo (5,270m). I planned to make first solo ascents of significant routes on each of these granite peaks.

In April, after the rainy season, I went to the southwest face of Gran Muralla (Grosse Mauer), and way over to the right found a great line on sound rock with lots of chickenheads. One of the pitches, up an offwidth and crackless face, was one of the most beautiful I've climbed on granite. I back-roped the climb using a Soloist, and called it Llegada de Bourne (Bourne Legacy, 6b).

The day before, I had made the first solo of Saturno's northeast ridge, following the Callisaya-Pratt Route (6a). Above the lower rock pitches, where there should have been easy snow, I found ice for which I was completely unprepared. I had to use a stone to cut steps for my rock shoes. I couldn't locate the descent in a snowstorm and thick cloud, so had to downclimb and rappel the route.

In preparation for a solo ascent of the Cuernos, I did two climbs of the northwest face with a talented Bolivian aspirant guide named Pacifico Machado Blanco. On May 9 I returned to solo Tyapi Khala (7 pitches, 6a/6a+), a line that appears to have been originally climbed in 1987 at 5+ A2. I self-belayed one pitch in the middle and the last two pitches.

Access to the Cuernos is five hours' brisk walk from the standard Kuchu Mocoya base camp; getting back down takes around four hours. My hope is that as more information on this area is published, more climbers will be encouraged to visit. There is still much potential for new routes.

ROBERT RAUCH, *Bolivian Tours*

La Flama, Buttkicker. On April 29, 2012, Gregg Beisly, Chris Clarke, and Robert Rauch climbed a six-pitch, partially new route on La Flama, a spear of granite northeast of Gran Muralla.

LINDSAY GRIFFIN, *Mountain INFO*

[This page] Gran Muralla from the southwest. (1) Northeast ridge (German, 1987). (2) Northwest face (German, 1987, reported to be 6a). (3) Northwest face (German, 1987, also reported to be 6a). (4) Unknown, but established by late 1990s. (5) Llegada del Bourne (6b). Behind and to the left lie the pinnacles (A) El Obelisco de Araca (Pico Penis) and (B) La Flama. *Chris Clarke*

Gigante Grande (5,750m), southwest face, Via del Minero. Traditional Aymara people have descriptive names for their mountains: Illimani is Water Bearer, Huayna Potosí is Thunderous Youth, and Mururata the Beheaded Peak. Our expectations were therefore high as we set off to climb Gigante Grande in the southern Quimsa Cruz.

Previously, this area has been difficult to reach, but high mineral prices and intense mining activity in recent years have ensured much-improved road access. Gregg Beisly (NZ), Chris Clarke (USA), and I reached the Laram Khota lake and mining camp at the foot of Gigante Grande in barely four hours from La Paz. From there, a mining road zigzags right to the start of the imposing 650m southwest face, at 5,100m.

USA climbers Dakin Cook and Kevin Starr climbed the southwest face in 1993. They were forced to bivouac near the summit, finishing the route the following day in a storm. A direct descent looked so difficult that they crossed the range instead and emerged next day at a mine. In the meantime, Dakin's friend, longtime Bolivian resident and activist Stan Shepard (USA), fearing they were trapped on the mountain by storm, drove from La Paz to organize a rescue and died tragically after his car veered off the road in snow. [*Editor's note: Cook and Starr are thought to have repeated the central line, the first on the face, climbed a month earlier by Teo Plaza and Iñaki San Vicente at UIAA V 75°. However, in the upper reaches these routes may take differing lines.*]

In 2001 Bruce Hendricks and Andy Selters climbed a new route left of the 1993 line, naming it Via Loco (*AAJ 2002*). They reached the west-northwest ridge but did not continue to the summit. They felt it might have been the most technical route in Bolivia at the time. The only two other known attempts on the mountain, by Bolivian mountain guides in 2013, were unsuccessful.

At 7 a.m. on August 1, as we walked toward the face, a local miner warned us that rockfall was common by midafternoon, and added that her husband had fallen to his death while mining on a nearby peak. We started up the right-hand couloir, roping up as the mixed ground became steeper and more technical. The climbing was engaging, with vertical sections of thin ice, mixed terrain, and long, moderate slopes of ice and névé. By midafternoon we'd climbed eight pitches but were still only two-thirds' height on the face, which was now receiving sun and sending down intermittent

[This page] Southwest face of Gigante Grande. (1) Via Loco (2001). (2) Plaza–San Vicente (1993). (3) Via del Minero (2013). *Erik Monasterio*

rock showers. Though we belayed from beneath overhanging rock, all of us took minor hits. The safest way was up, and rockfall became less severe as we homed in on the summit. At 4 p.m., after 12 pitches, we stood on top.

Our relief was short-lived. Our proposed descent of the northwest ridge looked ominous and threatened by loose rock. Chris, fearing altitude sickness, took off. Gregg and I descended more slowly, our pace determined by my lack of acclimatization and exhaustion (it was only five days since I'd left sea level). Nightfall caught us high on labyrinthine cliffs, making navigation a real challenge. Gregg guided me onto the final moraine wall, which became steeper as it spilled onto the glacier. We eventually had to rappel to the glacier, and three hours later, at midnight, we joined Chris. During a glissade, he had flipped over several times before coming to a stop, and was lucky to have survived without serious injury. We named the climb Via del Minero (TD+ AI4 M4).

ERIK MONASTERIO, *New Zealand*

San Luis (5,620m), René Flament; Huayna Cuno Collo East (5,600m), Charles de Seze. In July, Gabriel Fava, Carlitos Molina, and I went to the remote and little-visited southern end of the Cordillera Quimsa Cruz, specifically the Huallatani Valley, accessed via the village of Rodeo and Altarani Valley to the southwest. It took around six hours by 4X4 to reach the area, first on roads along the Altiplano and then via bad pistes. In the west lay Huayna Cuno Collo and to the east San Luis; between the two are three subsidiary summits, all unnamed on existing maps.

We established base camp at 4,950m on the north side of the large lake in the valley, near the ruins of mining houses, with a front-row view of the beautiful mountains immediately above. On July 1, Gabriel and I climbed San Luis by its west-southwest face (300m, D 55°), after approaching via 150m of mixed ground and 250m of glacier. We descended the southwest ridge (which at first heads more or less south), then slopes to the southwest. On both approach and descent we found deep snow, but the face was hard snow and ice. In the absence of previous known ascents, we named the route René Flament.

Because the forecast was bad for the next two days, we went down to Quime, a small and quiet village. For me it was an opportunity to recover: Unfortunately, just one year previously I was diagnosed with lung cancer, and had an operation to remove half of one lung.

Two days later we returned to base camp, and on July 7, after an approach of 350m, mainly over glacier, we climbed the east peak of Huayna Cuno Collo by its south face (350m, D+ 65°). We climbed the right and serac-free side of the face, a little left of an established route up the south spur. There was too great a risk of wind slab to continue to the main summit, so we stopped on the east summit, about the same time as bad weather moved in. We descended the east ridge, then south to the glacier. Again, we found deep snow on both the approach and glacier descent, but the face had hard snow and ice. Believing this to be a new route, we named it Charles de Seze. The Quimsa Cruz, which is wild, beautiful, and still with new route potential, really deserves to be more visited.

[*Editor's note: Yossi Brain, in his 1999 guidebook, notes that "there is more confusion over names and heights in the Quimsa Cruz than any other area in Bolivia". This is certainly true in the southern section, where "official" names, as recorded on the 1:50,000 Bolivian IGM map, are different from older maps of the region. At the AAJ website, Senior Editor Lindsay Griffin has partially clarified the history of climbs and naming in this area, dating back to 1939.*] 📷 🗒

HENRY BIZOT, *France*

SANTA CRUZ DE LA SIERRA

Chochis Tower, first ascent via west face, Furia del Viento. Federico Bueno Aloísio from Argentina, Jose Luiz Belmonte and Eduardo Ricardo Diaz from Bolivia, and I (originally from Brazil) made the first ascent of Chochis Tower in the Roboré–Santa Cruz de la Sierra region of Bolivia's eastern lowlands. This monolith of red sandstone is about 180m high, with sections of both good and bad rock. There are large sandstone walls in this area, but this appears to be the only prominent tower. According to locals, Chochis had been attempted previously by Peruvians, Argentinians, and Bolivians, all stopped by poor rock. We spent six days working on the route, using natural gear and 10 bolts, and reached the top on August 11, 2011: Furia del Viento (210m, 5.10c).

LEONARDO JULIANO MANGANO, *Bolivia*

[This page] The spectacular, red sandstone Chochis Tower. The first-ascent route follows more broken rock on the other side of the formation. *Leonardo Juliano Mangano*

ARGENTINA-CHILE

NORTHERN ANDES

Cerro Río Salado. In November, Glauco Muratti and Adriàn Petrocelli ascended an unclimbed volcano near Ojos del Salado: Cerro Río Salado (6,350m). They left their vehicle at ca 4,700m, and the next day reached a camp at ca 5,200m. On the third day the pair reached a col between the peak and Volcàn Huayco (which lies to the south). On the fifth day they reached the summit by the north face and north ridge, and they descended the same day.

Cerro del Nacimiento, south face. On December 20, Guillermo Almaraz and Pablo Bertoni ascended a new route up the south side of Cerro del Nacimiento, a peak located outside Catamarca in Argentina's northern Andes. The pair reached the highest summit of the massif, the northwest peak (6,460m), which has likely seen fewer than 10 total ascents.

Pico Número 3, southeast face. On November 15, Sebastián Aguiar and Fabrizio Oieni ascended the previously unclimbed southeast face of Pico Número 3 (a.k.a. Teniente Francisco Ibáñez, 5,550m), which is located in the beautiful Ansilta Range, near Mercedario, Argentina. They called the climb Tracción a Sangre (1,600m, PD II 60°).

Cerro Pachaco, Pijchu. In the San Juan Province of Argentina is an impressive limestone peak with many steep walls on its eastern aspect: Cerro Pachaco (ca 3,200m). In October, Willi Luhmann and Gabriel Fava established a new route to the peak's east summit. Their route, Pijchu (1,100m, 6b+), starts on an older, shorter route, Canal de la Guasa, and has 12 new pitches out of the total 18. It's gear-protected, utilizing a large dihedral and crack system, and was climbed ground-up. There are now five routes on Cerro Pachaco including the new one. The others are the first ascent (UIAA

IV/V), by Oscar Kummel, Erick Altrichter, and Germán Leuzzi in April 1958 to the west summit; Canal de la Y (800m, UIAA IV), by Fritz Altrichter, Oscar Kummel, José Miní, and Domingo Vega in March 1959; the Central Spur (UIAA V, very little information is known, it likely takes a line similar to the first ascent, but finishing on the higher east summit); and Canal de la Guasa (200m, 6a, *not to summit*), by Roberto Piriz and Aníbal Maturano in July 2012. 📷

Marcelo Scanu, *Argentina*

[This page] The east face of Cerro Pachaco. Pijchu climbs a system of left-facing dihedrals broken by ledges up the center of the face, then joins the left skyline to the summit. *Gabriel Fava*

[This page, left] The west face of Cerro Tolosa. See the AAJ website for a detailed topo of routes. *Gabriel Fava* [This page, right] The rarely climbed east face of Cerro Tolosa. *Gabriel Fava*

CENTRAL ANDES

Cerro Tolosa, west face. This fine peak (5,432m) is located near Aconcagua in Argentina's Central Andes. It was first ascended in 1903 by Countess Nadine Lougonine Von Meyendorff and Alois Pollinger. On October 27, Pablo Busso and Gabriel Fava traveled to the west face to attempt a new route. They established camp at the base. The next day they climbed a new route to the north summit of the mountain (slightly lower than the main summit). The pair named the route Por los Huevos del Hombre Cojo (1,000m, D+ IV M2 65°). There are four additional routes to the right of this route of similar length and difficulty; two of them reach the north summit, and two others reach the central summit.

Marcelo Scanu, *Argentina and* Gabriel Fava, *Argentina*

Pico Vivi Lotfi, south face. In the heart of Central Andes are "blank" zones ignored by mountaineers. The Santa Clara Range, situated at the southern end of the La Jaula Massif in the Cordillera Frontal, is one of these, and still houses 5,000m unclimbed peaks. Lotfi Mijel and I hoped to explore this remote region and summit an unclimbed peak.

Our expedition began in Punta de Vacas, on the Argentina-Chile border. On November 9 we approached by Tupungato Valley, walking 20km. On day two, we crossed the mighty Tupungato River and then hiked up Del Salto Ravine. On day three we reached ca 4,350m, where we established camp at the foot of the south face of an unclimbed peak. We started climbing on November 12 at 7:30 a.m. The maximum difficulty was 45° snow until we reached the upper ridge, which we followed to the summit. We named it Pico Vivi Lotfi and left a topo in a small cairn on top. We descended the north side.

Pablo David González, *Argentina*

Cajón del Mesoncito, Cerro Moai. Cerro Moai is a Chilean mountain (4,368m, 33°44′29″ S, 69°58′56″ W), first ascended in 1964, which had two routes and relatively few ascents. From April 19–21, Mariela Muñoz (German-Chilean), Luis Garrido, and Vicente "Vicho" Gamboa (both Chileans) climbed a new route called Los Porfiados. From a base camp below the mountain, they reached the summit in seven hours via ice up to 50° and some rock along a ridge. They descended the normal route, which is to the climber's right of the new line. [o]

MARCELO SCANU, *Argentina*

Cerro Calingasta, east face; Pico Maida, east face. In December 2011, Martín Neimark, Code Raguet, and I explored the barely visited western area of the Cordillera de la Totora. This beautiful range is located in San Juan Province in the Central Andes of Argentina—a remote area with lots of potential for moderate climbing on high peaks. A relatively new mining road allows a less tiring approach, if you get permission to use it. On our first trip, we ascended an often admired but unclimbed peak: Cabeza de León (5,045m). We also made the first ascent of a neighboring mountain that we named Alfil Peak (5,170m).

In December 2013, captivated by the area, we returned. This time we focused on two unclimbed peaks south of Alfil Peak. We drove from Calingasta, following the mining road to ca 3,700m. From that point, we hiked east to the complex Calingasta Glacier. At the upper part of the glacier we established camp at ca 4,600m, 7km from the road. From camp, we chose the more northern of the two peaks and climbed a straightforward snow slope (700m, 60°) up the east face to the ridge. After 150m, we reached the summit via a short but exposed section of loose rock (UIAA III). We named the peak Cerro Calingasta (5,330m) after the glacier. It took us five hours to ascend and three hours to descend the route (AD).

Unfortunately, the north face of the other peak wasn't in good condition and we decided to attempt another aspect. We first descended to the mining road and then hiked east for 8km through a valley, following a creek to establish a new camp at ca 4,300m, at the base of the mountain's east face. On December 19 at 8 a.m. we began ascending a snowfield (900m, 40°) to reach the upper part of a broken glacier. After a 350m traverse, we climbed the final portion to the summit, about 150m of easy and exposed mixed terrain. We descended by the same route (AD), reaching the road 14 hours after starting our climb. We called the mountain Peak Maida (5,291m). [o]

ANDRÉS BISCAISAQUE, *Argentina*

[This page] The east face routes on Pico Maida (left) and Cerro Calingasta (right). Cerro Alfil and Cerro Cabeza de León lie out of picture to the right of these peaks. *Andrés Biscaisaque*

NORTHERN PATAGONIA

COCHAMÓ

Pared Arco Iris, Positive Affect. On January 7, 2013, Drew Smith and I walked into Cochamó Valley with 160 pounds of food, climbing gear for any situation, and the intentions of having an adventure. After a week of climbing some established routes, we decided to explore the 1,000m Pared Arco Iris, which is dominated by striking dihedrals and large blank faces. It is one of the first faces you see when walking into the valley and looked to offer good free-climbing potential. Arco Iris had not seen a true bottom to top accent, and our goal was to put up a quality free route doing just that.

We worked in capsule style, first aiding and fixing ropes up the wall. Once we had a good idea how the pitches would be broken up, we bolted the anchors and started cleaning the pitches and adding necessary bolts on top rope. We spent a total of six weeks establishing the route. On average each pitch took two days to clean and bolt. In all, we put in 38 belay bolts and 64 protection bolts over 19 pitches. The climbing consists of delicate yet powerful stemming through the many dihedrals, connected by sections of straight-in crack and pure face climbing. Most pitches are 5.9 to 5.11, and there's one unforgettable pitch of 5.12, with powerful stemming for 40m.

Excited to check out the route, locals Daniel Seeliger and Mono Gallardo joined us for the first one-day ascent, climbing with Drew and me, which allowed us to confirm the grades and quality of the climb. The route took us 17 hours round trip. We named the route Positive Affect (975m, 19 pitches, 5.12b) in memory of my late wife, Jennifer Dinaburg, whose positive affect lives on. 📷 🔍

CHANCE TRAUB, *USA*

Atardecer, Doña Debora de Dedos. I've spent 10 seasons of my life climbing in the awesome big-wall destination of Cochamó Valley, and the devouring finger crack of my new route Doña Debora de Dedos (450m, 5.12b) is the best I've ever climbed. Others who have repeated it agreed and have since dubbed it "3D."

Jose Dattoli (Chile), Cristian Gallardo (Argentina), Ezequiel Manoni (Argentina), Chris Kalman (USA), and I all took part in opening this nine-pitch route, starting in March 2012 and finishing in January 2013. The route begins just right of Al Centro y Adentro (Haab-Seeliger, *AAJ 2012*), following obvious dihedrals that split the Atardecer wall in the upper valley of Anfiteatro.

[This page] Chance Traub leading pitch 18's 5.12b crux on Positive Affect. *Drew Smith*

The first six pitches climb some of the best finger cracks in existence—from tips to great locks to off-fingers. The two 5.12 pitches may scare away many, but they shouldn't—there's plenty of 5.11 climbing to be had. The third pitch (5.12a) is probably the most classic on the route, a continuous fingertip splitter that will leave most panting until its end. Pitch five (5.12b) falls into the same category, but on steeper rock in a left-facing dihedral. This will undoubtedly become a classic, must-do route in Cochamó.

DANIEL SEELIGER, *Chile*

El Monstruo, east face, Aprendiz del Monstruo. In late January 2014, Chris Moore, Katie Ryan, Cooper Varney, and I began to porter our gear across the strenuous 13km approach from La Junta to the base of El Monstruo. We set our eyes on a direct and sustained line on the east face, to the right of the one I completed last season, La Presencia de Mi Padre (*AAJ 2013*). At the top of the first pitch, we already knew we were onto something good. After a total of three trips to the wall, doing three- to four-day pushes each time, we completed our new route Aprendiz del Monstruo (1,300m, VI 5.12) on February 19. Of the 22 pitches, only five are easier than 5.10, and there are two pitches of 5.12. The quality of the climbing carries right through from bottom to top.

This is the second free route on the wall and avoids the upper snowfield at the top, negating the need for any snow equipment. We established the route ground-up, and the climb involved a number of bird beaks and other small gear in addition to some bolts. We first aided and cleaned a number of pitches before redpointing them. From the top of the formation, we descended the northeast ridge as the Polish team did from their route La Gran Raja (*AAJ 2006*). Going this way, you will need to downclimb moderate terrain until reaching the rappels for Pared Espejo in Anfiteatro, or continue to the pass at Valle Trinidad where there is an established fixed line. This descent, in its own right, would make for an involved mountaineering route.

Since 2013, a massive rock scar has adorned the far right side of the wall. The debris left a path that bisects La Gran Raja, appearing to have obliterated its initial pitches.

NATHAN CONROY, *USA*

[This page] El Monstruo showing La Presencia de Mi Padre (left) and Aprendiz del Monstruo (right). *Nathan Conroy*

Cerro Capicúa, A Tirar a la Rarita (not quite to summit). This season I hoped to complete a first ascent on one of the most impressive and beautiful walls in Cochamó, the west face of Cerro Capicúa. I'd chosen a line in the middle of the wall, following a very steep headwall. Trying to free as much as possible, and bolting if necessary to favor free climbing, it took three trips over three different years.

I first tried the route with my wife, Leslie Long (USA), in 2011. The possibilities in the lower part of the wall were limited, so we were forced through a slab, hand-drilling for progress. We were able to do just six pitches, with difficulties up to 5.10d. I came back two years later, in 2013, with Carlos San Juan (Chile). To avoid continuing up the slab we joined Tigres del Norte out left, climbing a finger crack in a corner, until we arrived at Plaza Cataluña (a huge ledge in the middle of the face with an *alerce* forest and running water). From here we followed an abandoned project started by Catalonians, climbing four pitches to the summit of a sub-tower (A3). We eventually freed the aid pitches by adding bolts, this time with a Bosch. The climbing was hard, up to 5.12a, and comprised of very thin slab climbing. Then we were forced down to Plaza Cataluña by a storm. Heavy rain kept us there for three days, soaking our clothes and sleeping bags. Eventually we bailed and rappelled through waterfalls—kind of epic.

On my third trip, in 2014, I teamed up with J.B. Haab (USA). We were armed with ropes to fix, bolts, and a tent to establish a real campsite on Plaza Cataluña. Four days of climbing brought us to pitch 20, where peckers proved very helpful (A3). Only six pitches remained to the summit; we decided to go for it, even though the skies were gloomy. The cracks up high were full of dirt, so progression was slow—cleaning and aid climbing. But the headwall was wild: an overhanging chimney, a huge roof, an exposed flake, a nice hand crack (finally!), and more filthy, slow aiding. By the time we were on top of pitch 25 it started to rain, just one short pitch below the top of the wall! We rappelled in the rain and kept cleaning the fixed ropes through the night.

Capicúa, in Catalonian, means a palindrome, a number that can be read the same way forward and backward. Thus, we named the route A Tirar a la Rarita (1,000m, VI 5.12a A3). Four slab pitches could be freed at solid 5.13 with the addition of bolts for protection. We did a thorough job cleaning the route up to pitch 18, and most of the anchors have two bolts. It was a bummer not to reach the summit after so much steep climbing—the final pitch is likely 5.7 or easier. But I'm not going back up there just for one pitch, that's for sure. 🔳

PATRICIO VYHMEISTER, *Chile*

[This page] Cerro Capicúa, showing A Tirar a la Rarita. *Patricio Vyhmeister*

[This page] Chris Kalman climbing a five-star pitch on El Filo la Aleta de Tiburón. *Austin Siadak*

La Aleta de Tiburón, El Filo la Aleta de Tiburón. In January 2014, Florian Haenel (Germany), Austin Siadak (USA), and I made the first ascent of an unclimbed feature left of Pared del Tiempo. (At first, it appears to be part of Pared del Tiempo, but it is separate from that wall.) The lower part of this feature is largely unbroken by cracks, dihedral systems, or other lines of weakness, and the only path up the wall that didn't appear rife with endless sections of hard hooking was a prominent arête starting left of a talus field. This trends left to join a prominent ridge on the southeast aspect (left side) of the wall. From the top one can summit Pared Atardecer on the left or Cerro Laguna on the right via 45 minutes of scrambling.

Over three days, we went ground-up on the route, bolting on lead by power and hand drill, and running out anything our cojones would allow. On a budget, I had settled for a fairly "Barbie" drill, which got us eight holes per battery at best. So we ended up doing more hand drilling and R/X climbing than any of us were really psyched on. We summited on the third day. All of our bolts had been drilled on lead, we had done minor cleaning, and the 11-pitch route had mostly 5.9–5.10+ climbing, but often run-out. The route was neither hard enough nor clean enough to appeal to stronger climbers, nor safe or clean enough to appeal to others. Our hope in the first place had been to establish a nice "beginner's route," so we decided to continue working on the line, making it safer and cleaner. We spent another three days on the route, simply working, and finally called it good when there were no more unreasonable run-outs.

We all believe this will clean up into a classic moderate line, and a good introduction for any visiting climber. We named the wall, which resembles a huge shark fin, La Aleta de Tiburón; the route is El Filo la Aleta de Tiburón ("The Shark's Fin Ridge," 525m, 5.10+). 📷

CHRIS KALMAN, *USA*

Pared el Fin de Tiempo, Siete Venas. After opening El Filo la Aleta de Tiburon (*see previous report*), I was set on finding a cleaner and harder route, full of splitter cracks. Near the back of El Anfiteatro, up a gully, was an amazing-looking buttress, still untouched. I was in need of a partner. Luckily, my girlfriend Megan Kelly and our new friend Dustin-Marco Hardgrove showed interest just in time.

A few access pitches led us to an amazing series of splitter cracks that form the bulk of the line, which is capped by a lightning-bolt-shaped squeeze chimney. On day two, Marco sat out and Zdzislaw "Tom" Lepert jumped in; however, we were only able to push the route one pitch higher, and with bad weather coming, as well as the end of Megan's trip, we had to put the effort on hold. After Megan returned to the U.S., Marco and I teamed up with Miranda Oakley to finish the line. That day we attempted to free the lower pitches, while carrying drilling and cleaning gear. I was able to free the first pitch "Index 5.11c" (which is maybe more like 5.12a); Marco led a 5.11/5.12 splitter on pitch three; and I came heartbreakingly close on the fourth pitch tips crack, which features two roofs, an offwidth-squeeze finish, and a deadpoint to a granite spike (proposed 5.12).

Above the crux we continued upward, free-climbing wet, vertical cracks (5.11) and mungy offwidths (5.9). Marco led the final pitch in the dark: a full 70m epic to the summit. We topped out around midnight, then made our way down the route, bolting as much of a rappel line as we could with our remaining battery. Unfortunately, we had to leave a few empty holes, as we ran out of bolts. A few rap anchors are comprised of wedged knots. We plan to return and establish a safe bolted rappel line for future climbers. We named the route Siete Venas (10 pitches, 5.12a C1) in honor of the seven distinct pitches of clean cracks on the route. The wall, which was previously unclimbed, we called Pared el Fin de Tiempo ("The End of Time Wall"). The route can be rappelled with a single 70m rope, but bring extra nuts to back things up. 🖾

CHRIS KALMAN, *USA*

Cerro Laguna, Surfing the Bamboo Chair. After a month of fighting cold weather in El Chaltén, my partners, Kivik Francois and Olivier Zintz (both from Belgium), and I decided to head north to the sunny granite walls of Cochamó. On January 11 we climbed a new line ground-up on Cerro Laguna, opening a direct route up the right side of this beautiful wall, following a large corner system with mostly thin cracks and several roofs. The climbing was excellent and sustained, with eight of the 11 pitches being 5.10 or harder. We didn't place any bolts, keeping the adventure intact. The line is on nearly perfect rock, with few ledges and many hanging belays. We called the route Surfing the Bamboo Chair (385m, 5.12b A0) due to the uncomfortable hanging belays and the bamboo belay chair Kivik made to combat them. Two pendulums might be freed.

Two days later, on January 13, we free-climbed the final pitch of the Cochamó classic Las Manos del Día. This pitch tackles a 10m horizontal roof crack with mind-blowing exposure, and goes free at 5.11+/12-. It's like Separate Reality, except it's 13 pitches off the deck!

LOGAN JAMISON, *USA*

Pared del Tiempo, Todo Cambia. In February, Cooper Varney, Elise Maillot, Laure Batoz, Caroline North, and Nick Heyward established a new route in El Antifeatro on Pared del Tiempo. The 8-pitch route, comprised of splitter cracks and roofs, was eventually free-climbed by Chris Moore and Cooper Varney on February 23. The route took five days of work, cleaning and adding bolted anchors (6 bolts total), with a mix of ground-up and top-down tactics, before it could be free climbed. They called the climb Todo Cambia ("Everything Changes," 450m, 5.11c). The recommended descent is via Doppler Effect (*AAJ 2013*). 🖾

Information supplied by Caroline North and Cooper Varney

TURBIO VALLEY

Cerro Mariposa, La Vuelta de los Condores. Paul McSorley initially told me about the Turbio Valley in the summer of 2008, after seeing a photo of Cerro Mariposa in the refugio at Aguja Frey near Bariloche. "Where's that?" he inquired. Nobody would tell him. However, blessed with fluent Spanish and a gregarious, charismatic nature, Paul eventually pried it out of the reticent locals: The wall was located deep in Rio Turbio valley, near the hippy farming town of El Bolsón. Back in Squamish, Paul relayed the rumors to me: endless machete-assisted bushwhacking, red-wine-guzzling gauchos, river rafting, and stacks of virgin walls. The place was just too intriguing. We had to go.

In February 2009 we went into the valley with Andrew Querner. A boat ride across Lago Puelo, followed by two days on horseback, led to about a week of thick, prickly bushwhacking. Intimidated by the rumors of rockfall on Cerro Mariposa, we switched our objective to the Piritas Valley— appetizing rock towers that weren't capped by a threatening glacier. It was a great trip, and we climbed two new lines on the Piritas. [*The first climbs in the Piritas Valley likely were climbed by Bicho Fiorenza (Argentina), who visited in 2006 with Pedro Lutti and in 2007 with Morsa Degregori. See AAJ 2009.*] After we were done climbing we rafted out the river in marginal, kiddie-pool rafts. The whole experience—from the horsemanship to the climbing to the rafting—was like being in a different world. I knew we weren't done with the enchanted valley.

In January 2014 I returned with Matt Van Biene, Marc-Andre Leclerc and Paul McSorley, intent on attempting Cerro Mariposa. Wary of the glacier on top, we desperately hoped to find a protected line on the northeast face. This time we came armed with burly rafts—on top of floating the river, we would have to cross a lake to reach the base of the wall. After the gauchos dropped us off, a week's worth of load shuttling saw us primed and ready below the very remote face. And after a half-day of fixing a few lines, we were ready to attempt the wall.

Aside from a couple of stomach-churning core shots on our ropes, the route went smoothly. We found a line more or less unthreatened by rockfall, left of the steepest section of wall, in a large

[This page] La Vuelta de los Condores, on the left side of Cerro Mariposa. *Matt Van Biene*

corner system, accessed by some difficult, glacier sculpted slabs. While on route, giant condors flew overhead, as if, we think, to encourage us. The hairiest lead came right at the top, where 21-year-old Marc tagged up the aid gear, then high-stepped on a marginal, upside-down knifeblade. We all held our breath, but the youngster showed us his repertoire of skills and led us safely to the rim. After another 45 minutes of snow plodding, we crested the sun-drenched summit. Following an open bivy near the top, we rappelled for a half-day back to our sleeping bags below the wall.

After a few days of hiking and rafting out, we clinked Heinekens on the banks of Lago Puelo. Miraculously, we had been blessed with a two-week spell of perfect weather for our climb. We didn't have a SAT phone, so we did weather forecasting the old-school way: squinting at the clouds. By the time we drained our first beers, the archetypal Patagonian winds and rain had returned. This was the first ascent of the wall and we called our route La Vuelta de los Condores (700m, 5.11 A2).

[*Editor's note: Cerro Mariposa lies on the Chile-Argentina border and is accessed from Argentina. Climbers are known to have visited the Mariposa valley at least as far back as 2001. During that year, as American Jerry Dodrill reported in a comment at Climbing.com, he and Willie and Damian Benegas scoped routes in the valley but were prevented by weather from attempting major ascents. While they were there, an Argentine team had an epic in which the leader on a big-wall attempt popped an aid hook and dropped his drill, which speared the belayer's leg, requiring an arduous evacuation down the wall, through the boulder-filled forest, and out the Rio Turbio by pack raft, where, according to Dodrill, "they capsized and nearly drowned." A report by Ryan Huetter in AAJ 2010 documents several ascents and attempts in the valley, including a repeat of the "Brazilian Route" (550m, 5.10+) on a formation called La Oreja.*] 🔲 ▶

WILL STANHOPE, *Canada*

AYSÉN REGION

Cerro Peñón, northeast face. On October 27, Felipe Cancino and I, both Chileans, made the first ascent of the northeast face of Cerro Peñón (2,424m), the second-highest peak in the Castillo Range, which is located south of Coyhaique. This prominent peak was first climbed by its east face, solo, by New Zealand climber David Waugh (*AAJ 1982*). It's unlikely to have been climbed again prior to our ascent, making our route the second on the mountain.

Our ascent was generally straightforward. We roped up while crossing the 2km glacier, then climbed solo up the northeast face for 700m (up to 70°). After this, we roped briefly to surmount a short rock step (5.5). Another 100m of 60° climbing brought us to just below the summit. From here, 10m of extremely loose and unprotected rock (5.7) and a short knife-edged traverse brought us to the top (850m, D 5.7 70°). 🔲

CHRISTIAN STEIDLE, *Chile*

Hama, La Via de los Seracs. Marco Poblete and Harry Brito (both from Chile) climbed a new route, La Via de los Seracs (5.9 60°), on an unnamed peak in the Aysén Region of Chilean Patagonia, which they called Hama (ca 2,400m). The peak is located near the Miller River valley outside of Puerto Sánchez.

The duo began from the town of Coyhaique on October 26, driving five hours south, and then approaching on foot for four hours to a camp at ca 1,400m. On the morning of October 27

they began up the route, climbing solid névé for the majority of the climb, and then reaching a short, steeper rock band (5.9). Above this they continued climbing moderate snow slopes (40°), reaching a point just 10m below the summit after 11 hours of climbing. They turned around at their high point, finding the remaining ridge to the summit too dangerous, with rotten ice and snow.

From a report at Desnivel.com

La Pirámide, summary. Yep, right there in the desert, just a two-hour drive from my house located outside of Chile Chico in northern Chilean Patagonia is Wyoming's Devils Tower on steroids: La Pirámide. The massive cliff hosts route potential up to 700' and is a great venue when the weather over the ice cap further south is bad—a not uncommon event.

The first development on the wall was done by fellow Americans Jay Smith, Jim Turner, Roger Schimmel, and myself starting in 2009. However, the area got a real boost this past year from visiting Brits Dave Brown and John Crook, who established three excellent new multi-pitch routes up to 5.11d. So far there are over 20 pitches of climbing established of varying lengths, with four excellent multi-pitch climbs in the 5.11a–5.11d range and some nice

[This page, top] La Via de los Seracs on Hama. The route stopped just shy of the pointy summit. *Marco Poblete* [This page, bottom] Corners and more corners: La Pirámide, viewed from the grassy camp area below the formation. *Jim Donini*

single-pitch climbs starting at 5.8+.

Reaching the cliff requires two hours of hiking from the road bordering Lago General Carrera, which lies on the Chile-Argentina border. This brings you to basecamp in a vast meadow below the wall where there is a good natural spring. Only soaring condors and noisy guanacos will disturb your solitude. From camp it's just a 35-minute approach up to the wall.

Future development on the cliff is likely to come from local climber Andres Bozollo, who has likely developed a trained cadre of young climbers in Chile Chico. So far, only three bolts have been placed for protection and there are a few bolted belays but the area is ninety-nine-percent place your own gear—definitely bring wires. 🔲

JIM DONINI, *USA*

Peak 1,960m, south face. After looking for a partner for days, I made the decision of going on a solo trip to climb the unnamed Peak 1,960m, which I had seen on a previous expedition. The peak is located on the north side of the Rio Leones, west of Claro River. A few locals refer to the peak by the nickname "Nariz de Eleuterio."

On March 5, I drove south from Coyhaique to Valle Leones to the Meliquina area. From Valle Leones I drove west on an old dirt road to reach my jumping off point. I then set up a pack raft to cross the Leones River from the north side to the south side. After crossing the river and approaching for a few hours on foot, I decided to set up camp. This is the same approach as for San Valentin, further northwest on the icefield. Early the next morning I set out for the climb. An hour approach brought me to the base of the south face. I took a rope and a set of friends and some slings just in case. On the first part of the wall I climbed through some steep and loose areas. Above, I reached a ledge below the most difficult part of the route (5.6). After around 45 more minutes of climbing I reached another steep section before the terrain eased off. My ascent took about two hours, and I did not find evidence of previous ascents (500m, AD, 5.6). I left a cairn on top with a note then mostly downclimbed the route. It took me two and a half hours to reach my car from the base, but not without some adventures crossing the river again. 🔲 🔍

PEDRO BINFA, *Chile*

CHALTÉN MASSIF

Chaltén Massif, summary. The 2013–2014 season was relatively cold and wintry compared with recent years, and many climbers focused on ice and traditional alpine routes more than pure rock climbs. This resulted in first ascents of interesting summits and a number of attractive new ice and mixed climbs.

At the south end of the Chaltén massif, Argentines Rafael Heer, Juan Jerez, and Juan Manuel Raselli did the first ascent of Punta Sordo, the last unclimbed minor summit on the west ridge of Cerro Grande, a voluptuously rimed point. They approached from the west, climbing the long west ridge of Cerro Grande, and descended to the east.

In November, Italians Tomas Franchini, Paolo Grisa, Ermanno Salvaterra, and Francesco Salvaterra made a daring attempt on the west face of Torre Egger. They climbed capsule-style, using portaledges, and spent 11 days on the wall before descending from their highpoint. The line climbs the very center of the steep and featureless face. Later in the season, Franchini and Francesco

Salvaterra climbed a dangerous new line on the south face of Cerro Rincón, tackling the obvious dihedral under the massively overhanging summit serac. They aptly named their line Ruleta Trentina (2,000', WI5 M5).

On Aguja Standhardt, Norwegians Robert Caspersen, Ole Lied, and Trym Atle Sæland did the first integral ascent of SCUD, a line that had been climbed to the junction with Exocet, but without continuing to the summit. They onsighted every pitch and proposed renaming the route Desarmada, believing that routes should only be considered "climbed" when they reach the summit.

On the east face of Aguja de la Medialuna, Argentines Jorge Ackermann, Tomas Aguilo, and Nicolas Benedetti climbed a pleasant seven-pitch new route called La Media Docena (1,100', 5.11). Farther up the Torre Valley, Scott Bennett and Coleman Blakeslee climbed an imposing 300' waterfall on the east face of Perfil de Indio (WI5+).

In the Marconi Valley climbers reached a number of unclimbed summits. Ben Erdmann (U.S.), David Gladwin (U.K.), and Kim Ladiges (Tasmania) climbed a tower on the west side of the north face of Cerro Domo Blanco, which they christened Punta de Los Tres Mosqueteros. Their 10-pitch line, which they dubbed D'Artagnan (1,300', 5.11+), climbs a steep and clean corner, and involves sustained difficulties. Immediately to the right, Mike Collins and Jonathan Schaffer (U.S.) did the first ascent of El Filo del Tornado (11 pitches, 5.11). Collins and Schaffer also climbed a new line on a buttress between the west pillar of Cerro Pollone and Aguja Tito Carrasco, reaching a point not far from the summit (1,300', 5.11). On the south face of Cerro Pollone, Canadians Tony Richardson and Jon Simms opened El Busca Jesus (650', WI4 M5), an alternate finish to Rayuela.

A number of other new routes were climbed on the west face of Aguja Tito Carrasco. Mike Collins and Jonathan Schaffer did the first ascent of Halle Berry (1,000', 5.11 C1), a line on the right side of the west face. Left of Halle Berry, Katsutaka Yokoyama, Ryo Masumoto, and Yusuke Sato (Japan) climbed Atari (1,000', 5.12), and later Yokoyama and Masumoto climbed Ippon (1,000', 5.12b A0) immediately to the left. Zigzagging between the routes Zigzag and Ippon, Joel Enrico and Adam Ferro climbed Terroir (1,000', 5.11 C1).

A number of small summits were climbed on the ridge between Aguja Tito Carrasco and Gran Gendarme del Pollone. The three to the south were christened Aguja El Tridente, the two

[This page] The dangerous and remote new line Ruleta Trentina on the south face of Cerro Rincón. *Rolando Garibotti*

farther north Cumbrecitas. Jack Cramer was involved in four of those five ascents and did the first ascent of El Tridente with Drew Smith via the east face, calling their route La Piqueta Voladora (230m, 75° M4). On the west face of the south summit of El Tridente, Justin DuBois, Allen Riling, and Edward Corder climbed one of the more difficult lines (400m, 6a C1WI4 M6 70°); however, they retreated off to the right without reaching the summit.

On Cordón Marconi, Dejan Koren and Bostjan Mikuz (Slovenia) did the first ascent of Aguja Dumbo, a big fin-like tower at the southern end of the chain. They climbed from the west, finding difficulties to 85° and M6.

On the Fitz Roy massif, Austin Siadak, Julian Poush, and Kevin Prince did the second ascent of the lengthy North Pillar Sit Start, climbing an important new variation from the very toe of the buttress (6,300', 5.11 C1). On the west face of Cerro Fitz Roy, Waldo Aravena, Gabriel Fava, and Roberto Treu (Argentina) climbed Tango Libre, a 1,500' alternate start to the Afanassieff.

Many new lines were added to Aguja Guillaumet. On the west face, Scott Bennett and Graham Zimmerman climbed Bossanova (1,300', 7a+ C1). On the east face, Iñaki Coussirat, Carlos Molina (Argentina), and Caroline North (Denmark) climbed Klettertren, which involves two variations to the Beger-Jennings route. Ben Collett and Josh Finkelstein climbed a variation to the Fowler route: So Long Charlie (300', WI4). Tony Richardson and Jon Simms (Canada) climbed the Richard-Simmons (300', AI4), a classy variation to the Coqueugniot-Guillot. On the pillar to the right of the Amy-Vidailhet route, Dave Macleod and Calum Muskett (U.K.) climbed a difficult new mixed line (600', M8).

On Aguja Saint-Exúpery, Matteo Della Bordella, Luca Schiera (both Italy), and Sylvan Schupbach (Switzerland) climbed a variation to Chiaro di Luna, heading up and right from the big ledge halfway up to reach the col between the two summits and continue via the Austríaca route to the summit. They called their line Can Accompany Only (800', 5.11+). Earlier the trio had climbed a sit start to the Californian Route on Cerro Fitz Roy, reaching the base via the couloir between Aguja de la Silla and the southwest face of Fitz Roy, "approaching" by the route Destreza Criolla, then continuing up the couloir to the Col de los Americanos (Robbins-Gutierrez, 2009). They then climbed the Filo Este of Aguja de la Silla, linking it the next day to the Californian Route. In all they covered close to 6,000' of vertical gain with difficulties to 6a+ C1 and M4/5, over four days.

[*Editor's note: First-hand reports describing some of these climbs in further detail can be found at the AAJ website.*]

Rolando Garibotti, *Pataclimb.com, Argentina*

[This page] Dave Macleod climbing a difficult mixed corner on Guillaumet. *Calum Muskett*

Aguja Volonqui, east buttress, El Lobito; Cerro Marconi Central, east face, La SuperWhillans; Cerro Pier Giorgio, east face (first complete ascents). During several of the short, cold and snowy weather windows in the 2013-2014 season, I turned my attention to neglected, smaller, but still fantastic peaks.

On December 4 I hiked into the Marconi Glacier with Sarah Hart to attempt an obvious ice gully on the east buttress of Aguja Volonqui (ca 2,200m) the following day. The route contained steep snow, moderate mixed climbing, one pitch of steep ice, a bunch of mellow ice, and one pitch of tricky, thin ice. The hardest climbing was on the final pitch (M5 A0), which involved one move pulling on a cam and then a mantel onto the ridge just 10m from the summit boulder. From the summit, we descended the Carrington-Rouse route (east face and south ridge, 1976) by rappelling and downclimbing. We named our route El Lobito (400m, AI4+ M5 A0), and I'd recommend it. Carrington and Rouse were turned back just below the summit by a rime mushroom, so this is likely the first ascent of the peak.

I hiked into the Marconi Glacier again on December 18 with Rolando Garibotti to attempt Cerro Marconi Central (ca 2,380m) the following day. We hoped to climb an obvious ice and snow ramp up the east face that I had attempted solo in September, before turning back because of poor ice conditions. Our ascent was enjoyable and fairly casual, with awesome scenery and excellent conditions. The rock is fairly compact and was rime-covered, so pitons are recommended. Our ascent took roughly five hours from the bergschrund to the summit at a moderate pace, and our descent took about five hours as well. We named the route La SuperWhillans (600m, AI3 M3) for its strong resemblance in form to Aguja Poincenot's famous Whillans Ramp, and also a play on the local classic La Supercanaleta. La SuperWhillans was repeated the very next day by Argentine climbers Carlitos Molina and Iñaki Coussirat and is recommended if conditions are right.

The only previous known attempt on Cerro Marconi Central was in 1966 by Argentine climbers Edgar Köpcke, Avedis Naccachian, and Enrique Triep, from the west side. Their attempt

[This page] The east and south faces of Aguja Volonqui, showing the Carrington-Rouse (left, not to summit) and El Lobito (right). *Colin Haley*

ended somewhere at or near the summit ridge, likely making ours the first trip to the summit.

With another weather window, Rolando and I left Niponino on January 23 at the leisurely hour of 8:30 a.m. to attempt the Skvarca-Skvarca route (*AAJ 1963*) up the central east face of Cerro Pier Giorgio (ca 2,700m). The first part is a chimney with mostly very enjoyable mixed climbing. There were two sections of A1, which would have been a time-consuming affair except that earlier attempts had left many pitons in-situ. After five pitches in the chimney we simul-climbed easy ice up and

left toward the summit. One more pitch of mixed climbing brought us to the col just south of the summit, and about 25m below the top, where a wooden wedge in a crack marked the highpoint of the Skvarca brothers. We first tried to climb to the summit directly, but found 30cm thick rime ice covering blank rock. Looking to the right, we found a flake and made a 15m diagonal rappel to the east side. From here we climbed directly to the summit via a narrow ice chimney—a bit like a mixed-climbing version of the Harding Slot, but fortunately easier! We reached the summit at 8:30 p.m., 12 hours after leaving Niponino.

Only after some days of research did we realize this was the first complete ascent of Cerro Pier Giorgio. In addition to the Skvarca brothers' ascent, a handful of other routes had been climbed to the summit ridge of Pier Giorgio, but no one had managed to traverse the gendarmed ridge to the summit. In this way Cerro Pier Giorgio is a bit like Chaltén's version of Les Droites: The summit ridge is very long, technical, and gendarmed, and traversing to the summit is in many cases just as difficult as the climbing up to the summit ridge. [*Editor's note: Cerro Pier Giorgio has also been spelled as "Cerro Piergiorgio" in recent reports. The peak was named after Pier Giorgio Frassati, a young climber in the early twentieth-century. The west-northwest wall is home to one of the sheerest big-walls in the area with 800m of vertical relief and few ascents. The east face also hosts future big-wall-style opportunities to the right of the Skvarca route.*]

These three ascents were by no means particularly difficult or significant climbs by today's standards, but it is astounding that in 2014 such prominent summits remained unclimbed. More than anything else, they are worthwhile simply because the peaks are wild, beautiful, and much more "alpine" than many of the mountains on the Chaltén Massif. 📷

Colin Haley, *USA*

[This page] The east face of Cerro Marconi Central. La SuperWhillans climbs the obvious snow and ice ramp. *Colin Haley*

Domo Blanco, southeast face, Super Domo. This year marked my eighth season of climbing in Patagonia. After spending three weeks further north attempting the east face of San Lorenzo, I arrived in El Chaltén December 10 to cold and snowy weather.

After not much climbing, a short but very cold weather window appeared the beginning of January 2014. The mountains remained icy but I had no interest in stepping into the conga line on one of the few ice climbs in the range. While looking at photos from the Manos y Más Manos traverse I did last year I saw a photo of the southeast face of Domo Blanco: Cutting across the face was a deep, unclimbed cleft with three distinct tiers. I instantly knew that was the objective.

After some rousting I got brothers Joel and Neil Kaufmann to commit. We left Niponino on January 2 at a somewhat casual 5 a.m. and by 8 a.m. we were at the base of the bergschrund, ready to go. I took the first block leading up moderate terrain of mostly névé with the occasional short step of water ice. We ran the rope out and simul-climbed the first section of in three fun pitches.

Joel took the lead up the second part, which started with an easy snow traverse leading to gradually steeper terrain. We probably simul-climbed close to 90m before Joel built a belay. This brought us to the base of a black dike and the mixed climbing crux. This great pitch led to a tricky rock traverse above that brought us deeper into the cleft. Finishing this second tier, we got a great view of the final tier (about 180m long). Up to this point the climbing had been incredible, but we now knew we were about to venture into some of the best climbing we'd ever done in Patagonia: The entire length was filled with perfect steep water-ice. We'd never seen anything like it in Patagonia.

Joel, being the most proficient ice climber, continued leading up this part. Two pitches of perfect WI4 deposited us at the base of the final 50m headwall, where the ice was iron-hard and blue-grey in color, and appearing to be hundreds of years old. Joel's now dull tools and crampons bounced off the vertical shield of ice many times before making purchase. However, we all had ear-to-ear grins on our faces knowing that we were in the process of picking one of the plumb lines

[This page] Joel Kaufmann leading the spectacular ice runnel on the upper part of Super Domo. *Mikey Schaefer*

left in Patagonia. Joel topped out the last pitch at around 7 p.m. and we all scurried the final couple hundred meters to the summit in strong winds. Though cold at the summit, we all felt the burning inside of having just completed one of the finest climbs in the range: Super Domo (500m, WI5 M5/6).

MIKEY SCHAEFER, *USA*

Fitz Roy massif, "Fitz Traverse." In mid-February, Tommy Caldwell and I were lucky enough to get a five-day weather window in Patagonia. We took advantage of it by climbing the "Fitz Traverse," a complete traverse of the Fitz Roy Massif. From north to south, the major summits on the traverse include Aguja Guillaumet, Aguja Mermoz, Cerro Fitz Roy, Aguja Poincenot, Aguja Rafael Juárez, Aguja Saint-Exúpery, and Aguja de l'S. It was my first real climb in Patagonia, and I have to say it was one of the most incredible climbing experiences of my life. One of the highlights was the fact that there was a full or nearly full moon for the entire traverse, and every night the glaciers would glow around us, staying light until dawn.

We started at 9:45 a.m. on February 12 from Paso Guillaumet, and even though the weather was perfect, conditions were far from ideal. Our progress up Guillaumet's Brenner-Moschioni Route was slowed by icy cracks and general snowiness, and the Argentina Route up Mermoz, our second peak, was a wet and icy nightmare—at least for me, since I have no experience with those kinds of conditions. We bivied that night between the summit of Mermoz and Aguja Val Biois.

On day two we traversed to the base of the North Pillar (a.k.a Goretta Pillar) of Fitz Roy and climbed the Casarotto Route with the Kearney-Knight variation in three glorious pitches by simul-climbing. The top of the pillar was a snowy, rime-covered mess. I thought we might be on Cerro Torre for a minute. Tommy led us the rest of the way to the summit of Fitz Roy, a heroic effort that involved aiding a river of freezing water in the dark. It was the only section on the traverse that

[This page] The skyline of the Fitz Roy massif, viewed from the east side. The Fitz Traverse, as completed by Tommy Caldwell and Alex Honnold, is shown. The duo started on the right and ended on the left. *Rolando Garibotti*

I jugged, super-grateful I didn't have to climb the icy abomination of a headwall. We camped that night on the summit of Fitz Roy. The next morning we ran into Whit Magro on the summit, and he helped us find the descent rappels down the Franco-Argentine Route.

We then continued simul-climbing across to Aguja Poincenot, possibly climbing an unclimbed spire along the way between Punta M&M and Aguja Kakito. This provided access to the Potter-Davis Route on Aguja Poincenot, which we short-fixed to the summit. We camped that night on top of Poincenot, hopeful that we would finish out the three remaining and smaller summits the next day. The descent off of Poincenot was one of the big unknowns of the whole traverse because it involved reversing a rarely climbed 1,000' big wall, but thankfully, after a lot of anxiety and searching, we managed to find the rappels down Judgment Day, nailing it on our first try.

Once at the Col SUSAT, we simul-climbed the Piola-Anker Route on Aguja Rafael Juárez and traversed the ridge to Aguja Saint-Exúpery before getting bogged down rappelling the Austríaca Route on Exúpery. We were forced to do the many rappels with just a 38m rope, as we had developed a core-shot near the middle of the lead rope, and it was too windy to use our tag line. In all we did over 20 short rappels with the remnants of our lead line before the wind calmed down and we could use our tag line again. When it got dark we decided to bivy that night below Aguja de l'S, the last spire on the traverse. It seemed prudent to rest and climb it in the light so we wouldn't botch the route finding or hurt ourselves crossing the glacier during the night. Needless to say we were very tired by this point. On February 16, we simul-climbed the north ridge Aguja de l'S in about a half-hour in our gloves and approach shoes, a bit of an anticlimactic finish to this amazing traverse.

As we summited the weather window quickly closed and the wind became nuclear. We rappelled and staggered across the glacier back to town, much worse for the wear after five days out. I had even developed snow-blindness. It took two days of full bed rest before we even considered trying to move around or get out of the house. It was quite the traverse. I can't recall all the exact stats off-hand, but anyone can look up a photo of the Fitz Roy skyline to get a sense of the scale. It's a lot of climbing.

[Editor's note: In all, Caldwell and Honnold climbed over 5km of ridge-line, with nearly 4,000m of vertical gain, and with difficulties up to 5.11d C1 65°. They simul-climbed throughout the majority of the traverse, reducing the 20-pitch North Pillar of Fitz Roy to a mere three pitches. The pair climbed Fitz Roy and Aguja Poincenot in rock shoes but did everything else wearing approach shoes.]

ALEX HONNOLD, USA, with additional information from Rolando Garibotti

TORRES DEL PAINE

South Tower of Paine, southeast face, Wall of Paine (not to summit). In October-November 2013, Jerry Gore, Raphael Jochaud, Calum Muskett, and Mike "Twid" Turner made the first ascent of the southeast face of the South Tower of Paine. The South Tower stands tallest among the three towers that form the massif, and the smooth southeast face offers more than 1,000m of climbing. Constant exposure to wind and storm greatly exacerbate its difficulty. Wall of Paine (900m, A3+) climbs 18 pitches of sustained, difficult climbing. The first half of the route contained poor rock but improved higher, allowing for more free climbing. Unfortunately, harsh winds up to 150km/h forced the climbers to retreat after topping out the wall, just 100m shy of the summit.

From a report on Desnivel.com

This page] The first ascent of Alas de Ángel via the northeast and southwest faces. *Camilo Rada*

CORDILLERA DE SARMIENTO

Cerro Alas de Ángel, Cerro Trono. The Cordillera de Sarmiento is the southernmost range of the Andes before they sink under the Magellan Strait. Although these peaks are all under 2,000m, the ragged ridges, sharp needles, and steep faces offer great mountaineering challenges, with the worst of the infamous Patagonian weather. After a rush of exploration and attempts through the 1990s, the range had not seen climbers in 12 years before Natalia Martinez (Argentina) and I visited in August 2012. [*See Recon: Cordillera de Sarmiento earlier in this edition for the full history of these spectacular mountains.*] On August 17 we set base camp near the toe of Glaciar Bernal on the west bank of the Fiordo de las Montañas, after a four-hour Zodiac ride from Puerto Natales. Following a week of load carrying in whiteouts and a couple of stormbound days in an igloo, we set high camp at 1,200m on a plateau near the headwalls of Cerro Alas de Ángel and Cerro Trono, the third- and second-highest summits of the range, respectively. [*These peaks were named Angel Wings and the Throne by the 1992 expedition led by American Jack Miller, but the consensus now is that Spanish names should be used.*]

The clouds broke for the first time on August 25, giving us the opportunity to quickly plan a route up Alas de Angel (1,767m). Following our plan to chase every single climbing opportunity, we launched an attempt amid constant wind and snow flurries, following the middle line of the steep glacier pouring down the northeast face. This involved a few short vertical steps on good ice. From the col between the north and south summits, we followed the southwest face up the northern peak, still in whiteout conditions. The crux came near the top with a steep pitch up a rime-covered wall. We reached the summit after six hours (550m, D+).

On the 27th we could see Cerro Trono (1,879m) for the first time, and we planned a route up its broad and rime-covered west face, which we attempted the next day in whiteout conditions. After linking a series of terraces with four pitches on rime and hard ice, we failed to penetrate the band of overhanging rime cauliflowers guarding the summit ridge.

We made a second attempt on September 2, the only day that we enjoyed a few hours of

[This page] Two of the peaks climbed on Peninsula Buckland: Cerro Jetaqána Taf (left; the name means "Arrowhead" in the local language) and Cerro Nous (right). *Rainhard Fuchs*

clear skies. We followed a similar route, but aimed first to reach the easier northern summit, which proved to be lower than expected. After returning to the col, we regained our earlier highpoint and continued to excavate rime and loose ice until we were able to climb five meters of overhanging ice, with several steps of aid, to gain the summit ridge. Easy terrain led to the summit, which we reached under heavy winds and whiteout conditions (500m, MD). 🖼

CAMILO RADA GIACAMAN, *Chile*

PENINSULA BUCKLAND

Cerro Cristal and other peaks. On December 15, Leopold Fuchs, Philip Schreiner, and I (all Austrians) left Punta Arenas by boat. The aim of our expedition was to explore and climb new routes on Peninsula Buckland, which holds a group of rugged, glaciated mountains west of Monte Buckland (and part of the same land mass), north of Monte Sarmiento, and just south of Isla Dawson. The highest point appeared to be a ca 1,200m rocky peak on the southern side of the peninsula, but we had targeted several other steep peaks, all unclimbed.

After setting up base camp a few meters inland on the north side of the peninsula, we spent two days exploring the area, eventually finding good access to the glacier that stretches about 10km in a northwest-to-southeast direction. With two days of full sun and a few hours without rain on other days we were able to manage five first ascents, including Monte Outland (1,046m), Cerro Cristal (1,206m), Cerro Jetaqána Taf, Cerro Nous, and Las Tres Botas, all of which were unnamed.

The most technical peak we climbed was Cerro Cristal, which we believe to be the highest summit on the peninsula. We climbed the peak by its north ridge up mostly rock (UIAA V) and a short step of water ice. The peak was composed of very friable granite making it hard to place protection. 🖼 🔍

RAINHARD FUCHS, *Austria*

CORDILLERA DE DARWIN

Cerro Coltrane (Mt. Beyond the Far), clarification of first ascent; other disambiguation notes. During the first longitudinal traverse of the Cordillera de Darwin, the French GMHM climbed a peak they called Mt. Beyond the Far, believing this to be the first ascent (*AAJ 2012*). However, during research for the Uncharted Project, mapping and documenting the history of peaks in Tierra del Fuego, we learned that this peak was climbed during an extraordinary and unreported expedition by Americans Douglas Krause and David Scheer in 1991. They named the peak Mt. Coltrane (2,011m, Chilean IGM map; 2,026m GPS). [*Editor's note: The Uncharted Project has uncovered many second or even third "first ascents" of peaks in the Cordillera de Darwin, as well as many ambiguous names. Camilo Rada has prepared extensive documentation of these errors and duplications, and his Cordillera de Darwin Disambiguation Notes can be found at the AAJ website, in addition to photos and an extraordinary new map of the Cordillera de Darwin.*]

NATALIA MARTINEZ, *Argentina, and* CAMILO RADA, *Chile*

Piramide Negra, Cerro Andrea, and other peaks. From September 29-October 18, Michael Ganter, Jörn Heller, Wilfrid Henselmann, Klaus Hildenbrand, Thomas Nieberle, Hans-Jörg Schelb, and I did the probable first ascents of a number of peaks in the Cordillera Darwin. We left from Punta Arenas, sailing south down the Canal Magdalena and then through narrow fjords to reach the Canal Beagle, upon which we traveled east. We used our sailboat to access minor fjords and completed a number of the climbs using skis.

In Fjord Martinez (54°28.073' S, 070°36.34' W) we climbed Cerro Condor (ca 870m), Cerro Aguila (ca 930m), and Piramide Negra (ca 1,120m). In Fjord Bahia King (54°26.065' S, 071°16.399' W) we climbed Aguja Anna (ca 790m). In Fjord Vetisquero we did a traverse of the Timbales Mountains (which range in elevation from ca 865m to 927m). We also climbed Cerro Nicole (ca 1,050m), Cerro Astrid (ca 1,080m, 54°49.753' S, 070°17.154' W), Cerro Nicola (ca 950m, 54°49.939' S, 070°17.729' W), and Cerro Novara (ca 935m, 54°49.753' S, 070°17.154' W). Lastly, in Fjord Pia, we climbed Brazo Pia Este and Cerro Andrea (ca 1,400m, 54°48.916' S, 069°28.473' W). 📷 🔍

ROBERT JASPER, *Germany*

TIERRA DEL FUEGO

Monte Olivia; Monte Toun; Cerro Cinco Hermanos; Torre del Pingui, new winter mixed routes. During the dry winter season of 2013, Argentines José Bonacalza, Ian Schwer, and Julián Fehrmann opened a number of new routes in Tierra del Fuego, outside the city of Ushuaia, Chile. On July 14 they established a new route on the south face of the well-known Monte Olivia (1,318m), which they called Eslabón de Lujo (190m, M5). On July 21 they made the first ascent of Monte Toun, calling their route Castorcitis (250m, M4/M5). On July 24 they climbed a new route on the east face of Cerro Cinco Hermanos (1,280m), called Pinguinos Voladores (150m, M5). And, lastly, on July 29, they climbed a new route on the southwest face of Torre del Pingui, which is located in the Torres del Rino group. They called this route Viaje Completo (230m, 50° M3).

MARCELO SCANU, *Argentina*

ANTARCTICA

ELLSWORTH MOUNTAINS

Sentinel Range, Vinson Massif. It was slightly quieter in the Sentinel Range than in past seasons, with 111 different climbers ascending Mt. Vinson (4,892m). During the 2013–14 season only five climbers ascended Mt. Shinn (4,660m).

A historical note on Shinn: Although it was reported correctly in AAJ 1986, Yvon Chouinard and Doug Tompkins' route on the big west face of Shinn has since been mistakenly placed on the south face. This means that Austrian Christian Stangl's 2008 ascent of the south face, as part of his Triple Seven Summits project, was probably an entirely new route.

DAMIEN GILDEA, *Australia*

HERITAGE RANGE

Various first ascents and traverses. Ralf Laier returned for his third expedition to the Heritage Range, climbing with Antarctic Logistics & Expeditions (ALE) guides Maria Paz "Pachi" Ibarra (Chile) and Seth Timpano (USA). They traveled by Sno-Cat from Union Glacier Camp northwest up the Schanz Glacier, with the aim of making a long, alpine-style traverse of the Soholt Peaks. Starting west of Hessler Peak on December 19, they made the first ascent of the northernmost peak, traversed over the summit, and then climbed the northern slope of Eley Peak (2,280m), which they also traversed. They descended to a campsite at 2,100m, and next day they continued south along the narrow crest, climbing over a number of small tops and one 2,300m summit, which they named Lillywhite Peak. After some tricky mixed climbing over gendarmes in high winds, they descended to a glacier, intending to continue their traverse the next day. However, forecasts of even higher winds forced a return to Union Glacier.

On December 26 they resumed their traverse, attempting the next peak south along their line, which they named Cerro Catedral. Unfortunately, they turned back 40m from the summit after finding loose 5.7 rock above an icy couloir. Moving over to the west, they made the second ascent of Macalester Peak, one of the highest of the Soholt Peaks, by the northwest ridge. Poor weather

[This page] Ralf Laier looks north along the Soholt crest from the col beneath Cerro Catedral. Mt. Craddock and the Vinson Massif are visible ca 120km distant. *Ralf Laier Collection*

[This page] High on the northeast spur of Dallmeyer Peak (1,600m) during an unsuccessful attempt. To the left is Mt. Inverleith, first climbed via the north face (*AAJ 2011*). *Phil Wickens*

prevented an attempt on Bursik Peak, and the trio finished by descending an icefall back to the eastern side of the range for a pickup on the Schanz Glacier.

Several of the Soholt Peaks, including Macalester and Eley, were climbed in January 1994 by the British Antarctic Survey team of Mike Curtis and Brian Hull. Other peaks in the area had been climbed by New Zealand geologists Paul Fitzgerald and Charlie Hobbs. 🔲

DAMIEN GILDEA, *Australia*

ANTARCTIC PENINSULA

Various ascents. I made two trips to the Antarctic Peninsula in late 2013 and early 2014. In December, operating from the yacht Spirit of Sydney with Sean Colyer, Matthew Flyn, and Glenn Wilkes, we visited Cuverville Island and made probably the first ascent of the most northerly couloir on the east face. At around two-thirds height we left the main couloir for a subsidiary branch on the right (250m, Scottish III). From the summit we descended the west slopes on skis.

On Lemaire Island we climbed the two most easterly summits (Pt. 600m and Pt. 650m), east of Rojas Peak. We ascended the east ridges of both at PD. We also made the first ascent of an unnamed peak of ca 700m two nautical miles southwest of Steinheil Point in Andvord Bay, using a camp on the Almirante Ice Fringe.

Next to Tournachon Peak, two nautical miles south of Spring Point in Brialmont Cove, we made the first ascent of Peak 949m via the east face (PD). We also climbed the northwest face of Mt. Hoegh and made an attempt on the unclimbed northeast spur of Dallmeyer Peak (1,600m), reaching an altitude of 1,350m (PD+), where we were stopped by an enormous crevasse.

In January 2014, I joined Jackie and Neville Nuckey, and Warren Dobe, on Icebird. Apart from climbing a number of popular peaks, we made the probable first ascent of a superb 10-pitch couloir (Scottish II) to summit an unnamed peak above the northern shores of Skontorp Cove in Paradise Harbour. 🔲

PHIL WICKENS, *Alpine Club, U.K.*

Mt. Walker (2,350m); Peak 1,712m; The Catwalk, traverse. A French-Canadian team aboard Spirit of Sydney made the second known ascent of Mt. Walker (2,350m). They also made the first ascent of a 1,712m peak above the Montgolfier Glacier, and completed a south-to-north ski traverse through the Catwalk, a narrow section of the Peninsula's spine connecting the Herbert and Detroit plateaus.

Walker was tried in 2002 by Alun Hubbard's team and first climbed in 2005, when it was thought to be one of the highest virgin summits on the Peninsula. Six members of a British Army

Expedition, under the leadership of Richard Patterson, made the ascent during the first traverse of the Forbidden Plateau, the long, narrow icefield extending from Charlotte Bay to Flanders Bay on the west coast of the Peninsula.

DAMIEN GILDEA, *Australia*

Various ascents and ski descents. I had the good fortune to visit the Peninsula in January 2013 with a great group of skiers from the USA, Germany, and the U.K. We climbed and skied numerous peaks, including several above a camp on the glacier that flows into Waddington Bay. Here we did at least two first ascents. Farther south, we climbed Cape Perez, making the second ascent, by a new route. (*See report below.*) A probable first ascent was the central peak of Lahille Island, a great ski peak that we named Mt. Louis (ca 545m). The full version of this report at the AAJ website has peak coordinates and photos. Additional photos can be seen at my website: Jimblyth.com. 📷 📄

JIM BLYTH, *France*

Cape Perez (ca 650m), north face and northwest ridge; First Sister of Fief (986m), east face. On March 5, 2010, New Zealanders Lydia Bradey, Penny Goddard, and Dean Staples made the first known ascent of Cape Perez (65°24'S, 64°06'W). Prior to this, on February 23, the three made what is believed to be a new route on the east face of the First Sister of Fief on Wiencke Island. They climbed 12 pitches of snow and ice at New Zealand 5. From the summit they descended the south ridge to the top of the couloir between the First Sister and Mt. Luigi, then made seven 60m rappels down the couloir, returning to camp after a 14-hour day.

For Cape Perez, the landing proved to be the most difficult part of the route. Once on shore, the three slanted right through a rocky barrier on the right side of the north face, reaching the northwest ridge above a prominent rock spire. They followed moderate snow slopes on or near the ridge until forced into a detour by a gulch. The summit was a spectacular point above the big walls of the southwest face, dropping into the ocean below. Perez was named after three Argentinian brothers by French explorer Jean-Baptiste Charcot in 1904. 📷

LINDSAY GRIFFIN, *with information from expedition members*

[This page] Cape Perez from the north. (1) January 2013 second ascent. (2) March 2010 first ascent (New Zealand). The impressive rock tower remains unclimbed. *Penny Goddard*

EUROPE

Most of the following climbs appeared on the "Super Big List" of ascents prepared for the 2014 Piolets d'Or jury by Claude Gardien (Vertical magazine) and Lindsay Griffin (AAJ/Mountain INFO). The online versions of most of these reports have links to additional information.

PYRENEES

Pyrenees traverse. Eloi Callado made a complete traverse of the Pyrenees, traveling 1,200km on foot over 67 days. During this odyssey he climbed 55 routes, including the Spigolo Sur of the Aiguilles d'Ansabère (7a+/7b), the Pilar del Embarradère (6c+ A1), and the north face of Vignemale (800m, V+). He did a total of 25,000m of climbing, with most routes graded between 5c and 6b.

NORWAY

Trollryggen (1,740m), not to summit. Tormod Granheim and Aleksander Gamme (Norway), and Andy Kirkpatrick (U.K.), did the first calendar-winter ascent of Suser Gjennom Harryland on Norway's celebrated Trollveggen (Troll Wall). Over 12 days, climbing in capsule style, they completed 18 pitches up to A3 on left side of the wall. They reached the east ridge at half-height and then descended.

Senja Island, Finnemannen. On a small peak on the island of Senja in northern Norway, Bent Vidar Eilertsen and Ines Papert established the 400m Finnmannen (M9+ WI7) in a 19-hour push, after an approach by kayak.

Lofoten Islands, new routes. In August, the international team of Simon Kehrer and Helmut Gargitter (Italy), Federico Pisani and Iván Calderón (Venezuela), and Fernando Gonzalez Rubio (Colombia) completed an old Italian project on the southwest face of Gaitgaljen (1,085m) to create Trolls Meet Latinos (350m, Norwegian 7/7+). They also established One Hundred Years Later (500m, 7+) on the Breitflogtinden (750m), above Kjerkefjorden. 📷 🔍

[This page] Ines Papert leading Finnmannen (M9+ WI7) in Norway. *Visualimpact.ch–Thomas Senf*

[This page, left] David Lama on the first winter ascent of the Sagwand in the Zillertal Alps. *Hansjörg Auer* [This page, right] Dreamliner on Sweden's Raitatjakka. *Krister Jonsson Collection*

SWEDEN

Raitatjakka (1,934m), Dreamliner. In April, Jan Axelsson and Krister Jonsson did the first ascent of Dreamliner (9 pitches, WI4+ M8) on the northwest face, ca 3km east of the Nallostugan cabin, in the Kebnekaise massif. Jonsson called this "maybe the best mixed route in Sweden." 📷 🔍

MONT BLANC RANGE

Grandes Jorasses (4,208m). Max Bionnet and Sebastien Ratel climbed a new route, Borat, on the east face between Groucho Marx and the Boivin Diaferia. The third pitch of the 750m route was led free at 7b, while the fourth was led at 7a with some aid, but followed free at 7b.

    Mont Blanc and Matterhorn speed records. On July 11, starting in the center of Chamonix, the Catalan ski mountaineer Kilian Jornet Burgada Jornet and French skier Mathéo Jacquemond ran to the summit of Mont Blanc, via the Grands Mulets route, in 3 hours 30 minutes. During the descent, Jacquemond was injured and Jornet continued alone, returning to Chamonix in a total of 4 hours 57 minutes 40 seconds, more than 13 minutes faster than the previous record. On August 21, Jornet broke the record for a round-trip on the Matterhorn by over 20 minutes. Starting in the Italian village of Breuil-Cervina, Jornet climbed and descended the Lion Ridge (southwest ridge) in a total of 2 hours 52 minutes.

BERNESE OBERLAND

Eiger (3,970m). On the north face, Robert Jasper (Germany) and Roger Schäli (Switzerland) made a rare repeat and first free ascent of the Ghilini-Piola Direttissima. The two climbed the 1,400m route in a 14-hour day at 7b/c.

ZILLERTAL ALPS

Hohe Kirche (2,634m). In temperatures down to –10°C, David Lama climbed a new route, solo, on the north face of this peak in the Austrian Alps at the start of December: Nordverscheidung (400m, VI/VII WI4 M4/5 90°).

Sagzahn. First winter ascent of the Sagwand via the 800m Schiefer Riss by Hansjörg Auer, David Lama, and Peter Ortner, at VI M7 80°, over two days in March.

DOLOMITES

Piccola Civetta (3,207m). A new mixed route on the north face was established over four days in May by Stefano Angelini, Alessandro Beber, and Fabrizio Dellai: Argento Vivo (1,200m, WI6+ M8 A2 5+).

Sass de la Crusc (2,907m). Josef Hilpold and Ulrich Viertler climbed Wüstenblume (400m, VIII+), using only trad gear. The route was climbed in sections, and with some fixed ropes.

Sassolungo (3,181m). First ascent of La Legrima, a coveted winter line up the north face. The 1,000m climb was carried out over two days in early January by Adam Holzknecht and Hubert Moroder, using natural gear: WI6 M6 V+, with two sections of A0.

Sass Pordoi (2,952m). A winter line based around the classic Fedele route on the northwest face was climbed by Jeff Mercier and Korra Pesce to give Ghost Dogs (750m, WI6 R/X M5 5+/6a). The climb was done over several days, using some fixed ropes at the start.

Molignon di Dentro (2,852m). Philipp Angelo and Andreas Tonelli opened a new route on the northeast face in two stages, climbing 11 pitches on March 5 and the final two on March 16 (650m, WI5+ M3).

SLOVAKIA

Tatra speed-solo and winter traverse. In early 2014, the well-known Slovakian alpinist Jozef "Dodo" Kopold traversed the full length of the Tatra Mountains, crossing 72km and more than 130 peaks in 72 hours of nearly nonstop running and climbing. Kopold began on January 5 with the Belianske Tatras, spent nearly 48 hours crossing the rocky High Tatras, and finished with the 42km snow-covered ridge of the Western Tatras. Kopold slept less than 30 minutes during the three-day effort, and was supported only by some drinks and a bit of company from a mountain rescue team near the end of the traverse.

The full Tatras traverse had only been done once before solo and unsupported in winter, by Pavol Pochyly, over 14 days during the late 1970s.

[This page] Stefano Angelini leads the sixth pitch of Argento Vivo, Piccola Civetta. *Alessandro Beber*

MIDDLE EAST

TURKEY

ALA DAGLAR

Lower Guvercinlik, Atomic Folder and Mostro Turco. In August, Carlo Cosi, Enrico Geremia, Nicolò Geremia, and I climbed two new routes up the impressive west face of Lower Guvercinlik (3,000m) in the Emli Valley. None of us knew the area, so our first two days were spent wandering through the park in search of rock to climb, until the majestic Lower Guvercinlik—known locally as Tranga Tower—threw its spell on us. This peak soars upward for 600m and is comprised of strange limestone: Good crimps are few and far between! To reach the base you need to walk for two and a half hours, so we decided to set up a small base camp beneath the face.

Brothers Enrico and Nicolò Geremia chose a line between the looming roof in the lower half of the wall and the Larcher-Oviglia route Come to Derwish (600m, 7b (7a obl), 2006). They used a variety of bolts, pegs, and cams to create Atomic Folder (600m, 7b+/c (7b obl) A1), which I reckon is a masterpiece. Knowing how to place gear and progress up technical slabs is the name of the game, all the way to the summit.

Carlo and I climbed a line circa 50m to the right, and in establishing Mostro Turco we decided to use bolts only, since the compact rock did not accept any trad pro after the first easy pitch. Pitch three is a spectacular 35m 8a on micro-holds, climbed by Super Carletto. The route then heads left along small cracks, slabs, ramps, and sections that ultimately were breached, after a grueling battle, with aid. With great regret for having failed to free this section, we continued until we joined pitch seven of Atomic Folder via a long traverse above the lip of an immense void. Oh well, Mostro Turco (650m, 8a (7b+ obl) A1) will be a great free-climbing project for our next expedition—or for other strong climbers! **PHOTOS, TOPO ICONS**

Andrea Simonini, *Italy, via PlanetMountain.com*

[This page] West face of Lower Guvercinlik: (1) Approximate line of Larcher-Oviglia, 2006. (2) Atomic Folder, 2013. (3) Mostro Turco, 2013. *Enrico Geremia*

Bes Parmak Sivrisi, El Pastor Electrico. Raul Gonzalez and Mikel Saez de Urabain climbed a new line on Bes Parmak Sivrisi (3,520m), at the head of the Cimbar Valley, in July. El Pastor Electrico (425m) ascends a shallow buttress on the northwest face, to the right of the original route on the wall (Alcay-Villarig, 1974), giving 12 pitches up to 6c. The two climbed it in a long day without leaving any fixed gear.

Information from MIKEL SAEZ DE URABAIN, *Basque Country*

Editor's note: In June, Italian climbers Jimmy Palermo, Tommaso Salvadori, and Ivan Testori made the first ascent of Cani Randagi (300m, 6b max, 6a obl) in the Cimbar Valley, on the southwest face of the canyon leading to Teke Pinari pass. Details are at PlanetMountain.com.

LEBANON

Tannourine el Tahta rock climbing. Lebanon isn't the first place that comes to mind for rock climbing—it's better known for beaches, nightclubs, and the threat of instability. The Lebanese civil war (1975–1990) and ensuing turbulence have kept tourists away and limited the development of climbing areas. We first visited in 2011 to retrace family roots, and went climbing one weekend at Harissa Tannourine, a crag established by the French military at the turn of the millennium, with about 40 bolted routes.

On our way back from the mountains, we stopped for a beer in a village dominated by immaculate limestone walls. We gazed up at the

[This page, top] The ca 450m northwest face of (A) Bes Parmak Sivrisi ("Five Fingers" Sivrisi). (1) Alcay-Villarig, 1974. (2) El Pastor Electrico, Gonzalez-Saez, 2013. *Mikel Saez de Urabain* [This page, bottom] Simon Rawlinson on Tawouk (7c) in the Schwarma Caves, one of about 50 new routes in the area. *Katy Anderson / R-A-D.org*

striking walls, ranging from 20m to 150m, in a band stretching up to the cedar line. We dreamed about it for a year before we could return, get permission from the municipality, and install the first bolts, working with local Lebanese climbers. After nearly two years and many return visits, we've established more than 50 bolted lines.

The first route to the top of the wall (100m, 6a, 6b, 6a+, 2013) is named after Georges Massoud, a local hero who climbed barefoot across exposed faces to hunt for quail to feed his family. His descendants still live at the base of the cliff. Not a day went by without them calling for us to sit with them on the terrace for coffee, walnuts, or oranges as we lumbered up the hill with our gear.

Tannourine el Tahta is at about 1,000m above sea level, and spring and autumn are the best times to go. Our website, R-A-D.org, has topos and useful information about traveling to Lebanon, including the relative safety of various areas. **PHOTOS, MAP, VIDEO ICONS**

WILL NAZARIAN *and* KATY ANDERSON, *R-A-D.org*

JORDAN

Wadi Rum, Sound of Silence and other ascents. In November, Steffen Krug and I spent three weeks in this very special sandstone area. After enjoying some classic big lines, we repeated a few of the modern routes, including La Guerre Sainte (7b, *AAJ 2001*), a 12-pitch bolted route on Jebel Nasrani. We found the grading for this stunning route—and generally for modern routes here—to be very soft compared to the classic trad climbs. We then went for what's considered to be the hardest route in Wadi Rum: Rock Empire (15 pitches, 8a, *AAJ 2006*), which is completely bolt protected. Coming from the traditional sandstone climbing area of Pfalz, we know that it is not a great idea to put expansion bolts in such soft sandstone, and we bailed after the fourth pitch. Unfortunately, many of the modern routes are equipped in such an inappropriate way, when glue-in bolts would last much longer.

Wadi Rum is still a paradise for exploration, and we opened a new route in Barrah Canyon, right next to the famous crack of Merlin's Wand. Sound of Silence has seven pitches up to 7a. From the end of the last pitch, 1.5 hours of easy scrambling leads to the summit, where the view is breathtaking. Descent is by rappelling the route with double ropes. **PHOTOS ICON**

JENS RICHTER, *Germany*

Editor's note: In November, a Catalan group did two new routes on the west face of Jebel Rum: Ivictus (Alemán-Coll-Sort, 250m, 6b) and Deliri (Bonsom-Gibert-Mas-Valés, 260m, 6c). Both routes were

[This page] Sound of Silence (235m, 7a) in Barrah Canyon. The arrow marks the classic crack line of Merlin's Wand (6a+). *Jens Richter* *climbed without protection bolts. (More info: Desnivel.com.)*

A Slovenian group established several very difficult sport climbs. In Wadi Rum, Klemen Becan put up Wadirumela (8b+), a 45m slab route. At a new crag called Araq Damaj in the Alijoun area, Becan climbed Same Same But Different (8c), likely the hardest rock pitch in Jordan (More info: PlanetMountain.com.)

YEMEN

Socotra Island, various ascents. In March my wife, Brittany Griffith, and I traveled to Yemen's Socotra Island, an incredibly diverse oval of isolated land in the Arabian Sea. Often called the "Galapagos of the Arabian Sea" for its 300-plus endemic species of flora and fauna, Socotra is actually closer to Somalia than Yemen, and due to the country's tumultuous economic, political, and tribal issues, it sees few visitors. Photographer Andrew Burr accompanied us on the trip.

Over the course of 10 days we did four new routes up to 5.12 on the rock spires of the Haggier Mountains, which dominate the skyline above the main town of Hadibo. We placed no bolts or pitons, and left only slings or single-nut anchors for rappels. Two of the spires were previously unclimbed. Our fixer/translator, Sammi, tried to ascertain for us the locals' names for the towers, but ended up with two or sometimes four different names for the same formation—different villages had different names. The sole exception was the central 800-foot tower in the massif, which everyone referred to as Mashanig. Heat was the chief concern, with temperatures breaching 100°F by 10 a.m. every day.

After establishing ourselves at a high camp, two hours of epic bushwhacking up a steep hillside brought us to the base of a clean, orange tower. Two pitches of 5.10+ later, we were on the virgin summit. We named our route Licking Pots and Chewing Qat, in reference to the freshwater crabs that would clean our dishes each night and for the mildly narcotic qat leaf that every man in Yemen, especially on the mainland, chews throughout every afternoon.

The following day we headed directly for an unclimbed gem we had scoped during the hike to camp: a 900-foot arrow of sheer granite on the right side of the massif. We climbed an impressively continuous corner system on the west-northwest face and topped out near sunset. Far below, the

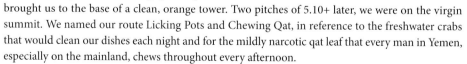

[This page] Brittany Griffith leading M.O.G. in the Fog (5.11) on Mashanig's north tower. *Andrew Burr*

Arabian Sea quickly faded from blue to black and we rapped off in the dark. It was one of the most inspiring and dramatic summits of my climbing life. We named our 5.12 route Battling Begonias, due to the flowers that sometimes choked the otherwise clean cracks.

After three days of exploring the island's stunning variety of sights, we returned to the mountains and climbed new routes on the two summits of Mashanig. [*Editor's note: The first known ascents of these towers were in 2009, by Josh Helling and Mike Libecki, who called them Daddy and Daughter towers (AAJ 2010). However, Libecki reported finding very old cairns on top of the larger tower, suggesting it was ascended generations earlier. The smaller undoubtedly has been climbed by locals as well.*] First we climbed the main summit in the broiling sun via a 650-foot 5.11 we dubbed Hammy Time. I suffered badly from dehydration but still managed to enjoy the stunning summit views in every direction. The following day we climbed the northern summit via a 420-foot 5.11 line we called M.O.G. in the Fog, in reference to the "Man of Girth," Burr, rappelling through the swirling fog for photos. The route started off a dramatic rock bridge that spans the chasm between the two Mashanig towers and followed obvious clean cracks directly up the east face.

We spent the final three days of our trip absorbing all we could of the island's world-class beauty: snorkeling with dolphins, hiking sand dunes, eating fresh lobster (and not so fresh lobster), deep water soloing, exploring kilometers-deep caves big enough to drive semi-trucks through, strolling down empty white-sand beaches, and enjoying the amazing dragon blood and desert rose trees.

JONATHAN THESENGA, *USA*

Socotra Island, various ascents. In late February and early March, Ethan Pringle and I did three new routes and some immaculate deep water soloing. Near Mashanig tower, which I had climbed in 2009, we did a 1,000-foot 5.6 up the west ridge of Thabbit's Tower (named after our translator/guide).

We then climbed a new route on the east side of Mashanig (800', 5.11b). Finally we moved to a new area I had reconnoitered in 2009 and climbed an amazing phallic spire: Kermit's Tower. Ethan was the rope gun on this, onsighting the 5.12+ R/X crux to the top. **PHOTOS ICON**

MIKE LIBECKI, *AAC*

[This page] The Libecki-Pringle route on Mashanig's east side. North tower is on the right. *Mike Libecki*

AFRICA

MOROCCO

ANTI-ATLAS MOUNTAINS

Timichcha massif, south side, new routes; Ait Makhlouf, east face. In mid-January, Andreas Parparinos and I climbed many new routes on the amazing south face of Timichcha (1,972m), which is clustered with large buttresses and towers.

In the town of Ighrem we found a very basic room to make our base camp. On January 10 we went to Timichcha and climbed the first new route, taking a crack system on the left hand side of Buttress No. 2: First One (110m, HS 4c). The next day we climbed the right hand side of Buttress No. 2: Cyprus Kourkoutas (140m, VS 4c). After descending we quickly climbed up the east ridge of Tower No. 3. On January 12 we drove north of Ighrem to Ait Makhlouf (1,686m) and climbed the far left side of the east face (150m, S 4b). On January 13 we returned to Timichcha and climbed crack systems on the right side of Buttress No. 3: Cyprus Monkeys (160m, HVS 5b). On January 14 we climbed Tower No. 1 up cracks in the center: Xaloumi Crack (80m, VS 5a). And on our final day we climbed Big Tower by cracks and chimneys on the left side, which provided a great adventure: Kerasaki sti Tourta (150m, E1 5c).

We numbered features on the Timichcha massif starting from the left as you look at them from the main road coming from Ighrem. The rock is generally good and is ideal for ground-up traditional climbing, with many good cracks. We did not place any pitons or bolts, and I suggest future climbers help to keep this magical place "clean." In January it was cold at night but pleasant during the day. It seems to always be windy. 📷

CONSTANTINOS ANDREOU, *Cyprus*

ATLAS MOUNTAINS

Jebel Tadrarate, southwest face, Azazar. In April 2013, Patrik Aufdenblatten (Switzerland), Ines Papert (Germany), and I climbed a new route on Jebel Tadrarate (2,803m) in Taghia, where there are many limestone walls up to 1,000m tall, with much potential. We chose a line 100m right of Antropecene (Albert-Arbones, 2007]. [*At least four other routes exist on the southwest face: Raum der*

[This page] "Big Tower," ca 150m high, one of many formations comprising the sprawling Timichcha massif. *Constantinos Andreou*

Wünsche (Helling-Kohbach-Petters-Whitehouse, 2009), La Rouge Berbère (Guillaume-Ravier-Thivel, 2002), Sul filo della Notte (Larcher-Oviglia-Paissan, 2003), and L'Axe du Mal (Bodet-Cortial-Petit-Piola-Robert, 2003.)]

We used a power drill to place bolts and returned to the ground each day; higher up we used a portaledge, climbing capsule-style. It's our belief that the route is not over-bolted—we placed 80 bolts over nine pitches, including belays. It often took us a full day to establish one pitch, sometimes even more. We reached the top after 10 days and it took a couple more for Patrik to free-climb all the pitches. The locals suggested we call the climb Azazar (400m, 8a), after a beautiful plant that grows in the area. 🖼 🔍 🗎

LISI STEURER, Austria

SUDAN

Jebel Kassala, The Rüppell Face. On Sudan's eastern border with Eritrea lies an impressive collection of granite walls and domes called the Taka Mountains. Inspired by past reports from Tony Howard (*AAJ 1999*) and David Jonglez (*AAJ 2003*), and other vague rumors of climbing, my wife, Brittany Griffith, and I traveled to the area in December. We landed in Khartoum, then made the eight-hour drive to Kassala, population 450,000, which abuts the Taka Mountains. Since camping in an urban area was out of the question, we stayed in a guesthouse. The midday heat reached 100°F.

We spent two days hiking around the mountains and scoping options in the scorching heat. Baboons howled among the boulders, and vultures circled high above as we approached the walls. With the heat, north-facing walls were the most realistic option. Most of the crack systems were discontinuous, leaving large expanses of unprotectable face climbing, and we had only brought an emergency bolt kit, presenting an interesting challenge.

Eventually we found a line with promising cracks on the 900' north face on the farthest north formation. Our first attempt ended 600' up when Brittany wisely chose to turn back below a 90' section of unprotected face climbing on fragile flakes and edges. We returned the next day, reclimbed the initial pitches, and I led the blank face, stopping to place a bolt from a tenuous, slabby stance. After that it was smooth sailing up straightforward cracks to the summit. We rapped off single-nut anchors as the Muslim call to prayer echoed from below. We named our route the Rüppell Face (900', 5.11c) in reference to the vultures and an obvious play on Nanga Parbat's Rupal Face. We also climbed two other fantastic 500' to 600' routes to different summits, but discovered bolts on one route and a haggard sling on the other. It's hard to know who may have climbed them first. 🖼

JONATHAN THESENGA, USA

[This page] The huge limestone walls above the village of Taghia, Morocco. *Franz Walter*

[This page] Viewed from the west, the domes of Jebel Kassala, which comprise the Taka Mountains in Sudan. On the left is the Totil massif, showing (A) North Totil, (B) Jebel Totil, and (C) West Totil. The Rüppell Face ascends (A), climbing just inside the sun/shade line. Brittany Griffith and Jonathan Thesenga also climbed a 500' route up the center of (C), where they found two bolts protecting an offwidth. The route follows obvious dihedrals, which they climbed in the morning to avoid the sun. The bolt hangers were Petzl, so it was likely established by European climbers, and it's possibly the same route described by David Jonglez as the "Turns of Jebel Totil" (*AAJ 2003*). (D) Unnamed dome. On the right is the Taka massif, showing (E) North Taka, (F) Jebel Taka, and (G) West Taka. Thesenga and Griffith climbed a 600' route on the southeast (back) side of (G), where they found an old sling. *Jonathan Thesenga*

ETHIOPIA

TIGRAY

Gheralta Massif, new routes; Adwa Mountains, new routes; Simien Mountains, reconnaissance; Gondar mountains, new routes. In January 2012, Magali Salle and I made a trip to Ethiopia, hoping to explore and climb new routes. First stop: the Gheralta region. The area is full of colorful sandstone, though we sometimes found places where it's more *sand* than stone. Despite the many others who have climbed here, the area still contains many towers and mountains yet to be fully explored. We climbed two new routes, both on the Gheralta Massif: Flying Magali (TD 6b+), on the "American Pillar," and Guebre (140m, TD 6a+) on Mt. Essamba.

Second stop: the Adwa Mountains. The rock here is volcanic and of good quality, often resembling the Hoggar Mountains of southern Algeria. We climbed routes between 140m and 300m, but we also saw walls 400m or taller. On Mt. Tihous we climbed: Relais sur Euphorbias (300m, TD 6a) and Vive Adwa (190m, TD 6a+). On Mt. Otowodiko we climbed: Timkat (180m, TD+ 6a+A1), 50 Ans et Toutes Mes Dents (180m, TD 6a), and Si Gentils (120m, D 5).

Third stop: the Simien Mountains (also spelled Semien or Simen). We didn't climb here but explored the area for six days. East of the village of Adi Arkay (on the road between Axum and Gondar) we found very impressive rock towers, but from a distance could not judge the rock quality. Using a 1:100,000 map of Simien Mountains National Park, it appears that a whole-day approach would be necessary to reach the base of these towers, and that's with mules and scouts. In the main Siemen Mountains the cliffs are impressive but quite grassy and loose, except for Mt. Buyait's east face, where the rock is clean and there are steep 200m walls. Most of the high cliffs top out around ca 4,000m. The temperature can be cold at night (below freezing) but after sunrise reaches good

[This page] The locals help with the approach to the Koraro Spires. *James Garrett*

climbing temperatures. A guide or scout is required, as is permission from the park warden in Debarek. Chennek or Debarek would be the best spot for staging an expedition.

Our fourth and final stop: the mountains south of Gondar. Prior to our trip, I had seen some shadows via satellite maps, but I could not have imagined so many rock spires! We only climbed two routes—one of poor rock and the other of great quality—but the potential is very high in this area. Generally, the mountains are not very concentrated. Addis Zemen or Gondar would act as a good base camp. We saw other magnificent mountains east of Gondar; however, I don't know how to approach them—a challenge for the next time! On Molalit (close to Meksenit) we called the higher quality route Aferan (200m, 5+). There's room for at least 15 more routes on that wall. For the other mountains between Meksenit and Addis Zemen, the approach ranges from a half hour to two hours, and the cliffs are between 200m and 300m high. A local scout or porter is highly recommended.

Throughout our trip, we established base camp in cities. You can do it in the wild, but it will cost more because you will have to employ guards or scouts night and day to look after your camp. We placed one bolt (for descending) on our new routes and left only three pitons in place. 📷 🔍

ALAIN BRUZY, *France*

Gheralta Massif, Koraro Spires, The Sharp One; Nebelet Spires, Slender Spire. Unclimbed, freestanding, multi-pitch desert spires are an ever-increasing rarity. For those seeking such treasure, the Tigray today likely inspires the same thrill as Fred Beckey's first glimpse of Moses Tower in the early 1970s.

My 2012 visit to Gheralta area was mostly a fact-finding mission. I returned in 2013 with enthusiastic Utah friends Erik Kelly and Peter Vintoniv. Our attention settled on an unfinished project I had started: a slender knife-like tower in the Koraro Spires, which the locals call Tewlihe, "The Sharp One." This was the last unclimbed, freestanding tower of the Koraro group. Featured, but with little in the way of continuous cracks, it became a labor-intensive project, and we enlisted the help of eager local boys to help carry our loads. [*Other freestanding Koraro Spires include Sheba, Squatty Tower, and HCP, all of which have been climbed, some by multiple routes.*]

We picked the wettest month of the year to visit: August—*don't ask!* Spectacular and scary thunderstorms arrived like clockwork almost every afternoon. On the fourth day we sat on the tower top and basked in the sunshine. We'd completed three long pitches of sandstone face climbing—mostly bolt protected and simply spectacular. We called the line Stealing Thunder (III 5.11d). We rappelled with two 70m ropes, and this line may prove to be the ideal route for travelers with little more than sport climbing gear.

Peter and I also visited the Nebelet Spires above the town of Nebelet, an hour's drive north of Hawzien, near the border with Eritrea. Lacking any information on previous visits, we chose to climb the southernmost tower, which we called Slender Spire. Two 70m ropes just made it back to the ground. Threatening weather thwarted a free ascent. Be aware that multiple names of formations have led to confusion in the area; it seems best to names things in correlation to the nearest town for clarification. 📷 🔍

JAMES GARRETT, *USA*

MADAGASCAR

TSARANORO VALLEY

Mitsinjoarivo Wall, Dancing with the World. In the fall of 2013, South African climbers Benj de Charmoy, Duncan Fraser, and Leo Le Roux established the nine-pitch route Dancing with the World (300m, 6c). The line climbs left of some prominent black streaks on the left side of the Mitsinjoarivo Wall, reaching the left-most summit. They established the route capsule-style over seven days, bolting ground-up, then climbed the route free in a day from the base.

From a report at ClimbZa.com

Chameleon Massif, Chameleon Air Society. In February 2013 I called Paul Byrne to bail on our spring trip to the Alaska Range. Luckily, we agreed on a new objective: the Tsaranoro Valley in the southern highlands of Madagascar. Our imaginations ran wild with the idea of climbing big, black and yellow, granite walls. Two months later, we flew to Antananarivo, then journeyed the long road to the Tsaranoro Valley. The steep, clean, and beautiful walls were devoid of other climbers.

After climbing a handful of big lines that rise out of various parts of the valley, and achieving our main objective, Out of Africa (580m, 7a) on Tsaranoro Kely, we turned our attention to the nearly virgin formation known as the Chameleon Massif. [*Only one other route is known on this formation: Solothorn 4+ (290m, 7a). This route was established at least four years ago, reportedly by a Swiss team.*]

[This page] Tyler Botzon starting the "Bering Sea" pitch (third pitch) on Chameleon Air Society: "amazing, sustained 5.11a face climbing for nearly 50 meters." In the background: Tsaranoro Be (center) and Karambony (right). *Paul Byrne*

The Chameleon protrudes from the center of the valley like a baboon's tooth, and it has a rock formation on its summit that looks just like a chameleon lounging in the sun. It was our first time lead-bolting—a totally thrilling experience. Every evening, we would rappel back to the ground after having our minds blown by an amazing day of climbing. Then we'd stash our gear at the base and enjoy the hour-long sunset walk through the villages and rice fields back toward our camp. Almost all the local villagers are incredibly kind, and love to exchange smiles and say "Salaam!" On the final day of our project, as I made my way up the last big pitch, I could feel the people of the valley below monitoring our progress. When I put the last bolt in, and moved through the final committing crux, the people in the fields erupted in celebration.

That evening, as the big African sun sank below the horizon, we both had grins ear to ear as we rappelled our beautiful new free climb. We named the all-bolted route Chameleon Air Society (800', 5.11a). It took us three days to establish, and it's all on clean, highly featured, black granite. The crux pitches offer phenomenal face climbing, and all the belays are equipped to rappel. The approach is easy in comparison to the other walls in Tsaranoro Valley.

TYLER BOTZON, *USA*

RÉUNION ISLAND

Zembrocal. Saint Leu, Réunion, 5 p.m. I'm sitting on the veranda of a little bungalow, the sun setting over a black sand beach. It is our last day on the island. I receive a text message: "I did it, thank you team." At first I don't understand. Then I feel a wave of happiness when I realize what has happened: Yuji has finished our climb! Yuji Hirayama and Sam Elias had returned for one last try on Zembrocal, the multi-pitch route we'd opened during three weeks of effort in June in the heart of this volcanic island. James Pearson, Jacopo Larcher, and I already had headed back to civilization to start packing. Yuji was still trying to free the crux fifth pitch, the last that hadn't fallen. The guys had settled around 8c+ for the grade: a 17m overhanging dihedral, with barely any footholds on the smooth gabbro rock, and just a thin crack that sometimes was too small for the fingers. Yuji's redpoint was the final, happy ending to our adventure, to my big project.

I grew up on this tiny dot on the map, east of Madagascar in the southern Indian Ocean. Here, I discovered climbing. But in this remote French department, climbing was all about competition.

[This page] The Chameleon Massif. Left: Solothorn 4+ (290m, 7a). Right: Chameleon Air Society (245m, 5.11a). *Paul Byrne*

We climbed on the rock, but our aims were indoors. I left Réunion when I was 16 to train in France, more than 9,000km from my family. I spent 10 years exploring my mental and physical limits on plastic. For me, competition was about giving the best you have in maximum-stress situations. Not that different from outdoor climbing, no? After reaching my goals in World Cups, I turned to the outdoors. I got a taste of fear, engagement, and of "real climbing," as some would say. It was time to go back to my people, my origins, and play a bit of the new game I had found.

Some childhood friends led me to the wall in the Cirque de Cilaos. Everyone knew about it, but no one had dared to try. Although there are many cliffs and difficult climbs on Réunion (including a possible 9a+), no one climbs trad. The concept is quite unknown. Opening the route was tough work, with many scary moments as we skirted huge boulders balanced on the virgin wall. There were many question marks: We always wondered if the next pitch would go, or if we would be stopped in our tracks. That's the very special thing with ground-up climbing: You soon realize that you aren't the one creating—it's more the route revealing itself to you. Amazing rock, beautiful shapes, surprising methods—every pitch turned out different, every section unique. I feel privileged to have been part of this adventure. My little island home now holds one of the hardest multi-pitch climbs in the world. [*Editor's note: Zembrocal has seven pitches (7a, 8a, 8a, 8a, 8c+, 6c, 7a). Two of the pitches are mostly bolted; most require a rack of protection. All of the pitches were redpointed, but the route has not had a continuous free ascent. A beautiful, highly detailed topo can be found at the AAJ website.*] 🖼 🔍 ▶

CAROLINE CIAVALDINI, *France*

[This page, top] Yuji Hirayama on the third pitch (8a) of Zembrocal. *Damiano Levati–The North Face* [This page, bottom] The mostly trad line of Zembrocal (7 pitches, 8c+) on the island of Réunion. *Damiano Levati– The North Face*

RUSSIA

[This page, top] The ca 13km-long Bezengi Wall from the north. (A) Main Shkhara (5,200m). (B) Main Jangi-Tau (5,085m). (C) Katyn-Tau (4,974m). (D) Gestola (4,860m). (E) Lial'ver (4,350m). *Provided by Anna Piunova, Mountain.ru.* [This page, bottom] Climbing Jangi-Tau West on December 31, 2013. Temperatures during the traverse averaged –30°C. *Viktor Koval Collection*

CAUCASUS

Bezengi Wall, complete winter traverse. The Bezengi Wall (sometimes spelled Bezingi) rises along the mountain frontier between Russia on the north and Georgia on the south. The sharp, ca 13km ridge links several of the highest peaks of the Caucasus: Lial'ver (4,350m), Gestola (4,860m), Katyn-Tau (4,974m), Jangi-Tau (5,085m, also spelled Dzhangi-Tau), Shota Rustaveli (4,960m), and Shkhara (5,200m). The full traverse had never been completed in winter.

A large portion of the ridge crest is located at around 5,000m, with steep, 2,000m glacier walls on either side. It alternates between snowy and rocky parts, with numerous gendarmes and cornices, upon which belaying is extremely difficult and confidence is needed. A peculiarity of the wall is the absence of simple routes up any of the peaks; descent from the traverse is practical only at the start and finish and in its middle, after climbing 6.5km.

The first summertime traverse of the Bezengi Wall was accomplished from east to the west, in

1938, by a team of Leningrad alpinists led by Evgeny Beletskoi, one of the strongest alpinists in the USSR at the time. The crossing took 18 days with advance caches. The traverse of the Bezengi from west to east was accomplished 15 years later, in 1953, by a team led by another outstanding Soviet alpinist, Kirill Kuzmin.

In winter, even at the foot of the wall, the temperature often drops to –25° to –30°C. Nearly all previous attempts at a winter traverse ended shortly after they began.

In the winter of 2007 a trio of alpinists from Moscow, using summer caches of food and fuel, managed to surmount the section from Shkhara to Eastern Jangi-Tau over a month of climbing, but the attempt ended tragically. The leader of the group perished, and the two other participants received injuries and frostbite. They were rescued on the 34th day via a grandiose operation with the aid of a helicopter.

In the last days of December 2013, a quartet of alpinists from St. Petersburg—Sergei Kondrashkin, Petr Kuzenkov, Nikolai Totmyanin, and I—began the traverse by climbing Lial'ver, on the west end. During the traverse there was stable weather, with an average daytime temperature of around –30°C or lower. We greeted the New Year on Western Jangi-Tau. In the area of Western Shkhara (5,057m), we were forced to sit for the night in an open bivouac; the short daylight hours did not allow us to find a good ledge to set up the tent. We descended from Shkhara on the 12th day of the traverse. We placed no advanced caches nor prepared the route. Approximate difficulty: Russian 6B.

VIKTOR KOVAL, *provided by Anna Piunova, Mountain.ru, translated by Henry Pickford*

It-kaya (3,193m), southwest face. We first saw the 500m walls of It-kaya, east of the village of Bezengi, while making the first ascent of Ak-kaya in January 2011. The area around It-kaya is strikingly beautiful, with many herbs, flowers, and boulders, making it a kind of paradise. Michaylo Mironchak, Vladimir Roshko, and I spent three days doing the first ascent of the southwest face. During the first day we climbed seven pitches (up to 6a/b), with problematic protection and broken limestone. We  often had to climb 15m to 20m without protection. On the second day the wall became steeper and reached a level of 6b+ A3. After six pitches on the third day we reached the summit. During the

[This page] The 500m southwest face of It-Kaya. *Mykola Shymko*

climb we placed one bolt. The route turned out to be quite interesting, with a variety of climbing. With knowledge of the route, it would be possible to do it in a single day. 📷 🔍

MYKOLA SHYMKO, *Ukraine, translated by Lidiya Tsoy and Max Kovtunenko*

Tyutyu, southeast face of Second West, Expromtus. The Tyutyu massif has five independent summits, up to 4,460m, and offers traditional rock and alpine routes in a gorgeous setting. After eight years away from this region, I stayed for 10 days as a student mountain guide in the summer of 2013. Julia Belozerskaya, my wife and climbing partner, and I made the first ascent of the southeast face of Tyutyu's Second West summit (4,420m), following beautiful granite cracks for eight pitches, plus some snow and scrambling. All but one small section of wet rock went free: Expromtus (635m, Russian 5A, TD 6a A2). 📷 📄

MAXIM FOYGEL, *provided by Anna Piunova, Mountain.ru*

KAZAKHSTAN

TIEN SHAN

ZALISKY ALA-TAU

Tuyuk-su area, various ascents. The Zalisky Ala-Tau has many peaks, the highest being Talgar (4,973m), with many established routes. But most climbers bypass the Tuyuk-su valley, despite its proximity to Almaty, the largest city in Kazakhstan. The Tuyuk-su is just above the Shymbulak ski resort, and the peaks can be reached in an hour's drive from the city center, plus one to three hours of walking.

On July 22, 2012, Alexander Chechulin and I took a new way up the left flank of Utchitel Peak's south side, by a narrow bastion that looked more difficult than it was (Russian 3A). That same afternoon we climbed another new route on the right side of Utchitel's south face (Russian 2B), with rock pitches up to 5a.

[This page] Michaylo Mironchak aiding pitch nine of the southwest face of It-kaya. *Mykola Shymko*

Five days later, Vitaly Komarov and I climbed a steep route up the west side of Maria Peak (3,750m). Five pitches (4b–5c) led to a ridge that we followed for 300m to the top. On July 31, Dastan Abdrakhmanov and I climbed the left side of the same peak's south face (Russian 4A).

In mid-September, Sergey Kadola, Nikita Simonov, and I walked into a separate valley to attempt a new route on Ushbinka (ca 4,030m). This mountain is located on the eastern side of the Tuyuk-su area, above the valley of the Left Talgar River. It is part of the long ridge extending eastward from Nursultan (4,330m, a.k.a. Komsomol). The south side of Ushbinka was still completely unknown, despite 80 years of alpinism in these mountains. Some years ago I observed the huge buttresses on this face and got the desire to explore them.

We spent one day hiking with heavy backpacks to the moraine of the Aristova Glacier. That evening we climbed a 30m pitch to test the rock and found it to be poor, with sharp, broken blocks. At sunrise we started our ascent from the lowest point of bastion. Miraculously, the rock was mostly solid after the start. By the most logical line, we climbed 14 long pitches (5a–6b) to the summit ridge and reached the top late at night. We bivouacked three pitches below the summit and finished the descent in the morning. This route (590m, Russian 5A) is now one of the most interesting in Tuyuk-su.

DENIS URUBKO, *Kazakhstan*

Nursultan, solo ascent of northwest face and descent with skis. In July, Jonathan Jay, an American living in Almaty, soloed the northwest face (750m, Russian 3B) of Nursultan (4,330m, formerly called Komsomol). After skiing a few turns down the normal route on the southwest ridge, he dropped onto the northwest face and skied and sidestepped a couloir through the upper face. Local climbers said both the solo and the ski descent probably were firsts.

Information supplied by Jonathan Jay

[This page] View from the east toward (A) Nursultan (4,330m) and (B) Ushbinka (4,030m). (1) South ridge from Komsomol Pass (Russian 2B). (2) Traverse from Snow Plateau (4B). (3) North ridge (3B). (4) Kadola-Simonov-Urubko route (2013, 590m, 5A). Arrow marks their descent. The northwest face (3B) is on the far side of Nursultan. *S. Guryev, courtesy of Denis Urubko*

KYRGYZSTAN

PAMIR ALAI

SABAKH REGION

Ashat Valley, Sabakh (5,300m), new variation on north face; Argo (ca 4,750m), new route; West Parus (4,850m), south-southwest buttress; Prometheus (3,900m), first ascent; other attempts and history. I first thought about visiting Sabakh back in the 1990s, a time when my blood started boiling just from the possibility of doing a first ascent. Even then very few mountaineers knew of this mountain valley, while the neighboring regions, Ak-Su and Karavshin, were gaining huge popularity. In 1997 our "Russian Way: Walls of the World" project started, and this led me far from the summits of Pamir Alai, but I never forgot about Sabakh.

The first mountaineers in the region were members of the "Spartak" Moscow team, who explored the area in the early 1980s, but did not climb. The huge north face of Sabakh (5,300m) was first climbed in 1985 by a team from Novosibirsk led by A. Plotnikov; a month later climbers from the Spartak team, under the guidance of Vladimir Bashkirov, climbed their own line on the north wall of Sabakh. In the following years Moscow mountaineers did many first ascents, but not all of these achievements had been recorded and graded. Nevertheless, we will try to restore some historical justice. A mountaineer from Spartak, Andrei Komolov, provided the following information about some early climbs, none of which are documented in the Russian Climbing Route Classification Record: West Parus (4,850m), north wall (Kolomyitsev-Komolov-Shibanov, tentatively 5B); Main Parus (5,053m), first ascent from the south (E. Moskovets, leader, tentatively 4A); and East Parus (4,800m), first ascent along the north ridge (S. Shorokhov, leader, 4B).

A team from Saint Petersburg led by A. Moshnikov climbed a beautiful line on the center of Sabakh in 1986. In 1989, Mityukhin and partners climbed a very steep route on the north side of East Parus. Another team, led by Egorov, climbed the southwest ridge of West Parus, and in 1990 a Spartak team climbed the north face of that peak. A team led by N. Petrov did the full traverse of the Ashat wall from east to west. A Ukrainian team with M. Zagirnyak as leader also did a new route on East Parus, but the exact location is unknown.

According to the local guide Nurdin, only two expeditions visited the region between 1990 and 2012: an Italian expedition at the end of the 1990s, and a Ukrainian expedition in 2008. The Italians climbed a beautiful line on East Parus and published a book about this climb, but the team

[This page, top] The north-facing wall at the head of the Ashat Gorge. (A) Dioskuri with (1) the peak's only route. (B) Ushbinka (ca 5,010m). (C) Argo with (2) Kolisnyk-Koshelenko, 2013 and (3) Petrov. (D) Svarog. (E) Sabakh with (4) 2013 variation to Plotnikov route, (5) Plotnikov, 1985, (6) Moshnikov, 1986, and (7) Bashkirov/Spartak, 1985. *Yury Koshelenko* [This page, bottom] The northwest face of Main Parus: unclimbed. *Yury Koshelenko*

from Odessa was less lucky: The climbers were caught under huge rockfall on the northeast wall of East Parus and a rescue was required, but fortunately there were no serious consequences.

Both of these teams climbed from the Uryam Gorge, on the east side of these mountains. No mountaineers visited Ashat Gorge for 22 years, though many commercial groups have trekked from Ashat into Ak-Su along two passes, with the help of the guide Nurdin.

In 2012 I decided to organize an expedition to this area. During our 20-day trip, Vasily Kolisnyk and I ascended a summit located above our base camp and called it Peak Prometheus (3,900m, east ridge, 360m, 3A). On August 5 we climbed seven pitches on the north wall of West Parus (4,850m) but were halted by blank slabs with no ice. (In March 2014, Alexander Zhigalov and Pavel Vlasenko from Krasnoyarsk completed this line.) Six days later we climbed the south-southwest buttress of West Parus (700m, 5A, with free climbing up to VI).

In 2013 I gathered a larger team of six. Four of my young friends planned to participate in the Russian Climbing Championship, while my friend Vasily and I would climb "for the soul." We

supported our young friends during their long Sabakh climb and helped them afterward, because one of them was slightly injured.

Vasily and I climbed a new line on the left side of the north face of Peak 4,750m in light style, with two very bad nights on the wall. Our route, Alkonost, was 700m, 5B. I have called the previously unnamed peak Argo because it resembled the ship of Argonauts.

We also attempted the west wall of Main Parus in deteriorating weather. We climbed 10 pitches and then spent two days on the wall waiting for better conditions, but then ran out of time as the expedition was ending.

Meanwhile, over five days at the end of July, A. Antoshin, I. Osipov, V Shipilov, and A. Vasilyev climbed a variation to the Plotnikov route on the north face of Sabakh (5,300m). After fixing pitches at the bottom, the four men spent five days climbing the 2,010m route.

Many possibilities for first ascents remain in the Ashat Gorge. Parus alone has three summits and seven worthwhile faces, including the unclimbed northwest wall of Main Parus and northeast walls of Main and West Parus. (Parus means "sail" in Russian.) Some of these walls have close to 1,000m of vertical relief. The whole north wall of Svarog (labeled Peak 4810m, but definitely higher than 5,000m) is unclimbed. This wall is probably the steepest in the region, with more than 1,000m of relief. Vladimir Bashkirov and his team tried to climb it in 1990, but since then there have been no attempts. More to the east, Argo has only two routes: N. Petrov's route in the right part of the north wall (6A) and our new route Alkonost. The east end of the Ashat wall is Dioskuri (Pollux on the east and Cator on the west), which is 4,700m according to the maps but definitely higher. There is only one route, following cracks and couloirs up the north wall.

There are many limestone peaks below Parus, along both sides of the Ashat Gorge, from which one sometimes has to rescue the local hunters, because they know how to ride a horse but not how to climb. In addition, the region has good blocks for bouldering—Vasily and I spent lots of time on these boulders as we watched our friends on Sabakh.

One definite negative of the Ashat wall is that the bases of most peaks are composed of loose shale, though this can often be avoided by climbing snow and ice. Also, the granite of the northern walls is considerably broken by melt-freeze, much more than in Ak-Su or in Karavshin.

From Uzgurush village, it takes 10 to 12 hours with donkeys to reach a base camp near the

[This page] The north face of West Parus (4,850m). (1) Vlasenko-Zhigalov, 2014. Black dot marks approximate high point of Kolisnyk-Koshelenko attempt in 2012. (2) Kolomyitsev-Komolov-Shibanov, 1990. *Yury Koshelenko*

terminus of the glacier in the Ashat Gorge. Nurdin, who owns a huge guesthouse in Uzgurush, can arrange everything. [*The online version of this report has many photos and logistical info.*]

YURY KOSHELENKO, *Russia, translated by Ekaterina Vorotnikova*

LAYLAK REGION

Blok Peak, new route on north face. In July, Sergey Maksimenko, Maxim Perevalov, and I headed to Kyrgyzstan to attempt a new route on the north face of Blok Peak (5,239m), named for the famous Russian poet Alexander Blok. July was unusually cold, with lots of precipitation. We had to wait 10 days for the weather to improve and strip the wall of ice. The approach from base camp (2,800m) usually takes five or six hours, but because of deep snow it took us no less than eight hours. The north face is about 800m, followed by a long but easier ridge to the top.

When we approached the wall Sergey Maksimenko was hit by a chunk of ice, breaking his arm. So, just two of us started up the route, following a line left of all established climbs on the face. The lower part was practically vertical. Overhangs protected us from falling ice, but in the afternoon a torrent of water ran in the corners. Higher up the corners were covered with ice, which was sometimes reliable but other times fell out in sheets. The upper route was typical mixed climbing, first not so steep, but then, just before the ridge, very steep again. We fixed 250m at the bottom of the route and then used a portaledge (which broke on the second-to-last night). The ascent and descent took nine days. Bolts were used only for rappel anchors and for setting up the portaledge.

ALEXANDER LAVRINENKO, *Ukraine, translated by Ekaterina Vorotnikova*

[This page] The north side of (A) Blok Peak East (5,100m) and (B) Blok Peak (5,239m) in an unusually heavy coat of snow and ice for July. (1) Filatkin Route. (2) Lavrinenko-Perevalov, 2013. (3) Efimov Route. (4) Bashkirov Route. (5) Aygistov Route. *Alexander Lavrinenko*

[This spread] Kichkesu peaks: (A) Chorku (6,283m). (B) Turkvo (6,243m). (C) 5,917m. (D) 5,408m. (E) Pogranichnikov (5,434m). (F) Meretskogo, climbed in 2013 by the left flank. *Yury Koshelenko*

TRANS ALAI

ZAALAISKY RANGE

Nura and Kichkesu regions, various ascents. In 2010, after a ski ascent and descent from Mt. Ararat, my friend Konstantin Babkin proposed that we look for virgin peaks for climbs and possible descents on skis, and in June of that year, along with Aleksey Bukinich, we departed for the eastern Zaalaisky Range (also spelled Zaalayskiy). The highest point of this region is the Kurumdy massif (6,613m), with the peaks of the Nura valley to the east and Kichkesu to the west.

We first headed for Nura, southeast of Osh, and investigated the peaks of the Kurum-Tor-Tag at the head of the Nura gorge—they didn't present any especial technical difficulty, but appeared rich in avalanche danger. We did an ascent on the side of the gorge, but poor weather prevented us from taking good photos. One new route was climbed in the Kurum-Tor-Tag massif in 2013: A group of tourists from Moscow, led by A. Lebedev, climbed Peak 5,985m, which in fact turned out to be a 6,000er (6,022m GPS). Judging from their account, this is the westernmost summit of the massif.

After 10 days in Nura we called a car from Osh and moved to the Kichkesu region. The car was unable to force a crossing of the Kichkesu River, so we had to carry loads to our base camp at the mouth of the Right Kichkesu Glacier (Pravii Kichkesu). The most outstanding peaks of this region are Mt. Chorku (6,283m), Mt. Turkvo (6,243m), and Mt. Pogranichnikov (Peak of the Frontier Guards, 5,434m), all of which were climbed during the time of the USSR.

It was drier in this area, and we succeeded in doing two first ascents. The first, relatively easy climb was above the middle arm of the Right Kichkesu Glacier, reaching a summit of 4,935m, which we called Ing Yan (Yin and Yang) because its southern slope presents a stone slab while the northern slope was snowy and icy. Our second climb, of medium difficulty, ascended a 4,800m peak at the mouth of the Left Kichkesu Glacier (Levii Kichkesu), which we called Mt. Meretskogo (Mt. M), because from the valley the mountain looks like the letter M and because L. Meretskii was one of the heroes of alpinism in my hometown of Rostov-on-Don. 🖸

YURY KOSHELENKO, *Russia, translated by Henry Pickford*

TIEN SHAN

KYRGYZ ALA-TOO

Ala Archa, Peak Korona, Box Peak, Ak-Too, various new routes. Many new routes have gone up in the mountains of Ala Archa National Park, south of Bishkek, as local climbers and foreign visitors take advantage of easy access to these superb mid-elevation peaks. Much of the activity was centered on the towers of Peak Korona (4,860m), above the Uchitel and Ak-Sai glaciers.

Willis Brown (Canada) and Seth Timpano (USA) climbed a new mixed line on the far right end of the north-facing wall above the Uchitel Glacier in October 2012. Their ca 500m route climbed the north-northwest face of Peak 4,300m, a summit along the ridge extending west from Korona. The crux was three sustained pitches (M6+, M5, AI5) sandwiched between lots of 50°–60° ice. A pitch of M4 led to the ridgeline. Brown and Timpano scrambled to an arbitrary high point at roughly 4,150m and descended the ice sheet to the west. Their nine-pitch route was called Privet Spasibo ("Hello Thank You").

Sergei Selivyorstov climbed two new ice routes farther east on the same north-facing wall. In January, he and Paul Vyazovetsky climbed a narrow ice couloir directly to the ridge (800m, Russian 5A 65°), then followed the west spur to the top of Korona. Then, in February, Selivyorstov soloed a new route starting at the same spot as the Canadian-American route from 2012 but heading left up an ice ramp and mixed ground to a finish right of the Novosel route (2002). Selivyorstov topped out on the ridge (850m, 4B) and rappelled.

On the far side of Korona, the west-facing Fifth Tower and Sixth Tower both got new routes. Over two days in March, Oleg Khvostenko and Igor Loginov climbed a line (Russian 5B) that slashes left to right across the 700m face of the Sixth Tower. The route followed a couloir to a prow, where the pair bivied, then continued up the south side to the summit. The climbers suggested the line would go free in summer at about French 6c.

In August, Konstantin Markelov and Anatoliy Syschikov completed a new route up the right side of the southwest face of the Fifth Tower over three days (725m, Russian 6A French 6c A2). The new line starts by the Ruzhevsky Route (5B, 1976) but stays to the right most of the way up the wall, before crossing it near the top for an independent finish.

On Ak-Too (4,620m), Nastya Cheremnikh, Andrew Erohin, and Arthur Usmanov climbed a new ice and mixed route (Russian 4B) up the left side of the northeast face, above the Ak-Sai Glacier.

On Box Peak (a.k.a. Boks Peak, 4,240m), near the terminus of the Ak-Sai Glacier, Arthur Usmanov, Constantine Markevich, and Sergei Selivyorstov climbed two new routes, both Russian 5B, on the steep, 700m rock wall of the north face. In late February they climbed a line to the right of the Michailava Route (*AAJ 1998*). They fixed ropes for two days and summited on the third. In early March, in the same style, the same trio climbed another new route farther to the right, starting up a snow and ice ramp and then continuing with aid.

DOUGALD MACDONALD,
with information from Anna Piunova, Mountain.ru, and Seth Timpano

[This page, top] Peak Korona, Fifth Tower (left) and Sixth Tower. (1) Egorov, 5A. (2) Sadowski, 5B, 1968. (3) Balezin, 6A, 1994. (4) Ruzhevsky, 5B, 1976. (5) Markelov-Syschikov, 6A, 2013. (6) Glukhovtsev, 5B, 1963. (7) Khvostenko-Loginov, 5B, 2013. *Ak Sai Travel (Ak-sai.com)* [This page, bottom] North side of Peak Korona (4,860m), above the Uchitel Glacier. (1) Gavrilov, 4A, 1956. (2) 4A, 1989. (3) Popov, 5B, 1976. (4) Smirnov, 5B, 1962. (5) Kalyugin, 5B, 1982. (6). Plotnikov, 4A, 1995. (7) 4A. (8) Selivyorstov-Vyazovetsky, 5A, 2013. (9) Novosel, 4B, 2002. (10) Selivyorstov, 4B, 2013. (11) Brown-Timpano, 2012, M6+. (12) Akimov, 3B, 1994. Several variations not shown. *Ak Sai Travel (Ak-sai.com)*

FERGANA RANGE

First ascents of four peaks. Our team of five British climbers explored Kyrgyzstan's relatively unknown Fergana Range, summiting four unclimbed peaks. This range runs southeast to northwest, west of the Torugart-Too, skirting the southern edge of the sparsely populated Arpa Valley. The full report can be found at the AAJ website.

DANIEL KELLER, *U.K.*

JAMANTAU RANGE

Mt. Kamasu, Mt. Kozerog, Pashalsta Peak, first ascents. The four-man team of Joe Prinold, Virgil Scott, Dominic Southgate, and Samuel Thompson began their expedition to the Jamantau Range, just north of the Arpa Valley and west of the At-Bashi, on August 24. After a 12-hour drive from Bishkek, they camped at the road head, and then, with the assistance of locals with horses, walked to base camp at 2,968m (40°56'25"N, 74°30'15"E), just to the northwest of Mt. Kamasu (4,505m, 40°54'44"N, 74°31'48"E). This unclimbed peak was the primary objective of the expedition.

Scott and Thompson climbed Kamasu on September 1. After a bivy on scree just below the foot of the glacier, the two climbed the glacier on the northwest face, with a crux icefall that was climbed on the right side in four pitches (70°). From a shelf atop the glacier, they followed a snow ridge to the summit (Alpine D). There was very little névé on the route—the vast majority was bulletproof ice, proving rather tiring on the calves! The descent was by downclimbing and Abalakov rappels, mostly following the ascent route.

Separately, Prinold and Southgate attempted Kamasu via the northeast ridge. After 1,100m of ascent, mostly on fairly steep scree slopes, they bivied on the ridge at ca 4,100m. The next morning easy ground led to a 60m snow slope of about 45°, at the top of which they found a sheer drop of about 50m. The two decided to retreat from this point.

On September 6, Southgate and Thompson attempted Peak 4,475m (40°54'20"N, 74°33'42"E). An overnight bivy was made at the top of the valley northwest of the peak (3,450m) about 100m below the start of the northwest-facing glacier. The two climbed this glacier (60°-65°) with a mix of pitched climbing and simul-climbing. This led to a snowy summit ridge, with a steep bergschrund at the very top (1,000m, D). The summit was slightly west of that shown on the Soviet maps, and was measured by altimeter was 4,450m. The team suggested a name of Mt. Kozerog.

[This page] Mt. Kamasu (4,505m). The first-ascent team climbed the long glacier system on the northwest face and then a snow ridge to the summit (1,000m, D). *Jamantau Expedition Collection*

Prinold and Scott made two attempts on the triangular Peak 3,861m (40°55'10"N, 74°29'16"E) before succeeding on September 8, starting from a bivy at 3,340m. The two climbed the left (southeast) arête on this rocky peak. About 10 pitches (no more than VS) plus simul-climbing led to a satisfyingly pointed summit. We named it Pashalsta Peak. The trip was supported by the Alpine Club and the British Mountaineering Council.

Information from VIRGIL SCOTT, *U.K.*

AT BASHI RANGE

Mustabbes Valley, various first ascents. A five-man British expedition comprised of Steve Brown, Paul Josse, Terje Lokken (Norway), Phil Morgan, and John Venier spent 12 days in late August exploring the glaciers around the western headwaters of the Mustabbes River. Various members of the team made the probable first ascents of eight peaks, ranging from 4,430m to 4,646m, and from F to AD in difficulty.

An ISM expedition led by Pat Littlejohn had journeyed up the Mustabbes River, on the south side of the At Bashi, in 2010, making the first ascents of eight summits above the eastern glacier (*AAJ 2011*). The 2013 expedition climbed above two advanced base camps, on the central glacier and below the far western glacier, as well as a base camp by the Mustabbes River. Among the fine peaks climbed was Peak Katushka (4,640m GPS), by the east ridge (Brown-Josse-Lokken, PD), above the central glacier. Brown, Josse, and Lokken later climbed Peak Chatir (4,646m), above the west glacier, via the southeast face and east ridge (PD). They then traversed south along the dividing ridge between the west and far western glaciers to reach Peak Kargan Semiz (4,550m, AD), before descending via the northwest ridge to the far west glacier. A full report on this expedition, with maps and photos, is available at the *AAJ* website.

DOUGALD MACDONALD, *with information from Paul Josse*

[This page] Peak Katushka with the line of the first ascent. *Paul Josse*

WESTERN KOKSHAAL-TOO

Dzhirnagaktu Glacier, various routes. Our group consisted of five female mountaineers from the Glasgow University Mountaineering Club: Hannah Gibbs, Carol Goodall, Imelda Neale, Libby Southgate, and me (Emily (Roo) Ward). We planned a lightweight, self-sufficient expedition. Sadly, our small expedition became even more lightweight when we lost two climbers before reaching base camp. Hannah caught a bad vomiting virus on the road to Naryn and returned home. Carol developed HAPE while carrying loads to base camp. Our sat phone was temperamental, and a stressful day was spent waiting for a helicopter to appear. Fortunately, she was safely evacuated to Bishkek.

In early September, Imelda, Libby, and I finished establishing base camp on the glacier with food for 12 days: significantly less time than we had hoped for! Our luck soon changed, however, as the weather and conditions were amazing. Most days were bluebird, and good névé covered the glacial ice. Cooler autumnal temperatures conveniently stuck together the loose shale.

As there were only three of us in the area with a faulty sat phone, we toned down our ambitions for technical climbing. Instead we aimed for routes in the PD to D– bracket. We climbed five new routes, with four of the summits being first female ascents. Two were insignificant peaks with little difficulty. The three more significant routes were all on peaks first climbed and documented by a Polish expedition three years earlier (AAJ 2011).

On Butterfly's Leg (4,865m), we climbed Point Zero Zero One Gully, a 300m, 55° couloir leading to the crest of the ridge between Rock Horse and Butterfly's Leg. From here we followed the south ridge to the summit via some crevasses and chossy scrambling. [*The peak's first known ascent was by the west ridge, though the Poles found a cairn on the summit.*]

We also climbed Pony (4,750m) by its north face and west ridge, ascending the second snow couloir on the north face with some interesting mixed steps at UIAA IV. From the top, we traversed the knife-edge ridge east, toward Rock Horse, until it was too chossy to continue. [*In 2012, Alek and Vladimir Zholobenko, part of an Irish expedition, climbed another line up the north face, starting farther east (AAJ 2013). The Poles did the first ascent of Pony in 2010 via a couloir on the south side.*]

On Night Butterfly (a.k.a. Nochnoi Motyl, 5,056m) we completed the route up the east ridge attempted by the Poles before they successfully climbed the peak by the south face. The aesthetic snowy crest is gained by an easy angled snow couloir. After a false summit, we dropped onto the

[This page] Climbing the aesthetic east ridge of Night Butterfly (5,056m). *Emily Ward Collection*

south face to avoid cornices, and then climbed a final slope with harder glacial ice up to 60°. There is a large bergschrund below the main summit that may be impassable in certain conditions. This route, which we called Flutterby, was our first ascent of a 5,000m peak and definitely the highlight of the trip! We owe gratitude to the British Mountaineering Council and the Mountaineering Club of Scotland for helping to sponsor our expedition.

EMILY WARD, *U.K.*

CENTRAL KOKSHAAL-TOO

Djangart Range, After You (Peak 5,318m), northwest face to north ridge; Buddyness (Peak 5,172m), northwest face; Mt. Skimmins (Peak 4,860m), northwest gully; Peak 4,580m, north face. Our expedition to Kyrgyzstan was made possible through the assistance of an AAC Live Your Dream Grant and the vision of team member Rob Gleich, an adventurous young man known for his alleged ascent of a 200' smokestack on the Tufts University campus and his penchant for ice climbing in a Speedo. None of us had ever completed a first ascent.

After arriving in Bishkek, Rob, Nick Levin, Austin Lines, Zach Matthay, Ryan Stolp, and I acclimatized in nearby Ala-Archa National Park, which was awe-inspiring, spectacular, and at times utterly miserable. On July 13 we crammed into taxis, mashrukas (mini-buses), and a 4WD van for an 11-hour cross-country bumpfest that took us through Karakol to Maida-Adyr airbase. We were one of the first expeditions to arrive for the 2013 season, and three days passed while waiting for our 30-minute helicopter ride to the Djangart. Just as cabin fever was setting in, the chopper picked us up and magically transported us to the northern terminus of the N1 valley, where it meets the Djangart River. Using a Delorme InReach–smart phone combination allowed us to track our flight in real time and gave us the confidence to burst into the cockpit and indicate our desired landing spot, narrowly avoiding an accidental drop-off at Djangart Pass.

On July 18 we established the Sandy Spit Camp at 4,000m on the east side of the N1 Glacier. Just southeast of camp towered our primary objective: Peak 5,318m. As the highest peak in the region and one of the most aesthetic, this summit had been the goal of multiple climbers, of which the most successful to date were Alex Brighton and Richard Tremellen (*AAJ 2012*).

On July 19 we attempted the northwest face. After reaching the corniced north ridge, we turned toward the snow-capped summit, but the early afternoon sun softened the snow and made upward progress impossible. We reached a high point of about 5,250m before starting down at 2:30 p.m. Four rappels brought us to open slopes, and after building the first V-threads of our lives we completed another 10 rappels to reach the glacier, where Rob successfully extricated himself from a hidden crevasse. Ryan had gone ahead, and a steaming-hot horsemeat dinner was ready for us when we arrived at 2 a.m.

Two days later we felt ready to try again. We departed at 8:30 p.m. on July 22, hoping to take advantage of better nighttime snow conditions. Hiking up a 300m talus slope to the south of the glacier, we reached the ice field and climbed through the night under a full moon. The sun rose as we crested the ridge. Ryan led an exposed mixed traverse and continued through a snow barrier to the summit ridge. Rob and Zach pushed the lead through varied snow features until we arrived on the summit, around 9 a.m. We began our descent less than 30 minutes later. By 6 p.m. we were back in camp and debating the name of our mountain, which we decided to call After You so we could tell both our moms and our girlfriends that we named it after them (ca 1,200m, M3 AI3).

[This page, left] Climbing the summit ridge on Peak After You. *Austin Lines* [This page, right] The first-ascent route up the northwest face and north ridge of Peak After You (5,318m), highest summit of the Djangart region. *Ryan Stolp*

After two well-earned rest days, our group split to try multiple objectives. On July 25, Ryan and I traveled south to attempt the west side of Peak 5,172m. We were drawn to a three-pitch ice line that took us through perfect rock to a hanging glacier. We had a tense moment when Ryan descended into a monster crevasse and the snow-covered floor collapsed under him. Eventually he struggled out of the dark hole and crawled across a snow bridge to the opposite side. We finally reached a crevasse-free area and set up camp at 4,700m.

The next day we climbed steep snow and ice to reach the summit at 9:15 a.m. in perfect weather. Nine or ten rappels brought us back across the bergschrund to high camp. We watched the sunset while eating a delightful dinner of cough drops from the first-aid kit, and in the morning made our way back to the Sandy Spit Camp. We named the peak Buddyness, and we called our route Last Crusade (5.3 WI3).

Meanwhile, Nick, Zach, Rob, and Austin had marched south to the border mountains. They roped up and frontpointed to a notch in the ridge. Taking off his gloves in the midday sun, Zach led easy fourth- and fifth-class rock to the summit of Peak 4,580m, where he was surprised to find an old bamboo pole. While this peak had been climbed before, perhaps the route had not. The guys named it Cigarette Direct (5.2 AI2).

On July 27, our pre-determined last day of climbing, this same four-person team climbed into a gully north of Peak 5,318m. As they paused to don crampons, rockfall came down and struck Nick in the kidney. Despite feeling somewhat nauseous, Nick continued climbing as the group ascended 50°–60° ice and some easy mixed ground to reach a heavily corniced ridge. The sunbathed, hanging snow features to the north prevented them from traversing toward Peak 4,885m, their original plan. Instead, the group reached a nearby high point to the south (ca 4,860m), which they named Mt. Skimmins in honor of a particularly obese feline friend in the U.S. They called the route Kidney Stone Gully (AI2 M2) to commemorate injuries old and new. 📷 🔍 ▤ ▶

JEFF LONGCOR, *AAC*

[This page, top] Peaks near the head of the Kichik Sauktor Glacier: (A) Peak Currahee, 5,025m, and (B) Peak Little, ca 4,850m. (1) Route to col where team split to climb each peak. (2) Descent from Peak Little. *Clay Conlon*

Djangart Range, seven first ascents. In August, Harry Bloxham, Clay Conlon, Al Docherty, Harry Kingston, Ross Davidson, and I (all from the U.K.) spent three weeks in the Djangart Valley. We had planned to attempt three 5,000m-plus unclimbed summits. Just before traveling, however, we learned that our primary objective, Peak 5,318m, now known as Peak After You, had been climbed a few weeks earlier by a team of Americans. Furthermore, the helicopter from Maida-Adyr airbase dropped us 10km from our preferred base camp.

Despite these setbacks, an initial exploratory trip onto the Kichik Sauktor Glacier turned into the successful ascents of two unclimbed peaks on the Chinese border. Following a tiring 12-hour approach from base camp, Ross, Clay, Harry Kingston, and I established advanced base camp at 4,300m. The following morning we left the camp at 3 a.m. and climbed to a col at 4,800m. Exhausted and with potential bad weather approaching, Harry and I chose to abandon the main target and instead summited a nearby unclimbed peak (Peak Little, ca 4,850m, AD-). Ross and Clay continued to the southeast and then east, finding difficult conditions that required them to pitch much of the corniced summit ridge. They summited Peak Currahee (5,025m GPS, D- III) at around 11 a.m., and returned to the col after 16 hours of climbing. Finding snow conditions too poor to continue the descent, they opted to bivy at the col and descend early the next day.

Harry Bloxham and Al were next to summit, climbing a cracking new line up west-facing snow slopes on previously unclimbed Peak Betelgeuse (ca 5,100m, AD-) in the N1 valley.

After a short period of bad weather, the team walked one day up the Akunguz Glacier (a.k.a. Akoguz Glacier). Harry Kingston, Ross, Clay, and I climbed Peak Kasparov (4,822m, AD), following snow up the north side to the rocky west ridge. The following day Ross

[This page, bottom] Harry Bloxham struggles to cross the fast-flowing Djangart River on his way back to base camp. *George Cave*

and Harry K. summited Peak Ozon (4,971m, AD), climbing snow and ice to the east ridge. Meanwhile, Harry B. and Al had walked west the length of the Djangart Valley to set up an advance camp on the Djangartynbashi Glacier. Here, they climbed two great new routes: the north face of Peak Feto (4,831m, AD+) and the west face of Peak Topor (ca 4,970m, D-), both previously unclimbed summits with some of the best alpine ice the team had ever encountered. The expedition gratefully acknowledges support from the Alpine Club, BMC, and Mount Everest Foundation. 📷 🔍

GEORGE CAVE , U.K.

Djangart Range, seven first ascents and high traverse. Tom Bell, Max Folkett, Richard "Reg" Measures, Neil Thomas, Hugh Thomas, and I arrived in Bishkek from the U.K. and New Zealand in early August. On 5th we traveled to Maida-Adyr, and the following morning we took a 25-minute helicopter flight to our base camp at the junction of the Djangart Valley and the N1 and N2 glaciers.

The team split into two parties for the whole trip and spent the initial few days acclimatizing and exploring the area, visiting the Chulaktor, Akoguz, N2, and N1 glaciers. Hugh, Tom, and Neil then made the first ascents of Peak Fotheringham (4,871m, 41°39'30.31"N, 79°0'32.88"E), up the east ridge and down the west, followed by Point Andrea (4,566m 41°40'19.94"N, 79°00'43.70"E). Two days later they climbed Peak Kinmundy (4,950m, 41°39'58.57"N, 79°1'32.80"E).

From the N2 glacier, Max, Reg, and I made the first ascent of Peak MacMillan (5051m, 41°41'43.24"N, 079°0'45.08"E). Our route was an aesthetic line up the northwest face (Frima Face, 900m, D- 45-70° Scottish III). Going light from a high camp at around 4,000m, we soloed 700m of 45°–70° névé to the west ridge—with the altitude this felt punishing. Taking care to avoid the cornices, we made our way to the top and descended the lower angled southeast face.

Two days later, on August 16, we made the first ascent of Peak Vinton-Boot (5,168m, 41°40'30.84"N, 079°1'37.91"E) via a stunning northwest-facing ice gully (Open Misère, 500m, TD Scottish V). Overcoming the bergschrund was awkward, and the pitches then gradually got steeper. The ice had formed over a layer of snow and didn't take screws well, and the rock was quite friable. Reg led the steepest ice, and then Max climbed some mixed to get around a thin, unprotectable section. After nine full pitches the angle eased off and we simul-climbed to the summit ridge. We descended the north ridge and a messy glacier, arriving back to camp after an 18-hour round trip.

On the 19th of August Reg, Max and I made an initial attempt from the N1 glacier on the traverse from Peak 5,274m (Djanghorn) to Peak After You (5,318m), the highest peak in the range, climbed by a U.S. team two weeks prior to our arrival. However this attempt was halted by rockfall, in which Max sustained minor injuries and our rope was cut. Over the next week, spells of bad weather limited activity to exploration and aborted attempts on Peak 5,112m (Sauktor Glacier) and Peak 4,911m (Akoguz Glacier).

On the 27th of August, Reg, Max, and I were ready for a rematch with the south ridge of Djanghorn (41°40'5.71"N, 078°59'21.70"E) and the traverse to Peak After You. Starting at 1 a.m. from our high camp, we went flat out, climbing as fast as we could through the rockfall danger to col at the beginning of the ridge. Immediately above the col were the crux pitches, which were steep and loose. Max led the hardest pitch in rock shoes. With a mixture of free and aid, he climbed an overhanging corner filled with flakes seemed posed ready to detach—which several did—at HVS A2 (5.9 A2). After seven very time-consuming, awkward pitches and several sections of tricky simul-climbing, we reached soft snow slopes leading to the summit.

We summited at 5:30 p.m. and started the 2.5km traverse of the other peaks. By the time

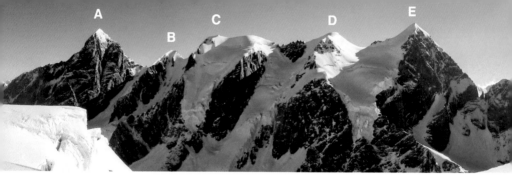

[This page] The east wall of the N1 Glacier, traversed from E to B (south to north) by Timothy Elson, Max Folkett, and Reg Measures. (A) Peak After You. (B) Peak Betelgeuse. (C) Peak Buddyness. (D) Peak 5,207m. (E) Djanghorn (Peak 5,274m), first ascent by the south ridge. *Hugh Thomas*

darkness fell we were over the next major summit, making the first ascent of Peak 5,207m. Stopping to melt water and eat, we contemplated biving, but it was too cold with no gear, so we pushed on, completing the second ascents of Peak Buddyness (5,172m) and Peak Betelgeuse (5,100m). Reaching the col before Peak After You at 1:30 a.m., we took the escape option back to our high camp. At our tent we checked the sat phone and discovered we still had no confirmation that our helicopter pick-up had been moved—meaning the helicopter was potentially arriving at 8 a.m. that morning! With this in mind we reluctantly collapsed the tent and walked four hours back to base camp, ending a 31-hour day. The helicopter didn't arrive until the following day. We would like to thank the Mount Everest Foundation, the Alpine Club, and the Austrian Alpine Club for supporting our expedition. 📷 🔍

Timothy Elson, *U.K.*

West Pogrebetsky Peak (6,487m), west face, Dasha Yashnaia. In August, Murat Otepbaev and I climbed a new route up the western wall of Pogrebetsky Peak's western summit (1,870m, Russian 5B, French 6c+). In all the ascent took four days: a day of approach and reconnaissance, two days to reach the summit, and a day to descend. We had reckoned on about five days and stocked food accordingly. Well, nothing proved to be of use.

We started climbing at ca 4,600m. The first day began with névé at about 60° for the first 400m, then it became steeper and the névé changed into a thin crust of ice over snow. Belay anchors were exceedingly difficult to find. We had set out at 2:30 a.m., and toward 4 p.m. we counted 22 pitches, but we could not find anyplace to spend the night. As we approached the rocky headwall, on pitch 27, it was 6:40 p.m. A strong wind made the search for a bivy site more difficult, and the advent of darkness did not cheer us up at all. We found a narrow shelf in the rocks, crawled into our tent, and began to heat water so at least something entered our stomachs. Food didn't make it.

We arose, as though by command, at 6 a.m. Neither of us wanted to abandon his warm sleeping bag. Our watches indicated 5,920m. We pulled ourselves together and sluggishly slipped into the cold. The metal gear stuck to our gloves; our bodies refused to cooperate. We returned to the route and climbed on ice-covered rocks, balanced on crampons. We climbed two and half pitches and bore down on the upper névé field. This led to a couloir, which in turn would lead us to the upper ridge. This gave us strength and confidence. But the couloir did not let us relax, and on the last two pitches we really had to toil. On the ridge the wind was howling. The summit was a stone's throw away, but sleep and hunger demanded we rest, so we dug in for the night. We felt no urge to eat—in vain did we drag so much food with us!

In the morning we descended the north slopes, below Pogrebetsky's main summit. We fell often in the deep snow and thick clouds tried to divert us from the path, but our desire for food and warmth was stronger. At 11:10 p.m. Dima Grekov met us in the kitchen at Camp 1 for Khan-Tengri. A profound thanks to him—the lights of the base camp were like a lighthouse for us.

GENNADY DUROV, *Kazakhstan, translated by Henry Pickford*

Editor's note: Pogrebetsky Peak (6,527m) was named for Mikhail Pogrebetsky, who led the Ukrainian team that did the first ascent of Khan Tengri in 1931. The mountain rises above the intersection of the Druzhba Glacier and the south arm of the South Inyl'chek Glacier. Three impressive climbs (including the Durov-Otepbaev ascent in 2013) have been completed on the north and west sides of the western summit of Pogrebetsky (6,487m). In 1980, a team led by E. Streltsov climbed the ridge splitting the west and northwest faces (Russian 5B). In 2006, a Krasnoyarsk expedition led by Alexander Mikhalitsin climbed the nearly 2,000m north-northwest face, then labeled the last unclimbed high-altitude wall of the former Soviet Union. This face had previously been attempted in 1984, 1989, and 1991. The Krasnoyarsk team spent seven days on the ascent of the north face, with another two days to descend. They found difficult climbing (6B overall) on compact marble and limestone, and were forced to spend several nights in sitting bivouacs in hammocks.

Cieza Peak (4,929m), east face. Spanish climbers Murcia Félix Gómez de León and José Antonio Pastor completed the possible first ascent of a 4,929m peak above the Dikiy Glacier, a branch of the South Inylchek Glacier extending southward to the Pobeda massif. Starting from a camp at 3,950m, the two climbed the east face, with most of the difficulties in the final 500m (snow and ice to 65°). They descended the south ridge and slopes to the east, and named the peak after their home town. 📷

DOUGALD MACDONALD, *from information at Desnivel.com*

[This page] (A) Pogrebetsky Peak (6,527m). (B) West Pogrebetsky Peak (6,487m), with (1) Krasnoyarsk Route, 2006, (2) Streltsov Route, 1986, and (3) Durov-Otepbaev, 2013. All teams descended the north slopes on the left. (C) Peak Voennih Topografov (Peak of the Army Topographers), 6,873m. *Supplied by Anna Piunova–Mountain.ru*

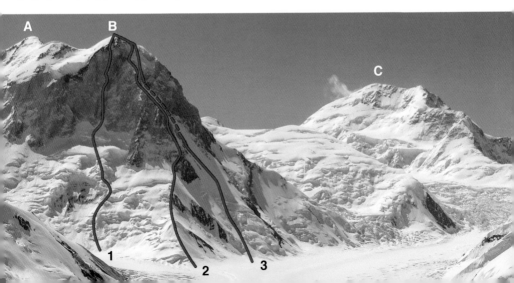

TAJIKISTAN

PAMIR

Sizdh Valley, Rakhsh (4,570m). In August, Peter Anderson, Jim Donini, Bo White, and I traveled to the Pamir Mountains in southeastern Tajikistan to teach wilderness medicine, climbing, and guiding basics to a group of local students from the Pamir Alpine Club, and to attempt new routes on alpine rock around Khorog. The trip was made possible by financial support from the Aga Khan Foundation and logistics support from the University of Central Asia.

During a free day with good weather, Anderson and I established a 350m rock climb on the east ridge of a previously unclimbed peak at the top of the Sizdh Valley (a tributary drainage of the Gunt River). The peak came to be called Rakhsh (4,570m), which is the name of the stallion of Rostam, a hero of the Persian epic tale Shahnameh. Other significant features in the area had previously been climbed and named after the Shahnameh by White and Donini (*AAJ 2012*).

Our route, dubbed Rhinocesaurus Ridge, consisted of about half a dozen pitches of belayed climbing (up to 5.8) with lots of simul-climbing on gneiss. The route stayed right on the crest, passing a significant gendarme ("The Rhino Horn") on the north side, and ended with hand and finger cracks to a knife-edged summit. We descended to the north by a 60m rappel, 300m of downclimbing, and a final 30m rappel from a bollard to reach the talus.

COREY LaFORGE, *AAC*

Shakhdara Range, Peak Karl Marx, ascent of southwest rib and attempt on northeast face. Doug Chabot, Steve Swenson, and had planned to climb in Pakistan. However, a few weeks before our planned departure, we still had not received our climbing permit, so we looked for options. Without much time to hash it over, we settled on Peak Karl Marx (6,723m) in the southern Pamir, and

[This page] Rakhsh (4,570m) in the Sizdh Valley. The Rhinocesaurus Ridge (east ridge) follows the right skyline past the prominent horn. The peak behind is ca 4,600m. *Corey LaForge*

[This page] Approaching the ca 1,800m northeast face of Karl Marx. The southwest rib, behind and right, was first climbed in 1946, for the first ascent of the peak. *Rusty Willis*

headed there in mid-July. We owe a huge thank you to Bo White, who has spent a lot of time in Tajikistan and helped us with logistics.

The launching point for the approach was a small village called Jawshangoz, where we were able to hire donkeys for the five-hour trek to base camp at ca 3,950m. A high-pressure system settled over the area, and we wasted no time in taking advantage of it. After only a couple days in base camp, we began climbing the southwest rib of Karl Marx, and we summited three days later.

Feeling more fit and acclimatized, we turned our attention to the ca 1,800m northeast face. In the 1970s, this face had been climbed, siege-style, by Soviet mountaineers. We planned to climb it alpine-style. However, there was one big question. There was a white band of rock about one-third of the way up the face; this looked to be marble and had no visible weakness. We had read that the Russians had drilled several hundred holes to climb the face, and we feared that we did not have the gear to get up it.

After much discussion, we decided we would do a reconnaissance climb up to the white band to have a closer look. Because the temperature was unusually warm, and we had seen water running down the face in the afternoon over several days, we decided to start at midnight so we could be above the initial ice face before the sun warmed the upper mountain. We woke at midnight as planned but did not cross the bergschrund until about 4 a.m.

Steve was leading the fifth pitch, about halfway up the ice face, when the sun touched the upper mountain. Doug and I were at the belay when we heard a rumble and saw the sky filled with rocks. Steve, despite having one tool ripped completely out of the ice by a rock, managed to stay on. Doug took a hit to his left shoulder and was not able to use his left arm, and I had my helmet caved in, but other than a headache and chipped front tooth I was fine. We quickly began rappelling, trying to reach the safety of the bergschrund. During the descent we were under constant rockfall, and Doug took another hit, this time to the face. There was a lot of blood, but luckily it was a clean cut and nothing was broken.

Back at camp, we decided the weather was too warm to get on any steep mountain faces, and we sent word for the donkeys to come get us. In the end, we felt fortunate that we were able to summit the peak so quickly, and other than the rockfall incident we had a great trip to a region that few foreigners see.

RUSTY WILLIS, AAC

Muzkol Range, Point SimSim (5,640m), north rib. In July, Jonathan Davey and I traveled to the Muzkol Range of the eastern Pamir to make climbs from the Bozbaital Valley. Unclimbed peaks up to just over 6,000m remain in this range. We accessed the area from the north, leaving the Pamir Highway near Lake Karakul, then driving southwest toward the range. The bottom of the Bozbaital Valley can be reached from this direction in a good off-road vehicle.

After a number of delays and two days spent carrying 25kg rucksacks in 45°C heat, we had established our base camp in the Bozbaital. Following acclimatization to 5,000m on the southern slopes of Muzkolski (*AAJ 1998*), we headed for an unnamed peak above the Aydemsi Glacier, to the east of Peak Frunze.

The first challenge was to cross the Bozbaital River, using a belayed pendulum traverse. On the first attempt I lost my footing and only the rope prevented me from ending up in the Aral Sea. For the second attempt we returned early in the morning when the river level was lower and succeeded. The Aydemsi Glacier is covered in rubble from its snout at the Bozbaital River right up to the point where it splits into two short tributary glaciers, so tent pitches for an uncomfortable night's sleep are plentiful.

The climb itself gained approximately 1,000m from glacier to summit, mainly moving together up classic 50° alpine ice slopes, with occasional opportunities for scrambling up rocky ribs (AD+). At the summit we were disappointed to find a slightly higher summit rose within spitting distance to the southwest. It was past midday and snow conditions were deteriorating, so it would not have been wise to attempt it. We descended the northwest face to the neighboring valley.

We named the top we climbed Point SimSim, after a beer brewed in Tajikistan costing approximately $1 a pint in Dushanbe. The higher summit that remains unclimbed would make an excellent ascent as the final stage of acclimatization for one of the 6,000m peaks at the top of the Bozbaital Valley. We would like to thank Gore-tex for awarding the expedition a Shipton-Tilman grant.

JOHN PROCTOR, *The Alpine Club, U.K.*

[This page] Point SimSim, above the west fork of the Aydemsi Glacier. The climbers descended the opposite side of the ridge to the east fork. An unclimbed higher top is hidden beyond. *John Proctor*

AFGHANISTAN

PAMIR

Koh-e-Wakhan Range, Peak 5,965m (6,060m GPS), south face; Peak 5,842m, northeast face, attempt.
In early September, Mick Follari, Aidan Loehr, and I traveled through Tajikistan to the Afghan border, where we were delayed crossing the frontier for more than a week by a cholera epidemic in northern Afghanistan. Once over the border in Ishkashim, Adab Shab, our agent, provided a driver and translator. We then drove two days to Ptukh, where I had been one and a half years earlier with three ski-mountaineering partners (*AAJ 2013*). After hiring porters, we reached our 2012 base camp in the Issik Valley via two easy days of walking.

The Issik Valley appears to be stocked with good granite and is not dissimilar to Chamonix, albeit 2,000m higher, with no people for hundreds of kilometers and endless, horrendous moraine. Our primary objective was the northwest face of Koh-e-Pamir (6,320m), but from our high camp at 5,100m on the glacier we could see it lay in the shade for all but two hours a day. September nights are long and cold, and none of us wanted to stuff fingers and toes into icy granite so late in the season. We turned instead to an unclimbed peak between Koh-e-Seh Aspe Safad and Koh-e-Helal. The Austrian map puts this at 5,965m (actually, the map marks it as 4,965m, but this is obviously a typo as the adjacent col is marked as 5,814m).

On September 17 we started up the south face in the small hours, climbing several pitches up a thin line of ice and rock (AI4+ M5) to a moderate snow couloir made up of the most awkward, bladed, mega sun-cups imaginable. We unroped, continued together, and at 5,800m roped up again for several pitches of moderate ice to the summit ridge. A quick jaunt led to the top, where a GPS measured 6,060m and an altimeter 6,030m. We now discovered we had forgotten the V-thread

[This page] Looking northeast from slopes below Peak 5,842m. (A) East ridge of Peak 6,041m. (B) Peak 5,798m. (C) Koh-e-Marco Polo (6,194m). (D) Koh-e-Pamir (6,320m). (E) Peak 6,009m. (F) Northern Issik Glacier. *Mick Follari*

tool, so Mick made a stupendous job of rigging 18 consecutive ice anchors down our route using a #6 Black Diamond Stopper instead of a V-threader.

Several days later we made our first attempt on Peak 5,842m, a summit with no known ascents that lies a couple of kilometers east of Koh-e-Seh Aspe Safad (6,101m). On the 21st we climbed unroped for 100m up an initial ice ribbon on the northeast face, and then belayed several pitches before reaching a steep section of rotten, white ice overlying a black-ice core. Aidan tried first, finding zero protection and breaking a pick. Mick then advanced the line by half a dozen moves and two ice screws. We went down, and after a rest day spent aggressively sharpening crampons, regained the same crux pitch. Aidan made steady progress over the bulge via some aid and desperate scratching. We then climbed several more pitches of AI5 M6 to reach an alcove approximately halfway up the face.

The sun had crossed the sky. The ropes were now frozen cables. The temperature was dropping, and we had not taken bivouac gear. I tried to imagine the horror of sport climbing back home with missing toes, and couldn't reconcile it. During lulls between each rappel we viewed the vast array of possibilities in this area awaiting any climbers prepared to brave the bureaucracy, visa dilemmas, poverty, security issues, and endless loose talus. The descent to civilization began next day. Having carried a paraglider to base camp, I elected to fly back to Ptukh.

On our ride back down the Wakhan, we discovered that battles were now frequent between the Taliban and Afghan National Army (ANA) in the Warduj district, a couple of hours south of Ishkashim. By dint of its ANA military base, an Ismaili Shia majority, and its appreciation for tourism dollars, Ishkashim itself is still fairly secure. That said, I'd encourage climbers to use prudence and discretion if you visit the Wakhan.

You should also ensure visas are in order. Aidan paid for a multi-entry visa to Tajikistan, but upon arriving back at the border discovered that in reality he only had a single-entry visa (which had already been used). By the time we learned of this, Aidan was already stamped out of Afghanistan and in effect became someone similar to the Tom Hanks character from *Terminal*—he was stuck in a no man's land between two countries. It cost him almost a month and a lot of money to get home. More info on the expedition may be found at Afghanalpine.com. 🔲

DYLAN TAYLOR, *AAC*

[This page] Climbing the lower section of the steep ice couloir during the attempt on the northeast face of Peak 5,842m. *Mick Follari*

[This page, top] The Qara Jilga group from the north. Three of the four summits are visible; the fourth is hidden in clouds on the left. The highest (6,094m) is the visible summit farthest back, the second highest probably the one in cloud. The forepeak (top of the attempted north ridge) may also be over 6,000m. The route to the crest of the north ridge at ca 5,400m is marked. Base camp was on the right side of the moraine below. *Alan Halewood* [This page, bottom] Richmond MacIntyre with his split helmet and a rock of similar size to the one that hit him. *Alan Halewood*

Qara Jilga (6,094m), north ridge attempt. Following my 2010 trip to Koh-e-Iskander, northeast of the Qara Jilga massif (*AAJ 2011*), I wanted to return and attempt one of the Qara Jilga summits. I persuaded Richmond MacIntyre (South Africa) and Rich Parker (U.K.) to join me. After two days' drive from Dushanbe we crossed the Tajik-Afghan border at Ishkashim.

In an old Land Cruiser we bumped, splashed, slid, and scraped our way up the Wakhan. We reached the end of the road at Sarhad-e-Boroghil. Seven days later, with the help of horses and mules, we walked to a base camp (4,815m) on glacial moraine below the north side of the Qara Jilga peaks.

During our descent from a scouting trip to 5,400m on the main north ridge, rockfall struck Richmond in the head, splitting open his helmet and rendering him unresponsive. The subsequent descent and evacuation was epic, and a testimony to Richmond's toughness. He suffered no permanent damage. [*The full account of the impressive retreat from these remote mountains can be found at the AAJ website.*]

ALAN HALEWOOD, *U.K.*

PAKISTAN

HIMALAYA

KHYBER PAKHTUNKHWA — KAGHAN VALLEY

Malika Parbat North (5,222m), north ridge ascents. In July 2012, Imran Junaidi from Islamabad and Jens Simensen (Denmark) climbed the north summit of Malika Parbat (5,290m), the highest peak in the Kaghan Valley, an area considered safe for local and foreign tourists. They approached via the Chitta Glacier, using the northwest flank to gain the crest of the north ridge (a section of snow at 70-75°), which they followed to the top. A similar line was followed on August 31, 2012, when Ahmed Mujtaba and Ahmed Naveed reached the summit after an open bivouac at ca 5,180m. (This route is different to that followed by Norman Norris and Gene White in 1967.) These are examples—and there are others—of the increasing number of Pakistani alpinists from the "lower regions," such as the capital Islamabad, taking on more technical climbs. A history of ascents on Malika Parbat and its northern summit can be found in the online version of this report. 📷 📄

LINDSAY GRIFFIN, *from information supplied by Imran Junaidi and Ahmed Naveed, Pakistan*

KARAKORAM

GHUJERAB MOUNTAINS

Koksil Sar V (5,830m, GPS), west face and southwest rib. Our all-Pakistan expedition to the Fourth Koksil Glacier took place from August 17–28 and comprised Kamal Haider, Sa'ad Mohamed, Ahmed Mujtaba, Syed Jawad Tashfeen, and me from Islamabad, and Arif Baig and Mohammad Yahya from Shimshal. Koksil Sar V was first climbed on June 16, 2000, by Karim Hayat, Ishfaq Karim, and Safdar Karim. They climbed the south face from the Fourth Koksil Glacier to the upper southwest rib, which they followed to the summit. They also made the first ascent of Koksil Sar IV on the watershed ridge to the south. We aimed to complete a new route on the peak.

We traveled the Karakoram Highway to Koksil Check Post (4,100m), 12km before the

[This page] Malika Parbat from the northwest, with the 2012 Danish-Pakistani route marked. *Imran Junaidi*

Khunjerab Pass, then walked south along the Koksil Valley for only two hours to establish base camp by a shepherd's hut at 4,200m. On August 23 we made advanced base at 4,800m, just below the Fourth Koksil Glacier snow line. High camp was made at 5,230m on the glacier, below the west face of Koksil Sar V.

In order to avoid rockfall danger on the southwest rib, we opted for the icy west face. On the 25th we began climbing in the dark. After a total of around a dozen pitches (generally soft but supportive snow over ice), and eight hours on the face, we reached the upper southwest rib at ca 5,650m. Moderate mixed ground led to the long summit ridge, where cornices and crevasses on adjoining faces required careful negotiation. After two hours all seven of us managed to crowd onto the small summit, which we measured by GPS as 5,830m (36°44.565'N, 75°20.864'E). Koksil Sar IV, south along an extended, corniced ridge, appeared much the same height. We downclimbed and rappelled our route, reaching high camp just before sunset.

AHMED NAVEED, *Pakistan*

Ghidims Valley, Yawash Sar Middle (5,786m), Panorama Peak (5,350m). In August-September 2012, Frank Gasser (Italy), Detlef Seelig (Germany), and Birgit Walk (Austria) visited the Ghidims Valley. The first people to reach the start of this valley, at a place called Mandi Kushlak, were Henry Montagnier and Captain C.J. Morris in 1927. (They did not enter the valley but instead turned west and went down the Ghujerab Valley.) In 2000 John Mock and Kimberley O'Neill penetrated the South Ghidims Valley and toward the head moved northeast to cross North Ghidims Pass (5,650m), descending the far side to the Akalik Glacier (*AAJ 2001*). Birgit Walk takes up the story of the 2012 expedition:

"On traveling to Karimabad and acclimatizing on nearby Khor (5,020m), we continued to Shimshal. Leaving here on August 27, in two days we had crossed the Boesan Pass and descended to Mandi Kushlag in the Ghujerab Valley. Next day we crossed the main river and entered the Ghidims Dur (valley), ascending it to where it splits. At this point we finally realized that our guide had no idea as to the location of our primary goal, Yawash Sar I (6,258m). The impressive north side of this peak had been photographed by Gasser in 2011, when he was a member of a small Polish expedition to the First Koksil Glacier (*AAJ 2012*). We decided to make base camp at the junction of what is known as the north and south Ghidims valleys, at an altitude of 4,475m on the Russian map.

On August 30, Detlef Seeling and the Pakistani Ilyas moved a little way down the South

[This page] South face of Yawash Sar Middle, showing route of ascent. *Frank Gasser*

Ghidims valley and then climbed south to a point of elevation 5,350m, on a ridge between two side glaciers. They named this Panorama Peak.

"The next few days were spent resting or in reconnaissance, but at the time we still could not identify Yawash Sar. Instead, we decided to attempt a peak situated at the head of the North Ghidims Glacier. On September 2, Gasser, Ilyas, and I established a high camp below the peak, but the following day bad weather and Ilyas' altitude sickness drove us back to base camp.

"Due to consistently unstable weather, Gasser and I again changed objectives, this time opting

for a peak west of our previous choice, as it appeared lower and technically easier. On the 6th we moved up to high camp in bad weather, but there seemed to be an improvement by 3 a.m. next morning, so we started up the south face at 4:15 a.m., and, finding good snow conditions (45°), reached the top via the upper southeast ridge at 7 a.m. We descended the ridge and regained our tent at 9 a.m., whereupon it began to snow. We continued down to base camp in poor visibility. We have called this peak Yawash Sar Middle."

JANUSZ MAJER, *Poland, and*
BIRGIT WALK, *Austria*

Ghidims Valley, Dosti Sar (6,063m), Umeed Sar (5,826m). After withdrawing from the Diamir Face of Nanga Parbat, following the terrorist attack, my next expedition was to the Ghidims Valley with Polish friend Anita Parys. After crossing Boesam Pass, Anita and I, along with locals Ilyas and Bulbul, reached the 4,475m base camp on September 7. After a couple of days of rest we attempted a snow dome, visible from Mandi Kushlak, but retreated from 5,300m.

At midday on September 17, Anita, Bulbul, and I established a camp at 5,160m on a different peak that had been visible from base camp. It lies on the ridge between the north and south Ghidims passes, northeast of the South Ghidims Glacier. When we woke at 3 a.m. the following day, the sky was clear and starry, and the temperature below –20°C. We left at 5 a.m. and reached the snowline at 7 a.m. The snow ridge above was not difficult, but there were a few crevasses before we reached the summit at 2:20 p.m. The final slope was 45°, and we could see all the great peaks of the Karakoram, from K2 to Rakaposhi.

We named the peak Dosti Sar (Dosti being Wakhi for "friendship"). I had known Bulbul since 1999, and Anita had shown great optimism and friendship after the Nanga Parbat terrorist attacks.

[This page] South face of unclimbed Yawash Sar I (6,258m). *Detlef Seelig*

[This page, top] View from the southwest over the Left Ice Flow of the North Ghidims Glacier: (A) Peak 5,820m, (B) Peak 5,920m, and (C) Yawash Sar II (6,176m, unclimbed). *Karim Hayat* [This page, bottom] Unclimbed peaks at the head of the South Ghidims Glacier and beyond, seen from the northwest. (A) Peak 6,093m. (B) Peak 6,047m. (C) Peak 6,200m. (D) Peak 5,913m. (E) Peak 6,000m. *Karim Hayat*

When most climbing and trekking expeditions canceled, Anita wrote to say, "I have booked a flight. Whatever happens I should come and climb this peak, and meet everyone." Our GPS registered an altitude of 6,061m (map height 6,063m). We regained camp at 5 p.m. and descended to base camp the following day.

We'd asked porters to be at base camp on the 21st for our outward journey. After breakfast on the 20th I set off alone. I told the others I was going exploring, but I'd already made up my mind to make a fast solo of one more peak. My goal was north of the Ghidims Dur, southwest of Yawash Sar I, and in front of Peak 5,901m. I reached the snowline at 11 a.m. and climbed 40-45° gullies to a final

50° slope. It was icy and I used three Abalakov threads to self-belay with my 20m of 5mm rope. The final two-meter-high cornice was 80°. I reached the 5,826m summit (map height) at 3 p.m. It was one of the greatest days of my climbing career.

At base the team had followed my progress through binoculars. By the time I reached the foot of the peak I was exhausted, having ascended 1,400m and descended the same way. Bulbul met me on the way back to camp, which we reached at 8:30 p.m. I have named this peak Umeed Sar (Hope Peak), dedicating it to the climbers who lost their lives in the terrorist attack. 📷

Karim Hayat, *Pakistan*

SHIMSHAL AREA – SHUIJERAB GROUP

Shuijerab Glacier, Koh-e-Gulistan (6,224m), southwest face and west-northwest ridge. Supported by the German Alpine Club, Harry Kirschenhofer, Michael Pfeiffer, Birgit Walk, and I reached Shimshal on August 13, and after a three-day trek along the Pamir-i-Tang, interrupted by a day of bad weather, set up base camp at 4,600m, close to the snout of the Shuijerab Glacier.

We had located four unclimbed peaks above 6,000m, which we labeled P1–P4, at the northern head of the valley, including one actually beyond the divide in the neighboring valley of Oprang. Unfortunately, I caught a throat infection and had to descend in order to recover. During

[This page, top] Looking east from high camp on the upper Shuijerab Glacier to peaks around the Shuijerab-Shuwert divide. Nearly all the peaks in this photo are thought to be unclimbed. *Provided by Christof Nettekoven* [This page, bottom] High camp on the upper Shuijerab Glacier. P3 on the left was climbed via a snow and ice slope off-picture to reach the left skyline ridge, which was followed to the summit. P1, on the right, remains unclimbed. *Provided by Christof Nettekoven*

August 17–22 the remaining team established a high camp and decided to attempt P3. Leaving at 3 a.m. on the 24th, they reached the foot of the southwest-facing flank of the west-northwest ridge, where a 350m, 50° ice slope, overlaid with a little snow, led to the crest (AD-). They followed the ridge to 5,950m, where a small rock step gave a section of UIAA II. Above, the crest was generally straightforward (PD+) but cut by a large crevasse at ca 6,100m. Fortunately, they could get across a snow bridge. After an exhausting plod through deep snow, Kirschenhofer, Pfeiffer, and Walk reached the summit, recording an altitude of 6,224m (GPS) and coordinates 36°35.525'N, 75°43.305'E. Because of the mass of flowers around base camp, we named the peak Koh-e-Gulistan, Wakhi for "mountain of the land of flowers."

Future expeditions should consider P1 (ca 6,106m), where a névé slope on the east face leads to the north ridge; P2 (ca 6,053m), via the south ridge; and P4 (ca 6,080m).

There are also four 6,000m peaks at the northern head of the Ganj-i-Tang (aka Ganj Dur) believed to be unclimbed. Coordinates for these mountains, as well as the P peaks, may be found in the online version of this report. 📷 📄

[Editor's note: Only two previous climbs from the Shuijerab Glacier are recorded. In 2002 a Japanese expedition attempted a ca 5,836m peak on the west rim of the West Shuijerab Glacier, retreating just 15m below the summit but naming the peak Halshamas Sar. In 2007 a Japanese mountaineer, with a local climber, went to the head of the East Shuijerab Glacier, then climbed onto the divide with the Shuwert Valley. From there the two followed the ridge south to the top of a fine snow pyramid, GPS measured at 6,152m (6,020m on the map). They named this peak Shuwert Sar.]

CHRISTOF NETTEKOVEN, *Germany, Wakhanexpedition2012.jimdo.com*

WEST KARAKORAM

Virjerab Muztagh, Khushrui Sar (5,900m), north ridge. Led by Krzysztof Wielicki, Maciej Dachowski, Wojciech Dzik, Wojciech Kapturkiewicz, Marian Krakowski, Anita Parys, Jerzy Urbański, Katarzyna Karwecka-Wielicka, and I visited the Virjerab Glacier in July 2012. We were the first to explore this glacier since 1925. The expedition was organized in Pakistan by Karim Hayat, manager of Mountains Expert Pakistan, who also organized our 2011 expedition to Koksil Valley (*AAJ 2012*). Hayat accompanied us, and we also had four base camp staff, three from Hunza and one from Shimshal.

The Virjerab Glacier was "discovered" by George Cockerill during his 1892–'93 expedition, and then visited for a second time, in 1925, by the Dutch couple Jenny Visser-Hooft and Philip Visser. Colonel R.C.F. Schomberg's book *Unknown Karakorum*, published in 1936, has a map of the

"Shingshal Mustagh Area," which includes the Virjerab Glacier. Nearly 80 years later, the Virjerab remains an attractive goal for exploration.

Difficulties in moving up the glacier due to lack of lateral moraines kept our expedition to the lower reaches, and we established our base camp at 4,058m, on the south bank (36°18.203' N, 75°35.993' E), three days' walk from Shimshal. On July 12, having several days previously put an advanced base at 4,700m in the Spregh Yaz Valley to the south, Dachowski, Hayat, Karwecka-Wielicka, and Wielicki climbed onto the eastern rim of the Spregh Yaz Glacier and bivouacked at 5,100m. Next day all four continued south up a ridge to the summit of a 5,900m snow and ice peak, which they named Khushrui Sar ("Beautiful Peak" in Wakhi).

Krakowski, Urbański, and I,

[This page, top] Looking south from the entrance to the First West Virjerab Glacier to the unclimbed peaks that form its east bank, the highest over 6,600m. *Janusz Majer* [This page, middle] Khushrui Sar from the Spreg Yaz Glacier, showing route of ascent via west flank and north ridge. The bivouac is at 5,100m, and the summit far left is Peak 6,099m. *Krzysztof Wielicki* [This page, bottom] Looking southeast toward unclimbed peaks in the upper Virjerab Glacier from a point before the entrance to the Chapachipond Valley. *Wojciech Kapturkiewicz*

together with two base camp staff, Farman and Noor Alam, moved southeast up the main glacier to the entrance to the First West Virjerab Glacier (as designated on Jerzy Wala's 2013 sketch map). Due to bad weather, we were unable to follow the Vissers' footsteps any farther toward the confluence of Second West and East Virjerab glaciers.

On the 17th, Hayat, Kapturkiewicz, Noor Alam, and Parys crossed from base camp to the north side of the glacier and bivouacked, their aim to climb a 6,570m peak in the Chot Pert group. On the 18th, Hayat and Parys climbed up to a bivouac at 4,800m, but on the following day the weather took a turn for the worse and they retreated. 📷 🔍

JANUSZ MAJER, *Poland*

HISPAR MUZTAGH

Khunyang Chhish East (7,400m), southwest face. Before its first ascent in July, Khunyang Chhish East (also commonly spelled Kunyang Chhish East) was considered the third-highest unclimbed peak in the world, and had thwarted attempts by a number of top mountaineers. Simon Anthamatten and Hansjörg and Matthias Auer completed the ascent via an alpine-style push up the 2,700m southwest face, with difficulties of about M4/5 at 7,000m. Hansjörg Auer's account appears earlier in this edition.

SPANTIK-SOSBUN RANGE

Sosbun Group, Solu Glacier, Pakora Brakk, Rodeoplatten; Pakora Brakk Puke (4,980m GPS). One year after our first expedition to the beautiful Solu Glacier (see *AAJ 2013*), Gaby Lappe, Clemens Pischel, and I returned with a load of big-wall equipment to the village of Bisil and pastures of Pakora. Once more, it was not only a climbing trip but also a cultural journey. From the many impressive unclimbed peaks we observed in 2012, we chose Pakora Brakk, immediately northwest of Pakora. Conveniently located directly above a lake with sandy beach, the huge southeast-facing walls of Pakora Brakk rise

[This page] From high on Pakora Brakk. Behind, to the southeast, the Sokha Glacier rises to largely unexplored peaks. *Kai Maluck*

high over the glacier, offering great views and solid rock.

After pitching base camp, we headed to the rocks, adding one pitch after another to create Pakora Brakk's first route. Rodeoplatten (570m of height gain, 860m of climbing) ascends the central face and offers 18 pitches of excellent climbing up to UIAA VI. We had completed the first four pitches, up a rock pillar, in 2012.

From the top of Rodeoplatten, at 4,529m, we continued to Pakora Brakk Puke, the next peak behind. A gully of ice and scree, with a few meters of thin 80° ice behind a chockstone, led to long, easy rock slopes of UIAA I and II, snowfields, a very exposed 70m ridge (UIAA V), and finally rock slopes (UIAA I and II) that led to the summit (35°58'28"N, 75°25'19"E). There is potential for many more routes on good rock on the impressive wall of Pakora Brakk. With a base camp located at 3,650m, it is also a useful stopover for acclimatization on the way to the unclimbed granite peaks further up the Solu Glacier. [*A full report (in German), with useful photographic documentation of the mountains in this region, is included with the online version of this report.*] 📷 🔍 ▶

KAI MALUCK, *Germany*

PANMAH MUZTAGH

Uzun Brakk (6,422m), west face. Uzun Brakk (formerly known as Conway's Ogre) is a prominent mountain on the true left (north) bank of the Biafo Glacier. In 2009 we admired it from the foresummit of Lukpilla Brakk, but there was a lot of snow that year and we did not find the courage to try. Memories remained.

Uzun Brakk (variously spelled Uzum and Uzen—it means "steep mountain" or "sheer mountain" in Balti) is an ideal objective for a lightweight, low-cost expedition, requiring neither permit nor guide. In July, after a three-day walk from Askole, Ondra Mandula and I established base camp at a place called Morpho Goro (a.k.a. Marpogoro, "red stones"), directly below the spectacular south face of Lukpilla Brakk. It was a nice, sandy spot with running water.

In good weather we went to inspect Uzun Brakk's southwest face, which rises directly above the Biafo. This was the flank attempted in 1993 by Americans Jim Donini and Jack Tackle. However, we found the bottom third of this face held huge seracs, which made it too dangerous. We continued into a side valley on the western side of the peak and walked up a glacier (sometimes referred to as Marpogoro) to 4,900m, where we found a campsite with great views of the impressive west face.

The following day we climbed an easy, unnamed peak of 5,600m on the opposite (west) side of the glacier. The summit, which we named Ktak Brakk ("sightseeing peak"), has great views and was the perfect place to study the west face of Uzun Brakk.

On August 5, after two days of bad weather, we returned to the unnamed glacier and spent the night at the foot of the west face (4,600m). Leaving at 3:30 a.m. on the 6th, we climbed unroped up a 400m, 60° snow couloir on the right side of the face. At the top, where snow turned to ice, we roped up and pitched moderate ice and mixed to the first rock band. We chose a red dihedral on the right, which gave nice, sustained climbing on good rock (6b). The leader climbed without a sack, while the second followed (no jugging) with a light pack. We hauled a 70L bag with tent, sleeping bag, and ice gear. After 14 hours we pitched our tent on a small ledge at 5,600m.

Next day, two moderate rock pitches and then eight easy but exhausting pitches of ice (60–70°), led to the summit rock band, where an interesting layback pitch gave access to a hidden ice/mixed corner. At the top of this (6,000m) we made our second bivouac. There was not enough

[This page] Looking east across the Marpogoro Glacier from Ktak Brakk. (A) Pt. 6,700m. (B) Baintha Brakk (Ogre, 7,285m). (C) Baintha Brakk II (Ogre II, 6,960m). (D) Uzun Col. (E) Uzun Brakk (6,422m), with ascent route marked. *Jiri Pliska*

room for the tent, but we spent a comfortable night on two separate ledges.

We began climbing again at 6 a.m., taking rock and ice gear, a stove and tent, but no sleeping bags. The day began with an excellent, if cold, finger crack (6b). We moved to the right side of the ridge, where the rock was reasonably sound, and climbed seven pitches to what we thought was the final rock tower blocking the way to the summit. However, we then discovered another monolithic tower that gave complex climbing. A short ice section was followed by drytooling a narrow crack to gain a thin traverse leading to more ice. From there we continued, pulling on gear for 10m, before finishing with fine free climbing.

Three pitches of easier rock and ice on the ridge brought us to the summit at 6 p.m. There was almost no wind, and the setting sun was turning everything to red, orange, and pink. There was no rush: We knew we would not make our sleeping bags before nightfall. We started rappelling at 7 p.m. and stopped at 11 p.m. for a cold but calm night on a small ledge at 6,200m, still 200m above our bags.

The following day we reached the bottom of the face at 10 p.m. The lower section is exposed to rockfall in the afternoon, and this shortened our ropes by 40m. We left two pitons, some nuts, and ca 30m of slings. Because of the nice weather and perfect climbing conditions we experienced, we named our line In the Right Place at the Right Time (1,600m, 35 pitches and 400m of unroped climbing, 6b C1 M5 70°). After we reached base camp, the weather turned bad and remained so until we left for home. 🖼

JIRI PLISKA, *Czech Republic*

Editor's note: Uzun Brakk, which lies just west of the true Ogre (Baintha Brakk, 7,285m), was thought to have been dubbed the Ogre by the British explorer Martin Conway, who traveled up the Biafo Glacier in 1892 on the first major expedition to what is now the Pakistan Karakoram. Prior to 2013 there were only two known serious attempts. The first was in 1980, via the east face, by Victor Saunders and Will Tapsfield. After two bivouacs, and at a point ca 150m away from the highest point, unstable double cornices on the crest proved too dangerous and the two retreated. In 1993, Jim Donini and Jack Tackle attempted the ca 2,000m southwest face from the Biafo Glacier. The weather proved unstable during their stay, but on their second attempt, four days' climbing took them to a point on the west pillar ca 300m below the top. Unfortunately, a prolonged snowstorm then forced them down. The Czechs' second bivouac (at 6,000m) was about two pitches below the Donini-Tackle highpoint.

Baintha Kabata (ca 6,250m), east face; Bobisghir (6,414m), south face and southwest ridge; Baintha Ahrta (ca 6,300m), west couloir; Biacherahi Central Tower (ca 5,700m), southeast face, attempt. In June the international team of Olov Isaksson (Sweden), Anton Karnoup (Russia/U.S.), Jesse Mease (U.S.), and I trekked to the Choktoi Glacier. Having been denied permission to enter the Chinese Karakoram, and denied official registration on a permit for the Charakusa, we were simply in search of freedom to climb without bureaucracy. Fortunately, in Pakistan everything below 6,500m is a "trekking peak", and the Choktoi offers technical trekking in the shape of granite big walls.

We arrived at Latok I north base camp on June 23. Our Askole porters were ably assisted by six strong Balti glacier ponies, which made it to within one kilometer of camp. In excellent weather we spent the first two days on reconnaissance treks. Karnoup, Mease, and I followed the East Biacherai Glacier north to the Biacherai Pass (5,270m), which afforded close-up views of the three rocky Biacherahi spires to the west, and of Bobisghir to the north across the Nobande Sobande. Then Isaksson, Mease, and I climbed to Sim La (5,300m/5,481m, various maps), on the way up passing to the north of Choktoi Spire (the "island" peak near the head of the Choktoi) and on the way down to the south side, thereby gaining optimal views of the Ogres and Latoks, as well as the Baintha Kabata group of low 6,000m peaks.

With good weather persisting, we all decided to make an attempt on Baintha Kabata, the peak north of Sim La, climbed in 2008 via its south ridge by Colin Haley and Maxime Turgeon, and again in 2009 by Aymeric Clouet, Julien Dussière, and Jérome Para. Rather than taking this complex and technical route, we were attracted (for acclimatization purposes) by the snow flutes of the east face, and thus climbed a short icefall southeast of the mountain to establish a 5,500m camp in the basin between Baintha Kabata and a neighboring, slightly higher peak. On the 27th all four of us climbed snow and névé to the summit ridge, finding very rotten snow/ice in the final meters to the top (also reported by Haley and Turgeon). The measured height was 6,250m, close to the reading of the French party, while the value reported by Haley and Turgeon seems to be at least 300m too low. Bad weather accompanied our return to base camp the following morning and continued for another five days, allowing us to experience some of the feeling encountered by Latok north ridge parties.

With the next good weather we set out for the Nobande Sobande Glacier, intending to climb Bobisghir. Crossing Biacherai Pass, we descended to the glacier by a short, steep, and very soft downclimb. A flat hike led to a forward camp at 4,800m, below the south side of the peak. On July 5 we made an early start to the northwest, climbing a snow face that narrowed to a thin ice gully. Mease led one pitch of low-angle but centimeter-thick ice to access the basin above the small icefall at ca 5,600m. We crossed the basin above the crevasse line, encountering some breakable crust and deep snow, then followed the rounded southwest ridge to the summit on excellent névé. In perfect weather we were rewarded with a marvelous 360° panorama, which included the Crown, K2, and the Hispar

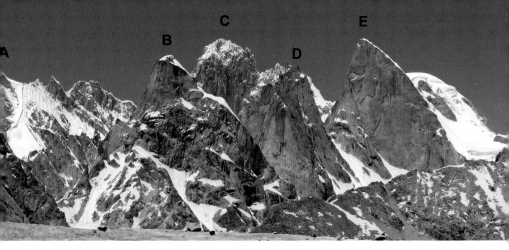

[This page, top] Looking west up the Choktoi Glacier. (A) Baintha Kabata. The 2013 ascent climbed the fluted east face visible here. (B) Biacherahi South Tower. (C) Baintha Ahrta. (D) Biacherahi Central Tower. (E) Biacherahi North Tower. *Bruce Normand* [This page, bottom] Bobisghir seen during an ascent of Braldu Brakk. The southwest ridge, climbed in 2013, is on the right, approached from the opposite side. The flat-topped extension to the left is known as Bobisghir North. The high peak in left distance is K2. *Pierre Neyret*

Muztagh. While descending, we waited some time at 5,600m for cooler conditions on the lower face, then made two rappels over the thin ice pitch, returning to base camp next day. [*Only one previous ascent of Bobisghir has been reported: in 1985 by Japanese climbers, via the southeast ridge. There have been several subsequent attempts, including one by the southwest ridge in 1995 by a British team.*]

An extended period of bad weather ensued, lingering longer on the Choktoi than in other regions of the range. After it cleared, and having established during the Baintha Kabata climb that the approach was crevasse-free and the neighboring peak could be reached by a long snow gully, I set out at 8 p.m. on the 16th for an overnight approach. I reached the ca 6,300m summit via the west couloir, a long gully of 50° snow and ice topped by a short, vertical ice step in blocky terrain and rotten snow around the corniced summit. Lingering morning cloud gave less of a view than intended, but cleared in time to cause some very soft snow on the descent, which was completed to base camp by midafternoon. We propose the name Baintha Ahrta (Horse Peak) for this summit, in honor of our uncomplaining assistant porters.

Meanwhile, Karnoup and Mease were attempting Biacherahi Central Tower (ca 5,700m), on a one-day push that saw them climbing soon after first light. Mease led nine pitches on the southeast side of the tower until stopped by blank rock about one pitch short of the south ridge, and some five pitches short of the summit. This line was followed in 1989 by the Spanish climbers Jon Lazkano and Javier Mugarra to make the first ascent of the peak. [*They graded their 20-pitch route up the ca 550m face 6a+ A3+; the pair report fixing 600m of rope over several days before jumaring to their high point and reaching the top in a 22-hour push.*] Karnoup and Mease found many pins and bolts, and much fixed rope. They graded their pitches 5.10 and surmised that the redder rock, of which much of the range is composed, is disappointingly featureless. 📷

BRUCE NORMAND, *China*

BALTORO MUZTAGH

Uli Biaho Tower (6,109m), south pillar, Speck. On July 21, Italians Matteo Della Bordella and Luca Schiera, and Swiss Silvan Schüpbach, completed a 40-year-old project by making the first ascent of the south pillar of Uli Biaho Tower. This spectacular granite column, west of the Trango Group, has captivated climbers ever since its photograph appeared in Eric Shipton's classic book of Karakoram exploration *Blank on the Map*. Subsequently, the remarkably few attempts—and even fewer ascents—have been misleading due to confused compass points.

The tower was not attempted until 1974, the year the Baltoro region reopened after being off-limits since 1961. Three young French made a spirited attempt, approaching via steep snow and ice couloirs to reach the south pillar (they referred to it as northwest), which would give the shortest route to the summit. Pierre Béghin, Jean Fréhel, and Dominque Marquis climbed the pillar until hit by a fierce storm. At this point they estimated only 30m of aid separated them from moderate snow and mixed terrain rising ca 150m to the summit.

To make the tower's first ascent in 1979, Americans Bill Forrest, Ron Kauk, Jon Roskelley, and Kim Schmitz accessed the east pillar directly via a ca 800m, objectively dangerous couloir, overhung by large seracs and subject to the ever-present threat of rockfall. In 1988, Italians Maurizio Giordani, Rosanna Manfrini, Maurizio Venzo, and Kurt Walde climbed a far safer couloir, south of the American approach, from farther down the Trango Glacier. Traversing to the foot of the south face, they climbed the southeast buttress, right of the French attempt, to create a 600m route at 6b+ and A3. This line has been consistently marked incorrectly on nearly all subsequent photo-diagrams of Uli Biaho. It was climbed again the following year by New Zealanders Guy Cotter, Nick Craddock, and Paul Rogers.

[This page] Uli Biaho from the south. (1) The new Italian-Swiss route. (2) The 1988 Italian route.
Jozef "Dodo" Kopold

In 2005 Jonathan Clearwater (NZ) and Jeremy Frimer (Can) discovered the safer Italian approach (which they thought new at the time), and followed it to the col at the foot of the south pillar. They fixed two pitches in an attempt to make the first free ascent of the tower, but abandoned their attempt after a storm pinned them in an uncomfortable bivouac on the col for three days.

Della Bordella, Schiera, and Schüpbach also used the 1988 Italian approach, hoping to attempt a new big-wall line between the existing Italian and American routes. They found this approach long and complex, with some technical terrain (a 200m icy traverse of 60–75°), but devoid of objective danger. However, the section of the tower they wished to climb did not sport any logical crack systems, the rock did not seem high quality, and the difficulty of the approach would have made it hard to bring up heavy loads and portaledges. Instead, they opted to complete the French line, which they estimate to be 500m high, with the last 150m or so over snow and mixed ground.

Although steep, it is well featured with flakes and cracks.

The route began from the small col 100m to 150m up and left of the southeast buttress, and the initial three pitches (6a/6b, then easier) trended right. The next 150m were direct, following a logical system of cracks and flakes (6a/6b). Above, they climbed an 80m chimney of 5+. To this point they had followed a series of ancient pegs, but once they traversed left to a 30m crack (A0 due to running water), all trace of previous passage disappeared. Higher, they traversed right to a small notch where they joined the 1988 route. Twenty meters down on the far side of the notch was a poor bivouac ledge, onto which all three squeezed for the night. Next day they followed the 1988 route for two pitches, then headed right to climb a short vertical section of ice around a hanging boulder, before following 50° snow slopes to the summit (a total of six pitches from the bivouac site, including several short pitches along the narrow summit ridge). A further day was necessary to descend. Despite the tricky approach and complex climbing on the pillar, the 17-pitch route, named Speck (500m, 6b A0 70°), is probably the easiest way to summit Uli Biaho Tower.

Later, from July 28–30, Schiera and Schüpbach climbed the Slovenian route on Trango Tower at 7b, then on August 1 climbed Great Trango Tower by its normal route, thus becoming the first team to climb all three towers (and in one season). Prior to these three climbs, the same pair made the first ascent of a small summit they named Submarine Peak (4,700m), by the 670m Via Andre (7a). *See report below.* 📷 🔍

LINDSAY GRIFFIN, *Mountain INFO*

[This page] Matteo Della Bordella, first pitch of Uli Biaho Tower's south pillar. *Silvan Schüpbach*

[This page] Seen from Great Trango Tower: (A) Paiju (6,610m). (B) Uli Biaho Great Spire (5,594m). (C) Uli Biaho Tower (6,109m). (1) Approach to south face. (2) Southeast Buttress. (3) Grmovsek-Karo. (4) Russian Roulette. (5) East Pillar–American Route. (6) North Face–Drastissima. *Jozef "Dodo" Kopold*

Uli Biaho Tower (6,109m), east face, Russian Roulette. Eugeny Bashkirtsov and Denis Veretenin climbed a new route in alpine style on the east face of Uli Biaho Tower. After previously climbing the Slovenian Route on Trango Tower in one and a half days, the pair approached from Trango Glacier up the same dangerous couloir followed by the 1979 American first ascensionists of the east pillar. This same couloir approach was used in 2006 by Slovaks Cmarik and Kopold to climb the north face.

The two Russians climbed unroped up the first third of the couloir, and then moved together with intermediate ice screw protection. They climbed fast for four hours, and then, when out of significant danger, progressed at a more leisurely pace for a further three hours to the base of the wall. The average angle of this 800–900m approach is 45–50°, and stonefall is a constant threat.

They started their climb up and right from the American route, with no portaledge ("too expensive to bring and no longer stylish"). On each day they climbed as far as weather would allow, although on day four this was only one pitch. The line mostly follows wide cracks and would have been psychologically easier had the team carried more than one large cam. For the most part, Bashkirtsov would lead, pushing up his only No. 5 Camalot. (Before getting the mountaineering bug, Bashkirtsov was a successful competition climber, with an onsight grade of 8a.) They climbed largely free—only around 10 percent of the route was aided. They were fortunate to find bivouac ledges each night.

Toward the top, the Russian line links with the American route for three and a half pitches (5c/6a), before forcing a more direct finish to the summit. The last section proved to be the crux: wide cracks through vertical or overhanging terrain.

From the top they went straight down the southeast face, rappelling "largely from bolts" (they took 10 in total, using all but three for protection and anchor points). They reached the snow close to the start of the 1988 Italian route on the southeast pillar, and from there crossed a spur to gain the relative safety of the Italian approach couloir, which they downclimbed. Summit to base camp took 16 hours; the round-trip ascent from base camp seven days. Difficulties on the 1,000m east face were graded 6c+ A2. 📷

ANNA PIUNOVA, Mountain.ru

Submarine Tower (ca 4,700m), first ascent by east face, Via Andre. Prior to their ascent of Uli Biaho Tower (see report above), Luca Schiera and Silvan Schüpbach made the first ascent of a smaller rock tower above the lower Trango Glacier, which they dubbed Submarine Peak. This tower forms the first point on the long ridge immediately left of the couloir used by the Italian-Swiss to access Uli Biaho. On July 17 the pair climbed the east (left) flank. Via Andre gave a total of 670m of climbing (7a) and forms a useful addition to acclimatization routes accessible from Trango base camp. 📷 📄

LINDSAY GRIFFIN, Mountain INFO

Great Trango Tower, northwest face, Bushido. On August 19, Marcin Tomaszewski and I completed a new route on the northwest face of Great Trango. We arrived at Trango base camp on July 29 and were carrying loads to the foot of the face the following day. On the 31st we carried loads and fixed five pitches, and the next day carried more loads and fixed a further three, climbing ground similar

[This page] Northwest face of Great Trango with approximate lines of (1) Krasnoyarsk Route (2007), (2) Out of Reality (2012), (3) Parallel Worlds (1999), (4) Krasnoyarsk Route (2007), (5) Bushido (2013), and (6) Azeem Ridge. The northwest face now has a total of eight lines; for more information see photos in AAJ 2012 and 2013. *Marek Raganowicz*

to but left of the 1999 Russian Route. On August 3 we hauled all our gear up to Camp 1 at the top of pitch eight. At this point we probably crossed the Russian Route. We continued capsule-style, following a beautiful clean-cut granite corner to the right, and then crack and corner systems to the top. On the terraces below the headwall we crossed the 2007 Krasnoyarsk Route.

Portaledge camps were made at the top of pitches 16, 19, and 26, the latter partway up the headwall. We were forced to carry all our water until we reached the terraces, where we found old ice. During the second half of the climb we had snowstorms and were able to melt fresh snow for water. Our route was independent for the first 38 pitches; pitches 38–45 more or less followed Azeem Ridge, Kelly Cordes and Josh Wharton's 2004 route on the southwest ridge. Our final day was more than 24 hours, climbing and descending through a bad storm. The top section of Azeem Ridge seemed somewhat overbolted; we were unaware at the time that these did not originate from the two Americans. [*Cordes and Wharton carried no bolt kit, making it likely these bolts were added in 2007 during the Krasnoyarsk ascent, which finished up the ridge.*]

During the climb we hand-drilled 21 belay bolts and eight rivets. We were forced to place two rivets beside the offwidth crack of pitch 39 (on Azeem Ridge) because it was snowing hard and there was no chance of free climbing. The rest of the drilled equipment was placed on our independent pitches, including the remaining six rivets on the pitch of A4. In the middle of the night and during a snowstorm, we reached a high point at the top of the ridge, on the long quasi-horizontal section leading to the 6,237m southwest summit. We did not continue along the crest.

The descent proved to be one of the biggest challenges in our mountaineering careers. Our gear was covered in snow, and at night our totally soaked ropes froze solid. We had to cut most of them and regained our top camp, exhausted, with only two 60m ropes remaining. Next morning we began two days of rappelling (ca 25 in total), the first day as far as Camp 3 on the terraces. We reached the bottom with totally shot ropes. Our route Bushido is VII- A4 UIAA VII+. 📷 🔍

MAREK RAGANOWICZ, *Poland*

Broad Peak (8,047m), west face, partial new route and tragedy. Our team of five, hoping to complete a new route on the west face, were Aidin Bozorgi (24), Mojtaba Jarahi (28), Pouya Keivan (24), Afshin Saadi (43), and me (47) as leader. Aidin, Mojtaba, and Pouya climbed the line in alpine-style above 7,000m, but died tragically while descending from the summit. Since then I've not stopped thinking about the ordeal, trying to understand what went wrong and what we might have done to save their lives.

We had dreamed about climbing a new route on Broad Peak since 1998, but until 2009 had not been able to finance an expedition. That year a strong team of 10 from the Arash Mountaineering Club sieged the first half of the face, joining the normal route at ca 6,800m, at which point they descended. [*See AAJ 2010. The line climbed by the Iranians in 2009 was more or less identical to that soloed by Carlos Carsolio in 1994, as far as Camp 3.*] Aidin, Afshin, and I were members of that team.

In 2011 six climbers from the club tried to complete the line by following the normal route to Camp 3 at 7,000m, and then traversing right, climbing new ground on the west face. They abandoned the mountain after having fixed 350m of rope on the traverse. Based on experience gathered during the two expeditions, we decided that climbing this top section in alpine-style would not only be possible, but also faster and probably safer. In 2009 we'd had a few close calls that were mainly the result of exhaustive rope fixing.

We arrived at base camp on June 26 and began acclimatizing on the normal route. It

[This page] Broad Peak massif from the southwest. (A) Broad Peak North. (B) Broad Peak Central. (C) Broad Peak Rocky Foresummit. (D) Broad Peak. (1) West-northwest ridge, first climbed in 1984 by Jerzy Kukuczka and Wojciech Kurtyka to start their traverse of the three main summits via the skyline ridge (3). (2) West couloir, first ascended in 2010 by Alberto Iñurrategi, Jiua Vallejo, and Mikel Zabalza, who first climbed Broad Peak North, then traversed the skyline toward Broad Peak. (4) West-northwest ridge (2008). (5) Normal route, as climbed today (first ascent unknown, though climbed to nearly 7,000m in 1954). (6) Original line (1957). (7) West-southwest spur (Carsolio, 1994, repeated by Iranians in 2009). (7a) Carlos Carsolio, solo (1994). (8) Iranian route (2013). (9) Southwest face and south ridge (2005). *Supplied by Ramin Shojaei*

was obvious that Aidin, Mojtaba, and Pouya were the strongest, and although I was the most experienced, I was not acclimatized, and so decided not to accompany them on a summit attempt. We estimated it would take them a day to climb from Camp 3 at 7,000m, through the technical difficulties, to ca 7,350m, then a second day on easier terrain to the summit. They took a spare day of food and fuel, just in case.

On July 13 they left Camp 3 at 7 a.m., but by 7:30 p.m. had only reached the end of the traverse; they pitched their small tent just above at a small col (7,050m). The ice had been much harder than two years earlier. On the 14th Aidin called to say they hadn't slept well, the ledge being too small. It then took them all day to reach 7,250m, where they were able to build a comfortable tent platform on snow. I left for the summit that night on the normal route, and by 6:30 a.m. on July 15 it was snowing. I turned around at about 7,700m. I contacted Aidin and told him to leave all the gear, go to the summit, and return the same way. He disagreed, saying they still intended to traverse over the summit. At 1 p.m. they told me they were only one hour from the top, but at 7:30 p.m. they thought they still had 45 minutes to go.

I didn't hear anything until 4 p.m. the next day, when Mojtaba called. He sounded tired and despondent. All three were exhausted and were still 30 vertical meters below the top. I was fairly certain they were still south of the main summit, and I urged them to bypass the summit, head to the foresummit, and descend the normal route to Camp 3. One hour later he called again, happy and energetic. "Sorry, Ramin, we disobeyed you. We've gone to the main top." I congratulated them, saying that Afshin and I would start up toward Broad Peak Col (7,800m) and meet them on the descent. However, we were far too slow, and after three and a half hours, I saw these efforts were pointless and returned to Camp 3. In the meantime the three climbers had contacted base camp to say they were stopping for the night between the two summits.

On July 17 the conditions deteriorated, and neither Afshin nor I were in a fit state to go up. Other climbers at base camp attempted to guide our three, who were asking for directions from the foresummit. Aidin called Iran that evening, confessing they had taken the wrong route and had been forced to re-ascend. The following day the three climbers were too exhausted to move. Various climbers selflessly came to our assistance, but they had no idea of the whereabouts of the stricken climbers, nor were they convinced they were still alive. On the 20th we were promised a helicopter with a professional German rescuer, Thomas Lammie. Then, at 2 p.m., Iran contacted us to say Aidin was still alive and begging for help. His last words were, "If nobody helps me, I will end up like the other two."

On the 21st helicopters arrived, one bringing Lammie. They flew up the mountain and took photos, but were unable to spot the climbers. Two days later we called off the rescue, concluding that even in the best of conditions our three climbers would be very hard to reach, and it was an impossible task with the work force currently at base camp. [*A fuller account of the Iranian climb and rescue attempts can be found at the AAJ website.*]

From a report by RAMIN SHOJAEI, *Iran*

MASHERBRUM MOUNTAINS

Aling and Masherbrum valleys, Double Peak, Hunchback Peak, and Cathedral Peak attempts; TIMI ascent from both west and east; Peak ca 5,220m. Ludvik Golob, Tomaz Goslar, Mojca Svajger, and I had planned to acclimatize in the Aling Valley, then cross 5,620m Gondokhoro La and make an alpine-style ascent of Gasherbrum I. We climbed in the Aling from July 17–31, then descended to Hushe, where we were informed the Gondokhoro La had been closed to foreigners. In the meantime our permit for Gasherbrum I had been canceled, following the Nanga Parbat massacre. In Hushe we were monitored closely by police. Eventually, they allowed us to enter the Masherbrum Valley.

First, however, on July 18 we established our initial base camp (35°31.693'N, 76°12.340'E), at 4,320m on the moraine of the Aling Glacier, at the junction of two side glaciers, one coming down from Double Peak. It had fresh

[This page] Looking west across the lower Masherbrum Glacier to: (A) Peak marked on some maps as Ice Cap; (B) Cathedral Peak; (C) Mitre, and (D) Sceptre. *Irena Mrak*

[This page] Looking north-northeast over the upper Masherbrum Glacier from Cathedral Peak. (A) Masherbrum far west peaks. (B) Masherbrum II/Masherbrum West (7,806m). (C) Masherbrum (7,821m). (D) Yermanend Kangri (7,163m). (E) Serac Peak (6,614m; behind it lies Broad Peak). (F) Gasherbrum IV. (G) Gasherbrum III. (H) Gasherbrum II. (I) Gasherbrum I. *Irena Mrak*

water, and we suggest future parties use the same spot, as the area has very limited campsites. Over the next several days we attempted Double Peak (6,700m) and an unnamed peak (*details at the AAJ website*). On the 25th we climbed to a summit on the watershed ridge between the Aling and Masherbrum valleys. We named it TIMI. Our GPS recorded 35°32.167'N, 76°15.096'E, and a height of ca 5,690m. On July 27 and 28, Golob, Svajger, and I attempted Hunchback Peak, but due to poor snow and ice conditions we retreated from 5,400m. We all then descended to Hushe.

After our difficulties with permits and police, we established a new base camp at 4,650m, on the west side of the Masherbrum Valley, on August 7. This was southeast of TIMI and a peak to its north that the locals call Masherbrum II and claim to be over 7,000m. Both this name and altitude are inaccurate; the mountain was originally known as Cathedral Peak (*see editor's note below*). We managed to climb to within ca 40m of the top of Cathedral Peak on two separate days, but were stopped by a large crevasse encircling the summit. On August 10 we tried via the east ridge, and on the following day more directly via the southeast face. Conditions were icy and we experienced much rockfall. We climbed 1,500m up to 60-70°, and estimated the summit to be ca 6,100m.

On the 20th, while waiting for the weather to improve, Svajger and I decided to climb TIMI from our current base camp (from the opposite side of our first ascent). In a weather window of a few hours we climbed a 690m, 50–70° ice slope to the summit. The following day we reached the standard base camp for Masherbrum, but found the glacier leading to this mountain too dangerous. Instead, we decided to explore the immediate area. Svajger and I ascended a small side valley on the east side of the Masherbrum Glacier and on the 23rd made the ascent of a small peak (35°34'40.47"N, 76°19'00.47"E; 5,220m Google Earth).

We feel this area provides a good acclimatization venue for parties planning an alpine-style ascent in the Baltoro (presuming that the political situation improves), but would suggest they visit earlier in the season, in order to find easier conditions. 📷 📄

IRENA MRAK, *Slovenia*

Editor's note: The name Masherbrum II has been applied to at least three peaks in the area. The true Masherbrum II would be the 7,806m southwest summit of Masherbrum. However, after an Italian team climbed the most westerly summit of the Masherbrum group in 1988, calling it Masherbrum Far West and reporting a height of 7,200m, a British guided expedition repeated their route in 1991 and referred to the mountain as Masherbrum II, possibly for commercial reasons. (Subsequent parties felt the height to be no more than 6,600m.) Then, in 1996, a Pakistan military expedition to Masherbrum climbed a 6,200m summit 12km south of the main peak, and also called it Masherbrum II. In 1961, Group Captain Tony Smyth's RAF expedition climbed four peaks from the Aling Glacier, including Mitre (ca 5,940m) and Sceptre, which lie on the ridge north of Peak 6,200m. The RAF team named the 6,200m summit Cathedral Peak, but did not attempt it. Cathedral is the summit attempted by the Slovenian women and almost certainly the peak climbed by the 1996 Pakistan expedition.

CHARAKUSA VALLEY

K6 West (7,040m), northwest face, attempt. In early July, Kenshi Imai, Kimihiro Miyagi, and Kenro Nakajima hoped to climb K6 West from the north (*the same line climbed later in July by Raphael Slawinski and Ian Welsted; see feature article in this edition*). Leaving base camp at 4,300m on July 4, the three Japanese reached the bottom of the northwest face (ca 5,250m) at 7 a.m. on the 5th, and that day climbed to 5,700m. The next day they continued up an ice gully to 6,100m. On July 7 heavy snow kept them at their bivouac, but on the 8th they were able to continue to 6,450m, just below the west ridge. More snow pinned them here for a further day, after which they decided to retreat.

HIROSHI HAGIWARA, *Rock and Snow, Japan*

TAGAS GROUP

Nangma Valley, Kapura South (ca 6,350m), southwest ridge. Paulo Roxo and I had not previously visited the Nangma Valley, and had no clear objective in mind. We made an initial reconnaissance and immediately found our goal. At the head of the West Nangma Glacier stood a beautiful peak, Kapura, with an elegant spur leading to Kapura South. It was our dream route, with no apparent objective hazards.

In late August we made an acclimatization trip and climbed the first part of the route, a broken rocky spur and ice slope leading to a prominent col at the base of the southwest ridge. The first 200m were easy scrambling, after which we climbed six pitches over ice, snow, and easy mixed ground. On the col we deposited a small amount of food.

After a spell of bad weather, we received a good forecast for September 5 to 11. On the 5th we left base camp and reached our single tent at advanced base in around five hours. At 3 a.m. the next day we set out, carrying a bivouac tent, and reclimbed 500m to our previous high point, which we had named Alam's Col (5,700m GPS), after our cook's son. We rested there until 1:30 a.m. on the 7th, when we started up the main part of the route. The face to the right of the ridge was 60-65°, with hard ice beneath a thin layer of snow, forcing us to belay the whole time.

At 7 a.m., after ca 500m of mechanical movement over ice, we reached the rock band cutting across the face above mid-height. We had to traverse right to find a passage around it, then slant back left above to gain the second ice slope, which we reached around midday. On the five traverse

pitches we found unconsolidated thin snow plastered onto rock, making for nervous moves.

Around 2 p.m., it was becoming clear that if we continued to the summit we would end up descending at night. But trusting the good forecast, and the prospect of sound Abalakov rappel anchors in the good ice, we elected to carry on. At 6 p.m. we reached the top of the ridge and a small but distinct, previously virgin forepeak, where we ended our ascent. Beyond, the ridge dropped into a notch before rising a little way to the south summit, perhaps 30-40m above. Rappelling from Abalakovs and rock pegs (fortunately, we were able to find decent cracks at night in the rock band), we reached the col at 3:15 a.m., after a nearly 26-hour day. Thirsty and tired, we decided to relax for the rest of the day. We left the col again at 3:30 a.m. on the 9th (to avoid the danger of rockfall) and began our descent to the glacier, reaching base camp at 11:30 a.m., eager for lunch.

We did not carry a GPS above the 5,700m col, but by comparing with the main summit of Kapura (6,544m) and using simple trigonometry on the distance and angle rappelled, we calculate our top to be at least 6,350m. We have called the route Never Ending Dreams (1,300m, 70° M4). It is the first route to be climbed on Kapura from the Nangma side. [*Editor's note: See the AAJ website for a brief history of climbs and attempts on Kapura's several summits.*]

Daniela Teixeira, *Portugal*

[This page, top] Daniela Teixeira traversing around the rock band on the summit day. Alam's Col is visible below. *Paulo Roxo* [This page, bottom] Never Ending Dreams on the southwest ridge of Kapura South. *Daniela Teixeira*

NEPAL

New Peaks for 2014. The Ministry of Tourism planned to open 103 new peaks to permits (many of which probably were climbed earlier, without a permit). Altitudes range from 5,647m Yalung Ri in the Rolwaling to 8,077m Yalung Kang West in the Kangchenjunga Himal. The French guide Paulo Grobel, officially brought onto the "technical committee," helped persuade authorities to standardize altitudes by using the HGM-Finn maps, and to add more summits to the permitted list in West Nepal. When all details are confirmed, the full list will be available at Himalayandatabase.com.

LINDSAY GRIFFIN, Mountain INFO

FAR WEST NEPAL

Api–Raksha Urai Himal, Raksha Urai III (6,609m), southeast face, east ridge, and south ridge. Christoph Kreutzenbeck and I left Kathmandu on September 25, 2012, for the Raksha Urai Range, with the intention of making a first ascent on one of the four Raksha summits, as designated by the 2001 British expedition (*AAJ 2002*). We flew to Nepalgunj, took a 20-hour bus drive to Chainpur, and then made a nine-day trek through the Seti Valley to establish base camp at 4,150m on a pasture east of Raksha Urai II and III. The military checkpoint in Chainpur informed us that we were the first Western travelers in this region since the French team that visited Raksha Urai in 2003 [though Americans were nearby in 2009.] Far West Nepal appears rarely visited by Westerners and the infrastructure for trekking is still poor.

It was not possible to find additional porters, yaks, or mules for our expedition, and we could only buy food in small amounts during the trek. For these reasons, we were forced to take a few rest days at Dahachar (a.k.a. Dalachaur, 3,700m) while our Kathmandu porters returned from their first food carry. This delay meant that by the time we arrived in base camp on October 8, we had only 15 days left to climb.

We first attempted unclimbed Raksha Urai II (6,420m), exploring a route up the east flank to the north ridge. On October 16 we left Camp 1 at 3 a.m. and climbed 60–70° ice and mixed slopes,

[This page] Looking along the north ridge of unclimbed Raksha Urai II. Beyond is the summit of unattempted Raksha Urai I. *Mirjam Limmer*

and as the snow on the ridge above was still deep, we decided not to continue.

In continuing poor weather and with only a few days left, we switched our objective to Raksha Urai III and the 900m southeast face attempted by the British in 2001. We started out at 3 a.m. on the 21st, climbing 16 pitches of 60–70° ice to the east ridge, where once again we found deep, unconsolidated snow. We followed the crest to where it meets the south ridge, and then continued north ca 300–400m, crossing several false tops as reported by the French expedition, before reaching the highest point. The south ridge had been mostly snow-covered, with sections of loose rock. On the 23rd we regained base camp, and then walked out to Chainpur. There is still much climbing potential in this region, though it is remote and serious. More information can be obtained at mirjam.limmer@gmx.de or from our website at Salon.io/mirjamlimmer/raksha-urai-expedition. 🔘

MIRJAM LIMMER, *Germany*

Editor's note: The first expedition to visit the Raksha Urai Range was a 14-member Austrian team in 1997, which observed III to be the easiest of the group, but failed before reaching the south ridge due to heavy snowfall. An Austro-German team tried again in 1999, retreating from 5,950m. The leader and four other Austrians returned in pre-monsoon 2001, this time following a different line to the south ridge, but got no higher than 5,800m. At the time, confusingly, these expeditions referred to this peak as Raksha Urai IV, defining the group as having six peaks, and designating them, from south to north, Raksha Urai I to VI.

A mostly British team tried the southeast face in the post-monsoon season of 2001, retreating from ca 6,500m, just below the east ridge. The 2001 expedition designated only four peaks in the Raksha Urai Range: I (6,370m), II (6,420m), III (6,609m), and IV (6,552m), a convention also adopted by the 2003 French expedition that made the first ascent of Raksha Urai III. Four members of this expedition—Arnaud Clere, Catherine Coulaud, Gael Faroux, and Keshab Raj Gurung—climbed the south ridge, but Faroux and Keshab Raj fell to their deaths during the descent.

Phupharka Himal, Vendée Himal (5,488m). Northwest of Simikot, the principal airport of West Nepal, lies the remote valley of Limi (a.k.a. Takuche Khola) and its three villages: Jang, Waljie, and Til. They are Tibetan in culture, isolated in winter, but linked to China by a road

[This page] Unclimbed Phupharka Himal, with the elegant north ridge dropping toward the camera. *Paulo Grobel*

[This page] Close to the Tibet border, toward the eastern end of the Chandi Himal. (A) Changwatang (6,130m). (B) Peak 5,988m. (C) Peak 6,022m. (D) Peak 6,024m (Snow Dome). (E) Chandi Himal (6,069m). *Guy Wilson*

Waljie, and Til. They are Tibetan in culture, isolated in winter, but linked to China by a road over the Lapche La (ca 5,000m) for three months of the year. Northeast of Simikot lies the Chuwa Khola Valley, descending from the Changla La, an ancient traders' pass across the border. Between the two there are ca 15 summits of 6,000m or above, all virgin and most unnamed.

We wanted to visit this paradise for exploratory mountaineering, ascending the Chuwa Khola before branching left and crossing the Nying La from the east. After this we planned to climb Ashvin, one of the 6,000ers. However, heavy spring snow blocked normal access routes to Limi. Desperate to reach Waljie and its four-faced Vairocana Buddha statue, unique in Asia, we decided to go west from Simikot to Yangar, and then cross the small Phupharka Himal to the north. Reaching a base camp proved easy with mules. We then left our Nepalese staff, crossed a snowy col (Phupharka La, 5,175m), and in passing a second ridge climbed a peak we named Vendée Himal. We reached the Limi Valley with just sleeping bags in our rucksacks. We were delighted with the statue and the hospitality of local villagers, but after we returned to a high camp on the Ardang Glacier, bad weather thwarted our plans to attempt Ardang (6,034m) or Tirawa Himal (5,876m). We forced a passage across the Ardang La (5,580m) and reunited with our Nepalese team.

Ardang, either by the easier south face or more directly from the north, presents an attractive objective. It should be on the list of new peaks opened by the government in 2014. I also suggest you look at Phupharka Himal (5,630m), especially its elegant north ridge. 📷

PAULO GROBEL, *France*

Chandi Himal, Peak 6,024m, northwest ridge; Chandi Himal (6,069m), southeast ridge, attempt. In November, Dave Chapman, Neil Warren, and I visited the remote Chandi Himal along the Nepal-Tibet border. As far as is known, no climbers had previously attempted any peaks in this range. Reaching base camp took five flights (ending at Simikot) and six days of trekking.

From Simikot we walked up the Dojam Khola, and then branched left into the Nying Khola, which leads to the Nying La immediately north of Changwatang. The journey proved slow, as mules found life difficult picking a safe route between steep bands of moraine. We established base camp at ca 4,950m below unclimbed Peak 5,895m, a cold spot where the surrounding mountains masked the sun for most of the day. On November 6, Dave and I moved west up the main valley and established advanced base camp at ca 5,450m in the bed of a dried-up lake, due north of Changwatang.

Next morning, in clear but windy weather, we ascended moraine and the snout of the glacier to reach easy slopes leading to the ca 5,950m col southeast of Chandi Himal. The route up the rocky crest. At ca 6,000m we met an extremely loose section, and with disappointment, retreated to the col. Not wanting to leave empty-handed, we climbed the northwest ridge of Peak 6,024m on the opposite side of the col, an easy snow dome but the first peak ever climbed in the Chandi Himal.

Despite a reputation for generally fine weather, the area was suddenly hit by prolonged, heavy snowfall. Several days passed, and there were no mules available. Abandoning most of our gear, and that of our local staff, we set off down valley carrying 30kg sacks. However, after three days we had covered only 15km, one quarter of the distance to Simikot. With further poor weather forecast, our agent stepped in with an offer of helicopter evacuation. The same day we were flown safely to Kathmandu. The expedition would like to thank the Shipton/Tilman Grant, Mount Everest Foundation, Alpine Club, and British Mountaineering Council for financial support. ▤

GUY WILSON, *U.K.*

KANJIROBA HIMAL

Strate Himal (5,323m), east couloir, and also by north ridge; Lambert Himal (5,100m), west ridge; Bijora Hiunchuli (6,111m), north-northwest ridge, attempt. Bijora Hiunchuli is a subsidiary summit on the northwest ridge of Kasi Dalpha (6,386m). The small, snowy top is clearly visible from Jumla airport, and access is relatively simple. In 2009, Sonia Baillif and I explored the approach to base camp in the Chaudhabise Valley, noting that the north-northwest ridge offered an elegant route to the summit.

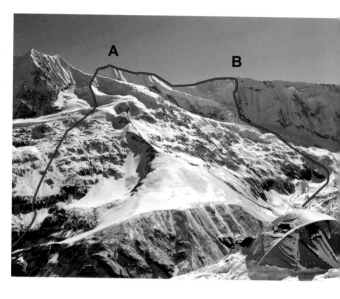

The spring season suffered from the effects of a heavy winter snowfall, which blocked many Himalayan villages. This meant our team's base camp was low. The weather was also unstable, but the main trouble was a case of cerebral edema to one of the party. In the end we climbed several small tops: Strate Himal by the east couloir (5,323m, AD-, François Damilano and Jean-René Talopp); the same peak again, but this time by the north ridge and descent of the southeast flank (F+, Frank Bonhomme, Stephane Castex, Sonia Baillif, Dhane Magyer, Zangbu Sherpa, Yves Exbrayat, and me); Jagdula Peak (*see report by François Damilano below*); and Lambert Himal by the northeast ridge (F+, Yves Exbrayat and Jean-Louis Perette). We only got a short distance up Bjora Hiunchuli, reaching the 5,272m col at the foot of the ridge and progressing up the crest to ca 5,600m. The beautiful north-northwest ridge of this peak is still there for the taking. ▤

PAULO GROBEL, *France*

[This page] The ascent, traverse, and descent soloed by François Damilano. (A) Peak 5,783m and (B) Jagdula Peak. *François Damilano*

Jagdula (5,764m) and unnamed peaks 5,783m and 5,750m. After having climbed Strate Himal on April 28 with Jean-René Talopp (*see report above*), I set out for a solo climb. Leaving base camp (4,021m) on the 30th, I walked up the lateral moraine of the Chaudhabise Glacier and then east to reach the bottom of the southwest face of Jagdula, a total of 7km. I then climbed this steep snow and ice face, with a tricky exit onto the summit ridge due to large cornices. From the summit I traversed the crest northwest to two more virgin summits (5,783m and 5,750m), before descending west down a beautiful unnamed glacier to rejoin the moraine, and so back to base camp, which I reached 22 hours after leaving. The overall grade was TD. I took only two bottles of water, some energy bars, and a 60m rope for rappelling and self-belaying.

FRANÇOIS DAMILANO, *France*

DAMODAR HIMAL

Chhubohe (5,640m GPS) southwest face and north ridge. In November, a team led by Brian Jackson did the first asents of three 5,500–5,600m peaks in the Chomochomo Danda range, above the valleys of Nar and Phu, including Chhubohe (pronounced Chub Chay). The team's full report can be found at the AAJ website.

BRIAN JACKSON, *U.K., Expeditionwise.com*

PERI HIMAL

Gyajikang and Nemju Himal, attempts. During the post-monsoon season, we found a useful new descent from the west ridge of Gyajikang and attempted Nemju Himal (6,404m). Our report is available at the AAJ website.

PAULO GROBEL, *France*

ANNAPURNA HIMAL

Peak 6,505m, southwest couloir. While acclimatizing for their alpine-style ascent of the Steck route on Annapurna's south face in October (*see feature article earlier in this edition*), Stéphane Benoist and Yannick Graziani (France) made the first ascent of Peak 6,505m, south of Annapurna III. They climbed the southwest couloir (700m, TD with sections of 90°).

LINDSAY GRIFFIN, *Mountain INFO*

Singu Chuli (6,501m), historical correction. While acclimatizing before their ill-fated attempt on the south face of Annapurna in 1982, and to inspect the east ridge as a possible descent, René Ghilini, Alex MacIntyre, and John Porter are reported in most references to have climbed a new route up the steep, fluted, west face of Singu Chuli. This is incorrect.

Instead, the three climbed Singu Chuli's south ridge, which they followed over the summit and up to Tarke Kang (Glacier Dome, 7,168m), then on toward Kangsar Kang (Roc Noir) until stopped by wind slab above 7,200m. It is not certain who did the first ascent of the south ridge of Singu Chuli, but it had been climbed at least once before. The grade was about D.

Retracing their steps, the trio gained the saddle before Singu Chuli, and then descended to the west. The first part of their route down was not ascended until 1984, and the lower section not until 2002. See online for more details and a photo of the 1982 ascent and descent. 📷 📄

LINDSAY GRIFFIN, *Mountain INFO*

Ghandarbha Chuli (6,248m), southwest face and west ridge. Formerly known as the Gabelhorn, Ghandarbha Chuli (a.k.a. Gandharva Chuli) lies on the ridge connecting Annapurna III (7,553m) to Machapuchare (6,993m), nearer to the latter. Before 2013 there had been no official attempt. The peak can only be attempted by a foreign team if it forms a joint expedition with Nepalis, so including cooks and helpers our expedition comprised two Romanians, Cristina Pogacean and I, and eight Nepalis. We reached base camp (3,857m GPS), at the confluence of the Modi Khola and the river that runs north from Singu Chuli (Fluted Peak), on May 2.

Next day, with three Nepalese companions, Pogacean and I made advanced base camp at 4,338m GPS on a grassy shoulder leading toward the glacier, on a ridge below "The Tower." The following morning Pogacean and I left before 4 a.m. and, after circumventing the Tower, climbed moderate mixed ground up the left flank of a southwest-facing spur. At 2 p.m. we were hit by an electrical storm that produced heavy snowfall. We continued to make upward progress, eventually stopping around 10 p.m. to spend an uncomfortable night in a half-erected tent at 5,438m.

We left at 10 a.m. next day, after a night of snowfall, and decided to move up to a better campsite and evaluate snow conditions. After four or five pitches, but well below the point where the spur meets the west ridge at a triangular rock buttress, we were able to dig a proper ledge for the tent (5,586m GPS) and spend a day appraising the situation. Avalanches fell down gullies to either side.

The weather cleared during the night, and we left at 3 a.m. on the 6th. We avoided the triangular rock buttress on the right via a difficult traverse on unconsolidated snow overlying hard ice. Once on the west ridge, we followed the crest, which proved quite sharp in places. A steep snow pitch (75° at the exit) gained the flat top of a large cornice formation. Increasing afternoon wind and the consequential spindrift slowed us considerably on the final section, as the slope steepened from 55° to 65–70°.

In discussions at Machapuchare base camp, the locals had appeared somewhat unhappy about

[This page] The southwest face and west ridge of Ghandarbha, showing camps. *Cosmin Andron*

the idea of our ascent of a "sacred mountain" (as they seem to see Ghandarbha Chuli as just an appendix of Machapuchare). We therefore had made the decision not to set foot on the very top, as a sign of respect. At 4 p.m. we stamped out a small platform one body length below the highest point. The GPS recorded 6,302m. We regained the tent at 10 p.m. and descended to advanced base the next day.

On the morning of the 8th we were greeted by three of our Nepalese team, who helped us pack, descend to our base camp, and then move onward to Machapuchare base camp. Here we discovered that the locals had not been thrilled on hearing the news of our ascent, but they remained reserved rather than hostile. We did our best to assure them that the top remains untrodden, and although they did not warm to us, we feel we made the best compromise. We began the walk out to Pokhara the following day. ⬛

COSMIN ANDRON, *Romania*

ROLWALING HIMAL

Gaurishankar (to Point 6,850m), south face, Peine Prolongée. Gaurishankar's twin summits were mistakenly considered by early explorers to be the highest in the world. For both Hindus and Buddhists, the peak has deep religious significance. To Hindus, Gauri, the name ascribed to the 7,010m south and lower top, is the goddess of fertility and beauty, while Shankar (the higher, northerly top at 7,135m) is not only the god of destruction but also of reproduction and restorative power.

The south face, above the Tongmarnang Valley, does not reach either summit directly, topping out on a rounded crest at ca 6,850m, behind which there is a slight dip before a long, gently angled snow slope rises to the south summit. The history of attempts on this steep and technical face is poorly recorded. Poles made the first significant attempt in the spring of 1983, reaching ca 6,000m. That fall, a 15-member Slovenian expedition made the first ascent of the face, climbing left of the impressive central pillar. They joined the 1979 British route at ca 6,500m, continued up the ridge, and bivouacked in a snow hole at 6,600m, before reaching the summit of Gauri the following day. A Japanese attempt in 1985 ended with Kensaku Sakai's fatal fall, and a German attempt in 2011 barely started because of poor

[This page] A hard mixed corner on the south face of Gaurishankar. *Pamalade 2013*

[This page] The south face of Gaurishankar. (1) Southwest ridge (1979, to Gauri, 7,010m). (2) Polish 1983 attempt and high point on south face. A similar line was followed by a Japanese team in 1985. (3) Slovenian route (1983). (4) Peine Prolongée (2013). (5) Southeast ridge (1984, to Gauri). *Pamalade 2013*

weather. [*See the online version of this report for a more complete history of these attempts.*]

In post-monsoon 2013 Mathieu Détrie, Pierre Labbre, Mathieu Maynadier, and Jérôme Para also experienced a long spell of bad weather, though this gave time for acclimatization. When it set fair on October 20, the four left their 4,900m bivouac and slanted up right above the bergschrund to gain the shallow couloir, stopping for the night at 5,900m. Next day they got up at 3 a.m. and climbed the couloir till 7 p.m., bivouacking at 6,500m. Above the couloir, a rightward-slanting ramp led to the base of the headwall. On the 22nd they were almost blocked two pitches below the top by a steep and difficult rock band. Here, they lost much time trying several options before winning through and reaching the small but distinct top at ca 6,850m, the apex of the south face. The rock had been universally poor, but fortunately the climbers had been able to stick to ice more or less throughout.

There was no time to continue to the summit of Gauri, so they rappelled. (Parties climbing the southwest and southeast ridges of Gauri most likely would have bypassed this high point, so the top was virgin.) The trials of the 1,900m French route are reflected in the name: Peine Prolongée or "prolonged pain" (ED WI5+ M5 A1).

> LINDSAY GRIFFIN, *Mountain INFO, from information from Lech Kiedrowski,*
> *Mathieu Maynadier, and Tone Skaja*

Bamongo (6,400m), second ascent, south face and west ridge, partial new route. On October 30 two strong Nepalese mountaineers, Mingma Gyalje and Pema Tshering Sherpa, and I made the second ascent of Bamongo. This is a pointed summit on the long west ridge of Kang Nachugo (6,737m); Bamongo was first climbed in 2008 by David Gottlieb and Joe Puryear en route to the first ascent of Kang Nachugo (AAJ 2009). Mingma was born in Na, directly below the mountain, and in Kathmandu he showed me a photo, saying he was looking for a climbing partner. I

[This page] Kang Nachugo from the south. (B) Bamongo. (1) Access to the west ridge used by Gottlieb and Puryear to make the first ascent of Bamongo and Kang Nachugo. (2) Chinese-Nepalese route to make the second ascent of Bamongo. The Gottlieb-Puryear start is marked; the Chinese Nepalese team followed the rock rib left of the icefall, then crossed the glacier to the foot of the face. (3) West ridge. (4) Gottlieb-Puryear attempt. (5) Kastelic-Santos completion of southwest face to 6,650m on south-southeast ridge. *Joe Puryear*

decided immediately to go with him.

From our base camp at 4,800m, we climbed a rock spur and wall to 5,440m (up to 5.8) on the 28th, then returned to base camp as a storm moved in. The next day we regained our high point and prepared for a single-push attempt on the face above.

We started at 5 a.m. on the 30th and reached the foot of the face through deep snow. The angle was between 40° and 60°, and conditions improved as we gained height. We needed to climb fast as we were traveling light (no bivouac gear), so we moved together with running belays. High on the face we climbed steep ice to avoid a rock band, and at 11:20 a.m. arrived on the ridge at an altitude of 6,000m. The crest above was sharp, the snow soft, and we were now exposed to a strong, cold wind from the north. With Mingma in the lead we made 10 pitches, and then continued for over an hour with running belays, occasionally stopping so one of us (mostly Mingma) could lead a steep step. My two companions moved so fast I had to ask them to stop a few times, just so I could catch my breath and take a few pictures. [Pema has climbed Everest 12 times.] We reached the summit at 2:35 p.m.

We reversed the route, and on the south face two of us rappelled, after which the third cleaned the belay and downclimbed. In this way we moved fast, reaching base camp by 9 p.m. It had been a round trip of 16 hours and we'd not stopped to eat or drink. Everyone was exhausted, and it's likely the fastest I've ever climbed at 6,000m. Our new route up the south face may also be the first by a Chinese on the south side of the Nepal Himalaya. Our line lies to the right of the 2008 ascent, and we named it Che Guevara (1,500m, 5.8 40-60°). 📷 🗒

LIU YONG (A.K.A. DALIU), *China*

Kang Nachugo (6,737m), southwest face, Monsoon (not to summit). I went to Rolwaling in search of an area in Nepal that is off the beaten track, yet still offers unclimbed peaks and faces. In the autumn, Santiago Padros (Italy) and I spent one month in Na, living in a lodge owned by a warm Sherpa family, and we became close with the friendly local community.

During our first few weeks in the area, we acclimatized to 5,000m, then went up the Ripimo Shar Glacier and climbed the south ridge of Ripimo Shar to 5,650m. From there we were able to see the huge climbing potential of the region. During the following days the weather worsened, and we could only make an ascent of Yalung Ri (5,650m), which we did in a fast one-day climb from Na. One and a half meters of fresh snow limited our options and aborted another proposed climb up the Ripimo Shar Glacier.

Back in Na we had only five days left for climbing. Tired of long approaches, we decided to attempt a peak "in our backyard." Kang Nachugo had only one ascent, and the southwest face remained unclimbed. It had been attempted by David Gottlieb and Joe Puryear, who in 2008 climbed for three days to 6,400m before forced to retreat in bad weather. A few days later they climbed the mountain by the long west ridge.

We reached the foot of the face on October 20 and pitched the tent. Next day we were able to climb around 1,200m. The first half of this we climbed unroped, but as the terrain became steeper we tied in and moved simultaneously. At around 3 p.m. we began to look for a place to pitch the tent, but the terrain forced us to continue to 6:30 p.m., when we finally found a poor ledge under a large rock barrier. There was not enough height for the tent, but it was enough for us to lie down and rest.

On the 22nd we climbed a few steep pitches on perfect snow and ice to the south-southeast ridge. We climbed up the crest a little way to a small, flat-topped prominence at 6,650m. It was midday, and although the distance to the summit, along an exposed, corniced ridge, was not great, we realized that continuing would require spending one more night on the mountain. We both agreed it would be best to go down, so we made 20 rappels and then downclimbed to the bottom of the face. We have named our line Monsoon (ca 1,500m, 75°). After our climb we decided to make a donation—the equivalent of the peak fee—to the Beding Monastery school, to support the education of kids in the valley. 📷 🗒

DOMEN KASTELIC, *Slovenia*

[This page] Emerging onto the south-southeast ridge of Kang Nachugo. *Domen Kastelic*

Likhu Chuli I (6,719m), north-northeast face of Pt. 6,660m, north flank and north ridge. On November 13 Ines Papert made the first ascent of Likhu Chuli I, reaching the summit alone. Her partner, Thomas Senf from Switzerland, remained in their top camp, fearing he might get serious frostbite in his toes.

Likhu Chuli I and its lower western summit II (6,659m) also appear on maps as Pigpherago Shar and Pigpherago Nup, respectively. A long ridge running north from Likhu Chuli I eventually crosses the well-known trekking peak Parchamo (6,279m), before dropping to the Tesi Laptsa Pass, a popular crossing point between the Khumbu and Rolwaling

The Likhu Group was officially off-limits until 2003, though in 1960 a French expedition, led by Robert Sandoz and exploring various peaks in the Rolwaling, climbed the steep and difficult west-northwest ridge of Likhu Chuli II, making the first and only known ascent. They established two camps before Alain Barbezat and Nawang Dorje reached the top. The only known attempt on Likhu Chuli I took place in 2007, when Japanese Koichi Ezaki and Hiroshi Kudo fixed

rope up the east flank of the north ridge to gain the crest at 5,950m.

Papert and Senf arrived in the Khumbu hoping to try a new line on the nearby north face of Tengkangpoche (6,487m), but lack of ice forced a change in plan. After a rapid acclimatization climb to the top of Parchamo, and a paraglide from a slightly lower altitude, the pair set off up the Likhu massif's north-northeast face, which leads to an eastern subsidiary top of 6,660m. Excellent conditions allowed them to climb half the 1,800m snow and ice face unroped. Above, sections up to 70° and waist-deep snow proved taxing, and a looming cornice forced them to bivouac just below

[This page, top] Ines Papert climbing the lower section of the north-northeast face. *Visualimpact. ch | Thomas Senf* **[This page, bottom]** Route of ascent of Likhu Chuli I with camps marked. *Visualimpact.ch | Thomas Senf*

the top. Next day they breached the cornice, gained the 6,660m top, and set up camp for a second, very cold night.

The following morning they realized climbing the east ridge to the main top would be impossible due to excessive amounts of powder, so instead they made a long traverse across the north flank of the summit pyramid and placed their third camp at 6,580m on the north ridge. Senf decided to wait, and on the following day Papert continued in high winds up 70° slopes to the summit, arriving at 2 p.m. The pair spent another night at the top camp before downclimbing the north ridge to a point where they could descend steeply east to the glacier. Both suffered some frostbite in fingers and toes.

LINDSAY GRIFFIN, *with information from Ines Papert*

Tengkangpoche (6,487m), northeast face, The Battle for Love (variant to Moonlight). In October, Galina Chibitok and Anastasia Petrova (Russia), and Marina Kopteva (Ukraine), climbed the 1,900m northeast face via a line they named the Battle for Love (VI 6b A2). The three started work on the route on September 23 and climbed for 18 days in capsule style, making nine camps, nearly all in a portaledge. The lower section of the face was characterized by moss-covered cracks and slabs, and the upper by ice-covered rock, which made protection and belays difficult to arrange.

At Camp 9, more or less out of food, they received a forecast for a three-day weather window, and so decided to climb nonstop to the summit. In a 52-hour return trip from their portaledge they

[This page] The upper section of the northeast face of Tengkangpoche. (1) Bullock descent route. (2) Nick Bullock, solo, 2003, as far as the east ridge. (3) Kenji Arai–Takaaki Nagato attempt to ca 6,250m in 2008. (4) Moonlight (2008). (5) Battle For Love, where different from Moonlight. *Yasushi Okada*

all in a portaledge. The lower section of the face was characterized by moss-covered cracks and slabs, and the upper by ice-covered rock, which made protection and belays difficult to arrange.

At Camp 9, more or less out of food, they received a forecast for a three-day weather window, and so decided to climb nonstop to the summit. In a 52-hour return trip from their portaledge they climbed 770m, reaching the top at 1:20 a.m. on October 9. By noon the following day they had descended to base camp. The three women climbed a total of 3,100m, placed 35 bolts, and endured snowfall on nearly all days.

At the time the women were not aware that this face had previously been climbed. In 2008, Japanese Hiroyoshi Manome and Yasushi Okada climbed in alpine style from November 12–15 to complete Moonlight (ED). The lower and middle sections of the Japanese and Russian-Ukrainian routes are more or less the same, but in the upper section the Japanese kept left, climbing steep

snow and ice to the east ridge. The three women worked up rock to the right, eventually finishing up the final section of the northeast pillar.

Lindsay Griffin, *Mountain INFO, from information provided by Anna Piunova, mountain.ru*

MAHALANGUR HIMAL

KHUMBU SECTION

Lungaretse, south face, Colombian Direct (not to summit). On November 4, Camilo Lopez and I climbed a direct line on the south face of Lungaretse, a peak immediately north of Kyajo Ri that people on the west side of the mountain refer to as Umjo-tse (Lake Peak).

We accessed the peak via Marlung (Marulung, 4,150m), a small village north of Thame in the Bhote Kosi valley, which we reached after a four-day walk from Lukla. We set up high camp at 4,800m above Marlung in order to acclimatize and scope lines on surrounding peaks. Prior to our arrival, two meters of snow had fallen in the cirque below the west face of Kyajo Ri, giving full winter conditions, but the weather had turned stable, with clear, cold mornings and thick cloud coming up valley from Thame in the afternoons.

We spotted an aesthetic, steep couloir on the south face of Lungaretse and attempted it from our high camp, only to realize we had misjudged the length. After ca 700m of climbing we were forced to retreat due to extreme cold and short daylight hours.

After a short recovery in Marlung, we discussed the idea of placing a higher camp and

[This page] Colombian Direct on the south face of Lungaretse. Unclimbed west face of Kyajo Ri to the right. *Camilo Lopez*

500m the couloir led onto a snowfield below the summit block. We reached a saddle between the main summit and a sub-peak to the left, with only a moderately angled slope leading to the former. However, due to the intense cold we had already decided we could not remain on the mountain at night. We descended from this point, making around 10 rappels plus downclimbing. We returned to camp in a whiteout, barely finding the tent. We have called the line Colombian Direct (ca 1,200m of climbing from high camp, TD AI4 90°). We saw no trace of previous passage on this mountain, which has no documented ascent.

[*Editor's note: Lungaretse, which lies roughly midway on the ridge between Kyajo Ri and Pharilapcha and is considerably smaller on the Machermo (east) side, has various quoted heights: The Schneider map gives 5,949m; NepaMap 6,070m; and Google Earth ca 5,870m (but also only ca 6,090 for Kyajo Ri, generally given 6,186m).*]

ANNA PFAFF, *USA*

Kyajo Ri (6,186m), east face, Stealing Beauty. In May, Vladimir Belousov from Russia and Marina Kopteva, the accomplished big-wall climber from the Ukraine, made the first ascent of the east face of Kyajo Ri, a coveted objective that had seen off many parties since the peak was officially opened in 2002. The mountain is the highest in a small cluster of peaks known as the Khumuchu or Kyajo Ri Himal.

In 2003 a Dutch team comprising Andreas Amons, Paul Bielen, Peter Valkenburg, and Michael van Geemen were the first to take on the challenge of the huge rock walls that form the triangular east face. They made one bivouac after five or six pitches, then after nine pitches (up to 6b A2) realized they had neither the right rack nor food and time to complete the route. Van Geemen would return to the east face in 2011 with Niek de Jonge, but the pair was forced to descend after a

[**This page**] (A) Kyajo Ri, (B) Pt. 5,900m, (C) Lungaretse (5,916m), and (D) Col 5,620m, seen from close to Machermo. (1) Southeast ridge (2006). (2) Dutch attempts on east face. (3) Stealing Beauty (2013). (4) Attempts on northeast face: (a) New Zealand (2011), and (b) Italian (2009). *Vladimir Belousov, supplied by Anna Piunova*

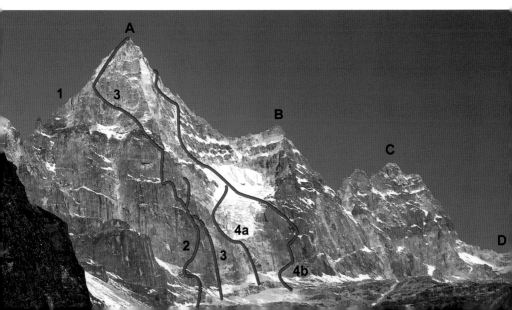

just three pitches when van Geemen fell ill.

In 2009, Germans Johannes Jahn and Michael Stacheder had another crack at this wall, and while it is not known whether their line was the same as the Dutch, the two climbed 700m over two days before tiredness and poor conditions forced a retreat. Their ascent to ca 5,800m involved difficulties of UIAA VII, M5, and aid. Attempts by Koreans are also strongly rumored, but no details are known.

Another Dutch pair, Roland Bekendam and Hans Lanters, attempted the face in late October 2012, but found that the sun disappeared from the wall by 11:30 a.m. and the temperature dropped rapidly to –10°C, making it rather chilly for rock climbing. They also found the wall completely devoid of snow and ice, and hence drinking water for their proposed three-day ascent. They quickly gave up and returned to Machermo.

In pre-monsoon 2013, Belousov and Kopteva arrived at Machermo lodge, and after three hours on a good path established a camp below the east face at 4,900m. From there to the foot of the ca 1,150m wall was just 30 minutes. Carrying a limited amount of food and fuel, the pair climbed the face, alpine-style, in five days, reaching the summit on May 14. A sixth day was needed to rappel the route.

The pair completed the line, named Stealing Beauty, in 28 pitches. The first four, up the steepest part of the lower wall, were 6b with one pitch of A2. The next three pitches in a corner system, leading to a sloping terrace at 5,300m, where they made their first bivouac, provided mixed terrain up to M6. Three more pitches (6b) led to a large scree terrace and a second bivouac (5,450m). Short rock walls and icy corners were followed to a couloir/ramp that slanted left across the lower headwall to reach the southeast ridge at around 5,800m. The climbing that day was nasty in parts, due to the poor snow and ice conditions and wet rock.

The Russian-Ukrainian duo was now on the 2005 American route. After a third bivouac, they kept to the left side of the crest on shattered rock and reached the top via a final 100m of icy slopes (65°, AI3). Some bolts were placed on the route.

LINDSAY GRIFFIN, *Mountain INFO, with information from Roland Bekendam, The Netherlands, and Anna Piunova, Mountain.ru*

Arakam Tse (5,904m), northeast face, Tatopani. Silvestre Barrientos, Alfonso Gaston, Ferran Rodríguez, and I (Spain) planned to try Cholatse's north face in the autumn. From October 2–16 we trekked in the Annapurna region and climbed Chuli Far East for acclimatization. We arrived in the Khumbu on the 18th to find that heavy snowfall above 5,000m had made many of the mountains dangerous. We tried twice to climb Cholatse, but there was a high risk of avalanche and huge cornices, so we gave up and moved northeast to Arakam Tse, which is lower and therefore had less snow and objective danger. We spotted a good line on the northeast face and set off from the village of Dzonglha at 2:50 a.m. on the 26th.

The approach to the face, through bad snow, took three hours, and we were expecting to find things just as unpleasant in the couloir. However, snow and ice conditions turned out to be perfect. We completed the first 400m unroped. The remaining 600m gave difficult snow, ice, and mixed climbing. It took seven hours to reach the summit and three hours to rappel our route, using nuts, pegs, and Abalakovs. We named the line Tatopani (1,000m, VI/5+ M5+). We returned to Dzonglha 21 hours after leaving. Local people said we were the first to summit this mountain. [*Editor's note: The HGM Finn map is wrong, in that it marks Arakam Tse as the summit of Cholatse, and Cholatse as*

[This page, left] Alfonso Gaston enjoys excellent ice conditions on Arakam Tse. *Josep Maria Esquirol*
[This page, above] Tatopani on the northeast face of Arakam Tse. *Josep Maria Esquirol*

climbing. It took seven hours to reach the summit and three hours to rappel our route, using nuts, pegs, and Abalakovs. We named the line Tatopani (1,000m, VI/5+ M5+). We returned to Dzonglha 21 hours after leaving. Local people said we were the first to summit this mountain. [*Editor's note: The HGM Finn map is wrong, in that it marks Arakam Tse as the summit of Cholatse, and Cholatse as Tawoche North. The true Arakam Tse, climbed by the Spanish, lies approximately 3km northeast of the true Cholatse. The true Arakam Tse is not on the Ministry list and appears to have no recorded ascents. It may be easiest from the southwest.*] 📷

JOSEP MARIA ESQUIROL, *Spain*

Tawoche (6,495m), northwest ridge, attempt. In November 2012, after climbing Kyajo Ri, Hans Lanters and I moved to Pheriche and attempted the unclimbed northwest ridge of Tawoche. We had been able to see it from both sides: steep sections up to the still virgin north summit (ca 6,350m), then a long knife-edge for 1km to the main top. Due to the excellent snow conditions on Kyajo Ri, we were optimistic.

The climb to the Cholatse-Tawoche col from the east is not simple. We made camp at 5,050m but found no snow until 5,400m. Every boulder moved. We had never come across terrain as bad as this in the Alps, and it was so tiring we had to make two load carries. On our first attempt to climb the couloir below the col we found no ice, only vertical, frozen rubbish. We turned to drier rock on the right and were successful next day. But it involved a scary ascending traverse, dry-tooling frozen debris to reach steep powder snow. We reached the col in early afternoon. Only one party had been there before us—a British team in 1983. An ancient fixed rope was still visible.

Next day, November 5, we set out for the north top. It had taken two days longer than expected to get here, making us low on food. Despite the cold (down to −25°C), we felt strong and climbed fast and unroped up the ridge above. In early afternoon we encountered an 80m, almost-vertical rock step covered with powder. Iced, it would give two perfect pitches, but now it was almost unclimbable, certainly unprotectable, and therefore too dangerous. Disappointed, we turned around.

Ama Dablam (6,814m), northeast face, attempt. The experienced team of Shin Dong-seok (48), Yoo Hak-jae (52, leader), and Yoo Young-jik (43) made an alpine-style attempt on a new route up the northeast face of Ama Dablam. The team established base camp on October 12 at 5,090m but were then stuck there until the 21st due to heavy snowfall. The three began their attempt on the 22nd, following a line that was similar, but slightly to the right in parts, to that attempted in 2007 by fellow members of the Corean Alpine Club (AAJ 2008).

On the first day Shin, Yoo, and Yoo climbed eight pitches of rock and snow (UIAA IV-V, 60-70°) in 10 hours, bivouacking at 5,750m. On the 23rd they continued over difficult rock and ice for eight hours, climbing six pitches (V, 70-80°) to a bivouac at 6,125m. On the following day they made a further five pitches (V-VI, 80-85°) to a high point of 6,300m (total climbing distance ca 1,600m). From this point their aim would have been to reach the upper north ridge at its characteristic shoulder and then follow it to the summit, therefore avoiding the large mushrooms on the upper east face. But while heavy snow cover was an advantage on the lower section of the face, once the angle increased the snow became soft and dangerous. It was also very difficult to find secure belays. Given the relatively slow progress on this upper section, they estimated it would take three more days to reach the summit.

After a bivouac at 6,250m, they retreated. All agreed that snow conditions on this face are the key: In perfect conditions, probably rare, the route wouldn't be too difficult, mostly mixed climbing with good rock protection. The central couloir is easier but too exposed to avalanche. This face has only received one ascent, in December 1985, by Carlos Buhler and Michael Kennedy, via the spur left of the central couloir. 📷

RODOLPHE POPIER, *The Himalayan Database, France, and Shin Dong-seok, Korea*

Kusum Kanguru (6,370m), southwest face. Vyacheslav (Slava) Ivanov and I were really surprised to find such a beautiful mountain with an unclimbed face so close to Lukla. What a stroke of luck! However, at that time we knew nothing of its history. We planned a quick, three- to four-day ascent before moving on to Lobuche Peak. Life makes its own plans.

Three couloirs penetrate the lower wall. The left, leading to the center of the face, is the most dangerous, with the St. Petersburg to Moscow train rumbling down at frequent intervals. We chose

[This page] Dry-tooling at the start of the Korean attempt on the northeast face of Ama Dablam. The 1985 Buhler-Kennedy route takes the mixed spur top left. *Shin Dong-seok*

the right couloir, which rises toward the south ridge. The trains here only started at 1 or 2 p.m.

We started on October 10 and for the first two days were only troubled by small avalanches and a little rockfall. After lunchtime we would hide beneath rocks. Eighty percent of the terrain was covered with 5 to 7cm of snow. There was no ice, and both protection and belays were hard to find in the largely crackless granite. If we placed three pieces of protection a pitch, that was pure joy. Sometimes we didn't place any, even though we wanted to, badly.

The first day I led 10 pitches. On the second Slava took over and added another 10. We belayed where it was possible, not at the end of the rope, so sometimes our pitches were as short as 35m. We also stopped in plenty of time to construct a tent site for the night, in order to save strength. By the end of the second day we had moved left out of the couloir and onto the bordering rock buttress. On the third day we climbed seven pitches in thick mist, stopping beneath an overhang at ca 5,800m. One hour of work and we had a nice, safe spot—if we had known then about the coming storm, we would surely have stayed there.

Next morning we traversed right to find a way through the rock barrier above. Snowfall accelerated rapidly, and Slava was hit by heavy spindrift. I followed the horizontal traverse with two sacks, and in the cacophony of roaring avalanches performed 10m pendulums, testing my bone strength against the rock. We had to hide as fast as possible, and managed to build a hasty, concave platform, the size of a bathtub. It would be our resting place for the next three days. Those days were terrible. Every three hours we had to get out and clear large amounts of snow between wall and tent—it threatened to tear us off the face.

Eventually we were able to continue. Slava climbed a hard, vertical pitch of dry-tooling, the only time his monopoints came in handy. (When the sun came out and the névé began to melt, they were useless.) Several times he took 5m to 7m falls, when snow over rock collapsed. The visions of Slava's falls are still in my mind. Once, he flew 7m and landed on his back, fortunately protected by his rucksack. He immediately got up as if nothing had happened and with a slight moan resumed climbing.

We had planned to climb fast, so had taken only a few days of food that did not need cooking, and only two 250g gas canisters. On the 19th, at an altitude of 6,145m, we ran out of both food and gas. The three-day storm had not only taken our supplies, but also our strength.

On the morning of the 20th we climbed 45–50° snow ridges to the summit—these were 45–50m pitches without protection. Our main belays were bags filled with snow and deeply buried, like deadmen. We continued along the crest toward the northeast summit (6,350m). Large snow mushrooms had formed on the ridge, and Sasha found it difficult in his monopoints and often flew, head down, into space. To belay him I had to dig a deep hole, like a mole, and sit in it. Finally, we

[This page] Vyacheslav Ivanov at a stance mid-height on the southwest face. *Alexander Ruchkin*

[This page] The southwest face of Kusum Kanguru. (W) West top. (M) Main (southwest) top. (1) New Zealand (2011, to west ridge). (2) Denz (1981). (3) Falling into the Void (2013). (4) Renshaw-Venables (1991). *Alexander Ruchkin*

reached the last summit and could see the descent onto the plateau. We had to make two rappels to reach it. The first was fine, but on the second I guess we were in too much of a hurry—it was extremely cold in a northerly wind. Our anchor was not buried deep enough and pulled. Riding a layer of snow, we both slid 20–30m onto the plateau. It was now dark, and we were fed up. We erected the tent and for the first time in five days we could lie flat. Next morning we continued our journey down the north face in knee-deep, or sometimes waist-deep, snow. We rappelled many times, and near the base narrowly missed being engulfed by a large avalanche.

We had now been without water for three days, just eating snow, but as we descended toward the valley the snow turned to small rivulets and we drank deeply. Unfortunately, crossing one of the bigger rivers, I slipped and plunged into the substance I'd dreamed of for so many days. I was immersed up to the neck, drowning my cameras. We finally reached a cairned trail that led to a clearing at 4,300m, which we presumed was the site of the north-side base camp. We had arranged for our sirdar to meet us here with food, but either due to a misunderstanding or the fact that we were lost, we never saw him. One trail led away from the clearing and we followed it for one hour until realizing it was definitely going uphill and not down. Sacha, who has less fat to lose than me, was very tired, falling behind constantly. We were unsuccessful in finding another trail down.

Next morning we spotted Monjo in the main Dudh Kosi valley, like a mirage 700m below. How were we supposed to get there? I suggested we try to rappel the steep, grassy slopes toward the village, but Slava, now nearing his limit, did not like the idea. We found later that he had lost 15kg, compared to my 12kg. We had one more option: a helicopter. Although we'd tried to the end, we phoned in our coordinates and a request to be rescued. We were evacuated to Lukla on the 22nd.

The southwest face is 1,400m, and our route had ca 1,600m of climbing (40 pitches). We named it Falling into the Void (Russian 6A, TD/ED WI5 M5).

Alexander Ruchkin, *Russia, provided by Anna Piunova, Mountain.ru, translated by Ekaterina Vorotnikova*

Editor's note: New Zealanders Peter Hillary and Murray Jones were the first to have designs on the southwest face. They reconnoitered the Kusum Khola in spring of 1979, before deciding it was too difficult to penetrate with porters. They made an attempt from the north instead. Several teams subsequently used their northerly approach, getting as far as the northeast summit but not the main top, before the arrival in Nepal of New Zealand's Bill Denz in October 1981. In what is now acknowledged to be one of the most remarkable first ascents of the lower Himalayan peaks, Denz, climbing alone, spent one and a half days ascending a mixed buttress to the left of the southwest face to reach the west ridge. He followed this to a second bivouac on the west top, and the next day he made a trying ascent to the main (southwest) summit, bivouacked, and then traversed the narrow connecting ridge to the ca 6,350m northeast summit. From here he descended the northwest flank and spent a further two days bushwhacking down valley to Monjo.

Denz's ascent remained largely unknown for many years, and the southwest face did not come to the attention of most climbers until after 1991. In autumn of that year, Dick Renshaw and Stephen Venables bushwhacked to the head of the Kusum Khola with their eyes on the face, only to find it regularly bombarded by rockfall. Instead they climbed 26 pitches up the right flank of a 900m buttress on the right, reaching the unclimbed south ridge. They finished up this via a magnificent rock pillar to the main summit. The 1,250m route was graded TD+.

In 2000, Bart Paull and Freddie Wilkinson also had designs on the southwest face, but like their predecessors saw it raked by incessant stonefall. Instead, they climbed an independent line up the center of the Renshaw-Venables buttress before following the 1991 route (pitches of 5.9) to 6,100m, at the start of the summit ridge. Here they were forced down by the onset of very high winds.

In 2001, Slovenians Jernej Bevk and Uros Samec were also put off the southwest face by stonefall, reaching ca 5,500m on the Renshaw-Venables. Also in the valley at around the same time were Pavel Chiznak, Ivan Foltyn, and Petr Strnadel, who completed Birthday Cake (5.8 M5 80°) to a 5,805m point on the south ridge, while fellow Czechs Roman Kamler and Slavek Vomacko put up West Buttress (5.9 90°), which leads to a 5,579m point on the west ridge.

In 2004 heavy stonefall stopped two unpermitted young Alaskans from trying either the southwest face or Renshaw-Venables, so they moved well right and climbed a rightward-slanting line almost to the crest of the south ridge.

Finally, in 2011, three New Zealanders, unable to get established on the face, climbed a rib to the left that they believe to be left of the line followed by Denz (but well right of the Czech line). This gave 1,000m of mixed ground (M5) to the west ridge, from where they descended (AAJ 2012).

Amphu I (6,740m), first official ascent. In early October, An Chi-young, Kim Young-mi, and I made the first known ascent of Amphu I, which lies between (and east of) the Amphu Lapcha (a.k.a. Amphu Labtse, a popular 5,780m trekkers' pass) and Baruntse North. While the official height (HMG Finn map) is 6,740m, the Schneider map has an altitude 100m higher.

The peak was opened in 2002 and since then it appears only two permits have been issued, to a German expedition in 2008 and a Japanese team in 2012. Neither expedition succeeded on Amphu I, though the Germans climbed Point 6,146m, the highest and most northerly of three unnamed summits between the Chhukhung and Amphu glaciers. [No doubt to comply with the permit, the Germans later referred to their mountain by the name Amphu Middle.] We feel it is rather confusing to refer to these peaks as "Amphu," as they are far away and in a different group from Amphu I.

After acclimatizing on Mera, we established base camp at 5,250m by the Panch Pokhari (the collection of lakes south of Amphu Lapcha), arriving on September 27. After two reconnaissance

[This page] Southwest face of Amphu I showing route of ascent, including base camp and Alligator's Mouth. *Oh Young-hoon*

I, though the Germans climbed Point 6,146m, the highest and most northerly of three unnamed summits between the Chhukhung and Amphu glaciers. [No doubt to comply with the permit, the Germans later referred to their mountain by the name Amphu Middle.] We feel it is rather confusing to refer to these peaks as "Amphu," as they are far away and in a different group from Amphu I.

After acclimatizing on Mera, we established base camp at 5,250m by the Panch Pokhari (the collection of lakes south of Amphu Lapcha), arriving on September 27. After two reconnaissance trips up to the glacier terrace below the face, which proved complex but not serious, we started our attempt on October 8. We planned to climb the southwest face via a deep couloir to the west ridge.

We crossed the bergschrund at 5,970m. Throughout the climb the wind was strong and we were troubled by snow showers and falling icicles. I led the first nine pitches, which were relatively easy, but the face got steeper as we progressed, and both An and Kim were hit by large falling icicles. Kim took over the lead on the 10th pitch. At 8:30 p.m. we found a small but ideal ice cave at ca 6,450m, in which to spend the night. Due to icicles in the roof, we dubbed it the Alligator's Mouth.

Starting next day at 8:30 a.m., Kim led, and then An, the face becoming almost vertical soft snow. The ridge, too, had soft snow and was quite sharp. Snow stakes sometimes gave no security. Higher, the angle eased, and we eventually reached the summit at 3 p.m. We had to belay down the dreadful ridge, as we could place no rappel anchors. We regained the Alligator's Mouth at sunset, and next day three hours of rappelling brought us to the glacier. We named the route Windy Couloir (1,300m, plus 500m glacier approach, TD AI5). 📷

OH YOUNG-HOON, *and Peter Jensen-Choi, Korea*

JANAK HIMAL

Syao Kang (6,041m) first ascent, Chaw East (6,404m), attempt. In post-monsoon season 2012, a New

of Yangma (4,200m), where we arrived on October 18. This settlement of 11 families is situated on sunny, south-facing terraces above fertile river flats. From the village a reconnaissance established a site for base camp, and explored possible routes onto Syao Kang and Chaw East. On the 20th base camp was set up on a grassy yak paddock close to the summer grazing village of Syao (4,400m).

We decided to attempt Syao Kang first, as it looked to be the less problematic of the two peaks. Local knowledge indicated a possible access route starting from the foot of the Ohmi Glacier and following a small tributary valley onto the peak's eastern flanks. This valley provided comfortable campsites at 4,950 and 5,300m, with spectacular views of Kangchenjunga and Jannu from the top camp. A day was spent negotiating a route through steep walls of rock and glacial ice above camp and onto the crevassed slopes above. We only belayed one and a half pitches on the final section of exposed ridge. At 3:30 p.m. on the 25th, John Cocks, Martin Hunter, Geoffroy Lamarche, Nick Shearer, and I summited Syao Kang. Two GPS readings indicated a height of 6,041m. Syao Kang has three summits: the north is clearly the lowest, while the south summit appears to be of similar height to the central summit that we climbed.

Back at base camp, John Nankervis, still suffering from altitude sickness, decided not to join the rest of us for an attempt on the more inaccessible Chaw East. Three days were spent pushing a route onto the Phuchang Glacier, where, on the 31st, a high camp was established at 5,600m.

[This page] On the summit ridge of Syao Kang with the Phuchang Valley behind. *Nick Shearer*

[This page] From high on the east side of Syao Kang, a wonderful panorama looking toward (A) Kangchenjunga (8,586m), (B) Danga (ca 6,350m), (C) Jannu East (7,468m), (D) Jannu (7,711m), (E) Sobithongie (6,652m), and (F) possibly Nupchu (6,044m). *Nick Shearer*

Shearer, and I summited Syao Kang. Two GPS readings indicated a height of 6,041m. Syao Kang has three summits: the north is clearly the lowest, while the south summit appears to be of similar height to the central summit that we climbed.

Back at base camp, John Nankervis, still suffering from altitude sickness, decided not to join the rest of us for an attempt on the more inaccessible Chaw East. Three days were spent pushing a route onto the Phuchang Glacier, where, on the 31st, a high camp was established at 5,600m. To get there we had followed the outlet of the Phuchang stream, which enters the Yangma valley behind Syao. Steep, scrubby ground on the stream's true right was followed by several kilometers of demanding terminal moraine. Until about 40 years ago, Yangma residents had used the Phuchang as a trade route into Tibet, crossing the Phuchang La (5,700m). However, glacial recession clearly put a stop to this, as an ugly cirque with 40m rock walls now forms a serious obstacle below the col.

A short icefall also barred our intended route onto Chaw's west ridge. On November 1 we climbed two steep ice pitches through seracs. Lower-angled slopes then led onto the west ridge of Chaw at an altitude of 5,850m. We followed this ridge a short distance before deciding to abandon the attempt some 500m beneath the summit.

On November 3 most of us left base camp, though John, who had not sufficiently recovered from altitude sickness, was evacuated by helicopter the following day. The remaining members crossed the Marsan La and Nango La into the Ghunsa Khola, where we regained the Kangchenjunga trail. ▣

PAUL MAXIM, *New Zealand*

Janak East (6,987m), southwest face and southeast ridge. Janak (7,041m) was first attempted in 1998 by a British-Nepalese party that reached the upper Broken Glacier, climbed peaks to the south, and noted a potential line up a spur on the right side of the southwest face, leading to the southeast ridge and then over the east peak to the summit. This line was attemped in 2004 by Romanians, who reached ca 6,400m. The following year Miha Habjan and Andrej Stremfelj climbed the face to the left, reaching the shoulder on the southeast ridge at ca 6,700m, where a storm forced retreat.

young members. We established base camp on the 24th, Camp 1 below the upper glacier on October 1, and Camp 2 (5,800m) beneath the face on October 8. Camp 3 was placed at ca 6,600m on top of the prominent serac barrier. On the 10th we tried to summit, but the ridge above the shoulder was not an easy snow slope, as we had imagined, but steep and mixed. We began again from Camp 3 on the morning of the 11th and reached the previously virgin top of Janak East at 12:30 p.m. We did not continue to the main top. Summit members were Yuki Honda, Masayuki Murakami, Tul Bahadur Tamang, Kitap Shing Tamang, Ram Kaji Tamang, and me.

HIROSHI HAGIWARA, *Rock and Snow, Japan*

KANGCHENJUNGA HIMAL

Anidesh Chuli (6,808m), northeast face to east ridge, attempt. Officially brought onto the permitted list in 2002, Anidesh Chuli (formerly known as White Wave) had no recorded attempts until April and May. The New Zealand team comprising Ben Dare, Andrei Dusschoten, Rob Frost, and Scott Scheele had planned to use yaks to reach base camp on the Ramtang Glacier. However, they were unable to move past the start of this glacier, and with porters unavailable, the team lost nearly a week ferrying loads to an upper base camp at 4,800m, and thence to an advanced base (5,100m) at the foot of the Ramtang icefall.

From here to Camp 1 (5,500m), the route went through the icefall, trending right toward the north-northwest ridge. One 30m section was left fixed. Above, the team climbed through a rocky buttress, then traversed flat névé below the northeast face (heavily threatened by a serac barrier) to place Camp 2 at 6,000m on a small snow rib north-northeast of Col 6,350m on the east ridge of Anidesh Chuli.

On May 2 all four climbers grouped at Camp 2, and two days later Dare and Scheele left for the east ridge. They planned to climb direct to the crest at ca 6,500m, place Camp 3, and the next day continue toward the summit. Dare and Scheele first climbed 200m of 30–40°, then linked snowy ramps separated by ice cliffs (up to 80°). On the last pitch below the ridge, transitioning from steep ice to snow, Scheele took an 80–90m fall, sustaining head injuries that left him unconscious for five minutes. It was 3:30 p.m. The cloud was thick and there was blowing snow. Dare reached Scheele and lowered him to 6,350m, where they bivouacked.

Still confused the next day, Scheele was lowered to Camp 2, which the pair reached at 2:30

[This page] Janak from the Broken Glacier to the southeast. (1) Slovenian Route (2006). (2) Japanese Route (2013). *Hiroshi Hagiwara*

[This page, top] Looking north across the Ramtang Glacier from Anidesh Chuli. (1) South ridge of Jaho (6,416m), climbed in 1974 by Danilo Cedilnik. (2) South face of Chang Himal (a.k.a. Ramtang Chang, 6,802m), climbed in 1974 by Janez Gradisar, Bojan Pollak, and Michael Smolej. (3) East Ridge of Ramtang (6,601m), climbed in 1930 by Erwin Schneider and Frank Smythe. (4) Mouse (6,260m), climbed in 1930 by J. Wieland. There are no other known routes in this panorama. *Ben Dare*

On May 2 all four climbers grouped at Camp 2, and two days later Dare and Scheele left for the east ridge. They planned to climb direct to the crest at ca 6,500m, place Camp 3, and the next day continue toward the summit. Dare and Scheele first climbed 200m of 30–40°, then linked snowy ramps separated by ice cliffs (up to 80°). On the last pitch below the ridge, transitioning from steep ice to snow, Scheele took an 80–90m fall, sustaining head injuries that left him unconscious for five minutes. It was 3:30 p.m. The cloud was thick and there was blowing snow. Dare reached Scheele and lowered him to 6,350m, where they bivouacked.

Still confused the next day, Scheele was lowered to Camp 2, which the pair reached at 2:30 p.m. Dare activated an emergency locator beacon, registered in New Zealand. This resulted in a call to Dusschoten and Frost's satellite phone—they were resting in base camp, and this was the first they knew of the accident. This pair set out the same afternoon and reached Camp 2 at 3 a.m. on the 6th. The team used a satellite phone to call for a helicopter, which arrived at 10:30 a.m., and both Dare and Scheele were flown to Kathmandu, arriving only 45 hours after the accident, a great credit to the crew from Fishtail Air.

The team feels the east ridge provides the easiest route to the

[This page, bottom] On the approach to Anidesh Chuli. The east ridge is on the left and north-northwest ridge descends toward the camera. *Ben Dare*

INDIA

[This page] The west ridge of Plateau Peak (7,287m). The route above ca 6,700m to the plateau is marked; the summit is much farther back. *Plateau Peak Expedition 2013*

EAST KARAKORAM

Plateau Peak (7,287m), west ridge. The Kolkata section of the Himalayan Club visited the Saser Kangri Group in July-August, with the aim of making the first ascent of Plateau Peak. Several teams have tried Plateau Peak, either from the west via the South Phukpoche Glacier or the east via the Sakang Glacier. Three of the most notable attempts were by the Indian Mountaineering Foundation in 2008, a joint IMF–Border Security Force team in 2009, and the Indian Air Force in 2010.

During our ascent of Saser Kangri IV in 2011, we had a close look at Plateau Peak and decided the only feasible route was the west ridge. In 2009 the IMF-BSF team reached ca 6,400m on this line, but were stopped by a rock tower and a sustained period of bad weather. We planned to circumvent this tower via a rather dangerous traverse across an exposed snow face.

We approached via the South Phukpoche Glacier, putting base camp at 4,706m and Camp 1 at 5,391m. Camp 2, on a broad snow shoulder on the lower section of the west ridge, was established on July 18 at 6,015m. The initial section above involved a rock buttress, then a sharp ridge of ice and broken rock. Camp 3 (6,366m) was placed immediately below the difficult rock tower—the high point of the 2009 expedition. We were able to fix the traverse around the rock tower before four days of moderate to heavy snowfall confined us to Camp 1.

On July 28 a Sherpa team set off to find a route on the upper pillar, and a safe passage through the capping seracs to the edge of the plateau at ca 7,150m. They returned late that night, having reached the edge of the plateau. All this section was fixed.

We all rested the next day and then left at midnight on the 30th. A long, 50–60° traverse on blue ice brought us to the upper rock wall. Here, narrow rock gullies, covered in a thin ice veneer, made the going tricky, despite the fixed ropes. We negotiated a 15m chimney, followed by a 6m vertical wall, before reaching 40-50° ice slopes between the top of the wall and the serac barrier. At 9:30 a.m. the first climbers reached the western end of the summit plateau.

When all had gathered, we headed east, covering more than 1.2km along the plateau, which is full of humps, before reaching the highest point, as indicated on the Russian map, at 1:30 p.m. on July 31. To the northeast were two more humps, but ours looked slightly higher. Summiters were Debraj Dutta (leader), Subrata De (deputy leader), Prasanta Gorai, and me, with Sherpas Dawa, Lakpa Norbu, Lakpa Tenzing, Mingma (Sr.), and Phurba. We regained Camp 3 a little after 9 p.m.

PRADEEP C. SAHOO, *The Himalayan Club, supplied by Rupamanjari Biswas*

Chamshen (7,017m), west ridge. Chamshen lies in the Saser Kangri Group, fairly close to the disputed territory and war zone of the Siachen Glacier. Access to these mountains is only possible for foreign climbers as part of a joint expedition with an equal number of Indians. Chamshen's lack of previous attention is largely due to mapmakers' decisions: In the past it has been marked as 6,965m, but a recent survey upped the altitude to over 7,000m. In July and August it formed the goal for an expedition comprising Divyesh and Vineeta Muni (India); Susan Jensen, Andy Parkin, and Victor Saunders (U.K.). There was a support team of six Sherpas for the Indian members (Ang Dorji, Chedar, Dawa, Mingma, Karma, and Samgyal), along with support staff and a liaison officer.

The approach from the Nubra Valley, north of Leh, was long, complex, and involved making the first crossing of a high and difficult pass: Sakang Col (6,150m). After establishing a main base camp on the glacier below the col, the team spent much time in reconnaissance, and made several attempts before crossing on August 10. The ascent involved steep climbing and was exposed to rockfall during the heat of the day. The group then descended to a glacial cirque between the high peaks of Saser Kangri III (7,495m) and II (7,518m), and then down to the large North Shukpa Kunchang Glacier. From here they ascended northwest to establish Chamshen base camp at 5,600m.

On August 14, the British members were planning to recross Sakang Col to resupply, and were camped on the edge of the cirque about one and a half kilometers from Saser Kangri II, when at 10 p.m. a massive avalanche swept down this mountain's serac-torn north face (see photo online). Although the main debris did not reach camp, the blast from the leading edge was so powerful that it lifted Parkin's tent into the air, over the top of Jensen and Saunders' tent, along the glacier, and into a deep crevasse. Parkin, still in his sleeping bag, fell through the floor of the tent and miraculously jammed ca15-20m down the crevasse on the only small snow bridge—a few meters either way and he would have gone to the bottom. Meanwhile, the tent containing Jensen and Saunders had rolled 30m across the glacier, coming to a halt just before the same crevasse. Parkin's axes and crampons, Saunders' axes and inner boots, the stove, and all food were missing. The party carried one rope, which Parkin would normally have commandeered for a pillow. Fortuitously, that night it had remained in Saunders' tent, allowing him to effect a rescue.

Several strenuous hours later, Parkin, his rucksack, and the remains of the tent were on the surface. With a back injury later found to be a minor fracture of the sacrum, Parkin was unable to stand. After pitching the remaining tent, and lashing it securely to the glacier in preparation for the inevitable second avalanche blast (which hit at 5 a.m.), the three sat out the remaining night.

Next morning, with the use of strong painkillers, Parkin was able to hobble 2km to the junction with the North Shukpa Kunchang Glacier, where he was left in a tent while the other two broke trail back to Chamshen base camp. Early on the 16th, Divyesh Muni, Saunders, and a team of Sherpas reached Parkin and carried him back to camp.

Many expeditions visiting Pakistan and Nepal take a satellite phone, and due to its tough build and better coverage in Asia and Europe, most mountaineers opt for a Thuraya. For the same reasons, and the difficulty of tracking conversations, this is also the phone of choice for terrorists. As a result, India forbids expeditions to carry any satellite phone (or GPS) in the mountains, and in 2010 banned the use of Thuraya throughout the country. However, Saunders had smuggled a Thuraya sat phone into India to use in an emergency.

Saunders phoned the expedition agent in Leh for a rescue, and this was carried out by Indian Air Force helicopters on the 17th, the pilots displaying exceptional flying skills in poor visibility. With Parkin safely in Leh, all remaining expedition members then had to endure a week of poor weather, stretching their food and fuel. With his cover now blown, Saunders decided he might as well use the phone to get a weather forecast, and received the promise of a clear spell. On August 21, after establishing camps at 6,000m and 6,500m, the whole team summited Chamshen via the west ridge. By the 24th they had recrossed Sakang Col.

On arrival in the Nubra Valley, Saunders was arrested and summoned to a court hearing in Leh, where he was threatened with a prison sentence of up to seven years and then let off with a fine of around $30. The team is indebted to the Indian Air Force and local agent Rimo Expeditions, as well as other friends who worked around the clock to arrange the rescue.

LINDSAY GRIFFIN, *MountainINFO, from information provided by Victor Saunders*

Rongdo Valley, various first ascents. A team of 12 mountaineers from the Indian Air Force, plus Sherpas, explored the little-known Rongdo Valley in May-June, summiting seven peaks, of which six were above 6,000m. Only two mountaineering expeditions have visited this region before (AAJ 2006 and 2013). The full report can be found at the AAJ website.

GP. CAPT. V.K. SASHINDRAN, *Indian Air Force*

[This page] Among their seven ascents, the team of Indian climbers in the Rongdo Valley climbed (A) Odgsal I (6,234m) and (B) Odgsal II (6,028m). *V.K. Sashindran*

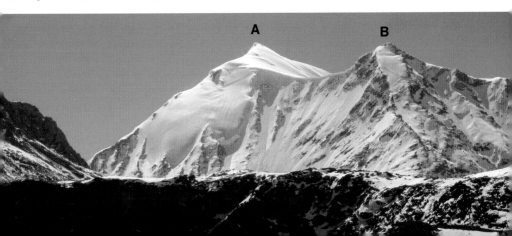

[This page, top] Jungdung Kangri from the west-northwest. (1) Attempt on west face of northeastern top. On retreating, Hall and Monypenny rappelled to the large horizontal snow ledge, moved across to its right edge, and then rappelled ice slopes. (2) Shaft of Justice. (3) Monypenny Hall of Fame. *Cory Hall* [This page, bottom] James Monypenny on the headwall during the west face attempt. *Cory Hall*

LADAKH

Palzampiu Valley, Jungdung Kangri, Shaft of Justice and The Monypenny Hall of Fame. With Pakistan travel plans falling through, my good friend James Monypenny (U.K.) and I quickly regrouped. With nothing more than a photograph and an incredibly vague topographical map, we set our sights on a previously unattempted 6,060m granite peak known as Jungdung Kangri in the Ladakh Range.

Jungdung Kangri lies hidden in the Palzampiu Valley, only a few dozen kilometers from the heavily militarized border with Pakistan. We first tried to gain access from the south through the town of Likir, thus eliminating the need for military permits. However, we were told the pass was uncrossable by mules. Instead, we secured nine-dollar military permits through a tourist agency in Leh and headed north by road over the Khardung La to the Nubra Valley. As these permits were only valid for seven days, we eventually decided to chance that we wouldn't be checked, and after 21 days our luck held. Climbing permits still need to be acquired well in advance, although recent reforms have simplified the process and dropped prices, as well as opening new areas.

After a two-day walk with a couple of mules, we reached base camp at 5,090m in a pristine alpine meadow. Above lay a playground of granite faces, alpine couloirs, and pointed summits. After hauling massive loads up moraine and glacial ice, we set high camp at 5,522m, below the west side of Jungdung Kangri.

We warmed up on what looked to be the easy central couloir. However, it soon steepened to 85°, with threatening cornices basking in the sun above. Our unacclimatized lungs burned, calves screamed, and heads spun. James led a pitch of 5.4 up to the central summit tower, and after many chossy dead ends I linked a 5.8 pitch to the central summit at 6,030m. We had established our first route, Shaft of Justice (630m, TD+ 5.8 80°), but in the process realized that the southwestern summit was actually higher.

Meanwhile, the large face to the left of the Shaft was calling, with 650m of icy, steep granite. A few days later, with a selection of rock and ice gear, but no bolt kit or bivouac gear, we launched into the unknown. Progress slowed as the brittle ice of the lower face steepened. A steep icy corner of M6, followed by an improbable 5.9 traverse, led to a 15cm offwidth—a lead that left me coughing blood. On a small, poorly protected ledge at 5,800m, we made an unplanned shiver bivouac. James led pitch after pitch of difficult aid and free next morning, but progress was slow. A second bivouac without water, food, fuel, or even a ledge was a daunting prospect. We bailed.

The main peak was still unclimbed, so once feeling fit we simul-climbed through mixed gullies to the right of Shaft of Justice, and in a few hours reached the col below the highest summit tower. I attempted a delaminated mixed pitch, but it quickly ended in unclimbable slabs. James then embarked on an epic three-hour aid lead, connecting discontinuous features via many large swings on poor gear, at one point tensioning off a pecker he pounded in with a belay device. We eventually stood on Jungdung Kangri's true summit with a route to be proud of: The Monypenny Hall of Fame (650m, ED1 90° A2++). 🖼

CORY HALL, *Canada*

Palzampiu Valley, Likir (5,619m GPS), east flank; Nia (5,681m GPS) west ridge. In August, Malgorzata Skowronska (Poland/U.K.) and a hired Indian partner climbed two previously virgin peaks on the southern rim of the Palzampiu Valley. Her full report is at the AAJ website. 🖼 📄

Kang Yissay Range, Cha Ri (ca 6,046m). A British party more or less made the first ascent of a previously unnamed 6,000m peak in the range running southeast from Kang Yissay (6,400m). Led by Douglas Briton, the three-member expedition left the Leh-Manali Military Road near the old monastery of Gya, about 70km from Leh, and trekked five days to the foot of the Yabat Glacier. Caroline McCann and Matthew Jones then climbed a nearly snow-free, unnamed mountain in a 13-hour round trip. The upper section held solid red granite, giving enjoyable climbing, but they stopped 8m below the top under a very rotten cone of rock. At their high point the GPS recorded 6,038m, and from this they deduced the summit to be 6,046m. They called the peak Cha Ri (Mountain of the Flying Bird); a lammergeier was seen circling the top most days.

LINDSAY GRIFFIN, *Mountain INFO*

ZANSKAR

Pensilungpa Glacier, Hidden Peak 5,802m, north-northwest ridge; Twin Peak East (5,825m), north face. Overshadowed by its more extensive neighbour, the Durung Drung Valley immediately east,

[This page, top] Looking south toward peaks around the head of the Pensilungpa Glacier. (A) Unclimbed Pt. 5,641m (attempted in 2013). (B) Unclimbed Pt. 6,197m. (C) Unclimbed Pt. 6,048m. *Derek Buckle* [This page, bottom] Seen from the east top of Twin Peak: (A) Sickle Moon, (B) Hidden Peak, (C) Twin Peak west spire, and (D) Pt. 6,048m. *Derek Buckle*

the Pensilungpa Valley is rarely visited. It does, however, have some fine unclimbed mountains, as Mike Pinney, Chris Storie, Tony Westcott, and I found on our visit in September. The Pensilungpa Valley, which rises southwest from the Kargil-Padam road where it crosses the Pensi La (4,485m), has five significant tributary glaciers flowing from the Pensilungpa–Durung Drung divide to the southeast. Marked glacial recession has meant that these are no longer contiguous with the main ice flow, and instead terminate in extensive, but negotiable, boulder fields. As numbered from the road, we explored the second, third, and fourth of these sub-glaciers, using four separate high camps.

The first objective, above Camp 2 at 5,223m on the third tributary, was a summit clearly identified from Google satellite images, yet hidden from any point in the valley by a dominant triangular peak north of the watershed that we called Pyramid Peak. On September 13, Pinney, Westcott, and I crisscrossed the maze of crevasses on the steep section of the glacier to reach a prominent rocky col to the south of Pyramid Peak. From here a short, steep snow climb up the north-northwest ridge of our chosen peak led to a compact, rocky summit at 5,802m GPS with extensive views over the Durung Drung glacier. We named it, appropriately, Hidden Peak (PD+).

Six days later, Pinney, Westcott, and I established Camp 4 at 5,186m on the second tributary. On the 21st we climbed from here to a snowy col at the head of the glacier and then up the north face of a mountain with two rocky summits that we called Twin Peak. We reached the first (east) summit (5,798m on the Indian map, 5,825m GPS; AD) but declined to attempt the slightly higher summit, an impressive sharp spire.

On the 17th a creditable attempt was made on the north-northeast ridge of Peak 5,641m at the foot of the fourth tributary. A combination of increasing technical difficulty and too low an assault camp resulted in retreat around 5,576m. We estimated this peak to be somewhat higher than the 5,641m noted on the Indian map. [*Editor's note: Over the years there has been much activity on the neighboring Durung Drung Glacier, including possible ascents of one or more 5,000ers on the divide between it and the Pensilungpa Valley, notably by Italians in the early 1980s. However, inconsistent peak heights and indefinite reports make these impossible to identify.*]

DEREK BUCKLE, *The Alpine Club, U.K.*

Under Moonlight (6,035m), southwest flank; Hana's Men (6,191m), east face; Hagshu (6,515m), southeast ridge, attempt. In June, Jonn Jeanneret, Dan Kopperud, Jake Preston, Gabriel Thomas, and I (Australian or American, all based in Asia) traveled to India to attempt a peak in the Gangotri. On the 17th, Uttarakhand state was hit by the largest flood in nearly a millennium, taking the lives of more than 10,000 people and flattening infrastructure. All access to the area was closed.

Zanskar became our alternative destination, and we reached base camp on July 8 at the northern foot of Hagshu, close to the Zanskar-Kishtwar divide. By July 14, after following the Hagshu Glacier southeast, in front of the east-northeast face of Hagshu, we had established a high camp on the upper plateau. The following day Dan, Jake, and I made an attempt on unclimbed Peak 6,191m to the east of Hagshu. Dan turned back due to illness one kilometer from camp (forgetting to give us the V-threader), leaving Jake and I to continue up a couloir on the south flank. About 200m below the top, we were hammered by a storm and tried to wait it out. After six and a half hours we headed down in a whiteout, having to downclimb the entire way. We regained camp after a total of 30 hours, exhausted, but hopeful for a second attempt later in the trip.

On the 19th the entire team attempted Peak 6,035m, which lies on the southern rim of the upper Hagshu Glacier plateau, and southeast from the summit of Hagshu. Thomas became ill three pitches up the east ridge, and Dan and Jake accompanied him down, leaving Jonn and I to continue (again, the V-threader went down with Dan!). After 20 pitches of snow and ice, we climbed the summit block around 1 p.m. (GPS readings of 6,029m and 6,032m). We found a walk-off descent (with a couple of rappels where we had to leave screws) on the south face, which unfortunately left us with about eight kilometers to return to camp below the north face. This entire descent took 14 hours, much of it in a full-blown storm. We regained the tents after a total of 25 hours, and named the peak Chand Ni Raat (Under Moonlight).

On the 26th we attempted to climb Hagshu (6,515m) via the southeast ridge. We spent two days reaching ca 6,440m and then retreated after climbing the first rock pillar. On the way back to base camp, we saw that we had been a fair distance from the summit longitudinally, but not much in altitude. We also noted

[This page] Hana's Men from the west, with camp on the plateau and route of first ascent. *Jeanneret Collection*

[This page] The much-attempted north face of Hagshu. Climbers have concentrated on lines right of center. *Jeanneret Collection*

that the south face, while difficult, has a direct line to the summit.

On the 28th, Dan, Jonn, and I headed back up Peak 6,191m. We had only one day's food left, but the weather was excellent. We were able to simul-climb the ice sections and reach the summit at 11 a.m., after a final scary pitch. GPS readings averaged 6,191m. This time we had the V-threader, so the descent went quickly and easily, and we were back at camp by 7 p.m. We named the peak Hana's Men, after my five-year-old daughter. 📷 ▶

BRYAN HYLENSKI, *South Korea*

Editor's note: The history of ascents of Hagshu, possibly the highest mountain in eastern Kishtwar, has not been properly recorded. Hagshu has been reported to be around 6,330m, but the Survey of India marks it as 6,515m. The 6,330m figure is mostly likely the height of the distinct north top, which sits above the much-attempted north face.

In 1988 a Polish expedition approached the mountain from Zanskar to the north. They ascended the glacier below the east-northeast face and eventually reached the plateau at ca 5,700m below the southeast ridge. In 1989 they returned, but this time from Kishtwar to the south. Approaching up the Hagshu Nala, they made a base camp and reconnoitered a way up to the plateau. They were then confined to camp by a long period of bad weather. Most of the team eventually decided to cross the Hagshu La (4,973m) and visit monasteries in Zanskar, but Pawel Jozefowicz and Dariusz Zaluski opted to stay.

The day after the others left, the weather cleared. The two Poles climbed through a crevassed area and then a 500m couloir (up to 60°) to reach the plateau. From here they climbed the southeast ridge in two days, reaching the summit on September 9; there was a rock step of UIAA VI- and a 15m ice step of 80°. They descended the same way and walked out to the north, arriving at the base camp of a British party. Their four friends, worried, had come back up the valley and found them. Exhausted, and with Jozefowicz suffering frostbite, they all went out to Srinigar, from where Zaluski returned to the south side to collect the base camp equipment (finding it had been damaged by bears). As the Poles did not have a permit, this ascent remained undercover.

The first official ascent was made just one week later, on September 16, by Phil Booth, Max

Halliday, and Ken Hopper (U.K.), who approached from Zanskar. They climbed a steep glacier system to reach the serac-torn east-northeast face, where they climbed a line up the center with two bivouacs. They took a day's rest at each bivouac site. The hardest climbing was above the second bivouac—a couple of pitches of Scottish 4. They followed the summit ridge southeast to the highest point (1,200m, TD, with much 55° névé).

Hagshu saw multiple visits by John Barry and various partners attempting the impressive north face; probably the best effort was in 1994, with Seb Mankalow, reaching ca 6,000m. After a hiatus of nearly 20 years, the peak was attempted again in 2010 by a large French expedition, which made little progress on the mountain.

HIMACHAL PRADESH

Kishtwar Himalaya, Kishtwar Kailash (ca 6,451m, Google Earth), southwest face. The start of this trip was particularly stressful, as the political situation in Kishtwar had become tense following the deaths of several people in a protest. As a result, our permit was only confirmed a couple of days before we were due to arrive in Delhi. But a permit we did get, and a few days later Mick Fowler, Mick Morrison, Rob Smith, and I found ourselves in India.

One of the conditions of our permit was that we travel to the road head at Gulabgarbh without passing through any Kashmiri towns or cities. This left only one real option: go via Manali using the new Udaipur to Atholi link road. Most climbers have traveled along impressive Himalayan roads, but this one is in a different league! My video of one frightening section went viral from Mick's Facebook page, getting over a million hits.

The approach to base camp requires four relatively big days, the first two on the popular pilgrim route to Machail, then two more up the Dharlang Nala, where we placed base camp an hour short of the Chomochior valley.

Kishtwar Kailash is one of the highest mountains in eastern Kishtwar. We had spotted the

[This page] Kishtwar Kailash from the upper Chomochior Glacier to the west, with ascent route and bivouacs four, five, and six. *Paul Ramsden*

peak the year before, when we climbed the north pillar of Shiva, getting good views of the south and east side of Kailash all the way up the route.

However, before arriving at base camp we weren't quite sure how we were going to climb it. Base camp gave us access to the south, west, and potentially northern sides, so we combined reconnaissance with our usual acclimatization outing. Unfortunately, almost every time we were in a position to view the mountain, the weather was poor. By the time we returned to base camp a week later, we had only managed to get partial views of the most feasible line on the southwest face.

While the route itself looked climbable, there were big questions about how we would get to the foot of the face. Easy access to the west side of Kailash is prevented by serac bands and steep rock walls. Fortunately, we spotted a small couloir that sneaked over a ridge on the south face, and gave access to a col just above the serac band. It took us two days to reach this col, with all the usual issues of poor rock and scary glacier travel.

Our planned line linked a series of snowfields via gully and chimney lines through very steep rock bands, a bit Eiger-like in nature. As this was a southwest face, early starts and early finishes would be the order of the day. Fortunately, the sections through the rock bands turned out to be reasonably sheltered from sun until midafternoon, so we managed to make reasonable progress each day. But once the sun did hit it was incredibly hot, and we were forced to stop and cut a ledge almost straight away. Day four proved to be the crux: a very steep and

[This page, top] Mick Fowler tackles a steep ice section on day four of the first ascent of Kishtwar Kailash. *Paul Ramsden* [This page, bottom] The unclimbed eastern aspects of Cerro Kishtwar (6,155m GPS) and Chomochior (6,322m, map height), seen from Kishtwar Kailash. *Mick Fowler*

occasionally overhanging gully section, poorly protected mixed passages, bad rock, and ice bulges. We managed to pitch the tent almost every night, even if much of the tent floor was hanging in space. The weather was perfect all the time we were climbing, and particularly good on the summit day. We arrived at the top on day six, the last pitch proving particularly challenging with very poor snow and rock. But it was all worth it for the first ascent of a very fine summit. The 2,000m route was ED, Scottish VI. The descent took two days, using Abalakovs all the way.

Unfortunately, Mike and Rob had not succeeded on their attempt of a nearby unclimbed peak. Winter arrived the day after our return to base camp, with snow falling all the way down to the valley. 🔲

PAUL RAMSDEN, *The Alpine Club, U.K.*

Upper Darcha Valley, Goat Peak (6,080m GPS); Para Handy Ridge. In 2012 the Scottish Zanskar Expedition attempted a couple of unclimbed 6,000m peaks in the Namkha Tokpo (AAJ 2013). One succumbed, but the other (G22) showed an unexpected lack of consideration. However, a potential route up the south face was spotted, and in June 2013 much of the same team (Rob Adams, Bob Hamilton, Steve Kennedy, Andy Nisbet, and I) returned to attempt an ascent from the Himachal Pradesh (as opposed to Zanskar) side of the range. We went a little earlier in the year for improved snow conditions, and spent June 12–July 1 at or above base camp.

The approach included a three-day walk from Zanskar Sumdo, where we watched a new track being bulldozed over the Shingo La. Heading north up the -Miyar valley, we hung a right at Kuddu and continued for a couple of days up a valley that was used for grazing but apparently had seen no other mountaineers. It hadn't seen many cartographers either—we established base camp at the foot of an unclimbed, unnamed 6,000m peak that was not marked on one of our maps, despite being only a day's walk from a well-used trekking route.

A reconnaissance of the southern side of G22 showed it to be an undertaking that would require a few days. Then it started to snow. Weather systems that caused havoc in Uttarakhand also made it possible for us to build rather large snowmen at base camp.

When the weather finally cleared, a time shortage made the proximity of the 6,000m peak above base camp irresistible. We established an advanced base camp at 5,200m on the south ridge, and the following morning crossed the glacier to reach the southwest ridge, which we climbed on crusty but safe snow (up to 50°) to reach the sharp summit at 6,080m (PD). We named the summit Goat Peak in honour of the 60th birthday of the Goat of Barten (Andy Nisbet, who lives in the Scottish village of Boat of Garten).

With time now running out, we turned to a very attractive ridge west of base camp, on the other side of the river. Profound cultural discussions led us to name the ridge after Para Handy, a character from a series of short stories published in a Glasgow newspaper in the early 20th century. The first top ascended, by the two that had to return to work (Adams and Kennedy), was named McPhail's (ca 5,450m). This was followed by Dougie (ca 5,390m), Sunny Jim (5,200m), and Vital Spark (5,150m), all named from the same series. All were PD to AD, generally on snow with some rocky steps.

Hamilton, Nisbet, and I then made a couple of attempts on a summit with map height 5,930m, southeast of base camp. Unfortunately, melting snow produced substantial rockfall. Thwarted, we returned to base camp to finish the whisky before the arrival of the porters. 🔲

SUSAN JENSEN, *Scottish Mountaineering Club*

Miyar Valley, Masala Peak (5,650m), Los Crotos (not to summit); Neverseen Tower (5,750m), Changa Style (not to summit). For 20 days in September, Carloncho Guerra, Aztlan Madio, and I visited the Miyar, intending to climb new rock routes. We took a public bus to the road head and didn't hire porters, horses, or even a cook for base camp. With bad weather and heavy sacks, it took six days to reach base camp on the moraine of the Chhudong Glacier.

After waiting out more bad weather, a window suddenly appeared, and on September 16 we climbed the north face of Masala Peak. Although we probably made the first ascent of this great rock wall, we didn't go to the summit, stopping at ca 5,500m because we had brought no ice gear for the final, nontechnical, section. We rappelled our line, which we named Los Crotos (705m, 6b+), regaining our tents at midnight.

Two days later, in continued good weather, but with the walls still heavily iced, we attempted the left pillar of the west face of Neverseen Tower. Starting left of the 1992 Italian route, Horn Please, we climbed six pitches and then made a cold bivouac on a narrow ledge. Next day we climbed four pitches and just about reached the Italian route. At this point increasing ice in the cracks was making progress difficult and time-consuming. We descended after having climbed 520m to 6c, naming our variant Changa Style. 📷

LUCAS ALZAMORA, *Argentina*

Miyar Valley, Sanjana Peak (5,937m), southwest ridge; Mt. Sealth (5,968m) east ridge; David's 62 Nose (4,950m), southwest face, Emerson-Owen Route. In August, Sandeep Nain, Jason Schilling, and I headed up the Miyar Valley with two cooks and eight horses, against the flow of shepherds and their flocks moving to the lowlands of Himachal and the Punjab. Three days of pleasant trekking brought us to the standard base camp.

Over the next three weeks we made two separate forays to the upper Takdung Glacier, climbing two new routes. Reaching the upper glacier is a tedious affair. Many hours of boulder hopping are needed before gaining the vast snowfields above. We established high camp at ca 5,180m. On the 27th it took all day to climb 14 pitches, up to 5.10b A1, to the unnamed peak between Trento and Om Shanti (both climbed by Italians in 2008). Darkness descended on top, and we decided it was best to shiver for 10 hours there until morning.

At first light, we discovered we were not actually on the summit, but still had another tower to climb. Zombies may very well have climbed the next two pitches faster, but Sandeep

[This page] West face of Neverseen Tower. (1) Changa Style incomplete variant (2013) to (2) Horn Please (1992). (3) Mai Blau (2005). *Carloncho Guerra*

[This page, top] Los Crotos on Masala Peak. Across the Chhudong Glacier lie (A) Neverseen Tower, (B) Lotos Peak, (C) Geruda Peak, (D) Mont Maudit, and (E) Double Peak. *Carloncho Guerra* [This page, bottom] Left: Om Shanti (2008). Right: Sanjana (2013). *Tim Halder*

bravely aided across a horizontal crack to bring us to the summit around 9 a.m. We named the peak Sanjana.

On September 3 we climbed onto the crest of the watershed ridge between the Takdung and the large glacier to its northeast. On the glorious morning of the 4th we climbed unroped to the highest peak at the head of the Takdung Glacier via a southeast-facing snow/ice headwall and a rimy summit scramble. We named it Mt. Sealth in honor of our home, Seattle. As usual, by late morning the weather deteriorated quickly, and we descended in a fog and graupel.

On the 8th, Jason and Sandeep finished the trip by putting up a new line on David's 62 Nose to the right of Lufoo Lam (350m, UIAA VII+, Grmovsek-Grmovsek, 2007). Climbing on solid granite, they reached the summit just as the daily dose of graupel fell from the heavens. They called their line the Emerson-Owen Route (350m, seven pitches, 5.10a). [*Editor's note: This route appears to start left of Clandestine (2008), possibly sharing common ground with Shim Nak (2004) at around half-height, and climbs similar terrain to D'yer Ma'ker (2009) toward the top.*]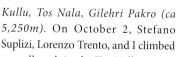

TIM HALDER, *AAC*

Kullu, Tos Nala, Gilehri Pakro (ca 5,250m). On October 2, Stefano Suplizi, Lorenzo Trento, and I climbed a small peak in the Tos Valley. From Manikaran, via Tos village, we followed the Tos River for three days to a base camp at Samshi Thacth (3,800m). From here we had to cross to the east bank

down to base camp. We managed to reach a bivouac at 4,700m below the side glacier, but it snowed during the night and we returned to base camp. On the way down, Lorenzo fell and fractured his left hand. Fortunately, at base camp we met a group of Indian trekkers, one of whom was a doctor who was able to treat the fracture.

Two days later we returned to our bivouac, only to find that an animal had made off with the food. At 5 a.m. next day we left for the summit in beautiful but very cold weather. We climbed the west face of our peak via a steep rock and ice couloir, gained the south ridge, then continued up the long and icy crest. A final steep rock buttress led to the summit, which we reached at 1 p.m. We descended the north ridge over difficult mixed terrain. Lorenzo performed well with a broken hand.

We called the summit Gilehri Pakro (the gilehri is an animal that lives at high altitude, and pakro is a thief). Our route was named Broken Hand (700m, 4 70°). On the summit my altimeter read 5,250m; Google Earth coordinates are 32°07'45.81"N, 77°30'45.44"E (and 5,142m).

[Editor's note: Although the Tos Nala has been visited by many expeditions and the mountains at its head are well known, no records have been kept for climbing on smaller peaks down the valley.]

MASSIMO MARCHEGGIANI, Italy

LAHAUL

Bara Shigri Glacier, Khhang Shiling (6,360m), northeast ridge via west flank; Kulu Makalu (a.k.a. Lal Qila, 6,349m), northwest face, attempt. From July 20–August 10, Vasile Dumitrica, Mihnea Prundeanu, and I took part in Climbathon 2013, an event organized by the Indian Mountaineering Foundation. There were several objectives: exchanges of information and experience between Indian and Western mountaineers, with a focus on alpine style, and ascents of several peaks in the region. With 10 instructors, three

[This page, top] Gilehri Pakro, showing (1) ascent via west face and south ridge, and (2) descent via north ridge. *Massimo Marcheggiani* [This page, bottom] Attempted Romanian route on the northwest face of Kulu Makalu, halted by a rockfall accident. *Cosmin Andron*

foreign, and over 60 "student" participants (nearly all Indian), it was a large and complex event.

After several days of preparation and acclimatization around our base camp at Concordia, four teams, each with an instructor, planned to attempt Shigri Parvat (6,536m). Once at the base, I decided the mountain was too busy and unsafe at the time, and I looked for a different objective for my team. Directly opposite was the west side of Khhang Shiling. On August 4 we left advanced base at 2 a.m. and summited at 7:30 a.m. Summiters were Bharat Bhusan, Subrata Chakraborty, Prerna Dangi, Karn Kowshik, and Bhupesh Kumar (India), Vasile Dumitrica, Mihnea Prundeanu, and me (Romania), and Angel Robledo (Brazil). [*Editor's note: The only previous ascent of this peak took place in 2004, when an Indian party, led by Divyesh Muni, climbed from the east to reach the col between Shigri Parvat and Khhang Shiling, and then up the northeast ridge of the latter to the summit.*]

After the Climbathon had finished, Vasile, Mihnea, and I attempted Kulu Makalu by the unclimbed northwest face, approaching up its northern flank. On August 9, Vasile was in front, having just climbed over an ice bulge, and Mihnea was a couple of meters above me, when there was a large rockfall—a truck load, no exaggeration. Mihnea's helmet was broken, and a table-top-sized block hit him in the back. (The eventual diagnosis was a damaged sciatic nerve and hairline fracture of a lumbar vertebra.) We managed to rappel to the bottom of the face, and Mihnea, still in shock, crawled to base camp. The next day, with porters, we made it safely to the road at Batal. 📷 🗒

COSMIN ANDRON, *Romanian Alpine Club*

GARHWAL HIMAL

Bhilangna Valley, Satling peaks, first ascents. In the post-monsoon a team of eight German females made first ascents in the Satling group south of impressive Thalay Sagar. The Satling Valley had been visited by Martin Moran (AAJ 2003) and Tom Dauer (AAJ 2005), but while both described the high potential for first ascents, no subsequent expedition had come here.

After a four-day approach following the Bhilangna River, we established base camp at 3,700m, then after acclimatization and load carrying made two advanced bases. Charlotte Gild and Dörte Pietron went to the Dudhganga Glacier on the south side of the Satling range, planning to climb the triple-headed peak Brahmasar from the south [the south, but not the highest, summit was reached from the south in 2002]. They climbed the south couloir (50° snow) between Brahmasar and Cream Topping, but then decided to retreat. Later, they made the first ascent of a 5,360m peak opposite Brahmasar, which they called Pala Devi. The pair climbed the east ridge at UIAA II, 40° (snow).

Meanwhile, the rest of the team operated from an advanced base at 5,050m on the Satling Glacier. Yvonne Koch, Ursula Wolfgruber, and I made the first ascent of the west summit of Ice Wave (5,618m) via north-facing couloirs (450m, M5 70°). Caroline North, Ursula, and I also climbed 5,180m Point Lilliput (200m, M2 and three pitches of III–V), a small peak southwest of the Cathedral.

Caroline and Christina Huber made the first ascent of Left Rabbit Ear (5,500m, 50° snow and two pitches of M2). [The Right Ear was climbed in 2002.] The same two repeated the original 2002 route to the north summit of the double-headed Cathedral. They also climbed the south summit, suggesting this top, at 5,292m, was around five meters higher than the north summit. Later, with our team doctor Julia Thiele, they reached a small summit southeast of the Cathedral, moving simultaneously up three pitches of easy rock and mixed, and naming the peak Punta Alaja (5,222m).

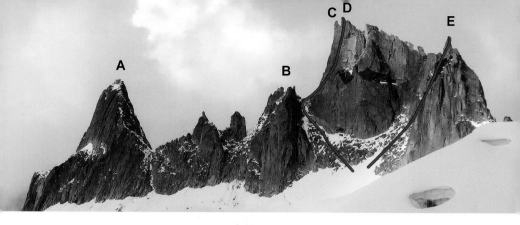

[This page] On the north side of the Satling Glacier. (A) Point Walker, climbed in 2004. (B) Point Lilliput. (C) Cathedral north summit. (D) Cathedral south summit with 2013 route. (E) Point Alaja with 2013 route. *Mirjam Limmer*

Satling means "seven phalluses," and Caroline, Christina, Ursula, and I went off to look for the eighth. A rock tower east of the Satling glacier plateau seemed to fit the bill, and so for the final ascent of the expedition we climbed the 8th Phallus (5,500m, VI M3 50°snow). 📷

MIRJAM LIMMER, *Germany*

WESTERN GARHWAL

GANGOTRI

First crossing of Chaukhamba (Meade's) Col (6,093m). Chaukhamba Col lies northeast of Chaukhamba I (7,138m), on the ridge connecting it with Januhut (6,805m). A crossing of this col, from the Bhagat Kharat to Gangotri glaciers, forming the most direct route between the two famous pilgrimage sites of Badrinath and Gangotri, was first tried by English mountaineer C.F. Meade in 1912. Meade reached the col from the east and looked down onto the Gangotri Glacier. Shipton and Tilman failed to make the crossing (or even to reach the col) from the east in 1934, as did Harish Kapadia in 1997. In 1995 a three-member British team reached the col from the west in an attempt on Chaukhamba I.

In May a team of five Indian climbers and four experienced high-altitude porters accomplished the feat. They started from Mana village, beyond Badrinath, on May 18, reached the col on the 26th, and descended the full length of the Gangotri Glacier (despite one injured climber). They reached Tapovan on May 30 and Gangotri the next day. In February 2014 the Himalayan Club presented this achievement with the annual Jagdish Nanavati Award for Excellence in Mountaineering. 📖

LINDSAY GRIFFIN, *MountainINFO, with info from Debabrata Mukherjee and Ritobrata Saha*

KUMAUN HIMALAYA

Kuchela Dhura (6,294m), north face and east ridge. From the summit of Kuchela Dhura, a sharp, three-kilometer ridge runs southwest toward Nanda Kot (6,861m). In 2012 I organized an expedition that reached this ridge from the northwest and then followed the crest northeast until stopped at 6,206m by a V-shaped notch. The IMF asked me to lead another attempt in the post-monsoon season of 2013. This time we would climb an icefall on the north face.

Negotiating landslides and wiped-out bridges as a result of the June 16 disaster in Uttarakhand, our team trekked from the road head via Martoli to a base camp at 4,173m, on the true right bank of the Lawan Gad—the same approach as used to climb Nanda Devi East. On August 30 we established advanced base at 4,922m.

The next day we began on the icefall, fixing 400m of rope. In total we would fix 1,000m up the north face before establishing summit camp at 6,064m (GPS) on the east ridge. On September 4, Wallambok Lyngdoh, Vijay Singh Rautela, Chitramohan Singh Chauhan, and I set off from advanced base with three days' food. After a rest day at our high camp, we reached the highest point (30°18'22.2"N, 80°05'19.6"E) on the 6th. The next day we descended, removing all garbage and ropes. 🔘 📑

Abridged from a report by DHRUV JOSHI, *India*

SAHYADRI RANGE

Harischandragad Fort, Kokankada, Left Route (second ascent, mostly free). Kokankada is the ca 600m concave cliff, over 1.5km in length, on the southwest side of Harischandragad Fort (Maharashtra). In December 1985 a team from Mumbai made the first ascent of the south face via the Left Route. Eight climbers and a support team spent 17 days on the route, using fixed rope and placing stainless steel 8mm bolts. This was the first big wall climbed in the Sahyadri, and a fine performance given the equipment available in India at the time.

We first tried the line in February 2012, retreating from a height of ca 200m. The technical difficulties were high, and there were other factors like extreme temperatures, strong winds, rotten rock, continuous rockfall, poor protection, scorpions, and poisonous snakes.

On our second try we decided to approach from the top (easy walking), rappel the route, preplace minimal protection, and then climb the face. On the morning of January 17, 2014, Rohit Vartak, Sharad Chandra (photographer), and I started down the wall. We soon realized there had been dramatic changes in the route in the 28 years since the first ascent. Cracks had widened and were choked with debris. Many old bolts were unusable. Using a power drill, we placed 24 bolts. We then climbed the route over two days. We used aid on a total of 18m, and felt many pitches were now 6c/7a, with cruxes 7a/7b. 📑

SAMIRAN KOLHE, *India*

[This page] The south face of Kokankada showing Left Route (1985/2014). *Sharad Chandra*

CHINA

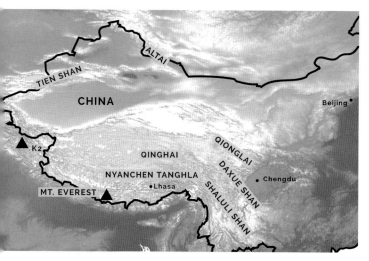

XINJIANG

WESTERN KOKSHAAL-TOO

Kyzyl Asker (5,842m), southeast pillar, all free ascent. Due to the terrorist attack in Pakistan, we had to change our summer expedition plans. After a couple of weeks' research we decided on the Chinese side of the Western Kokshaal-Too. Permits proved slow to obtain and were pretty pricey, and even with them it was not guaranteed we would get there. On our journey we passed seven checkpoints. Finally, at the end of August, Stéphane Hanssens, Sean Villanueva, Evrard Wendenbaum, and I entered the promised valley. Being a lot more alpine than expected, it was very different from our previous expeditions. [*The team approached via the same valley most likely first traveled by foreigners in 2000 (Libecki, AAJ 2001), then took the left glacier branch leading north toward Kyzyl Asker. The head of this glacier has been visited a number of times by parties approaching over Window Col from Kyrgyzstan.*]

After a week of exploration and acclimatizing, we spent the next 15 days surfing on the southeast pillar of Kyzyl Asker. The climbing was absolutely spectacular, with compact, orange granite, sometimes forming crazy hueco shapes. The weather was rough, with many snowstorms, and the temperatures dropped to –15°C at night. At the warmest time of the day they barely rose to –5°C, and our water bottles would freeze solid by midday. Taking off gloves and wearing tight rock shoes in these conditions sometimes felt ridiculous. But the unique scenery of the surrounding snow-plastered mountains made up for the suffering, helping us to keep going.

On our 13th day of vertical living we made the final push to the summit. Because the rock was too icy, we switched to mixed climbing for the last 400m (which also counts as free climbing, I guess). This was an exciting new experience for virgin mixed climbers like us. The summit was a lot farther than we estimated, and we didn't reach it until 10 p.m., in total darkness and biting cold. By the time we reached the portaledges, Stéphane's toes were hard and cold, like a piece of chicken coming out of the freezer. He had serious frostbite. There is no rescue in this region, so we descended quickly, rushed out of the mountains, and as soon as we reached civilization Stéphane was dispatched to Belgium. The good news is that he should be able to keep all his toes, but he would need around six months for total recovery.

After a new integral start, our climb lay very close to the 2007 Russian Route (6B, mixed free

[This page, top] After a day of hauling in a snowstorm, the Belgian team established Camp 2 on the southeast pillar of Kyzyl Asker. The climbers spent 13 days on the route. *Evrard Wendenbaum* [This page, bottom] Looking southeast from Kyzyl Asker into China. (A) Unclimbed, unnamed peak over 5,500m. (B) Unclimbed peak, 5,665m. (C) Unnamed glacier flowing south from Kyzyl Asker, used for the approach. (D) Great Walls of China, highest summit (5,186m). (E) North top (ca 5,120m) climbed by Dutch team (see next page), following snow and ice in left center of the shadowed face. (F) Peak 4,622m. No mountaineer is known to have visited the glacier visible in front of this peak. *Evrard Wendenbaum*

and aid, 30 pitches, Mikhailov-Odintsov, Ruchkin) as far as our Camp 3. We knew about their route and hoped to find a completely independent line to the left. But above Camp 3 it was logical to join their route. The pillar is 1,200m high. We did about 1,400m of climbing in capsule style, all free at 7b+ M6/7. 🖸

NICO FAVRESSE, *Belgian Alpine Club*

Great Walls of China (5,186m), northern top (ca 5,120m), Double Trouble. From July 27 to August 25, Vincent van Beek, Vincent Perrin, Bas van der Ploeg, Bas and Saskia van der Smeede, and I visited the western sector of the Western Kokshaal-Too. Following the usual approach through Kyrgyzstan, we reached the unnamed glacier south of Kyzyl Asker. Our goal was to establish rock routes on the ca 700m east face of the Great Walls of China, where previously only two ice routes had been climbed (*AAJ 2005 and 2012*). Unlike other expeditions, we managed to drive to base camp without any problems, and established advanced base on the glacier after 10 days of load carrying.

Once we got a text promising a good weather window, we split into three parties and set off for the lines we'd each chosen. Vincent Perrin and I tried a line on the main wall, with Bas and Saskia attempting another a few hundred meters to the left. Bas van der Ploeg and Vincent van Beek were much farther left, on the tower left of the main face (a little right of the two ice routes).

Unfortunately, Saskia was hit by rockfall, and although not seriously injured, was unable to continue. At the same time, Vincent and I were struggling with wet rock and serious aid (A2/3). Our line turned out to be exposed to icefall, and when we couldn't find a safe spot for the portaledge, we retreated. Van Beek and van der Ploeg made much better progress, but eventually had to abandon their climb when they ran out of water and found they needed bigger cams to progress.

A little later, as Perrin, van der Smeede, and I were on the glacier and watching the other pair, we scoped a snow and ice line on the north face. We were only able to find three ice screws among our big-wall gear, so we decided to bring a big beak as an extra piece of ice protection. On August 16 the weather was clear and cold, and it felt great to climb in alpine style after struggling

[This page] Kyzyl Asker from the southeast. (1) This ice couloir is the most attempted major line in the Western Kokshaal-Too and still awaits an ascent. (2) Southeast Pillar, Belgian Route. (3) Southeast Pillar, Russian Route. (4) Southeast face, Belorussian-Russian attempt, 2009. *Evrard Wendenbaum*

with aid. However, the higher we climbed, the more difficult it became: Solid black ice was hidden under the white cover. Vincent led the first technical pitch, which involved 10m of 80°. Higher, Bas had the opportunity to lead another fine section of AI3+. Although the final bit was not steep, we kept belaying, since snow conditions were tricky. The wind had created huge vertical cornices in a way I had never seen before. We couldn't see if we reached the exact high point of the long horizontal ridge, but quickly agreed it was too dangerous to swim any further. Although happy with our success, we now had to descend 800m with a single 60m rope.

We named the route Double Trouble (800m, TD- AI4) after our tricky ascent/descent and the usual stomach problems climbers experience during an expedition. The overall difficulty and quality were comparable with the Swiss Route on Les Courtes in the Mont Blanc Massif. Back at base camp we realized that we had finished at the northernmost top; the main summit lies more to the south. 📷

BAS VISSCHER, *The Netherlands*

Run for the Bolder. In August, Ethan Pringle, Liv Sansoz, and I, along with photographer Keith Ladzinski, traveled to the remote border area of China and Kyrgyzstan, on the south side of the Western Kokshaal-Too. We approached up the long valley leading to Peak Byeliy (a.k.a. Grand Poobah), an area I had visited three times before, and did the first ascent of a 1,000-foot wall on the east side of the valley. Run for the Boulder (5.12 R) had scary rockfall but also world-class splitters, as good as we had ever seen.

MIKE LIBECKI, *AAC*

[This page] Ethan Pringle and Mike Libecki climbing pitch four of Run for the Bolder. *Keith Ladzinski*

ALTAI

Keketuohai National Geologic Park, various routes. In June several friends and I traveled to Keketuohai, and as during my previous trip in 2012, we were welcomed by the park authorities (AAJ 2013). Permission to climb was granted after fulfilling a number of basic requirements. Currently, non-Chinese nationals are unable to stay overnight inside the park due to border regulations. Public transportation is available to the park from Keketuohai town. To Divine Bell it is a distance of 23km, and a one-day round-trip costs 49 RMB for two people.

    We put up a number of shorter routes (on Tongs Wall and Crocodile Hill), and longer climbs on a new crag named the Flock and on Small Bell Mountain. The Flock is a very broad dome downhill and left of Shepherd's Rock. Garrett Bradley, Sarah Rasmussen, Bryn Thomas, Zhuo Lei, and I put up five routes, from one to five pitches.

    On Small Bell Mountain we repeated a nine-pitch route with leads up to 5.10+/11-. [*For Whom the Bell Tolls, Tommy Caldwell and party, 2010.*] Bryn and I then started up the first five pitches of this route to the tree ledge, then made a double pendulum out right to reach the start of a parallel crack system, which we climbed in a further five pitches, the first being 5.11. Tour de Bell provided a great day out with loads of finger and hand cracks, exposure, and fun. A No. 6 Camalot would be useful for the 5.10 chimney/offwidth on pitch eight.

    Farther to the right, Sarah and I climbed Small Bell Chimney Route in 10 pitches to 5.11-. This follows the major chimney system in the middle of the Bell and is reached by breaking out right after the first pitch of For Whom the Bell Tolls. The climbing is fairly sustained at 5.10/10+. All routes on the Small Bell have a walk-off to the left. 🔘

MIKE DOBIE, *China*

QINGHAI

Tanggula Shan, Sangay Ri (ca 6,000m) and Longyala West (6,000m). For nine years I had toyed with the idea of climbing in Qinghai, which has many virgin summits. With only two weeks to spare, I focused on a small glaciated system in the Tanggula Shan, 100km north of the border with Tibet. The Tanggula Shan is crossed by the Golmud-Lhasa road at the Tanggula Shankhu, which at 5,300m is one of the highest motorable passes in the world. The venue of choice lay a little to the northeast, at 33°06'N, 92°03'E.

[This page] Small Bell Mountain. (1) For Whom the Bell Tolls. (2) Tour de Bell. (3) Small Bell Chimney Route. *Mike Dobie*

Mohd Rozani bin Maarof and I traveled 600km south from Golmud by 4X4, and after inspecting northern approaches, we drove to the western end of the Dongkemadi Glacier. We camped at ca 5,000m near the glacier outflow and moved up next day to an advanced base at 5,400m.

On September 23 we left at 8:30 a.m. and headed east to an unnamed peak, which we climbed by its west-northwest ridge. The climb was PD-, but the rapid altitude gain and strong wind made it feel harder. On top our GPS recorded 6,000m, and we named the peak Sangay Ri (Lion Peak).

On the 25th we left at 5:30 a.m. and took an unexpectedly long time to cross a small but crevassed glacier. In light winds we headed southwest up broad slopes of good névé to reach the col between Longyala and Shar Ri, the latter a ca 5,800m summit directly above base camp. From here we climbed east over the west shoulder of Longyala to a false summit (Longyala West) at ca 6,000m. What had appeared from below to be an easy traverse to the main top (6,100m) was in reality a 50m drop and then a rising traverse along a double-corniced ridge. A stronger team would have pushed on, but one's approach to risk changes when in a remote situation with no possibility of rescue. We descended, and two days later began our drive back to Golmud. ▣ 🗎

DAVID LIM, *Singapore*

Qiajajima Range, Gujon Ri (5,490m) and the Mekong headwaters. The Mekong River, the 10th longest in the world, rises in the historically Tibetan province of Kham and flows ca 4,350km to the Mekong Delta in Vietnam. It's hard to believe that its source was not reached until 1994, but it lies hidden in a remote and unknown massif of south Qinghai. The Japanese explorer Tom Nakamura feels its discovery solved "one of the world's last great geographical mysteries."

In 2007 geographers reached an agreement that the true source (33°42'38.8"N, 94°41'45.4"E) lies at 5,175m, at the base of a glacier running northeast from a peak named on maps as Guozongmucha (5,490m). This summit is situated in the northwestern part of a large range of peaks. The highest, toward the southeastern end, is referred to as Qiajajima I (5,930m, climbed in 2004 by Japanese).

After climbing in Sichuan's Shaluli Shan Josito Fernandez, Dani Martin, and I crushed our bums for four long days of travel northwest to the town of Zadoi (Drito) in Qinghai. It was the start of high season for picking caterpillar fungus, and we were fortunate to find a taxi driver willing to take us 70km west toward the mountains. Snow blocked the dirt road at 4,700m. We shouldered heavy sacks and walked for three days to reach the Lasawuma Valley, below the Mekong source, making our third camp at 5,089m. We then climbed the northeast spur of Guozongmucha (500m, PD– 45-50°) to the summit at 33°42'18"N, 94°41'27"E. We had completed our romantic quest of reaching the "real" source of the Mekong, the point where the first drop of the river forms. We named our route El Rio de la Vida. [*The summit reached was the 5,490m northwest top, directly above the Mekong source; the southeast top is higher at 5,514m.*]

At a Khampa shepherd camp on the way out, we were invited for tea, and on showing pictures of the mountain we had climbed, were told with complete conviction that this was not named Guozongmucha, but Gujon Ri. According to local people, Guozongmucha (on some maps called Saitso Shan) lies to the northwest of Gujon Ri and rises to 5,632m (5,685m Russian Map). A full report with maps, photos, and topos is available as a download. ▣ 🔍 🗎

SERGI RICART, *Spain*

[This page, top] Unclimbed 5,400m peak in the region of the Mekong headwaters. *Tamotsu Nakamura*
[This page, bottom] Nyainbo Yuze massif from 4,398m Ronggeshan Pass to the northwest. The main summit is the snowiest pyramid left of center. Nyainbo Yuze II is the large, black rock peak to its left. Unclimbed granite walls abound. *Tamotsu Nakamura*

Unclimbed peaks near the Mekong headwaters. In June, Tadeo Shintani and I traveled to Zadoi with the aim of exploring unknown peaks and glaciers around the headwaters of the Mekong River. We were able to reach Hongse (4,700m, 33°24.887' N, 94°36.433' E) to the west of the mountains, but June and July are prime months for caterpillar fungus collection, and there was no one available to organize onward transport by horse caravan.

The area around Zadoi has many fascinating peaks between 5,300m and 5,800m that have yet to be surveyed or explored. Between Zadoi and Yushu to the east lie two clusters of wonderful 5,200–5,400m rock peaks that will attract climbers in the future. One group lies a little east of Zadoi, the other close to the 4,712m Changlashan Pass. North of Yushu are many impressive 5,400–5,700m snow and rock peaks. There is now a new airport at 3,800m, 30 minutes north of Yushu.

Tamotsu Nakamura, AAC Honorary Member

Nyainbo Yuze (5,369m), north-northeast face. A Chinese party including Li Yuan and Zhang Xaiohui climbed the north-northeast face of Nyainbo Yuze in the summer of 2011. This was their second attempt, the previous in 2009. Approaching from the tourist center, via the Ximen lake and valley to the northeast of the mountain, the team made Camp 1 on the glacier at 4,910m, with the peak clearly visible. On summit day they crossed the glacier and made a direct ascent of the face, with 400m of ice and snow, capped by a 30m vertical rock gully to the right. They summited at 2 p.m. and descended the east ridge. This is the first known ascent of the peak, though it seems unlikely it was unclimbed. In 1989 Yasuyuki Takeuchi and a Japanese team from Kyoto reached the summit of the slightly lower Nyainbo Yuze II to the northwest.

Although not a high massif, the Nyainbo Yuze group is an extensive collection of predominately granite peaks with challenging rock walls, and could potentially become a little alpine paradise. 🔲

From information provided by Tamotsu Nakamura, AAC Honorary Member, and Xia Zhongming, Germany

SICHUAN

SHALULI SHAN

Jarjinjabo Massif, Rim Route; Peak ca 5,500m, south ridge and upper west ridge. In October a team including Andrew Hedesh, Sylvain Millet, Claire Thomas, Thomas Vialletet, Zhuo Lei, and I visited the Jarjinjabo Massif, north of the Zhopu pastures. We climbed a number of new routes, including but not limited to, those described below. Residents of the nearby monastery were friendly, and the locals didn't mind us climbing. The best months for rock climbing are July and August. There is a chance of rain at this time, but the weather clears for long periods.

Andrew, Zhuo Lei, and I climbed Rim Route on the flanks of the rock peak southeast of Peak 5,382m (PLA map). Andrew and I then made an all-free ascent. This is a great climb that follows a prominent feature rising out of the valley floor to the summit of a pointed tower. Single-bolt anchors (with a carabiner) were placed for rappelling to the top of pitch eight, after which downclimbing and rappels from trees led to the ground.

From Zhopu Lake, walk northeast, past the monastery, until a large gully and waterfall appear on the left. Rim Route climbs steep rock to the right of this, reached by working up through the forest. We completed the line in 16 pitches (one of which is a diagonal rappel) and some walking/scrambling. The crux, on pitch 14, is 5.10b.

In the same month Zhuo Lei and I climbed Peak ca 5,500m, a fine moderate mountaineering route following a nice couloir and ridge with steep snow and easy glacier travel. From the monastery we ascended northeast to a higher valley and lake, where we camped. Next day we scrambled up a

[This page] Rim Route is situated a little way above the monastery and Zhopu Lake in the Jarjinjabo Massif. *Mike Dobie*

talus slope to the hanging valley below rocky Peak 5,556m (PLA map), and then climbed a snow couloir on the right to gain a watershed ridge. We followed this north, and near the top worked right, across the glacier, to reach the west ridge of the triangular snowy summit of Peak 5,550m, which we followed to the top. We then reversed the route to our tent. 📷

MIKE DOBIE, *China*

Chola Shan and Gangga Massifs: Khai Ri (ca 4,940m), northwest face, Horses; Tangaryama Ri (5,063m), traverse; Tsara Mashe Ri (5,150m), west face, Taxi Driver. Josito Fernandez, M'Paz Garrido, Dani Martin, and I explored the mountains of northwest Sichuan, basing our activities around the villages of Ganzi and Manigango on the Sichuan-Tibet Highway. On April 16, having set up base camp at 4,160m in the Okopo Chu valley, ca 25km east-southeast of Manigango, I almost made the first ascent of Khai Ri (local name, ca 4,940m) via the northwest face. The 750m route, named Horses (AD–), started with a long, easy couloir (35-50°), topped by a steeper gully (55-60°), followed by 65°

[This page, top] Tsara Mashe Ri from the west. (1) Descent on the northwest face. (2) Taxi Driver. *Sergi Ricart* [This page, bottom] Dani Martin on the first pitch (M5+ R) of Taxi Driver, Tsara Mashe Ri west face. *Sergi Ricart*

and UIAA IV+ climbing on the summit ridge. I didn't climb the last 10m on the summit tower, stopped by exposed rock slabs covered with loose snow.

All four of us then traveled the Sichuan-Tibet Highway to Yolba (3,425m), south of the Chola Shan. On April 25 we walked east to below the Redak La (4,155m), on the 26th to the tiny village of Amula (4,126m), and on the 27th north to the Dzin Tso (lake). Just before crossing the Dzin La, we turned west and summited previously unclimbed Tangaryama Ri (5,063m). We ascended the southwest face (PD–, 30° II) in deep snow but with few technical difficulties, and descended the northeast face (45°).

We now wanted to visit a group of mountains in the Gangga Range, west of the main summits. From Ganzi we traveled west along the highway for 20km to the village of Lanyi Nge (Lani Cun), then walked south for three hours to pitch camp at 4,090m at the snout of the glacier between Tsara Mashe Ri (5,150m) and, to its northwest, Tsara Yashe Ri. On April 30, Dani, Josito, and I started up the west face of Tsara Mashe Ri, following a steep goulotte clearly visible from the road. The first two pitches were rather runout M5+ and M5, after which an enjoyable third pitch (75° M3) led into the upper snowy couloir, which we climbed unroped for 200m (50-60°) to the summit ridge. Josito then led the easy but extremely loose rock ridge north for 80m to the summit (III). We named the route Taxi Driver (450m, ED1), and we descended the shorter northwest face with two rappels plus downclimbing at 45°. 🎞️ 🔍

SERGI RICART, *Spain*

QIONGLAI SHAN

SIGUNIANG NATIONAL PARK

Eagle Rock (ca 5,300m), south face, 353 Years Old Dreaming. On August 23 our team reached base camp at 4,400m below Eagle Rock, the south summit of Potala Shan (a.k.a. Putala Peak). Eagle Rock lies above the valley of Shuangqiao, and was believed to have been climbed only once, by a three-man Swiss team, via the south face (*AAJ 2006*).

From August 25–27, Heng Jhao, Jinyon Dong, and I climbed a 13-pitch line to the right of the Swiss route, finding classic slab climbing, often with very little protection. On the fourth pitch I managed to place only one piece of pro in 60m. At the end of pitch three we found an 8mm bolt and karabiner, remnants of a Japanese attempt that was stopped by bad weather. Above the sixth pitch we moved out right, aiming for the main crack system we planned to follow. Reaching this direct would have involved drilling through a blank section of rock, but a circuitous route to the right offered poorly protected free climbing. The ninth pitch and the pitch above were 5.10+. On the 12th pitch I met the unexpected: three pegs, one and a half meters apart. Who had placed them? They were not new and not on the Swiss route. This pitch was the crux at 5.11a. I was pleased to climb it free but also frustrated to learn someone had been here before.

I arrived on the summit ridge at 7:30 p.m., in the gap between the low and middle tops of Eagle Rock. About 200m away and one pitch up is a higher top, a small eminence that cannot be seen from anywhere in the Shuangqiao. We descended from the gap, and at 3 a.m., 21 hours after leaving, we regained the tent. An hour later a thunderstorm struck and the noise of rockfall echoed around our camp. Was Eagle Rock expressing its feelings for our ascent?

One day later, three more members of our expedition, "Griff," Jiang Qiu, and Yong Zhang,

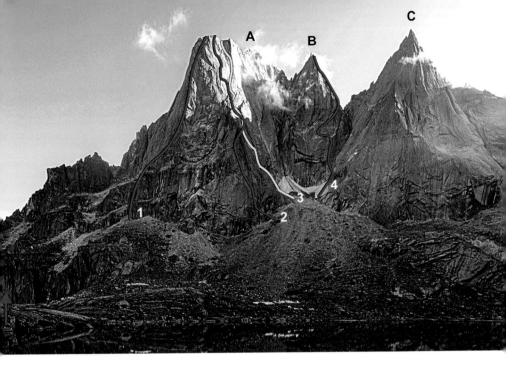

[This page, top] (A) Eagle Rock (ca 5,300m). (B) Central Tower (ca 5,380m). (C) Warglesei (ca 5,300m). (1) Invisible Hand (Costa, 2013), continuing to true summit behind. (2) I Hate Camping (700m, 7a A3, Durr-Looser-Ruggli, 2005). (3) 353 Years Old Dreaming, 2013. (4) Japanese Route, 2013. Arrow marks top portion of Invisible Hand Sit Start and Hagoroamo (both 2013). *Wang Zhiming* [This page, bottom] Speed Indeed on the west face of Peak 5,180m. *Marcos Costa*

repeated the route. We used a total of 15 bolts, one on each belay, and a couple off-route on pitch eight. We named the climb by adding the ages of all team members and our old guide, because we all had the same climbing dream: 353 Years Old Dreaming (650m, 13 pitches, 5.11a). 📷 📄

Abridged from a report by WANG ZHIMING, *translated by Sean Wang,*
and provided by Demin Ma, China

Eagle Rock (ca 5,300m), southwest face, Invisible Hand and Invisible Hand Sit Start; Peak 5,180m, west face, Speed Indeed. Although I'm originally from Rio de Janeiro, I've been living in China for the last six years, doing my best to develop the climbing. I'd focused mainly on sport climbing, but in 2013 concentrated more on alpine routes. In September I visited the Shuangqiao Valley for the fifth time, keen to climb Eagle Rock, having seen the face while ice climbing in the valley the previous winter.

I established base camp by Baihaizi Lake and on September 13 started up the west-southwest face, solo, reaching the top at 6:45 p.m. Around 70 percent of the route consisted of perfect hand cracks, with the rest divided evenly among finger cracks, offwidths, and normal alpine face climbing with loose rock. I bivouacked about 25m away from what I thought was the summit block of Eagle Rock. The wind was very strong, and, unable to sleep, I boiled water and stayed in my bivy sack until late morning.

At 10 a.m. on the 14th I began the 60+m of vertical gain and ca 200m of ridge traverse to the true summit block of Eagle Rock. Reaching it, I started my descent immediately, but could not find the rappel anchors from the Chinese party that had climbed the south face three weeks earlier. I managed to descend this face with a 50m rope, making 13 rappels and downclimbing almost two-thirds of the wall. I named my ascent Invisible Hand (650m, 5.10+).

Prior to this, I had tried a "sit start" version on the southwest face, well to the right. The wall here is ca 300m high and slightly overhanging. Unfortunately, it was completely wet after 12 consecutive days of rain. It took me all day to climb 45m, and the next day a crack needed multiple No. 4 Camalots, which I didn't have. Back down in the valley, I met Pat Goodman and Matt McCormick, who kindly helped me out with bigger gear (ultimately, I was only able to finish the route due to this). [*Editor's note: Goodman and McCormick made unsuccessful attempts on three separate lines on the west face of Seerdengpu (5,592m).*] On October 7 I returned with my roommate, whom I'd taught to use ascenders, and gave him a real workout, jumaring at 4,300m. We took four days to complete the route, after I'd spent a total of three days fixing the first 100m. Invisible Hand Sit Start is 330m, 5.12- A2+.

Climbing in the valley with Kanehara and Onodara, I learned that Peak 5,180m, due east of Baihaizi Lake, was still unclimbed. Temperatures were now dropping and I had ice gear with me. On October 12, when the weather improved, I left the tent at 5:30 a.m. and took 40 minutes to reach the bottom of the west face. I gained the summit at 8:30 a.m. and was back at the tent by 10 a.m., before the sun had hit the wall. This was fortunate: Between 11:30 a.m. and noon I witnessed the largest rockfall I've seen in this valley, when two- to three-meter-high boulders cascaded down the ramp I'd not long ago descended. Speed is indeed safety in the mountains. I named the route Speed Indeed (580m, 5.8 M3 70°).

MARCOS COSTA, *Brazil/China*

Central Tower (5,380m GPS), southwest face and south-southeast ridge. South of Potala Shan, above the Shuangqiao Valley, the Central Tower lies between Eagle Rock (ca 5,300m) to the west and Warglesei (ca 5,300m) to the east. As these three peaks form a cirque around the head of a hanging valley containing Baihaizi Lake (White Lake, 4,600m), we have tentatively called these the Three Baihaizi Mountains.

On July 30, Naoki Ohuchi and I set up base camp by the lake. We began climbing the 510m southwest face on August 2. The approach took more time than imagined, with moraine followed by three pitches on snow leading to the foot of the wall. Ohuchi led up thin cracks and over bulges

using aid, while I carried the loads that we eventually deposited on the upper terrace. We rested at base camp on the 4th, then began again the next day. After two bivouacs we reached the ridge between Central Tower and Warglesei. We then descended to civilization, where we met two other friends, Koji Sano and Yusuke Yamazaki.

On the 15th all four climbers reclimbed six pitches and cached equipment, took a rest day, and then on the 17th began climbing in two pairs. That day we climbed 12 pitches, led by Ohuchi and me (up to VI+ A1). After a bivouac on the south-southeast ridge, Yamazaki led pitches 13 and 14, I led 15, and Sano led the last two to reach the top, just left of a 15m monolithic summit block.

Hiroo Yonezawa, *Japan*

Shizi (5,057m), east face; Fenghuang (4,901m), southeast face; Xiao Peak (4,785m); Eagle Rock (ca 5,300m), southwest face, Hagoroamo. In August and September, two teams from Keio University Alpine Club climbed three possibly new peaks from the Shuangqiao Valley; they also did one second ascent and completed the fourth ascent of Eagle Rock via a new route.

The first team, Yusuke Kimura, Takaaki Morikami, Kengo Nagamo, and Kengo Tagai, operated from August 3–22. Morikami and Nagamo set up base camp at 4,000m near the entrance to the Dagou Valley and then spent two days attempting unclimbed Peak 5,120m, which lies on the west rim of the valley, on the ridge south of Dayantianwo. They gave up due to rockfall, and instead climbed Peak 4,970m to the east, on the Dagou-Changping divide, unaware that it had been climbed in August 2011 by Chinese He Chuan, Ye Feng and Zang Yunpin. (AAJ 2013). Both parties climbed the southeast ridge.

Their next target was Shizi on the ridge immediately south of Peak 5,120m. Kimura, Morikami, and Tagai made the first ascent on the 15th, climbing the 570m east flank in 13 pitches at 5.10c. The ridge running southwest from Shizi crosses Ohuchi Peak, and then a second summit of map height 4,901m. Morikami and Tagai climbed this on the 19th via the 340m southeast aspect (seven pitches, generally 5.7-5.8, with one pitch of 5.10a). They named the summit Fenghuang. On the 21st, the same pair also climbed Xiao Peak, a summit midway between Haobangah and Dagou West, discovered during reconnaissance from the Changping Valley.

Keita Kanehara and Kenji Onodera arrived on August 31, but it rained for two weeks. On September 13 they climbed the east face of Niuxin Shan for acclimatization. On the 15th they camped at Baihaizi, and set off on the 16th for a new line on the lower southwest wall of Eagle Rock. They climbed this in eight pitches following flakes, cracks, and corners. There was a little rain and

[This page] Japanese route for the first ascent of Shizi. *Keio University Alpine Club*

some rockfall, but the line is steep enough that they were not affected. In the middle they had to climb a wet crack, and in the upper section a grassy slab.

The upper wall is ca 700m high, and they made a rising rightward traverse up it on easy broken ground to reach the headwall, where they joined the original Swiss route. They then connected with the Chinese route, 353 Years Old Dreaming, climbed the previous month, and followed this, using existing bolt belays, to the summit. The route on the initial wall was named Hagoroamo (eight pitches, 5.11) and the whole route gave ca 1,100m of climbing. **PHOTOS ICON**

Supplied by Tamotsu Nakamura, *AAC Honorary Member*

Dayantianwo (5,240m), southwest face, Three Sheep Bring Prosperity. On September 15 a multi-national expedition completed the first ascent of Dayantianwo, above the Shuangqiao Valley. This granite pyramid lies south-southeast of Baihaizi Lake and is the first summit southwest of Peak 5,180m. Chaohui Zheng of China, Szu-ting Yi of Taiwan, and I climbed the ca 600m southwest face at 5.10 R/X 60°. We were part of a larger expedition, organized by Zheng, that attempted the peak earlier in the month. At that time a series of storms covered the mountain in heavy snow. After a week of good weather that melted most of it, we three, along with the Tibetan climber Laoyao Xu, returned to our high camp at the base of Dayantianwo, and the following day started up two separate routes on the southwest face.

After seven pitches the two routes intersected, Xu decided to descend, and Zheng joined Yi and me. After reaching the summit we rappelled during the night, returning to camp after a 16-hour round trip. Yi and I named our route Three Sheep Bring Prosperity, after the Bharal mountain sheep that ran past us across fifth-class terrain close to the summit. Zheng named his variation Top of a Dream.

[This page] Dayantianwo from the south, showing (1) Three Sheep Bring Prosperity and (2) Top of a Dream. Behind and right lie the Three Baihaizi Mountains and Potala Shan. *Dave Anderson Collection*

Prior to this, on August 25, Yunching Li (China), Yi, and I established Playing with Fire, a ca 450m, nine-pitch route (5.10-) on the south ridge of Seerdengpu. The route ends at a saddle on the ridge, probably 1,000m below the summit, and was completed with one bivouac during the descent.

DAVE ANDERSON, AAC

Joey Shan (5,178m), Jianifornia Dreaming. On October 11, Erik Harz, Felix Parham, and I reached the top of what we believe to be a previously unclimbed peak in the Changping Valley. Joey Shan, named for the incredible spirit of our friend Joey Hernandez, a Californian climber who passed away from cancer while we were on the mountain, is the first peak west of Bipeng Pass, on the north side of the upper Changping.

We'd traveled to China as part of Fred Beckey's expedition to attempt Celestial Peak, but snowy conditions led us further up the Changping, looking for dry rock. From a high camp we hiked up steep, grassy trails made by Himalayan blue sheep, puffing hard at the elevation, to reach a nice bivouac at ca 4,500m under a massive granite boulder below the west face.

Setting off in a cold, clear dawn, we gained the southwest ridge near a prominent gendarme, via the northwest flank. We then traversed onto the south face. From there we climbed directly to

[This page, top] Dave Anderson leading the southwest ridge of Dayantianwo. *Dave Anderson Collection*
[This page, bottom] Joey Shan from the southwest showing Jianifornia Dreaming. *Felix Parham*

rejoin the southwest ridge and followed it to the summit, a distinct perched block in a dramatically exposed location. It was 6 p.m., my altimeter read a little over 5,180m, and we had climbed 12 pitches of good alpine rock and snow in perfect weather. We descended to the north, walking down steep snow, and then made two rappels to return to our bivouac.

To our surprise the translation of California in Mandarin Chinese is Jianifornia, so we named the route Jianifornia Dreaming (450m, IV 5.9). During our three weeks in the Changping Valley, starting in early October, we experienced mostly cold, snowy weather. Although conditions for climbing dry rock appeared briefly, planning for snow or mixed routes would give more flexibility.

Our operator, Zhang Jiyue of Sichuan Earth Expeditions, did much to make our trip successful. Many thanks to the legendary Fred Beckey for organizing and funding the expedition. Fred's love for wild mountains, and his amazing determination over decades of alpinism, continue to inspire us.

NEIL KAUFFMAN, *AAC*

Daogou West, north ridge, first and second ascent details. The Daogou peaks (East, 5,466m; West, 5,422m) are steep, rocky mountains, the eastern flanks of which are accessed from the upper Changping Valley. The name comes from their location. Head north and then northwest into the upper Changping, then turn back southwest into a subsidiary valley: Daogou means "reverse valley."

The peak was first climbed in 2006 from the Shuangqiao Valley to the west. In 2008 (mentioned, with no detail, in AAJ 2011), Chen Hui, Gu Qizhu, and Pen Xiaobing made the second ascent via a new route up the northeast couloir and north ridge. Over five days in October 2013, Chen Hui, Pen Xiaobing, and Yang Xiufeng repeated this route, which can now be described. The approach couloir (scree and snow to 50°) gave about 930m of climbing above base camp at 4,350m, and Camp 2 was placed at the couloir's exit at 4,900m. Next day they climbed the 40–50° snow ridge/face above to Camp 3 at 5,100m, and the day after they climbed 55m along the crest (M3) to Camp 4 at the same altitude, then reconnoitered four more pitches, leaving a rope on the second. On the 12th they climbed a total of seven pitches on the final tower (5.9+ M4+) to reach the summit. Belay bolts were placed on some of these pitches (and at the head of the couloir). A further day was needed for the descent.

Supplied and translated by XIA ZHONGMING, *Germany*

Pomiu (a.k.a. Celestial Peak, 5,413m), southwest face and south-southwest ridge, Warm. In 2012 Chinese Chen Hui and Pan Xiaobing made a late-November ascent of Pomiu via a partial new line. On the 17th, using horses to carry equipment, they reached base camp southwest of the mountain at 4,100m. Next day they climbed through scree and grassy slopes, interrupted by one loose rock pitch of 5.10a, to reach Camp 1 at 4,442m, below the southwest face. Over the next four days they climbed about 14 pitches, up to 5.10, to the left of the route followed by three Chinese climbers in 2005 for the third ascent of the peak (*AAJ 2013*). The pair moved slowly due to Chen Hui leading every pitch of the route, descending, and then reascending with both rucksacks. Once on the south-southwest ridge, they followed the ridge to the summit in two more days. The ca 1,200m route (24 pitches, 5.10a) was named Warm.

Supplied and translated by XIA ZHONGMING, *Germany*

TIBET

NYANCHEN TANGLHA WEST

Peak 5,955m and Peak 6,192m. On September 14, Zhou Peng and I climbed Peak 5,955m, a summit among the small knot of peaks south of the main road that runs southwest from Yangbajain, along the south side of the Nyanchen Tanglha. The following day we climbed Peak 6,192m (29°51'21.73"N, 90°12'58.71"E), the highest mountain in this group. We accessed both peaks by walking up the long river valley running south from the road. We climbed the steep north face and west-northwest ridge of 6,192m, and the northwest ridge of 5,955m. 📷

LI SHUANG, *China*

HIMALAYA

Ice Tooth (6,200m), east ridge; Phola Gangchen (Molemenqing, 7,703m), east pillar attempt. My main project for the year was an expedition to Tibet in October with Miha Gasperin (doctor), Luka Krajnc, Tadej Kriselj, Nejc Marcic, Marko Prezelj, Luka Strazar, and Martin Zumer. There is an obvious unclimbed line on the south face of Phola Gangchen, and to me it looked perfect.

We established base camp in a beautiful setting at 5,000m by a lake. Our first ascent was on Ice Tooth (6,200m, a peak south of Nyanang Ri first climbed in 1983 by Tone Skarja and Andrej Stremfelj from the west). Luka Strazar, Nejc, Marko, Martin, and I climbed the east ridge, which was difficult rock at first but became easier when we reached mixed and snow climbing on the upper part of the route. We made one comfortable bivouac.

Only Marko and I were motivated to try the line on the south face of Phola Gangchen. The approach was complex, taking much time and energy. In the moraine, we had to roll large rocks out of the way to make our passage safe. Our next obstacle was an extremely broken glacier. Less than 100m below the plateau under the face, I realized that it would be too dangerous to continue. Marko had already sensed this but stayed silent, knowing I would not be satisfied if I didn't try.

[This page] The east ridge of Ice Tooth (6,200m). *Marko Prezelj*

[This page, bottom] The east side of Xixabangma, showing the only two routes attempted to date. (1) British attempt, 1987. After making the second ascent of (A) Pungpa Ri (7,486m) via the southeast face and south ridge, the British traversed below it and continued up the ridge toward (B) Xixabangma, before retreating at ca 7,650m. (2) The 2013 Slovenian attempt on (C) Phola Gangchen. *Lindsay Griffin*

Instead, we looked at the east face, which has steep rock and mixed terrain in the lower section, followed by beautiful snow arêtes. Marko and I decided to try this line, joined by Luka Strazar, Nejc, and Martin. On our first day we climbed sections of ice and steep mixed, with difficulties around M6. Next day we climbed steep snow ridges to a perfect tent site at 6,600m. However, on the following morning it started snowing heavily, and the trio that had joined us the day before decided to rappel.

Marko and I climbed one more pitch through increasing snowfall and wind, stopping at ca 6,800m. We returned to the bivouac and decided to wait for the storm to pass. The forecast promised only one day of storm with little snow, and we had enough food to sit this out. Half a meter of snow fell that night, and the next day was no better. By the following morning we knew we had to escape. Visibility was bad, and it proved difficult to find rappel anchors.

We eventually gained flat terrain and began breaking trail through chest-deep snow. Despite being exhausted, we were still in good spirits. After many hours of tough travel, light from the moon enabled us to see through a gap in the mist to the lake where our second camp was located. What looked like a two-hour mission from this point took almost six hours. We then spent another hour digging out the tent.

On a normal day it would have taken three and a half hours to get back to base camp from our lake camp. But it wasn't until midnight that we reached safe ground on top of the moraine, and we needed all the following day to return to base, where we waited for Luka Krajnc and Tadej, who were still breaking trail from the other side of the valley. They had attempted Eiger Peak (6,912m), climbing ca 600m until forced down.

As a team we started a difficult descent to Nyalam, leaving our equipment at base camp to be retrieved after the snow melted. 📷

LUKA LINDIC, *Slovenia*

Chomolhari Kang (7,034m, 7,054m GPS), north face. In May, Zhou Peng and I saw Chomolhari Kang (28°09.869'N, 90°10.951'E) for the first time. We were traveling from Pumajiangtang village to Kangma with the aim of getting a closer view of peaks on the Bhutan-Tibet border. We had no idea if there was a road leading south to Kangma, as none of the maps we found in shops or on the Internet showed one. But a local cattle herder assured us there was a passable road, though in some places barely visible, as it had not been used much in recent years. After 52km of bumpy travel, we reached the mountains.

In May the land becomes very soft during the warm day; the risk of getting a vehicle stuck is high. We decided to return in the autumn, and on September 26, after an acclimatization ascent in the Nyanchen Tanglha range, Yang Bo, Zhang Hao, Zhou Peng, and I reached the base of Chomolhari Kang, hoping to climb the mountain on skis.

We were lucky, as it proved possible to drive to 5,800m, where we set up base camp close to the snow line. The forecast predicted heavy snow for the 28th, so we decided to attempt the mountain in one day from camp. At 5:50 a.m. on September 27, Yang Bo, Zhou Peng, and I left the tents and took just 30 minutes to reach the snow line. We roped up in case of crevasses, though once the sun rose we could see the slope showed no sign of any.

After an exhausting climb we reached the top at 5:15 p.m. The total distance from base camp was 11.5km, and our GPS showed 7,054m. Although our ascent had been gentle in angle, we could tell that on the Bhutan side the mountain was precipitous. Despite constant sunshine, the temperature remained low all day. The descent was far more pleasant: We skied down to base camp in just two hours. 🖸

LI SHUANG, *China*

Sursun Ri (6,535m), first known ascent, via northeast ridge. After six weeks in base camp and one attempt at the British Route on the southwest face of Xixabangma (a.k.a. Shishapangma), the weather got worse, with a lot of fresh snow at altitude and a strong northerly wind. We could see a one-kilometer horizontal plume stretching from the summit of Xixabangma. There would be a high risk of windslab.

As an alternative, Sébastien Moatti and I looked at the northeast ridge of Sursun Ri (Triangle Peak in Tibetan; named by the 1982 British team), an unclimbed, shapely peak situated on the Nepalese border and obvious on the approach to base camp. With mostly snow slopes, it looked quite straightforward. Furthermore, after one week of bad weather at our homely base, eating far too many French fries and Snickers fritters, we needed to get some exercise and lose some weight.

After a windy night at our advanced base and a long crossing of the Nyanang Phu moraines, we reached the foot of the peak at 5,200m on October 8. We ascended goat terrain until the beginning of the snow ridge at 5,900m, where we bivouacked.

An early start was rewarded by a wonderful sunrise over the Himalaya. We walked up the snow ridge until the terrain became steeper, reaching the crux at around 6,400m. Two mixed pitches (around M4 with good protection) through a rock barrier gave nice climbing. Snow slopes and exposed ice flutes at 60-70° led to the final mushroom, which we turned on the Langtang side to reach the summit at 3 p.m. The overall standard of the route was about D, and we were able to regain our tent that night.

MAX BONNIOT, *GMHM, France*

[This page] The northeast ridge of Sursun Ri. The frontier ridge, rising left, leads toward Pemthang Karpo Ri (a.k.a. Dome Blanc, 6,830m). *Max Bonniot*

SEVEN SUMMITS

Completion of Triple Seven Summits. The Austrian Christian Stangl has become the first person to climb the three highest mountains on each of the seven continents. While many people now have climbed the so-called Seven Summits, only Stangl has—seemingly unequivocally—climbed each of the second highest as well as the third. Apart from Ojos del Salado, which he climbed in 1996, Stangl climbed all of these peaks from 2008–2013.

There has been debate in recent years on which peaks should rank as the second- and third-highest summits on several continents, particularly Australasia. Stangl measured his summit elevations by GPS, and his list, corroborated by the Asian authority Eberhard Jurgalski, from Germany, is as follows:

Second Seven Summits:
K2 (8,611m)
Ojos del Salado (6,893m)
Logan (5,959m)
Dykh tau (5,205m)
Batian (5,199m)
Tyree (4,852m)
Sumantri (4,870m)

Third Seven Summits:
Kangchenjunga (8,586m)
Pissis (6,795m)
Orizaba (5,636m)
Shkhara (5,193m)
Mawenzi (5,148m)
Shinn (4,660m)
Puncak Mandala (4,758m)

NEW ZEALAND

SOUTHERN ALPS

Mt. Burns, northwest ridge. Kieran Parsons and I made the first ascent of the northwest ridge of Mt. Burns in December. It's an enormous feature that dominates the head of the Landsborough Valley, a large but fairly isolated valley immediately southwest of Aoraki / Mt. Cook National Park. The ridge is made up of impressive slabs of overlapping schist, which we had expected to climb, but we found the majority of the rock could be avoided by snowfields on the north side. We spent two days approaching the base from the west coast via the Karangarua River, climbed the ridge on December 20, and then spent two nights in the hut at Baron Saddle waiting out a storm. On the fifth day we descended via the Mueller Glacier and exited to Mt. Cook Village—an extremely satisfying alpine journey through an awesome variety of terrain. Overall the climb was NZ 2+ (technical), V (commitment). 🔍 📷

ROB FROST, *New Zealand*

DARRAN MOUNTAINS

Mt. Tutoko, west face. Guy McKinnon soloed the first ascent of the west face of Mt. Tutoko (ca 2,723m), the highest peak of the Darran Mountains, near the southern tip of the south island. The ca 1,900m face had only one recorded attempt, in 1974, when three climbers reached the upper headwall before retreating.

McKinnon bivouacked at the base of the west face and then climbed the wall in 8.5 hours on July 11, following ice and snow up a gully system. He bivouacked again near the summit and then attempted to descend the northwest ridge (the 1924 first-ascent route on Tutoko). Cliffed out near the bottom, he was forced to reclimb much of the ridge in order to descend the north face and ultimately walk out the Tutoko Valley, reaching the road 21 hours after beginning his descent. McKinnon described "utterly superb" conditions on the climb, with "nothing overly hard, just a lot of it." He graded the route VI 4+, but noted that if the Darrans' commitment grading were open-ended, the climb would have been given VII.

Information supplied by GUY McKINNON, *New Zealand*

[This page] The 1,900m west face of Tutoko and first-ascent line. The photo is from the winter of 2011. *Guy McKinnon*

Marian Peak, south face, Maid Marian. In early March, Ben Dare and Daniel Joll made the first complete ascent of the south face of Marian Peak (1,000m, 21 A2). The two did the route in a 28-hour round trip from the Homer Hut, and they said the climbing was excellent and likely would go free at New Zealand 23.

Information from The Climber, New Zealand

MALAYSIA

TIOMAN ISLAND

Nenek Semukut, Damai Sentosa. In April the international team of Stephanie Bodet and Arnaud Petit (France), Yong Liu (China), and I, with help from local Tam Khairudin Haja, climbed a new route on the south tower of Nenek Semukut (a.k.a., the Dragon Horns or Nekek Semukut). Our line is to the right of Batu Naga (Rivera-Wright, 2011), following well-featured slabs on the right side of the southwest face. Damai Sentosa ("In the Name of Peace") is graded 6c+ (6b+ obl.), with 280m of rock climbing and ca 150m of steep jungle climbing. We opened the route ground-up, and it is mostly bolted, with only a few cams needed. On May 4, together with Tam Khairudin, I redpointed the line.

Nenek Semukut is among the highest rock faces in Southeast Asia. As of early 2014 there were seven routes. [*The author has prepared three photos showing all route lines on the Dragon Horns, along with very helpful information on climbing in the area, all of which can be found at the AAJ website.*] 📷 🔍

DAVID KASZLIKOWSKI, *Poland*

[This page, left] The horns of Nenek Semukut, about an hour's walk above the village of Mukut. *David Kaszlikowski* **[This page, right]** Yong Liu leads the fourth pitch (6c+) of Damai Sentosa. *David Kaszlikowski*

BOOK REVIEWS

Note: Some of these reviews have been edited for length. The full-length articles are available to read at the AAJ website: publications.americanalpineclub.org.

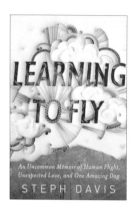

Learning to Fly: An Uncommon Memoir of Human Flight, Unexpected Love, and One Amazing Dog. Steph Davis. Simon & Schuster, 2013. 304 pages. Hardcover. $24.99.

Steph Davis' second book picks up shortly after the release of her first, *High Infatuation: A Climber's Guide to Love and Gravity*, in which readers move through her childhood, her introduction to adventure sports, and some of her more notable climbing feats (a one-day ascent of Torre Egger and free-climbing Salathé Wall, among others).

In *Learning To Fly*, we meet Davis as she leaves for a countrywide tour to promote her first book. She is managing the fallout from what she refers to as "the incident": her then-husband Dean Potter's controversial 2006 ascent of Delicate Arch in the Utah desert, which led to a media uproar, a heated community-wide discussion, and both Potter and Davis being dropped by their primary sponsors. By page 13, she writes that she "was without a marriage, without a paycheck, and pretty much without a career. In a life defined by risk and uncertainty, almost all of my anchors were gone."

So Davis did what the rest of us wish we could do when we get fed up with climbing: She took her dog, Fletch, and her pickup truck to Colorado and spent a summer learning to skydive. Living on savings, she couch-surfs near the drop zone, jumps out of airplanes as often as possible, and finds a new life philosophy: "When death holds no more fear and when you've lost the things most precious to you, there's nothing more to be afraid of." By the end of summer she has grown to love the feeling of falling, come to terms with her failed marriage, and found her way back to climbing with a free-solo of the Diamond on Longs Peak.

By the time Davis and Fletch make their way home to Moab, Davis is at peace. There are setbacks, of course—a broken pelvis, challenging interactions with her ex-husband, the painful aging of her sweet pooch—but her story perks up when she meets Mario Richard, a local pilot and experienced BASE jumper. It's no surprise to readers when she writes, "I've never questioned emotion. I've lived my life for it. It wasn't hard to see that over the last several months, I'd been falling in love as much as I'd been falling into air." Davis and Richard marry in Castle Valley, Utah, and celebrate their union with a wedding-day BASE jump.

Davis' account is honest and vulnerable, and it hints at both the boldness and the single-minded self-assurance that is required from any professional athlete. I was consistently inspired by Davis' focus on reaching her dreams, and loved reading about the inner workings of a badass female athlete. However, my favorite pages were the ones in which Davis let down her guard. Case in point:

Despite being a little over-saturated with dog references, I cried like a baby when Fletch died.

In August 2013, shortly after the release of *Learning To Fly*, Mario Richard died while BASE jumping in Italy with Davis. He was 47. Davis had successfully made the same jump just a few minutes before. I was dumbstruck when I heard the news; Davis and Richard seemed so careful, so full of life. After reading *Learning To Fly*, the parts of their story that I will remember most are Davis' closing words, which describe the feeling of a jump: "The world spread around in all directions, vast with possibility. I stretched my wings, floating up slightly, trading speed for buoyancy as I savored the sensations of flight, seeing, hearing, feeling.... I watched it dispassionately, eaglelike, free now of questions. High up in the sky, it was so easy to see. The green meadow lay out ahead, far beyond the cold mountain. I plunged down, tucked my wings, and flew."

CHAROLETTE AUSTIN

Rock, Paper, Fire: The Best of Mountain and Wilderness Writing. Marni Jackson and Tony Whittome, editors. Banff Centre Press, 2013. 295 pages. Paperback. $21.95.

On the face of it, an anthology of pieces written by students in any kind of writers' workshop sounds like a really bad idea. But in the Banff Centre's Mountain and Wilderness Writing Program, thanks to the inspired leadership of editor/teachers Marni Jackson and Tony Whittome, minor miracles seem to be wrought annually. *Rock, Paper, Fire*, a collection of pieces written by students in the program, bears witness to this conflagration.

Granted, some of the contributors to Rock, Paper, Fire—including Bernadette McDonald, Freddie Wilkinson, Katie Ives, and Maria Coffey—were pretty experienced writers even before they signed up for the Banff program. But what makes the anthology work, I think, is that all the aspirants are wilderness junkies, some of them at the cutting edge of climbing, sea kayaking, sailing, or skiing. The fervor that animates their three weeks together, I suspect, owes much to the fact that as they critique each other's projects, they're engaging in the endless colloquy that lies at the heart of adventure. How did we get into this mess? How are we going to get out of it? Why do we keep doing it, knowing we could die? Why is there nothing else in life that compares?

By now, in my more jaded moods, I like to think I've heard and dismissed all the specious rationalizations for why we continue to tiptoe on the edge of disaster as we play at being, in Lionel Terray's pithy phrase, "conquerors of the useless." But in *Rock, Paper, Fire*, I learned something new on every other page. From McDonald's rueful meditation on Tomaz Humar's all-but-inevitable pilgrimage toward death on a lonely Himalayan ledge. From Steve Swenson's account of a tragedy on Denali that he wonders to this day whether he could have prevented. From Jon Turk's rolling the dice under the sea ice closing in on Ellesmere Island. From Niall Grimes' linkage of grief over his mother's death to the joyful rediscovery of his childhood crags. From Don Gillmor's evocation of the bond between downhill speed on skis and the downward trajectory of aging. From Helen Mort's rekindling in poetry of the transcendent climbs of Dorothy Pilley and Alison Hargreaves.

Pick up a copy. You'll be surprised—and moved.

DAVID ROBERTS

THE ALCHEMY OF ACTION
DOUG ROBINSON

Why do people climb mountains?
Because it gets us high.
But adrenaline junkies we are not,
and beta-endorphin isn't behind runner's high either.
The surprising answer reveals natural psychedelic transformations
at work deep in the brains of adventure athletes.

The Alchemy of Action. Doug Robinson. Moving Over Stone, 2013. 188 pages. Paperback. $24.

First, full disclosure: Doug Robinson is an old and good friend. I am a fan of his writing in general and am included in The Alchemy of Action as both friend and example/illustration of its premise.

This is a beautifully written, deeply researched, insightful, and groundbreaking contribution to human understanding (and consciousness). It is a great read about climbing, among many other human activities, but it is bigger than that in the same way contemplation from the summit encompasses more than summit-inspired chest thumping. Because Doug is a climber he poses this question and answer on the front cover:

"Why do people climb mountains?"

"Because it gets us high."

Well, yes, but it's not adrenaline and it's not just climbing. On the first page of the introduction Doug quotes William Burroughs: "Buddha? A notorious metabolic junky…. Makes his own, you dig? So Buddha says, 'I'll metabolize my own junk…. I'll metabolize a speedball and make with the Fire Sermon.'" While some (not all) devoted, traditional Buddhists might (with good reason) take issue with Burroughs' inserting speedballs into the Eightfold Noble Path, *The Alchemy of Action* explores such improbable connections and many more. Doug comments, "Buddha's own speedball is a mixture, a blend, a hormonal cocktail arising from the brain blender when it's activated by a lot of sweat and a bit of fear."

A lot of sweat and a bit of fear is an apt description of climbing as well as the alchemy of action. This book is for climbers, but it also explores such diverse activities as running, hiking (long distance as well as day treks), skiing in the backcountry, and skiing for speed, and it delves into states of mind as familiar and diverse as depression, euphoria, catatonic exhaustion, and rapture. *The Alchemy of Action* is a well-placed step along the path to answering the question every climber has posed to himself or herself, and with which Warren Harding used to greet me nearly every time we met: "Have you figured out yet why we keep doing this?"

Well, yes, because it gets us high. But it's not exactly the first kind of high that comes to mind. You can't buy it on the street. To paraphrase Burroughs' description of Buddha, we metabolize our own junk within ourselves with nothing more than a balanced mixture of sweat and fear. That oversimplifies the more complicated reality contained in a definition of "metabolism: n. 1. The chemical processes occurring within a living cell or organism that are necessary for the maintenance of life. In metabolism some substances are broken down to yield energy for vital processes while other substances, necessary for life, are synthesized."

Energy for vital processes necessary for life is a topic worth understanding by every climber, and Robinson has expended an enormous quantity (and quality) of his own energy to help us with that effort.

One of my favorite sections of the book involves, of all people, Roger Bannister. It begins, "A funny thing happened on the way to the four-minute mile. In the spring of 1954 Roger Bannister was in the best shape of his life, running so well. But he had stalled out. He was stale, maybe overtrained…. His body was bored and his mind had gone flat." He and his training buddy Chris Brasher needed a change, so they went to Scotland for four days of climbing. It was a risk, and Brasher even took a leader fall, but they returned to their training refreshed in mind and spirit, and a few weeks later Bannister ran the first sub-four-minute mile, 3:59.4 on May 6, 1954. Robinson writes, "Roger Bannister's climbing interlude...was the perfect thing, just the right antidote to padding around and around. Dizzyingly around. An endless, droning slave to the inside track. Which actually wasn't quite dizzying enough; only driving him deeper into his own rut. So it became necessary, essential even, to revert to wildness to get the juices flowing again." Metabolically speaking.

Sixty years later Bannister wrote, "The urge to struggle lies latent in everyone. The more restrictive our society and work become, the more necessary it will be to find some outlet for this craving for freedom....We run, not because we think it is doing us good, but because we enjoy it and cannot help ourselves." With *The Alchemy of Action*, Doug Robinson helps us understand that enjoyment and how we can help ourselves. Thanks, Doug.

DICK DORWORTH

Everest–The First Ascent: How a Champion of Science Helped to Conquer the Mountain. Harriet Pugh Stuckey
Lyons Press, 2013. 424 pages. Hardcover. $26.95.

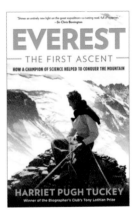

This superb, wonderfully researched, and readable book does several impossible things impossibly well. It tells the story of the '53 British Everest expedition again and makes it new. It brings into plain sight a member of that expedition previously erased—like a liquidated member of Stalin's central committee reappearing in a photograph. It portrays that man, an eccentric English scientist named Griffith Pugh, as the essential figure in high-altitude physiology in the 20th century. The way we climb now—the clothes we wear, the food we eat, the fluids we drink, how we acclimatize—comes from Pugh's meticulous in situ experiments.

Pugh was an expert skier selected for the 1936 British Olympic team. A medical officer in WWII, he trained mountain troops and made observations about fitness and adaptation to altitude. Like other British mountaineers of his era he was stoic, but unlike others he did not think that suffering was ennobling, especially not the suffering of men ill-trained and poorly clothed and fed.

One of Pugh's insights had to do with the need to remain hydrated at altitude. Previously, in the Mallory days and the slightly later Shipton-Tilman era, copious fluid drinking was considered bad form, a moral weakness perhaps, but Pugh proved experimentally that low fluid intake led to fatigue and a host of cascading physical anomalies at altitude. In the face of sneering opposition he quietly made his case, and climbers on Everest became avid brewers of tea. One proof is that Ed Hillary, previously one who had called the water-drinkers sissies, arrived at the summit and promptly urinated on it.

Everest–The First Ascent is a misnomer. That title seems calculated to rope in those of us who are not yet quite stuffed full of Chomolungma lore, who will throw dollars at any handsome (and this book is very handsome) work promising a few happy hours mulling over once again the pluck of the early expeditions with men who climbed to 28,000 feet wearing sport coats and thin leather boots. What this book is, rather, is a brilliant biography of a historic field scientist, one who did essential work in high-altitude medicine and addressed other fascinating problems in exercise physiology.

Interestingly enough the author is Pugh's daughter. Consumed with anger at her often absent, often hurtful father, anger which turned for reasons of self-preservation to bleak indifference, she has turned the immense energy of that suppression into an act of beautiful resurrection. We have as a result a book so brimming with truth about certain dimly understood famous personalities (Hillary is one; John Hunt, leader of the expedition, is another) that serious scholarship about the conquest of the 8,000-meter peaks, how it was actually done, by what type of people, can be said to have started anew, here, in these pages.

ROBERT ROPER

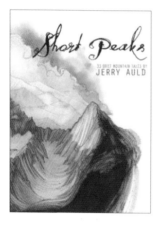

Short Peaks: 33 Brief Mountain Tales. Jerry Auld. Imaginary Mountain Surveyors, 2013. 280 pages. Paperback. CAN $25.

Climbing fiction has always been problematic, perilously close to an oxymoron. During the bad old days in Camp 4 we used to read aloud from James Ramsey Ullman's trite stuff such as *And Not to Yield*, intoning his purple prose into the firelight and howling with derision. If that guy ever had any feel for the reality of climbing, it had long since slipped beneath the cushion of some overstuffed chair. I can only recall two pieces with respect: Jeff Long's moody saga of the Valley, *Angels of Light*, and James Salter's exploration of the life of Gary Hemming, *Solo Faces*. But Salter was a "real" writer, with the respect of the larger literary world, not just a climber. Fiction, apparently, was for better writers than climbing could muster.

So it was with a certain trepidation that I accepted a chance to review the stories in Jerry Auld's *Short Peaks*. I've never been that fond of plot. Boy meets girl. Boy acts like a dick; girl goes on the rag. Whatever. So maybe it's just me, but when Jerry Auld evokes the tension in climbers on a ledge "with all of them tied in, pressed together like sticks of dynamite" it just lights my fuse.

One favorite story, and not such a short one, revolves around the mystery of George Mallory. I won't spoil the twists of the tale, but read "Proof." I got riveted when "The old man's voice is like the rumble of stones under ice." I came back for a second serving, steeping again in that voice, coming from "a wheelchair under a pile of blankets." I've heard out old men before. Norman Clyde for one, and his tales were way worth it. This guy, spun out of Jerry Auld's imagination, had been on the 1924 Everest expedition, and lingering out of that trip is climbing's hoariest mystery. Now we have an ice axe and a body, both discovered high on the summit ridge. But still no camera, Mallory's "pocket Kodak." Still no proof. So we are all set up to hang on the words coming from this gravelly voice on the veranda of an old soldier's home in the Darjeeling foothills.

This is what fiction is for, really: to carry us a ways beyond what we know. Could be a little, could be a lot. Loosened, as by the second beer, to wander beyond the bounds of proof. I haven't finished these short "peeks." But I hear the editor knocking, again, so I'll just quickly say: "Read this, I think you'll like it.'" I'm happy to say that rumors of the death of climbing fiction have been greatly exaggerated.

DOUG ROBINSON

The Seventymile Kid: The Lost Legacy of Harry Karstens and the First Ascent of Mount McKinley. Tom Walker. Mountaineers Books, 2013. 304 pages. Paperback. $19.95.

Tom Walker's *The Seventymile Kid* is an antidote to one of the least-read books from the highest peak on North America: Archdeacon Hudson Stuck's The Ascent of Denali. "The preacher," as his partner Harry Karstens referred to him, wrote in stilted and lofty language, deterring all but the most determined Denali aficionados or historians. Until Walker's skillfully researched book, a dearth of information had elevated the Archdeacon as a visionary leader. This quirk of history passed over the pivotal role played by the laconic Harry Karstens in the first ascent of Denali.

Walker's "just the facts" biography of the forgotten Harry Karstens introduces his early mining and mushing days, including deeds on the Seventymile River in eastern Alaska, until the narrative moves, with Karstens, to his work around "the Great Ice Mountain." Through Walker's substantive mining of forgotten letters and diaries, the climbs preceding the 1913 first ascent are put in a unique Alaskan light.

At times, the author uses vernacular such as climbers "conquering a ridge." Or he mistakenly describes the Harper Icefall as "unclimbable except by technical experts," not knowing that its frequent and thunderous collapses would turn the best technicians to jelly.

Still, Walker gets it mostly right and uncovers a lot of forgotten gold. Nuances of the early climbs—detailing the sponsors and personalities—are newly revealed, despite no shortage of books on the pioneers. We learn that the lordly Stuck proved a burden to his three partners, who were forced to carry his weight, cook for him, and put up with his sing-alongs. While Stuck confessed to his diary about having teammates "who will save me all they can," Karstens alternately blew up at the English preacher or told him "to quit his whining.... We were out roughing it, not at a first class hotel. He promised to do better but forgot about it the next day."

To set the record straight, "the Archdeacon of the Yukon" (his self-anointed honorific) was an ambitious, prickly, yet generous soul. As recorded in Walker's book (after Harry Karstens is thoroughly introduced), Stuck inoculated, educated, and defended the natives of Alaska and the Yukon. Unlike most missionaries of the day, Stuck foresaw the dangers of assimilation and fought to preserve indigenous customs and language. He also became an outspoken champion for restoring the mountain's original name, Denali.

When he first began visiting remote Alaskan villages, being guided on dogsled and riverboat trips, the mountain proved an irresistible beacon to the Archdeacon. While Stuck had once been guided up Mt. Rainier, and was a hardy, well-educated soul, he didn't have the resources or the stamina to climb the mountain on his own. So Stuck shrewdly enlisted the legendary Seventymile Kid as both leader and guide.

Walker definitively shows that Denali would not have been climbed in 1913 without Karstens. With no climbing experience, the Seventymile Kid kept everyone alive, found the route, avoided (or, strangely enough, built bridges over) crevasses, and chopped miles of steps. Rather than castigating the petulant Stuck, Tom Walker carefully analyzes the seldom-seen diaries and letters, then brings the neglected Harry Karstens to life, showing a pioneer ascent rent by personality conflicts.

JONATHAN WATERMAN

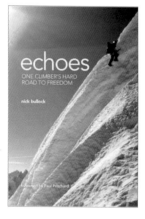

Echoes: One Climber's Hard Road to Freedom. Nick Bullock.
Vertebrate Publishing (U.K.), 2013. 256 pages. Hardcover. £20.

Nick Bullock's new book *Echoes* opens with a violent revenge attack inside a prison, in which one prisoner beats another's head open with a steel weight. The scene is written in a high adrenaline flashing lights sirens blood everywhere style that gets your attention and leaves you freaked out.

During his prison career Nick Bullock figures out that what he really wants to do is to climb. The story that evolves is the trajectory of a very keen climber who is perpetually torn by dual voices, one telling him to follow his passions (be a climbing bum), the other telling him to play it safe (keep your job).

Nick's insights into criminals and the system that locks them up are his strong suit. We get the feeling that prison is defining the author a bit too much, as well. When he is on the Grandes Jorasses in winter he describes ice climbing like this: "Crash, another placement. Crash. I saw my stave breaking bone. Crash. One hit is self-defense, the second is assault."

Nick is a fitness fanatic, and he becomes a trainer inside the walls of the prison, helping the incarcerated blow off steam rather than one another's heads. As he tries harder climbs—rock, ice, alpine—he falls. A lot. In fact, as I read this book it struck me that the only climbing writer I know who has written as much about falling off things is me. Like the prison violence, the parts about falling are vivid. I don't want to be a spoiler, but when I read the part about him trying the necky sea-cliff classic The Bells!, my palms sweated as I thought, "Oh, no, please no, please don't..." Other journeys get him to the Himalaya, where he has epics good enough that they don't need summits. A big climb on Jirishanca in the Andes demands frightening commitment.

The writing isn't cute or funny. He's sometimes sweepingly opinionated. But there is drollery, understatement, and naughtiness. Like when he overtakes, solo, two climbers on an ice route in Scotland: Nick seems to be off-route, and the pair are not at all happy when Nick's crampons cut out from the ice above their heads, or at the bombardment he gives them as he smashes with his picks. The punch line comes at chapter end, when Nick is home and he gets a phone call. The ensuing conversation is a near-perfect mime of the irascible Ken Wilson spitting out to Nick, and then hanging up, that he's just (unwittingly) stolen a new route out from under those same two lads.

Only after I read the last chapter did I see the author's overall design. This is a story about getting trapped and breaking free. In between, there is climbing. It works, and it invites more from Nick Bullock.

GREG CHILD

Climbing Fitz Roy, 1968: Reflections on the Lost Photos of the Third Ascent. Yvon Chouinard,
Dick Dorworth, Chris Jones, Lito Tejada-Flores, Doug Tompkins. Patagonia Books, 2013. 144
pages. Hardcover. $35.

The iconic 1968 climb is reflected on here, 45 years after the fact, by all its luminary principals except Chouinard (who is behind the scenes as publisher). The climb is deservedly well-known as inspiration for Chouinard's business ventures, Tejada-Flores' film (*Fitzroy Patagonia: Mountain of Storms*), and for embodying Chouinard's prophetic (and oft-cited) statement from his essay "Modern Yosemite Climbing" (AAJ 1963): "Yosemite Valley will, in the near future, be the training ground for a new generation of super alpinists who will venture forth to the high mountains of the world to do the most esthetic and difficult walls on the face of the earth." It was also, of course, one hell of an adventure.

The photos, lost by Jones in a 1996 wildfire, were found years later by Dorworth, who had copies stored in various caches. The book has the feel of an archival family document authenticating the stuff of legend. The photographs have been lovingly restored, but are clearly "historic." Though the essays are necessarily reflective, i.e. backward-gazing, they are fresh and interesting, which should not be surprising considering the accomplishments of this rare assemblage of characters.

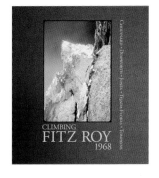

Two takeaways here: What would you most hate to lose in a wildfire? Back it up! And, don't forget to have your own "trip of a lifetime." This is a beautiful and essential artifact.

DAVID STEVENSON

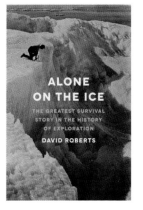

Alone on the Ice: The Greatest Survival Story in the History of Exploration. David Roberts. W. W. Norton, 2013. 368 pages. Hardcover/paperback. $27.95/$16.95.

Douglas Mawson's 1911–13 Antarctic journey was riddled with horrific crevasse falls, near starvation, polar-madness, and disheartening sled dog meals. No surprise then that *Alone on the Ice* opens like a thriller. But as told by David Roberts, this bio-adventure is both compelling and scholarly.

In the opening "Forgotten By God" chapter, Roberts explains why anyone steeped in more famous explorers' deeds should read this story: "Since the second decade of the twentieth century, Mawson has lurked in the shadow of his contemporaries Scott, Shackleton, and the great Norwegian polar explorer Roald Amundsen. In part this is because he was Australian." More importantly, Roberts explains, Mawson had no ambitions for the pole and was driven to "explore land that had never before been seen by human eyes."

For those readers already familiar with the popular (yet, according to Roberts, "vastly oversimplified") 1977 book *Mawson's Will*, this epic was ready-made for Roberts' keen character analysis. Mawson is revealed through the author's generous portrait, and even more profoundly from Mawson's diary, which Roberts calls "a telegraphic blueprint of exhaustion and grim pragmatism." Here, to rival anything Scott of the Antarctic wrote while going down in flames, Mawson also thought he was penning his last words: "This is terrible. I don't mind for myself, but it is for Paquita [his fiancé] and for all the others connected with the expedition that I feel so deeply and sinfully."

Still, despite the deaths of two partners, there's little morbidity and nothing saccharine about the narrative. In classic form, Roberts employs his mathematically precise bullshit detector, ferreting out various personality quirks, including the many soiled-pants-type nuances of an expedition member's insanity; the ongoing tension with another teammate who can't get back to college to resume his Rhodes scholarship; the "choleric," "fulminating," "gloomy," (27 years young) "Old Man" Captain Davis; or the widow Kathleen Scott's libidinousness and speculated attempt to bed Mawson. All of which, should be noted, make it a page-turner of fully fleshed-out character portraits. Thanks to scores of letters, memoirs, and diaries, Roberts quotes directly from the explorers, often with haunting immediacy.

Photo-rich, nuanced, and impeccably researched, *Alone on the Ice* showcases David Roberts' deft investigatory style. His re-creation of the Mawson saga is without peer—among one of the greatest survival stories in the history of exploration.

JONATHAN WATERMAN

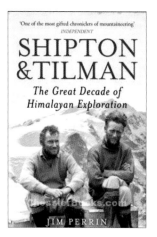

Shipton & Tilman: The Great Decade of Himalayan Exploration. Jim Perrin. Hutchinson, 2013. 416 pages. Black-and-white photos. Hardcover. £25.

Perhaps the most celebrated of all mountaineering partnerships, and certainly among the most productive in mountaineering accomplishment, was that of Eric Shipton and Bill Tilman. In Perrin's biography these two subjects emerge as very different men who, if it were not for the climbing bond, would probably never have met or become friends. The two Englishmen met, improbably, in Africa in the late 1920s. Shipton, nine years Tilman's junior, was already an experienced climber thanks to several seasons in the Alps. Tilman was a novice at climbing, but had a formative experience of a different sort, shipping out to France in 1915 and being wounded and decorated for bravery.

Shipton and Tilman shared two essential characteristics. One was a preference for small, lightweight expeditions rather than the huge siege campaigns that were then the fashion in Himalayan mountaineering. The second was that they were both gifted writers, and together left a legacy of some of the best expeditionary mountaineering accounts ever written.

An accomplished climber in his own right, and one of Britain's best known mountain and travel writers, Perrin is well qualified to write this account of Shipton and Tilman's lives and achievements—particularly since he befriended Tilman in that climber's last years. Through a close reading of the expedition accounts, private correspondence, and Shipton's unpublished notebooks, Perrin traces the growing bonds between the two men. In their African climbs, Shipton was the expert, Tilman the novice. By the time they explored the Nanda Devi sanctuary, they were equals: "There is a growing mutual trust and reliance here, a recognition of pooled perceptions and shared responsibility."

Perrin's biography has many virtues, but it also has limitations. He is a self-indulgent writer, with a penchant for irritable and sometimes bizarre asides. (He obviously has a strong dislike for George Leigh Mallory and for Wade Davis, author of a recent history of early Everest expeditions—neither of which he bothers to explain.) Is Perrin's biography worth reading? Absolutely. Is Perrin absolutely objective and reliable? Given his penchant for curmudgeonly license, unfortunately not.

MARICE ISSERMAN

The Summits of Modern Man: Mountaineering after the Enlightenment. Peter H. Hansen. *Harvard University Press, 2013. 392 pages. 24 halftones. Hardcover. $35.*

Climbing has recently attracted increasing attention from major university presses. This is Harvard's second book (after Taylor's *Pilgrims of the Vertical*), and Yale published Isserman and Weaver's *Fallen Giants*. Peter Hansen's book is the most academic and wide-ranging. "Mountain climbing did not emerge as the expression of a preexisting condition known as 'modernity,' but rather was one of the practices that constructed and redefined modernities during debates over who was first." This sentence gives the tone of this ambitious, fascinating, but often difficult book.

This is a work of cultural history. Its vocabulary is often that of contemporary theory. Thus references to Walter Benjamin, Foucault, and "the Baudelairean aesthetic of modernity." Hansen is never pompous, but he is not always easy. His main argument is that mountaineering and the Enlightenment emerged together. Climbing was part of a broad movement toward individualization and secularization. As Alpine dragons were dispelled, "conquest" became a popular word in Alpinism.

Hansen has done prodigious research over a long period, some in foreign languages including Chinese (with some assistance). The result is rich and challenging. Anyone interested in the origins and cultural significance of mountaineering should read this one.

STEVEN JERVIS

Northern Exposures: An Adventuring Career in Stories and Images. Jonathan Waterman. *University of Alaska Press, 2013. 250 pages. Paperback. $30.*

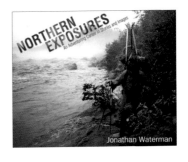

Waterman's 12th book encapsulates a rich body of work from a climber and explorer enamored with the northern regions. "[Alaska] is a nondenominational temple built for everyone," he posits. The 23 stories and 99 color photos will serve as a point of reference for some, a motivational guide for others, and a how-to guide for many. But for Waterman, they are an attempt to shake those of us still blind to our planet's changing face from our stupor. "It amazes me that most adventure writers…stick to their narratives of adventure mastery and leave the politics to the nature writers and environmentalists," Waterman laments.

Many of the pre-published stories simply capture Waterman's fascination with the North: an encounter with a curious polar bear, a tedious climb up Mt. Logan's west ridge, a quiet kayak across calm waters. But at the root of the work remains an urge to action. Waterman says his book might "serve as a template for forging a career in the outdoors." As one such person attempting to do just that, I will reinforce the idea that this template comes with an important caveat: to make a living in the outdoors is to fight for its preservation. One cannot consciently walk through wild places, writing about and photographing their splendor, without choosing to speak for them.

SHEY KIESTER

IN MEMORIAM

EDITED BY DAVID WILKES

Note: Many of these articles have been edited for length. The full-length tributes are available to read at the AAJ website: publications.americanalpineclub.org.

DOUG ABROMEIT, 1948–2013

Doug Abromeit, 65, the retired director of the Forest Service National Avalanche Center, died suddenly from an apparent undiagnosed heart condition while mountain biking with friends last spring.

Doug grew up on a family homestead on Lake Pend Oreille near Sandpoint, Idaho, where he spent his time in the woods and on the water, hiking, hunting, picking berries, and fishing. He graduated from the University of Idaho in Moscow with a degree in education. Doug and his wife and lifetime soul mate, Janet, worked as teachers in Nuiqsut, a traditional whaling village on Alaska's North Slope. He also worked as a ski patroller and smoke jumper before he landed a job as a Forest Service snow ranger at Alta, Utah. That's where I first met him, in the fall of 1986. As with a friendly golden retriever in a city park, everyone always seemed to gather around him—a quality that served him well in his long career in the avalanche business.

In his early days as a snow ranger, Doug noticed the disarray of the program that used military weapons for avalanche control, and he dove in and started organizing a fractured community of ski areas, highway forecasters, and U.S. Army personnel. Doug, John Hoagland, and I joined forces to create the Forest Service National Center of Excellence for Avalanches, which eventually became the Forest Service National Avalanche Center. Doug often described it as being a "program with a big name and a very small staff," as he was the only employee until the prominent avalanche scientist Karl Birkeland joined him 12 years ago.

Doug was a longtime instructor at the National Avalanche School, and he produced the educational video *Think Like an Avalanche*. He also represented the avalanche community and the Forest Service on countless national committees and organizations.

Doug lived his 65 years to the fullest, always fit and healthy and an avid backcountry skier, climber, and mountain biker. Although he accomplished a lot, he seldom let his work interfere with his enjoyment of life.

BRUCE TREMPER

STANLEY W. BOUCHER, 1927– 2013

Stanley Wayne Boucher passed away on September 30, 2013. He was born and raised in Colorado Springs, and he graduated with honors from Colorado College, where he majored in English and history. Drafted into the Army during the Korean conflict, he worked as a social work technician in an experimental psychiatric unit serving all of the Eighth Army north of Seoul. He subsequently made a career as a psychiatric social worker, ending up as the Director of Mental Health Continuing Education for the Western Interstate Commission for Higher Education.

He maintained a lifelong interest in mountains, especially those in Colorado. He was a life member of both the Colorado Mountain Club and the American Alpine Club, joining the latter in 1952. He frequently led hiking, climbing, and cross-country ski trips for the Boulder Group of the Colorado Mountain Club. Contributions to the Stanley Boucher Memorial Fund, American Alpine Club, 710 10th Golden, CO, 80401, will support the digitization and online accessibility of Stanley's unpublished mountaineering manuscript, *The World at Our Feet*.

VIRGINIA BOUCHER

JOHN EWBANK, 1948–2013

John Ewbank, legend of Australian rock climbing, died in New York on December 2, 2013. Few other climbers could lay claim to doing the first ascent of the hardest route on a continent, inventing the system by which it was graded, and then seeing that grading system be adopted in three countries and recognized worldwide.

Born in England in 1948, Ewbank learned to climb in Yorkshire before emigrating to Australia as a teenager. The gray and orange sandstone escarpments of the Blue Mountains quickly became his spiritual home, as well as the center of his legacy to Australian climbing.

The young English lad paired up with the best climbers of the day and set about establishing dozens of hard new free climbs. A trip back to England greatly influenced him and, much to the consternation of the old guard, he became obsessed with training and using newfangled chocks and nuts as protection. Ewbank developed his own early chocks, known as Crackers. He wrote articles promoting the use of natural protection, confronted those who still used pitons, and railed against excessive bolting.

Ewbank not only pushed grades far higher than

they had ever been but also rewrote the grading system, scrapping the convoluted British system used in Australia at the time. The open-ended Ewbank Grading System was introduced in his 1967 guidebook, *Rock Climbs in the Blue Mountains*, and was immediately adopted throughout the continent. It is now also used in New Zealand and South Africa. Ewbank gradually retired from climbing during the early 1970s and eventually moved to New York to pursue a career as a singer and songwriter. His unique character will be sadly missed.

GLENN SHORT

ARTUR HAJZER, 1962–2013

Artur Hajzer, one of Poland's best high-altitude climbers from the "golden age," was killed while retreating from Gasherbrum I on July 7, 2013. Born on June 28, 1962, in the Silesia region of Poland, Artur graduated from the University of Katowice with a degree in cultural studies. His interests in music, history, and art remained important throughout his life. He started climbing as a boy and soon progressed to increasingly difficult routes in the Tatras and the Alps, in both summer and winter.

His Himalayan adventures began at the age of 20, with expeditions to the Rolwaling Himal, to the Hindu Kush, and to the south face of Lhotse. Although the Lhotse expedition was unsuccessful, it was the beginning of his climbing partnership with Jerzy Kukuczka. Together they did the first winter ascent of Annapurna in 1987, a new route up the northeast face of Manaslu, and a new route on the east ridge of Shishapangma. Artur climbed seven 8,000-meter peaks and attempted the south face of Lhotse three times, reaching 8,300 meters on the formidable face.

When Kukuczka was killed on Lhotse's south face, Artur stopped climbing for 15 years. Instead, he went into the outdoor equipment business with Janusz Majer. But in 2010 he launched an undertaking that would occupy the rest of his life: the Polish Winter Himalayan Mountaineering Project 2010–2015. He nurtured the cadre of keen Polish alpinists who succeeded on Gasherbrum I and Broad Peak. It was common knowledge among the Polish climbing community that Artur's dream was to lead a team to the summit of K2 in winter. Now it will be up to someone else to fulfill that dream in his memory.

BERNADETTE MCDONALD

POP HOLLANDSWORTH, 1915–2013

James Guy "Pop" Hollandsworth, Sr., beloved founder of the Asheville School mountaineering program, first director of the North Carolina Outward Bound School, and past president of the Carolina Mountain Club, passed away at age 97 on June 21, 2013. Pop was not big or tall (no more than 5-feet-5-inches), but to the thousands of young people he introduced to the pleasures of mountaineering and wilderness travel, he was a mountain of a man.

Pop Hollandsworth grew up in a coal-mining town in southern West Virginia, where his father was the high school principal. By age 14, he had not only earned the rank of Eagle Scout but also (for reasons obscured by time) gotten the nickname "Pop." In 1937, Pop graduated from Berea College and began teaching in a one-room school in a coal camp near home. After World War II, he began what became a 38-year career at the Asheville School, a private school in North Carolina. In addition to his duties as a science teacher, and eventually as a dean, Pop was the founder and head of the school's mountaineering program. Through a longtime collaboration with Wyoming guide Vince Lee, countless students had life-changing experiences in the mountains. As the mother of one wrote to Pop afterward, "I sent you a boy…and you sent me back a young man."

BOB JONES *and* VINCE LEE

LAYTON KOR, 1938–2013

Layton was such a beautiful man. That warm, happy face, those rich eyes, his intense look as he moved toward a face of rock. We were friends for 53 years. I did more climbs with him, I think, than did any other climber. He often addressed me by my middle name, Oliver. We both were in poor health these last several years, and he often sensed when I felt bad. He would phone and crack one of his jokes. Just the look he got on his face could be gut-splitting.

There are individuals who seem fated, or preordained, who have the charisma and all the natural enormity of spirit, to be stars. In the early 1960s we awoke into a kingdom of sandstone. If to climb was our world, and if such an Eldorado was real, Layton was the preeminent spirit. Layton climbed with a fury and did so with more inborn skill than any climber I knew. Every moment with Layton was an electrifying experience. He stepped to the rock, and then there was an explosion upward of grace and speed. Also madness. He sometimes raced past the point at which there were holds enough to stay on the rock. My devotion to Layton must have been profound, for without reservation I was, again and again, prepared to put my life on the line.

I will never forget the sun-warm winter day in 1961 when we made the second ascent of the Naked Edge. I see vividly his brilliant unprotected lead of the final headwall of Rogue's Arête, on Bear Peak above Boulder in 1963. Then there was a day he broke off a block and fell past me on the Bastille Crack. It was a miracle I held him, both of us for one thrilling moment supported by a single, half-placed angle piton that shifted in the crack. That was as close as we came to eternity, until April 2013, when Layton's heart stopped on a hospital bed.

My friend has touched climbers throughout the world. He is there forever in the beautiful rock of Yosemite or the Black Canyon, or in the high yellow spurs of Eldorado. He is in the sheer granite reaches of the Diamond of Longs Peak. Adios, pardner.

PAT AMENT

THEODORE (NICK) NICOLAI, 1935–2012

Theodore (Nick) Nicolai, scion of a prominent Oregon family, who died in September 2012, was Oregon Section Chair in 1969 and 1970, succeeding Lute Jerstad. In 1971 he was first elected to the AAC Board of Directors, and in 1974 he was re-elected to the Board and made vice president. Unfortunately, he was forced to resign later that year to deal with a crisis in the family business.

During the Korean War he had trained with the Army's cold-weather forces in Alaska, which gave him a taste for high-standard climbing in cold conditions, and he subsequently led three *direttissima* climbs in the Oregon Cascades that were possible only in winter conditions. In April 1970, he led an expedition to Mt. Hayes in the Alaska Range, which, owing to fierce storms, did not succeed in its principal objective of a new route on the west ridge, but did achieve the first ascent of nearby Mt. Skarland.

Temporarily turning his back on the mountains, Nick acquired a 53-foot ketch, which he named Free Sprit, and with his family spent 16 months sailing to Polynesia. When Bhutan finally opened, he was one of the first to organize an expedition for trekking and climbing there. After successfully negotiating a sale of the family business and subsequently losing his wife, Cicely, he divided his later years between the mountains of Ketchum, Idaho, and the coastal waters of the Queen Charlotte Islands, British Columbia. Energetic and a born leader, he invariably made a vivid impression on all who knew him.

T.C. PRICE ZIMMERMANN

DENALI SCHMIDT, 1988–2013

Denali was enchanted with the world—he was obsessed with the color blue, because it was the color of the sky. He held wonder in his striking blue eyes, love in his smile, and a playful wisdom beyond his years. The day we met, he talked delicately about the quiet of winter in the Sierra and the clarity of the stars, holding the words in his mouth like precious gems.

Denali was a child of the world who grew up between Australia, New Zealand, and the United States. From a young age, he displayed talents in the arts and outdoor sports, two opposing but complementary interests that would pull him throughout his short life. His father, Marty Schmidt, named him after his first love, the mountain on which he started his alpine adventures. Denali possessed the natural climbing abilities of his dad, and joined him to summit his namesake in 2011

and 2012, putting up a new route, Dad and Son, on the lower southwest face (*AAJ 2012*). They also became the first father-son team to summit Broad peak together, immediately before their attempt on K2, the mountain that took their lives in an avalanche. Together they sought to find the edge of what was possible—the fine line between life and death that taught them both a deep appreciation for life itself.

Denali came to the United States to work as a ski patroller in Bear Valley, California, and became known for the extreme lines and jumps he would take. At California College of the Arts, he studied painting, embracing a type of gut-driven expression that made sense with the grunt of the climb—the drive came from a similar place. He had just graduated with promising talent and the second-highest GPA in his class, with plans to continue to travel the world, exhibit his artwork, and explore as much as possible. He made the future seem shiny and golden with all the things he wanted to do.

Whenever he called from his climbs in Pakistan, it brought me back to the day we met—he couldn't contain his excitement with each experience, his love for the world. And now he is a part of it, boundless forever, sharing with us the beauty he found around him.

LARISA MINERVA

MARTY SCHMIDT, 1960–2013

From a young age Marty was passionate about going to the hills. The mountains were the one place on this Earth that truly nurtured his soul. Guiding clients was his calling: to bring them to stunning, breathtaking places in the mountains, where the heart stands still in a moment of awe.

Marty's climbing philosophy was holistic, in line with his spiritual nature. No oxygen and no Sherpas past base camp. Known as one of the fastest and strongest climbers, he was well-respected by the Sherpa community and his climbing mates. He was a lovable, charming, and sensitive man with bucket loads of energy—an irrepressible bright light that seemed indestructible. His enthusiasm made you feel special, and that anything and everything was possible. With the skills Marty learned during his years as a Pararescue jumper in U.S. Air Force Special Operations, he was ready to give up everything to help a person in need, in keeping with the Pararescue motto, "That others may live."

Marty traveled the globe extensively, and his love for culture and nature would always bring him back to Aotearoa (New Zealand), his adopted home. He loved the people and his simple lifestyle, growing vegetables and looking after Mother Earth, a true Kiwi at heart.

GIOVANNINA CANTALE

WILLIAM THOMAS, 1926–2013

William Hewitt Thomas, an AAC member for over 50 years, died October 19, 2013, in Carlsbad, California. He was 86. Bill served the AAC for many years, reviewing research proposals as a member of the Scientific Committee.

Bill became interested in both mountaineering and science as a teenager in Riverside, California. When he was not in school, working for the USDA Salinity Lab as a technician, or experimenting with growing beans with nutrient solutions in the garage, Bill learned the rudiments of technical climbing at Tahquitz and on trips to Southern California's Mt. San Jacinto and to the Sierra Nevada. He graduated early from high school in 1944 and enlisted in the Army Specialized Training Reserve, studying electrical engineering. In the program he met Willi Unsoeld, who became a climbing partner and lifelong friend. Bill and Willi headed for the hills at any furlough—hitchhiking from Kentucky to Colorado to climb Longs Peak, and later to a three-week exploration of the Selkirks.

After his discharge from the Army, Bill entered Pomona College, where he earned a B.S. in chemistry in 1948, then earned an M.S. and Ph.D. in plant physiology at the University of Maryland. In 1954, wishing to return to the West and its mountains, Bill accepted a one-year position as a phytoplankton researcher at Scripps Institution of Oceanography in La Jolla. He was there for more than 50 years.

Bill became very active in the local chapter of the Sierra Club, particularly the Rock Climbing Section. He met Sara "Topper" Sussman on a club outing, and they were married in 1956. Both were instructors in the chapter's basic mountaineering courses, and they made numerous climbing, backpacking, and skiing trips to the eastern Sierra Nevada and beyond.

Beginning in the 1970s, Bill began to study red snow algae in the Sierra Nevada. Although he retired from Scripps in 1988, he continued to maintain a lab and renewed his research in the eastern Sierra. He often laughed that he'd finally found a way to "do oceanography in the mountains."

ALAN THOMAS

NECROLOGY

In addtion to those covered above, AAC members who passed away during 2013 included:

Charles Flather	George R. Merriam M.D.	Reinhold A. Ullrich M.D.
Paul R. Galipeau	Rich Olsson	Tom Unger
Charles B. Huestis	Joseph M. Riddle	John Wylde
Robert Klimek	Paul W. Tamm	John M. Zivec

CLUB ACTIVITIES

EDITED BY FREDERICK O. JOHNSON

Alaska Section. The Alaska Section partnered with the Hatcher Pass Mountaineering Huts Group to support motorized vehicle–boundary education and incident reporting around the Snowbird Hut. This involved posting boundary signs, handing out brochures with motorized-boundary maps, and speaking at various functions. Together, we hope to support the Department of Natural Resources in maintaining the present boundaries, in order to allow safe non-motorized passage to the Snowbird Hut.

Harry Hunt and Cindi Squire treated the hut to a major mold-remediation project this summer. The interior walls were sterilized and sanded, and then a special mold-killing primer and paint were applied. Venting was installed to combat moisture buildup when the hut is in use. The remedies are proving to work well, and the mold has not reappeared. The hut continues to be well-used in winter and summer.

Many of our members are making a difference. Particular thanks are due to Clint Helander for the time he dedicates to speaking and giving slideshows for local climbing groups.

HARRY HUNT *and* CINDI SQUIRE, *Co-chairs*

Sierra Nevada Section. Our "Climb-munity" gatherings continued to be popular and well attended throughout the year. These included ice climbing in Cold Stream Canyon near Truckee, rock climbing at Pinnacles National Park, a June weekend on Donner Summit, and our much-loved Pinecrest event with Royal and Liz Robbins and Tom Frost. An outstanding presentation by Freddie Wilkinson highlighted our annual holiday dinner in Berkeley. Freddie's "Mountain/Story" wove tales of his own adventures with stories of the Sherpas at the heart of the 2008 K2 tragedy and Bradford Washburn's legacy of work in the Alaskan mountains.

The section's conservation activities included a weeklong stewardship project with the National Park Service in Tuolumne Meadows and hosting the Western Regional Fall Highball Craggin' Classic in Bishop. With national sponsorship from C.A.M.P. USA, this ever-popular event drew more than 250 attendees and contributed more than 400 volunteer hours to cleaning up the Buttermilks. At the climbers' reception hosted by New Belgium Brewing, over $8,000 was raised for Western Region Live Your Dream grants. The party featured a joint slideshow by Matt Segal and Will Stanhope, as well as the 2013 Reel Rock Film Tour.

Members, rangers, and climbers alike enjoyed our free climbers' coffee every Sunday morning in Yosemite. As part of the climbers' interpretive program, AAC Yosemite Committee Chair Linda McMillan and her husband, Tom, continued to lead the free Saturday evening slideshow series in Yosemite, generating goodwill and exposure for the Club.

KAREN ZAZZI, *Chair, and* JEFF DEIKIS, *Western Regional Manager*

Southwest Section. We had four main events in 2013: a climbing/restoration weekend in Joshua Tree in March; a stewardship day at the third annual Idyllwild Climbers Festival in May; helping with the work party and a fund-raiser for the section's Live Your Dream grant program at the Fall Highball in Bishop; and a successful winter dinner in November. In addition, we met frequently at Cal Tech for programs such as the Reel Rock Festival and the Banff Film Festival, sponsored by the Cal Tech Alpine Club.

On November 30, the section hosted its holiday dinner at Taix French Restaurant, featuring a slideshow and film by Freddie Wilkinson. With the assistance of a no-host bar and appetizers, the crowd enjoyed visiting with old friends and making new ones. The evening included a silent auction that raised $1,000 for the section. Thanks to Jeff Deikis, AAC regional manager, for his help with this event and the Fall Highball.

JIM PINTER-LUCKE, *Chair*

Arizona Section. In addition to rock climbing outings in the Superstition Mountains, east of Phoenix, and the McDowell Mountains of Scottsdale, the Arizona Section added a canyoneering event to its list of activities. Canyoneering is very popular in the Southwest and has significant crossover appeal with climbers. We also continued to support the Forks Fest Climbing Festival, a large gathering and celebration held in Paradise Forks. Among our social events were a screening of Reel Rock films in Flagstaff and a gear swap in Phoenix in conjunction with the Arizona Mountaineering Club. One of this year's highlights was the Arizona Section's first Annual Holiday Dinner, held at Boulders on Broadway in Tempe.

ERIK FILSINGER *and* JEFF PAUL SNYDER, *Co-chairs*

Idaho Section. Our section completed many events in 2013, focused on developing the Idaho climbing community. Among these, Jim Donini spoke at two dinners, one in Boise and the other in Sun Valley, providing stories of adventure that inspired everyone in attendance. We also partnered with the North Idaho Climbers Alliance to complete a trail project at Laclede Rocks. A motivated group of volunteers worked to build and maintain trails and improve eroding belay stations. Additionally, the group cleaned hundreds of pounds of trash from the roadside. Our section is co-chaired by Kammie Cuneo in the south and Jason Luthy in the north.

JASON LUTHY, *Co-chair*

Western Slope Section. Our first major event this year was in support of the Western Colorado Climbers Coalition's (WCCC) annual fund-raiser in April. The proceeds will go to possible land purchases in Unaweep Canyon, south of Grand Junction. Activities included a bouldering competition at the local climbing gym, an after-party with the band Zolopht and the Destroyers, a raffle stocked by the AAC and several gear companies, a used-gear swap, beer, and more. The event raised approximately $1,400 and included upwards of 90 participants.

Our second major event was the annual anchor replacement weekend in June at Penitente Canyon in the San Luis Valley. With approximately 25 participants, over a dozen routes were upgraded or modernized in the main canyon, with the specifics posted to Mountain Project. The group returned a week later to upgrade a few more routes. The AAC held a gear raffle, and John Strand and his wife once again generously provided the beer and BBQ.

LEE JENKINS, *Chair*

Front Range Section. Two activities stood out last year in the extremely engaged section on Colorado's Front Range. We formed a group called the Climbing Posse that met after work to climb. The dates were announced in our monthly e-mail, and each meeting was organized by a volunteer. Besides getting on the rock, the purpose of this group was to foster a sense of AAC community and "ownership" in the section, develop new volunteer leaders, mentor less experienced climbers, and give new members a chance to network. About 25 members participated, and we hope to expand this program in 2014.

The Front Range Section dinner, an affordable grass-roots event designed to attract all members, was held at the American Mountaineering Center in Golden. The legendary George Lowe was the speaker. Highlights included a costume contest (black-tie thrift store) and a storyboard contest. Approximately 140 people showed up, with at least half of them in costume. The most humorous storyboard portrayed George Lowe landing his plane and following Sasquatch footprints to a cave, where he discovered Jim Donini inside. We plan to make this dinner an annual section event.

CAROL KOTCHEK, *Chair*

Great Lakes Section. The Michigan Ice Fest continues to be the largest gathering of Midwest climbers and our section's biggest event, with 434 participants descending upon Munising for the best ice conditions we have seen in decades. Climbers from 10 states and two countries were represented. Participants came to enjoy Midwest camaraderie and the chance to climb the beautiful ice formations at Pictured Rocks National Lakeshore and Grand Island. Over the weekend we signed up 42 new members for the AAC and the Access Fund, and exposed hundreds of first-timers to the sport of ice climbing.

In the fall our section hosted Climb Up 2013!, a four-day event on the south shore of Lake Superior. Members gathered to climb, socialize, and celebrate another year of adventure.

BILL THOMPSON, *Chair*

New England Section. In February our section helped International Mountain Equipment sponsor the 20th annual Mt. Washington Valley Ice Festival in North Conway, New Hampshire. It was an honor to be chosen as the beneficiary of the Friday-night festivities, and we were able to raise over $2,500 for the Northeast Live Your Dream grant.

Bayard Russell was guest speaker for the annual section dinner at the Henderson House in Weston, Massachusetts. He kept us enthralled with his presentation on cutting-edge mixed climbing in the Northeast. In early May, AAC Regional Manager Sarah Garlick hosted a volunteer summit in the Gunks. Representatives of several sections were present, sharing in a lively discussion on the direction of the club, followed by some outstanding climbing in amazing weather. We rendezvoused for dinner at the Grist Mill before retiring to the Duck Pond in the Mohonk Preserve for a lively campfire.

In September, we had our second annual Craggin' Classic festival in North Conway with evening events including slideshows by John Bragg and Madaleine Sorkin, music from a local band, and a pig roast. We also held our two annual BBQs at the base of Cathedral Ledge in North Conway, and a couple of after-work "Bouldering and BBQ" evenings at Hammond Pond, near Boston. Chad Hussey hosted the sixth annual "It Ain't Over Til It's Over" cragging day at Ragged Mountain, Connecticut, in November.

NANCY SAVICKAS, *Chair*

Upstate New York Section. Our section has had a great introduction since New York split into Upstate and Metro New York sections last year. Over the Columbus Day weekend, we hosted a very successful BBQ for 20-plus members and other climbers at the High Peaks Cyclery Guide House at Lake Placid. The section also provided free morning coffee to climbers at the Adirondack International Mountainfest in Keene Valley. We are planning additional gatherings.

WILL ROTH *and* MARK SCOTT, *Co-chairs*

Metro New York Section. The year 2013 will stand out for a memorable 34th Annual Black Tie Dinner. Fifty years earlier, Americans, for the first time, stood on top of Mt. Everest. Of all of the exploits of that historic expedition, none has stood the test of time like the west ridge climb by Tom Hornbein and the late Willi Unsoeld. It was therefore fitting for us to celebrate that Golden Anniversary in New York with Tom as our special guest. A swift sell-out, the dinner drew an enthusiastic crowd. Spirited bidding engineered by auctioneers Steve Schofield and D. Byers raised a record sum to support the club's causes. Among the items that went under the hammer was a wooden ice axe autographed by both Tom Hornbein and Jim Whittaker, which fetched an eye-popping $8,000!

Tom gave a warm and self-effacing presentation, leaving no doubt that his climbing legacy will live forever. Since Tom was a tough act to follow, his keynote was preceded by a short video narrated by Fred Golomb, who, at age 88, has taken up paragliding and maintains an intimate, if sometimes bruising, relationship with the French Alps. Robert Anderson, leader of the 1988 Anglo-American expedition to the Kangshung Face, took us on a breathtaking 3.6 billion–pixel tour of Everest, with images created by David Breashears.

With perhaps the best ice climbing conditions seen in the Northeast in years, the section sponsored outings to the Adirondacks in January and the Catskills in February. When the temperature warmed up, we returned to the Adirondacks in early June as guests of the historic Ausable Club. A highlight of the weekend was a presentation by Vanessa O'Brien on her "Explorers Grand Slam," reaching the Seven Summits plus both north and south poles. We also helped organize informal dinner shows at Manhattan's Explorers Club. Presenters were Olaf Soot on Mt. Waddington, Ted Vaill on his efforts to find the real Shangri La, and Don Healy on his Seven Summits quest.

For the first time, we honored those who had completed the Seven Summits with a handsome plaque: Robert Anderson, Yonsuk Derby, Vanessa O'Brien, and Victor Vescovo. We hope to repeat this ceremony in future years, as New York has perhaps a disproportionate share of Seven Summits climbers.

Special thanks go to our impressive cadre of volunteers, including Jonathan Light and Howard

Sebold, who masterfully cope with our AV needs. Mike Barker, Lee Elman, Julie Floyd, Vanessa O'Brien, Andrea Salerno, and Martin Torresquintero assist in event planning. Conor Moran, section webmaster, keeps us all abreast of members' activities and photos on our unique section blog: Nysaac.blogspot.com.

PHIL ERARD, *Chair*

D.C. Section. The section's major climbing trip was held over Columbus Day weekend. With help from the Southern Appalachian and Mid Atlantic sections, we organized a joint meet at Seneca Rocks. Despite uncooperative weather, members ascended various Seneca classics between storms. Our section also held a Christmas dinner with the Potomac Mountain Club, along with other climbing and social events.

In April we joined AAC Executive Director Phil Powers for a day of climbing at Carderock. The subsequent dinner provided an opportunity to quiz Phil about the future direction of the club. In August, Rob Graver and Mike Baur gave a noteworthy presentation on their ascents of the Ham and Eggs couloir and Shaken Not Stirred on the Mooses Tooth in Alaska's Ruth Gorge.

Members completed ascents in Alaska and the Wind Rivers, on Mt. Slesse and Mt. Rainier, and throughout the Northeast. Several others climbed in the U.K., making two separate ascents of the Old Man of Hoy. Members climbed a number of South American volcanoes, while Chris Clarke, currently based in La Paz, put up new routes in the Bolivian Andes.

SIMON CARR, *Co-chair*

Southern Appalachian Section. In 2013 we held 31 events, ranging from climbing video nights and first-aid classes to full-on banquets. The commitment of numerous volunteers and local business partners made this record year possible.

Last year the section responded to the rappelling death of a local climber by committing to the development of free public clinics to promote safer rappelling. The resulting Rappelling Best Practices Clinics absorbed the bulk of the section's energy in 2013. Fourteen clinics were hosted by excellent partners across North Carolina, and additional clinics took place at Stone Summit Climbing and Fitness Center in Atlanta. In all, 172 climbers attended the clinics. Our heartfelt thanks goes out to all who provided financial support, instructional time, venues, and promotional assistance. Special thanks to our developers and instructors— Aram Attarian, Danny McCracken, and Patrick Weaver—and to partners Appalachian Mountain Institute (AMI), REI, and Rescue Dynamics.

I would also like to offer huge thanks for the help I have received over the eight years of my tenure as section chair. Starting on January 1, 2014, Danny McCracken took on the challenges and pleasures of leading the section. Lead on, Danny!

DAVID THOENEN, *Chair*

Thanks to James Benoit for additional editing assistance.

INDEX

COMPILED BY RALPH FERRARA & EVE TALLMAN

Mountains are listed by their official names. Ranges and geographic locations are also indexed. Unnamed peaks (eg. Peak 2,340) are listed under P. Abbreviations are used for some states and countries and for the following: Article: art.; Cordillera: C.; Mountains: Mts.; National Park: Nat'l Park; Obituary: obit. Most personnel are listed for major articles. Expedition leaders and persons supplying information in Climbs and Expeditions are also cited here. Indexed photographs are listed in bold type. Reviewed books are listed alphabetically under Book Reviews.

A

Abromeit, Doug *obit.* 372
Absaroka-Beartooth Wilderness (MT) 126-9
Ackermann, Jorge 228
Acopan Tepui (Venezuela) 193-4, **194**
Adamson, Scott *art.* 23-31, 64-71; 147-50
Adwa Mts. (Ethiopia) 251-2
Afghanistan 279-81
After You, P. (Kyrgyzstan) 270-1, 273-4, **271**, **274**
Agdierussaksasit (Greenland) 185
Aguiar, Sebastián 216
Aguila, Cerro (Chile) 237
Aiarpoq (Greenland) 185, **184**
Ait Makhlouf, Morocco 249
Ak-Too (Kyrgyzstan) 265-6
Ala Archa (Kyrgyzstan) 265-6
Ala Dagar (Turkey) 244-5
Alas de Angel (Chile) *art.* 80-89; 235-6, **235**
Alaska *art.* 23-31; 140-65
Alaska Rg. (AK) *art.* 23-31; 142-6
Alboran, Punta "Half Dome" (Greenland) 183-5, **184**
Alfil P. (Argentina) 218
Aling Valley (Pakistan) 300-1
Almaraz, Guillermo 216
Altai (China) 350
Altar, El "Kapak Urku" (Ecuador) 194-5
Alzamora, Lucas 340
Ama Dablam (Nepal) 320
Amelunxen, Conny 169
Amphu I (Nepal) 323-4, **324**
Anderson, Dave 359-60
Andes (Chile/Argentina) 216-37
Andrea, Cerro (Chile) 237
Andrea, Pt. (Kyrgyzstan) 273
Andreou, Constantinos 249
Andron, Cosmin 309-10, 342-3
Angel Wings (Chile) *see* Alas de Angel
Angel Wings (Sierra Nevada, CA) 118-20, **119**
Angel, The (Revelation Mts., AK) 140-1, **141**
Angelini, Stefano 243
Anidesh Chuli "White Wave" (Nepal) 327-8, **328**
Anna, Aguja (Chile) 237
Annapurna (Nepal) *art.* 12-21
Annapurna Himal (Nepal) 308-10
Antarctic Peninsula (Antarctica) 239-40
Antarctica 238-40
Anthamatten, Simon *art.* 32-7; 289
Anti-Atlas Mts., Morocco 249
Antoshin, A. 262-3
Api-Raksha Urai Himal (Nepal) 304-5

Apocalypse (Revelation Mts., AK) 141
Araksam Tse (Nepal) 318-9, **319**
Aravena, Waldo 229
Argentina 216-37
Argo (Kyrgyzstan) 260-3, **261**
Arizona (US) 120-1
Asgard, Mt. (Baffin Is., CAN) 178-9
Ashat Gorge (Kyrgyzstan) 260-3, **261**
Astrid, Cerro (Chile) 237
At Bashi Range (Kyrgyzstan) 268
Athelstan, Mt. (CAN) 169
Atlas Mts., Morocco 249-50
Auer, Hansjörg *art.* 32-7; 289
Auer, Matthias *art.* 32-7; 289
Ausangate, Nevado (Peru) 201-2
Austin, Charlotte 368-9
Auyuittuq Nat'l Park (Baffin Is., CAN) 177-9
Axelsson, Jan 242
Aysén Region (Chile) 225-7

B

Baffin Island (CAN) 177-9
Baintha Ahrta (Pakistan) 292-4, **293**
Baintha Kabata (Pakistan) 292-4, **293**
Baltoro Muztagh (Pakistan) 294-5
Bamongo (Nepal) 311-2, **312**
Bara Shigri Glacier (India) 342-3
Barnes Wall (Greenland) 182-3, **183**
Barrille, Mt. (Ruth Gorge, AK) 157
Bashkirtsov, Eugeny 296-7
Bear Glacier (Wrangell-St. Elias Mts., AK) 162-3
Bear's Tooth (Alaska Rg., AK) **27**
Beglinger, Ruedi 172-3
Beisly, Gregg 210-1
Bekendam, Roland 319
Belousov, Vladimir 317-8
Bennett, Scott 140-1
Benoist, Stéphane *art.* 19-21; 308
Bermúdez, Julio **190**
Berry, Nik 131-3
Bes Parmak Sivrisi (Turkey) 245, **245**
Betelgeuse, P. (Kyrgyzstan) 272, **274**
Beyer, Jim 125
Beyond the Far, Mt. (Chile) 237
Bezengi Wall "Bezingi" (Russia) 256-7, **256**
Bezingi Wall (Russia) *see* Bezengi
Bhilangna Valley (India) 343-4
Biacharahi North Tower (Pakistan) **293**
Biacherahi Central Tower (Pakistan) 292-4, **293**
Biacherahi South Tower (Pakistan) **293**
Bialek, Anne 204

Irvine, Mt. (Sierra Nevada, CA) *art.* 102
Ishinca (C. Blanca, Peru) 196-7
Isserman,Marice 376
Italia, P. (C. Real, Bolivia) 206-7, **207**
It-Kaya(Caucasus Mts., Russia) 257-8, **257**
Ivnarssuaq Great Wall (Greenland) 180-1, **180**

J

Jackson, Brian 308
Jaco (Chile) *art.* 80-89
Jagdula (Nepal) 307, **307**
Jaho (Nepal) **328**
Jamantau Range (Kyrgyzstan) 267-8
Jamison, Logan 223
Janak (Nepal) 327, **327**
Janak East (Nepal) 326-7
Janak Himal (Nepal) 324-7
Jannu (Nepal) **326**
Jannu East (Nepal) **326**
Jarjinjabo Massif (China) 353-4
Jasper, Robert 242
Jati Khollu (C. Real, Bolivia) 209, **209**
Jay, Jonathan 259
Jebel Kassala (Sudan) 250, **251**
Jebel Tadrarate, Morocco 249-50
Jeffcoarch, Daniel 120
Jenkins, Mark 132-3
Jensen, Susan 339
Jervis,Steven 376-7
Jetaqána Taf, Cerro (Chile) 236, **236**
Jobo LeCoultre (Nepal) *art.* 64-71
Jobo Rinjang (Nepal) *art.* 64-71
Joey Shan (China) 360-1, **360**
Joffre, Mt. (Coast Mts., CAN) 169
Johnson, Mt. (Ruth Gorge, AK) 153-5, **155**
Johnson, Samuel 161
Jordan 246-7
Jornet Burgada, Kilian 242
Joshi, Dhruv 344-5
Junaidi, Imran 282
Jungdung Kangri (India) 332-3, **332**

K

K6 West (Pakistan) *art.* 38-44, **40**
Kaghan Valley (Pakistan) 282
Kalman, Chris 222-3
Kamasu (Kyrgyzstan) 267-8, **267**
Kang Nachugo (Nepal) 313, **312**
Kang Yissay Rg. (India) 333
Kangchenjunga (Nepal) **326**
Kangchenjunga Himal (Nepal) 327-8
Kangchenjunga Himal (Nepal) *art.* 52-57
Kanjiroba Himal (Nepal) 306-7
Kapak Urku *see* El Altar
Kapura South (Pakistan) 302-3, **303**
Karakoram (Pakistan, India) 282-9, 329-31
Kargan Semiz, P. (Kyrgyzstan) 268
Karl Marx, P. (Tajikistan) 276-7, **277**
Kasparov, P. (Kyrgyzstan) 272-3
Kastelic, Domen 313
Kaszlikowski, David 186-7, 367
Katushka, P. (Kyrgyzstan) 268, **268**
Katxalote, El (Greenland) 185

Kauffman, Neil 360-1
Kazakhstan 258-9
Keena, Seth 109-10
Kehrer, Simon 241
Keketouhai Nat'l Geologic Park (China) 350
Keller, Daniel 267
Kelley, John 163
Kennedy, Hayden 134
Khai Ri (Gangga Massif, China) 354-5
Khhang Shiling (Lahul, India) 342-3
Khumbu (Nepal) *art.* 64-71; 316-24
Khunyang Chhish East (Pakistan *art.* 32-7, **34**; 289
Khushrui Sar (Pakistan) 287-8, **288**
Khvostenko, Oleg 265
Khyber Pakhtunkhwa (Pakistan) 282
Kichatna Mts. (AK) 142
Kichkesu (Kyrgyzstan) 264, **264**
Kichkesu Region (Kyrgyzstan) 264
Kidd, Mt. (Rocky Mts., CAN) 176
Kiester,Shey 377
Kimura, Yusuke 358-9
Kingfisher (Fisher Towers, UT) 126
Kingsbury, Tom 126-7
Kinmundy, P. (Kyrgyzstan) 273
Kirkpatrick, Andy 241
Kishtwar Himalaya (India) 337-9
Kishtwar Kailash (India) 337-9, **337**
Kishtwar, Cerro (India) **338**
Knott, Paul 166
Koh-e-Gulistan "P3" (Pakistan) 286-7, **287**
Koh-e-Wakhan Rg. (Afghanistan) **279**-81
Kokankada (Sahyadri Rg., India) 345
Kokshaal-Tau (Kyrgyzstan) 269-75
Kokshaal-Tau, West (Kyrgyzstan) 269-70
Kokshaal-Too (China) 346-9
Kokshaal-Too *see* Kokshaal-Tau
Koksil Sar V (Pakistan) 282-3
Kolhe, Samiran 345
Kopold, Josef "Dodo" 243
Kopteva, Marina 317-8
Kor, Layton *obit.* 375-6
Koraro Spires (Ethiopia) 252-3
Korona, P. (Kyrgyzstan) 265-6, **266**
Koshelenko, Yury 260-3, 264
Koval, Viktor 256-7
Kozerog (Kyrgyzstan) 267-8
Krajnc, Luca 362-3
Krause, Douglas 237
Kuchela Dhura (India) 344-5
Kulu Makalu (Lahul, India) 342-3, **342**
Kumaun Himalaya (India) 344-5
Kurum Tor-Tag (Kyrgyzstan) 264
Kusum Kanguru (Nepal) 320-3, **322**
Kyajo Ri (Nepal) 317-8, **316, 317**
Kyrgyz Ala-Too (Kyrgyzstan) 265-6
Kyrgyzstan 260-75
Kyzyl Asker (Kokshaal-Too, China) 346-8, **348**

L

Ladakh (India) 332-3
LaForge, Corey 276
Lahaul (India) 342-3
Laier, Ralf 238-9

the AMERICAN ALPINE club

AAJ

INTERNATIONAL GRADE COMPARISON CHAR

SERIOUSNESS RATING:

These often modify technical grades when protection is difficult

R: Poor protection with potential for a long fall and some injury

X: A fall would likely result in serious injury or death

YDS=Yosemite Decimal System;
UIAA=Union Internationale des Associations D'Alpinisme;
FR=France/Sport
AUS=Australia;
Sax=Saxony;
CIS=Commonwealth of Independent States/Russia;
SCA=Scandinavia;
BRA=Brazil

Note: *All conversions are approximate. See AAJ online for further explanation of commitment grades and waterfall Ice/ mixed grades.*

YDS	UIAA	FR	AUS	SAX	CIS	SCA	BRA	UK	
5.2	II	1	10	II	III	3			D
5.3	III	2	11	III	III+	3+			
5.4	IV- / IV	3	12		IV-	4			VI
5.5	IV+		13		IV	4+			S
5.6	V-	4	14		IV+	5-	4a	4a	HS
5.7	V		15	VIIa		5		4b	VS
5.8	V+	5a	16	VIIb	V-	5+	4 / 4+	4c	HV
5.9	VI-	5b	17	VIIc		6-	5 / 5+	5a	E
5.10a	VI / VI+	5c	18	VIIIa	V	6	6a	5b	
5.10b	VI+	6a							E
5.10c	VII-	6a+	19	VIIIb		6+	6b		
5.10d	VII	6b	20	VIIIc	V+	7-	6c		E
5.11a	VII+	6b+		IXa			7a	5c	
5.11b	VII+	6c	21	IXb		7	7b		
5.11c	VIII-	6c+	22	IXc	VI-	7+			E
5.11d	VIII	7a	23				7c	6a	
5.12a	VIII+	7a+	24			8-	8a		E
5.12b	VIII+	7b	25	Xa	VI	8	8b		
5.12c	IX-	7b+	26	Xb		8+	8c		
5.12d	IX	7c	27				9a	6b	E
5.13a	IX+	7c+	28	Xc		9-	9b		
5.13b	IX+	8a	29				9c		
5.13c	X-	8a+	30	XIa		9	10a	6c	E
5.13d	X	8b	31		VI+		10b		
5.14a	X+	8b+	32	XIb			10c	7a	E
5.14b	X+	8c	33				11a		
5.14c	XI-	8c+	34	XIc		9+	11b	7b	E
5.14d	XI	9a	35				11c		
5.15a	XI+	9a+	36	XIIa		10	12a		E1
5.15b	XII-	9b	37		VII		12b		
5.15c	XII	9b+	38	XIIb			12c		E1